# *fly-fishing*
# SOFT-HACKLES

# *fly–fishing* SOFT-HACKLES

## NYMPHS, EMERGERS, AND DRY FLIES

ALLEN McGEE

STACKPOLE
BOOKS

*Guilford, Connecticut*

Published by Stackpole Books
An imprint of Globe Pequot

Distributed by NATIONAL BOOK NETWORK

Copyright © 2017 Stackpole Books
Photos by Allen, Hyun, and Harrison McGee unless otherwise credited
Illustrations by Dave Hall

British Library Cataloguing in Publication Information Available

**Library of Congress Cataloging-in-Publication Data Available**

ISBN 978-0-8117-1684-0 (paperback)
ISBN 978-0-8117-6562-6 (e-book)

♾™ The paper used in this publication meets the minimum requirements of American National Standard for Information Sciences—Permanence of Paper for Printed Library Materials, ANSI/NISO Z39.48-1992.

When you begin to understand the technique of the wet fly, the search for places where fish are lying becomes fascinating. The more you practice it, the more you realise that it is far from being merely a question of promenading a train of flies under water. It is full of tricks and subtleties, and requires an eagle eye and quicker reflexes than does the dry fly. For this form of fishing, the rod is no longer a shooting machine but a receiving post, with super-sensitive antennae, capable of registering immediately the slightest reaction of the fish to the fly.

—Charles Ritz, *A Fly Fisher's Life*

# Contents

# Introduction

Perhaps it serves to perceive tradition as a stream. I prefer that to thinking of tradition as a museum of old things—though there is that, too. There are actual things that are iconic to the fly fishing tradition, objects to be admired for their beauty and utility, the thought and craftsmanship contributing to their making—and these beautiful tools, the fine rods and reels, brilliantly conceived flies and gear, do serve as visual, working proof of a tradition holding rich craft and aesthetic values. We love looking at these things. As one who has sipped an entire glass of whiskey while savoring and admiring a single well-tied salmon fly I am no exception. Many find a lifetime of pleasure collecting the trappings of our sport, and some collect while seldom or never wetting a line. Ours is a faceted passion. And though I take pleasure from all aspects and elements of the fly fishing tradition, I won't lie, more than anything I love to hook fish and feel a tug, so it is the ideas and concepts behind those things in tradition, born of observation, experience, and connection through time on the water, that interest me the most. Tradition is the archive of what worked. Something works enough times to be truly noteworthy, and it is kept. Tradition is a living river, its authentic elements fractal and expansive. We may take what we need from that nourishing stream, and what we take, we may duplicate, refine, or carry in a new direction.

What makes us who we are as anglers? Does our connection to the natural world have anything to do with it? Are we influenced by where we live, or have lived? Are we "men of the country," informed by energetic signals unique to our particular regions? Well, yes. More or less. I think so. Possibly more than we may know. Everything's connected. Anglers are adaptable and absorbent predators, come down the ages bearing a formidable arsenal. Knowledge of lake and stream. We learn what is valuable to keep and come to see how that both serves and defines us.

I met Allen McGee while seeking initiation into The International Brotherhood of the Flymph, a talented group of artist practitioners who kindly invited me to join their circle. An honor that humbles me, to say the least. I am fortunate to have met Allen, as we have been kicking an interesting conversation on soft-hackle design and, turns out, we are both inspired by the design approach of the great Charles Brooks. Like Brooks, McGee is the kind of fly designer I call a "bait fisherman." Form follows function. Looking at Allen McGee's fly designs I am struck that they seem so authentic to tradition, "classic" you might say, while at once new and fresh. Allen combines the effective traditional elements in ways that make perfect sense, then abstracts from there as needed and without regard for convention. The choices of body materials, hackle, and coloration are more sharply defined than what used to be associated with the simple soft-hackle style of the old North Country Spiders and other ancient designs, Allen's flies reflecting deeper observation. I suspect there are more than a few savant designers out in the woodwork secretly fishing killer soft-hackle patterns and not bothering to write about it, and that is as it should be. Imagination has no boundaries. But we are fortunate that Allen McGee is on the job sharing his fly patterns and observations in writing and photography, as his designs represent a significant interpretation and direction. These flies are not fanciful constructs, but workhorse patterns meant as good baits, plain and simple.

—Steven Bird, 2015

# Acknowledgments

I want to thank a few fellow anglers and fly tiers I feel are at the forefront of wet-fly experimentation. Steven Bird lives on the American reach of the Upper Columbia River in northeastern Washington. His blog *Soft-Hackle Journal* is an amazing look at someone who lives trout fishing, and knows what he's talking about when it comes to soft-hackles. He is always experimenting with new materials for flies, but at the same time feels that the Pflueger Medalist is the best reel ever made, and still fishes the two he bought back in the 1960s as a teenager. As he puts it, "Both are imbued with the mojo of a thousand rivers." His flies also reflect his wisdom. Lance Hidy is the son of Pete Hidy and continues his father's work with flymphs and wet flies. Lance is a direct connection to some of the most innovative development of wet flies ever. Michael Brucato lives in Massachusetts. He has guided in the area for over a decade and continues to introduce many to the power of fishing soft-hackles. Sandy Pittendrigh, of Montana Riverboats (http://montana-riverboats.com), fishes out of Bozeman, Montana, were he builds drift boats. Many of the naturals he has photographed are shown here to illustrate Western trout-stream insect species. Jon Rapp lives and fly-fishes in central Missouri and is actively involved in Trout Unlimited. He often visits his local trout streams just to collect, photograph, and identify the biomass, to better understand his home waters. I appreciate all of these friends who contribute to the genre, and I think you will find their work to be valuable as well. Most of all, I sincerely thank my wife, Hyun Soon, who captured many of the photos in this book, and my son, Harrison, both of whom have accompanied me on many a long fishing trip.

The smaller waters around Island Park, Idaho, offer the angler a chance to find solitude and some of the greatest soft-hackle trout fishing available in the world.

# *Defining the Genre*

eaving the great waters of Roscoe, New York, on my way to visit my brother in Catskill Park, I didn't know what to expect as far as the trout streams were concerned. I'd fished the Beaverkill, the Willowemoc, and the East Branch Delaware River tailwater many times but had never found time to venture farther up into the Catskills until now.

Margaretteville was a sleepy little town that I might never have explored, but for this trip. I soon found myself walking down Frog Lane to the bridge crossing the upper East Branch of the Delaware River. There I found a fast-water run that I felt sure would hold some trout. I cast across-stream and mended the line to slow the drift. The bead thorax Hare's Ear

Soft-Hackle sank, and my mind zoned in on the drift. I tried to keep the fly in the drift lane as long as I could, to give any fish that might be there as much opportunity to strike as possible. Amazingly, on the first cast the line paused just as it was beginning to swing into the current of the fast channel, and I lifted the rod tip slightly. The hook bit, and I was into a fish. Then, whatever it was got serious, and I got excited. The heavy fish dove to the streambed. The water was fast and deep in the middle channel, and as it got deeper, I couldn't follow downstream much. The fish started to run. I was trapped. The fish was now below me, and the weight and the water velocity strained my 5X tippet.

Hooked into a brown trout on the Firehole River in Yellowstone National Park. Fishing soft-hackle dry flies in late May and September during *Baetis* hatches works well on this insect-rich river. Soft-hackles are extremely effective; trout take them like a cat pounces on an escaping mouse.

I decided to try to let the fish tire itself out by using side pressure on the rod, holding it horizontally to the water, and choking up on the rod blank. It worked well enough that the fish wasn't running anymore. I was then able to negotiate the fish across the deep middle channel, over to my side. I regretted not having a net. I played it as gently as I could, hoping the hook would hold. After nearly 15 minutes of eternity and multiple close tail grabs, I finessed the trout close enough to put my hand underneath to support it. It was a beautiful 16-inch brown that appeared to be wild. I removed the fly and supported the fish facing upstream in the slower current long enough to feel that it had regained its energy, then let it swim away. As I walked back up the gravel road to my brother's house in near darkness, I felt a sense of accomplishment and pride in knowing that my flies and techniques had worked well on a stream that I'd never fished before.

The International Brotherhood of the Flymph, June 2012, Livingston Manor, NY. Left to right: Lance Hidy, William Anderson, Bob Kern, Allen McGee, Jim Slattery, Ray Tucker, Mark Libertone, Chris Stewart, John Shaner, Bill Shuck, Mike Hogue, Vicki Shadlock, Bob Dietz, Doug Duvall, Tim Didas.

Over the last few years, I've been excited about the resurgence of soft-hackles in fly boxes, fly bins, catalogs, blogs, message boards, and, most importantly, on and in the water. I feel that many anglers are realizing the true potential of this style of flies. They represent not only the physical shape, but also the movement of the natural stream insect. Soft furs make the bodies of these flies breathe and move like gills on the natural. Soft-hackles from a wide range of feathers pulse in the currents. Modern synthetic materials give the fly the flash and translucence of the nymph's natural exoskeleton. By fishing them with the correct behavior of the natural in mind, we complete the process of imitation.

My first book, *Tying and Fishing Soft-Hackle Nymphs* (Amato, 2007), explains wet-fly philosophy, tying methods, traditional and modern soft-hackle nymphs, and the tackle and methods used in fishing them. This new book expands on the field, and I hope it pushes the boundaries of how we think about soft-hackle flies and what they can imitate. Soft-hackles imitate not only the life stage, shape, and color of the natural insect, but its life as well, through the combination of soft-hackle collars, translucent fur, or synthetic body materials that move and breathe in the water currents, and sometimes abdomens that move in imitation of the swimming nymph. This imitation of life triggers an instinctive response from trout.

While many may think of soft-hackles as small, lightweight flies fished only on or near the surface, you can fish them from the bottom to the top of the water column. A skilled angler can present his flies to the level of the fish, which is of

A Soft-Hackle Dry/Wet Caddis imitates a Smokey Wing Sedge well in both form and function, and changing hook size and body color will adapt it to match other sedge species as well.

A Pale Morning Dun *Ephemerella excrucians* imitation, tied with elements of both traditional design and modern wet-fly materials. The UV Ice Dub wing is realistic in color, sparse for translucence but still visible.

utmost importance—fish don't want to move far for a fly, and often won't in fertile streams, choosing instead to eat food that comes to them. Soft-hackles can be fished in technical match-the-hatch situations, with specific methods designed to imitate the behavior and movement of a specific species.

Traditionally, wet flies fall into three general classifications: spiders or wingless wet flies, winged wet flies, and flymphs. Spiders are perhaps the most well known as they are commonly envisioned when someones mentions a soft-hackle. The sparseness of their design imitates mayflies well. Winged wets are traditionally tied with opaque wing feathers often from turkey slips. Howevery, by using feather tips or modern translucent fly materials we can now imitate the wings of sub-surface mayflies more realistically. Flymphs are the buggiest wet flies of all; the bodies often are made of fur or fur/sparkle synthetic dubbings that bring more movement and life to the fly in addition to soft-hackle collar. They can be tied with or without tails as desired and intended for matching species as such.

Electric Spider, a modern variation of a spider.

Featherback, an example of a modern winged wet fly. In larger sizes it can imitate the Western Green Drake Emerger or in smaller sizes a diving egg-laying *Baetis*.

Yellow Crush, a modern variation of a flymph.

I have expanded the types and uses of soft-hackles. I use them to fish from streambed to surface, and to imitate all the life stages of trout-stream invertebrates. The terms flymph and nymph define the maturity of the insect the flies are matching. Soft-hackle nymphs and flymphs work from the streambed to the surface, where floating emergers, soft-hackle dry flies, and spinners then take over. Sunken spinners finish the cycle. The hook weight, material used, or any other added weight, and proper presentation methods all contribute to the drift depth, and therefore the fly's match with the natural's life stage.

## SOFT-HACKLE PROSPECTING FLIES

These impressionistic, nondescript patterns are fished as searching patterns when trout aren't rising to a specific hatch. Prospecting flies include various nymphs, flymphs, and dry flies, and work well when fish are feeding opportunistically and not keying on specific life stages of a specific species. They can be fished with many presentation methods, and adapted to fishing depth by using weight on the fly or leader.

Many traditional wet flies are prospecting flies, but I don't limit prospecting flies to only wet flies. Prospecting soft-hackle dries work effectively on small streams or as indicators for dry/wet droppers, and as depth suspenders for soft-hackle nymphs and flymphs.

The Wet Krystal is an example of a prospecting wet fly.

## SOFT-HACKLE NYMPHS

- Full nymphal form;
- Often fished deeper near streambed, but sometimes near or on the surface as an ascending or floating nymph during a hatch;
- Weighted or unweighted, depending on the depth of the natural imitated at a given time.

Soft-hackle nymphs imitate the nymphal life stage of the mayfly. The body design can be bulkier, and hackle collars denser. When fishing deep, you sometimes need to have more movement in the materials and a more easily detectable target to catch the eye of the trout, due to lower light levels at depth and/or faster velocity the fly is traveling. The contradiction in a bulkier design is that a sparser fly will sink faster through the water column. The choice of design requires careful consideration of the variables of the water, including depth, turbidity, and velocity.

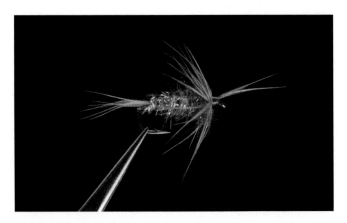

Trail Creek Swinger.

While realistic nymphs look nice, I would be much more confident fishing a bug that has life, movement, and action. It not only looks more alive; the movement also better catches the trout's attention by entering its peripheral vision and generating an instinctive response. The tied-in-the-round style of the soft-hackle nymph fits these needs perfectly. The action of these flies is unmatched, and especially difficult in the smaller #16-20 sizes of most standard anatomical nymphs. However, proportionally tied soft-hackle nymphs can still be active moving in the water. They just look buggier to angler and trout alike, with obvious results once you start to fish them effectively.

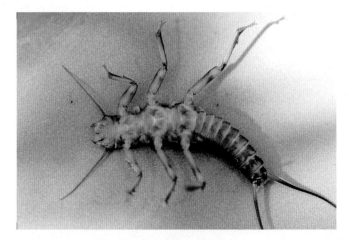

The Golden Stonefly natural. MONTANA RIVERBOATS

The combination of materials in this stonefly soft-hackle imitates the movements of the legs and body of the Golden Stonefly. It's an example of how synthetic material and natural fur and feather can work effectively together.

## FLYMPHS

- Imitate a transitional emerger or adult stage of mayfly or caddis;
- Usually fished just about a foot under or just under the water surface;
- Unweighted or lightly weighted;
- Often tied with hyrdofuge natural furs that hold air bubbles;
- A vulnerable life stage easy to catch, fish often key in on them during hatches.

The term "flymph" is a portmanteau, the blending of two words—in this case "fly, or wet fly" and "nymph"—into a new meaning. Flymphs are designed to imitate the transitional life stage between the immature form of caddis, mayfly, stonefly, or midge, and the adult form. Vernon "Pete" Hidy coined the term "flymph" in 1963, and defined it as "a wingless artificial fly with a soft, translucent body of fur or wool which blends with the undercolor of the tying silk when wet, utilizing soft-hackle fibers easily activated by the currents to give the effect of an insect alive in the water, and strategically cast diagonally upstream or across for the trout to take just below or within a few inches of the surface film."

Hidy's definition describes not only the makeup of the fly and what it imitates, but also the manner in which to fish the fly to simulate the behavior of the emerger. Presenting the fly upstream from the trout allows the fly to sink a few inches underwater before it reaches the fish. At that point, the fly will then rise again on the swing in front of the fish, imitating the behavior of the emerging naturals.

Action Flymph.

I use the term flymph not so much as a strict definition in terms of materials, but rather to describe the transitional life-cycle stage of the nymph to adult mayfly, or caddis pupa to adult. Traditional fly materials work well with modern fly-tying materials, combining into designs that enhance the capability of flymphs and make them even more adaptable to specific hatches.

The pocket behind the soft-hackle collar and the thorax of a flymph traps air bubbles, imitating the small glistening air bubbles that many naturals have when emerging. Natural-fur-fibered bodies also trap these air bubbles as they enter the water. Midge and caddis pupae generate a bubble of gas under their pupal shuck to help in ascension, and egg-laying caddis capture air for breathing when they dive underwater to lay eggs. Caddis then use this air bubble to buoy themselves back up to the surface, where they either fly off, or die and drift spent. Some don't make it to the surface, as the highly reflective bubble makes them easily visible prey for trout.

Fully mature mayfly nymphs also generate a gas bubble under their exoskeletons to raise them to the surface. As the wings of these emerging insects open and unfold, they have a thin film of air on them due to their hydrofuge water-resistance.

Ice Dub and other sparkle dubbings catch light and reflect it in an ever-changing, eye-catching way. Also, notice that the hackle collar traps air bubbles, characteristic of many emergers and diving egg-laying adults of all species.

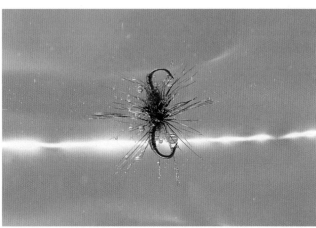

Floating soft-hackles give the impression of a natural trying to break through the surface film. The Flashabou under clear scud back abdomen gives the appearance of translucence, simulating the exoskeleton of invertebrates. Furthermore, the hackle simulates not only appendages like legs and antennae, but movement and struggle. A fur or synthetic dubbing thorax that traps air bubbles creates the hydrofuge flymph. When a fly is only inches underwater, the water acts as a mirror and reflects it, making it more noticeable and alerting fish to a food source. A flymph will become waterlogged after repeated drifts or catches. Restore its ability to hold air bubbles by using a tissue to dry it.

# FLOATING SOFT-HACKLE EMERGERS

The floating soft-hackle emerger represents mayfly and caddis species in match-the-hatch situations, imitating a natural nymph or pupa as it crawls out on the water surface. It can also simulate a crippled or stuck-in-the-shuck natural. This is one of the most vulnerable stages during hatches, as the natural cannot fly off the water until it has fully emerged and dried its wings enough to take flight. Fish key in on these, more often than on adults. An important distinction is the contrast between the nymphal or pupal abdomen and adult thorax. Also, keep in mind that some mayflies are lighter or darker when they first hatch. For example, an *Isonychia* emerging dun is light green when emerging out of the nymphal exoskeleton, but soon darkens to brown.

*Isonychia* Emerger.

## SOFT-HACKLE ADULT DRY FLIES

Soft-hackle dries imitate mayfly emergers/duns/spinners, caddis pupae/adults/egg layers, stonefly adults, midge pupae/adults, and terrestrials floating on top of the water in the surface film. These flies are meant to be fished dead drift in the classic dry-fly manner, or skittered, depending on the behavior of naturals at the time. The soft-hackle collar imitates legs instead of wings on these flies. They can also imitate emergers, stillborn adults, or sunken spinners by fishing them subsurface. Tie them with either hook-shank-length bodies up to about size 14, or extended bodies (#10 and larger) to keep them able to float, the better to imitate the larger Drake mayflies.

Snake Stonefly.

## FLOATING MAYFLY SPINNERS AND SPENT CADDIS

These dry/wet patterns imitate low-profile surface-floating mayfly spinners or egg-laying caddis adults. The behavior of the specific species should dictate the presentation method. Just like with soft-hackle adult dry flies, floating spinners can be fished only dry, only wet, or both on the same presentation. These flies are effective in fishing spinnerfalls and caddis ovipositing, as well as for general prospecting. Fished wet, they will sink about a foot underwater; they are tied on dry-fly hooks to enable fishing them as floating patterns as well.

Brown Drake Spinner.

## SUNKEN SPINNERS AND DIVING EGG LAYERS

Mayfly spinners eventually sink after floating in the surface. This happens even more quickly with species like Sulphurs that lay their eggs over riffle water, fall spent soon after, and get pulled under in the turbulent water. Fish hold in the riffles, feeding on these sunken spinners. Many caddis species lay eggs by diving, and many mistake seeing caddis in the air or trees for a hatch. In fact, they are mating and will soon either skitter along the surface or dive underwater to lay eggs. Both ways, they eventually end up underwater. Sunken adults also make good prospecting flies. The Sparkle Organza wings on sunken spinners catch light and scatter it, creating an eye-catching flash that can cause trout to instinctively strike.

Diving Caddis.

## BEHAVIORAL RESPONSE

One of the primary reasons that soft-hackle flies elicit strong behavioral strikes from trout is moving action of the fly resulting from the combination of materials and presentation that complements the fly design. I call it action for action. My goal is always to design and fish fly imitations with life-like behavior and movement matched to each insect-species life stage. When I'm fishing, I'm conscious of keeping my eyes open for any naturals emerging, and when they are most vulnerable. I take this into account when designing my flies, breaking down the body into materials that best imitate the movement that the natural exhibits. For instance, soft-hackle collars are just one of the body segments that can effectively imitate the behavior of the natural bugs. Bodies or thoraxes tied with a mixture of natural fur—rabbit, hare, squirrel, mole, muskrat—and sometimes combinations of synthetic or natural flash, like peacock, also imitate movement, the flash functioning as a sign of life. Articulate abdomens on large flies for more realism. Add wings to wet mayfly emergers to imitate the ultraviolet reflection that the natural mayflies exhibit in their wings, on which trout cue, particularly species that fully emerge underwater like some Quill Gordons and PMDs. Winged patterns also imitate overlooked sunken spinners.

After a day on the water, we take away observation and information on trout, water, and insects, learned while on-stream. Observation helps us understand how an insect truly appears to trout. By that I mean not just size, shape, and color, but also where certain species live and hatch, how they are suited to the water conditions, and if they live amid streambed vegetation, rocks, or silt. Observation, though, is most important in learning how to fish the fly. I encourage fly fishermen to study nymphs, pupae, and emergers, their movement and behavior, in a controlled environment like a fish tank or tray of water, to see just how much movement many of these species exhibit.

Observing the reaction of trout to insects at the surface can also give us insight into what attracts and holds their focus. The fact that trout have splashy, sometimes breaching, takes of caddis pupae as they emerge shows the caddis' strong swimming ability to reach the surface quickly, and transition rapidly. A sipping rise to mayflies can indicate that many naturals are stuck in the shuck, which would favor fishing a flymph that has elements of both the nymphal shuck and the adult attempting to emerge. In other words, the natural fly's behavior influences trout behavior. The better anglers understand the fly species' behaviors and how trout key in on them, the better they can design soft-hackle flies to be fished in an irresistible way that other fly designs, without all the elements needed to fully imitate life, simply cannot achieve.

The way the hook sits in the trout's jaw gives us insight into subsurface takes. If the hook is in the tip of the jaw, the trout was chasing the fly when it was hooked. If the hook is seated in the back corner of the jaw, as seen here, the trout was holding stationary and took the fly as it was drifting into and alongside the fish.

# B. A. M.

For a soft-hackle to imitate a caddis, mayfly, stonefly, midge, terrestrial, or baitfish, it should not only look naturally alive in color and size, but also have action and movement. Too much realism in a fly is often a detriment when it makes them stiff and inflexible. They don't move. The best flies have a look of life to them, and appear alive in the water. The traits of this realism have three components: Behavior, Action, and Movement, or B. A. M.

All soft-hackles should have elements of B. A. M. It's not just the action and movement of these flies that make them effective. It's also the added element of natural behavior that makes them most effective, because they look fully alive.

## Behavior

- Certain mayfly species emerge on the streambed, like the Orange Sulphur (*Epeorus vitreus*) and Quill Gordons (*Epeorus pleuralis*). A winged wet fly is appropriate in this case.
- Caddis pupae use their legs to swim and emerge. Their soft-hackle collars should be active. They emerge quickly at the surface, so an active emergence presentation is realistic.
- Stoneflies crawl to shore to emerge on structure out of the water. During a stonefly hatch, it is effective to fish nymphs close to the shoreline and banks of the stream.
- Midge pupae ascend vertically to emerge, but are most vulnerable at the surface, hanging under the surface film.
- Nymphal behavioral drift (when nymphs intentionally move to find new homes) occurs in the early morning and late evening. Theoretically, this is when the low light offers them protection from predation; however, trout look for the nymphs at these times and feed heavily on them.

- Soft-hackle dries allow two different life-stage imitations in one cast: an adult at the beginning and an emerger or egg-laying diver at the end.

*Hydropsyche* Diver.

## Action

- An articulated soft-hackle nymph is effective because the fly has movement not only in the hackle, but also in the body, adding up to more action.
- Is the mayfly a swimmer, clinger, crawler, or burrower? This will determine the swimming ability and the amount of movement the nymph will exhibit while in the current flow.
- Depending on the species, employ stripping, mending, and other line manipulations, combined with the nymph's soft-hackle collar and body construction, to emphasize animation in the fly.
- Wet flies can be fished with one, two, or more line manipulations in one drift, to achieve different drift levels and imitate the appearance of specific species' action.
- Mayfly nymphs use their abdomen to propel themselves when swimming and emerging. Marabou tails and articulated abdomens represent this well.

Drake ArticuNymph.

## Movement

- Fly design and presentation affect the depth in which the fly is fished
- Drifting an immature nymph in one current lane is realistic, as the fly would not be moving toward the surface to emerge.
- Swinging nymphs across many current lanes can appear unnatural unless done slowly or to imitate ascending emergers.
- Movement is controlled through line mending and manipulation techniques, and the stream current itself.

Green Drake Emerger.

## RECIPES

### ELECTRIC SPIDER

| | |
|---|---|
| **Hook:** | #12-18 Mustad S82 |
| **Thread:** | Olive 6/0 Danville Flymaster |
| **Body:** | Green Flashabou |
| **Rib:** | Hareline Natural Rabbit Dubbin |
| **Hackle:** | Hen pheasant |

**Note:** This is a modern variation of a Spider. For the ribbing, touch dub the dubbing on the tag of the tying thread. You can also use a Mustad R30 dry fly hook, depending on desired sink rate.

### FEATHERBACK

| | |
|---|---|
| **Hook:** | #16 Mustad S82 |
| **Thread:** | Olive 12/0 Benecchi |
| **Tail and Abdomen:** | Olive mallard flank |
| **Thorax:** | Hareline Caddis Green Rabbit Dubbin |
| **Wing:** | Hareline Clear Wing |
| **Hackle:** | Medium dun India hen neck |

### YELLOW CRUSH

| | |
|---|---|
| **Hook:** | #12-18 Mustad S82 |
| **Thread:** | Yellow 6/0 Danville Flymaster |
| **Tail and Hackle:** | Pale yellow Whiting Pale Brahma hen saddle |
| **Body:** | Cheek of hare's mask |

**Note:** This is a modern variation of a flymph. The body dubbing is touch dubbed on the tying thread and wound over the underbody. You can also use a Mustad R30 dry fly hook, depending on desired sink rate.

### WET KRYSTAL

| | |
|---|---|
| **Hook:** | #12-#16 Tiemco 206BL |
| **Thread:** | Black 8/0 UNI-Thread |
| **Tail and Hackle:** | Brown partridge |
| **Abdomen:** | Red Flashabou (leave gaps to allow thread to show) |
| **Thorax:** | Black Hareline Rabbit Dubbin |
| **Wing:** | Furnace hen cape tip |

## TRAIL CREEK SWINGER

| | |
|---|---|
| **Hook:** | #10-18 Tiemco 5262 |
| **Thread:** | Rusty brown 70-denier Ultra Thread |
| **Tail:** | Ginger Wapsi hen neck |
| **Abdomen:** | Golden Brown Hare' E Ice Dub |
| **Rib:** | Orange Holographic Tinsel |
| **Thorax:** | Peacock Hare' E Ice Dub |
| **Hackle and Antennae:** | Ginger Wapsi hen neck |

## ACTION FLYMPH

| | |
|---|---|
| **Hook:** | #12-16 Dai-Riki 070 |
| **Thread:** | Orange 6/0 Danville Flymaster |
| **Body:** | Amber Hareline Rabbit Dubbin and Sulphur Orange Nature's Spirit Hare's Mask Dubbing |
| **Hackle:** | Bleached partridge |

**Note:** Variations may be orange, yellow, and green. Dubbing is hand mixed and roughed up with Velcro brush.

## ISONYCHIA EMERGER

| | |
|---|---|
| **Hook:** | #12 Tiemco 100 |
| **Thread:** | Camel 8/0 UNI-Thread |
| **Shuck:** | White and brown Z-Lon |
| **Abdomen:** | Brown Superfine Dubbing |
| **Rib:** | Tying thread |
| **Wing:** | Coastal deer hair |
| **Thorax:** | Caddis green Superfine Dubbing |
| **Hackle:** | Medium dun hen cape |

## SNAKE STONEFLY

| | |
|---|---|
| **Hook:** | #6-16 Tiemco 200R |
| **Thread:** | Orange 6/0 Danville Flymaster |
| **Rib (optional):** | Gold UTC Ultra Wire |
| **Body:** | Natural rabbit fur |
| **Wing:** | Light dun CDC |
| **Hackle:** | Brown partridge (shown) or tan Brahma hen |

**Note:** Body touch dubbed on tag of tying thread.

## BROWN DRAKE SPINNER

| | |
|---|---|
| **Hook:** | #14 Mustad R50 |
| **Thread:** | Coffee 6/0 Danville Flymaster |
| **Tail:** | Moose body fibers |
| **Body:** | Brown, light olive, and tan Superfine Dubbing mixture |
| **Wing:** | Coastal deer hair |
| **Spent Wing:** | Sparkle Organza |
| **Hackle:** | Grizzly hen cape |

**Note:** Hackle hen cape marked with BIC Tiki Hut Tan.

## DIVING CADDIS

| | |
|---|---|
| **Hook:** | #12-18 Mustad S82 |
| **Thread:** | Tobacco brown 6/0 Danville Flymaster |
| **Body:** | Light Hare's Ear Plus dubbing |
| **Hackle:** | Gray partridge in front of natural CDC |

## HYDROPSYCHE DIVER

| | |
|---|---|
| **Hook:** | #14 Tiemco 2457 |
| **Thread:** | Coffee 6/0 Danville Flymaster |
| **Abdomen:** | March Brown Hareline Rabbit Dubbin |
| **Rib:** | Black UTC Ultra Wire (small) |
| **Thorax:** | Rusty brown Hareline Rabbit Dubbin and golden brown Hareline Ice Dub mixture |
| **Hackle:** | Tan CDC |

## DRAKE ARTICUNYMPH

| | |
|---|---|
| **Hook:** | #14-16 Tiemco 3761 |
| **Thread:** | Tobacco brown 6/0 Danville Flymaster |
| **Tail:** | Rusty brown Woolly Bugger marabou |
| **Abdomen:** | March Brown Hareline Rabbit Dubbin |
| **Rib:** | Brown ostrich herl |
| **Thorax:** | Rusty brown Hareline Rabbit Dubbin |
| **Wing Case:** | Brown ostrich herl |
| **Hackle:** | Mottled gray Whiting Brahma hen saddle |
| **Bead:** | $3/32$" gold |

## GREEN DRAKE EMERGER

| | |
|---|---|
| **Hook:** | #10 Tiemco 200R |
| **Thread:** | Black 6/0 Danville Flymaster |
| **Tail:** | Olive partridge |
| **Abdomen:** | Olive DMC #832 Embroidery Floss |
| **Rib:** | Green ostrich |
| **Thorax:** | Olive Hareline Rabbit Dubbin |
| **Wing:** | Olive Z-Lon |
| **Hackle:** | Olive partridge and black marabou |

# Progressive Fly Materials and Tying Methods

An angler who designs and ties soft-hackles can customize the fly to match the particular color and size of insects in his or her own trout streams. Combining hackle collars with effective body materials creates a fly that looks and behaves alive. Guard hairs picked out from the body of furs like hare, rabbit, and squirrel pulsate and move underwater with the current, simulating a live insect's gills or body undulations. Many new fly materials are also available for enhancing and customizing flies to achieve life-like effects. Weight is the first consideration of design because it will determine where the fly rides in the water column, what it matches, and how it will be fished.

## WEIGHT AND SINK RATE

There seem to be two kinds of fly tiers: those who think it is all right to weight nymphs, and those who don't. Those who don't contend that since real nymphs are weightless, weight makes the nymph appear unnatural, and that light nymphs drift better in the water currents. But if you want to fish deep with lightweight nymphs, you have to weight the leader with split shot. The weight on the leader affects the drift, is more cumbersome to cast, and makes point-fly strikes harder to detect since you are not in direct contact with it.

I use all weighting options, depending on the water-current velocity, depth of water, and where the fish are holding.

The Teton River at Rainey Bridge in Driggs, Idaho, at sunset. If you fish here in the summer, don't leave too early, as warm evenings will trigger the caddis hatches and egg-laying flights at dusk. Fishing actually gets better in the low light, when you can fish soft-hackle caddis imitations to the sound and sight of rising fish.

I use a weighted nymph and add split shot to the leader as necessary, to get the fly to the depth needed to reach fish. If I'm sight-fishing in shallow, clear water, an un-weighted nymph may be all I need to reach the fish. You simply have to put your fly in front of trout to catch them.

The hook style and materials affect not only the appearance of life in the fly, but also the weight. When I design a fly, I consider how deep I will fish it, and weight the fly as needed to sink it. Sometimes this means as light as possible, and sometimes this means weight. Even fine copper or gold wire wrapped around the shank before tying the fly adds just enough weight to quickly break the surface tension of the water, and doesn't add unnecessary bulk to the appearance. Remember that 90 percent of a trout's diet is subsurface food.

A wire underbody adds enough weight to sink a fly like this May-Cad Nymph at different depths depending on your presentation. Touch dubbing over copper wire creates a lifelike vibrance, and the water acts as a mirror, alerting fish to a food source.

A sparse, smooth abdomen or body sinks faster than a dubbed fur body but has less enticing movement of fibers to project realism. You must decide the most important factors for the purpose of a particular fly, and then take into account any other flies that may be on the rig, to achieve proper appearance and drift.

The weight of the fly must match its intended purpose. A floating soft-hackle needs to be light, and also have materials that will aid in flotation, such as lightweight ribbing (if any), waterproof dubbing, and a hackle collar that can help carry the weight of the fly in the surface film. The weight of the fly will link to the life stage of the insect you want to match, and this will determine where in the water column you want the fly to ride. Of course, immature nymphs should be fished near the streambed. Emerging nymphs can be fished at all depths, but often the presentation is to raise the emergers toward the surface in front of the fish, to imitate a natural on its journey to the surface. Some of my favorite deep nymph bodies have abdomens made from copper wire in various colors. The wire creates a segmented look, has flash, gives a slim profile to the fly that cuts through the water

column quickly, and adds weight to sink the fly faster and keep it sunk. For flies #20 and smaller, I use the extra-small wire; #16-18, the small wire; #12-14, Brassie size; and #10 and larger, medium-size wire.

You can get a feel for a fly's weight and ability to sink (or not) by dropping it from about 12 inches onto the hard surface of a fly-tying desk, and listening for the sound it makes. A dense or faster-sinking fly will let you know it, while a more buoyant fly will be much quieter as it hits the table's surface.

This Light Cahill nymph imitation has a copper-wire abdomen, which is a good way to add weight, segmentation, and flash. The gills undulate in the water's currents.

Here are the weighting methods I use, from lightest to heaviest:

- Dry-fly hook (on top of the water surface to a few inches below)
- Wet-fly nymph hook (flymph, 4 to 15 inches below the surface)
- Copper-wire underbody (ascending flymph 24 inches below and up to the surface)
- Glass-bead head or thorax (deeper nymph)
- Copper-bead head or thorax
- Lead-strip underbody: .020 (#10-12), .010 (#14), .015 (#16)
- Lead-wire underbody: .020 (#10-12), .010 (#14), .015 (#16)
- Tungsten-bead head or thorax
- Bead and copper-wire underbody or abdomen
- Bead and lead-wire underbody

Fishing two or three flies on the leader allows you to fish three water levels, using a heavy point fly, a medium weighted dropper, and the light dropper as the top fly. Fishing three different water-column levels allows you to present your flies to more fish, and increases chances of a double, or even a triple catch. Putting the heaviest fly on the point often avoids having to use split shot, allowing for easier casting and better strike detection when I can feel the point fly and all the droppers directly, without the hinge effect of the split shot.

# FLY SINK-SPEED TESTING

Knowing the sink rate of a specific fly helps you choose the right fly for the water conditions you encounter, and determine how deep the fly will sink in a short amount of time. This lets you choose flies to target the depth at which the fish are holding, and to imitate any insect life stage, given hatching bugs and the time of year. The sink rate is the number of inches per second a fly will sink without any drag (excluding factors like heavy current). It informs us of how much mending we need to make to keep the fly sunk and dead-drifted. With the sink rate known, we can even silently count down the inches per second to become familiar with what our nymphs are actually doing once they are in the water and sinking to level.

Take a glass pitcher you can fill with 10 inches of water. Drop a fly in the pitcher. Use a stopwatch (like the one on your smartphone) to time the rate it takes the fly to sink to the bottom. Divide the time by 10 to get the inches-per-second sink rate, which can help you determine fly weighting for optimum water-column drift depth. To retrieve the fly and test another without making a mess, use a small rare-earth magnet, superglued to the end of a wooden dowel long enough to fish the fly out.

| SINK RATE | | | | |
|---|---|---|---|---|
| Fly Pattern | Hook | Hook Type | (ips) | Notes |
| Bead Head Orange Hare Thorax Nymph | #14 | nymph | 15 | 1/8" tungsten bead |
| Bead Thorax Marabou Pheasant Tail | #16 | nymph | 8.18 | 3/32" brass bead |
| Heavy Metal Nymph | #14 | nymph | 8.18 | 3/32" copper, wire abdomen |
| Bead Thorax Pheasant Tail Soft-Hackle | #16 | nymph | 8.18 | 3/32" brass bead |
| Heavy Metal Nymph | #16 | nymph | 5.62 | copper wire abdomen |
| Minimalist Marabou Flymph | #12 | nymph | 4.73 | no body, only exposed hook, thread and hackle |
| Yellow and Snipe | #14 | dry | 4.5 | small wire underbody and ribbing |
| Partridge and Orange | #14 | nymph | 4.2 | smooth silk floss body |
| Marabou Winged Wet Fly | #14 | dry | 4.09 | hen hackle tip wing |
| Ice Caddis Pupa | #16 | nymph | 3.75 | V-Rib body |
| Wet Ant | #14 | nymph | 3.75 | Loon Hard Head body |
| Marabou Winged Wet Fly | #14 | nymph | 3.75 | hen hackle tip wing |
| Partridge and Orange | #14 | dry | 3.75 | smooth silk floss body |
| Partridge and Orange | #14 | dry | 3.6 | silk thread body |
| The Bumblebee | #12 | dry | 3.46 | Coats and Clark thread body |
| Mayfly Soft-Hackle Dry | #16 | dry | 2.57 | deer hair wing |

Holding the fly underwater in a glass pitcher with a dowel and magnet lets you examine which materials will darken and which won't (usually synthetics) when exposed to water. Test the action of the fly by moving it around.

## HOOK SHAPE

Though most fly hooks have straight shanks, aquatic insects are rarely straight. Even if the fly doesn't have all of the natural's moving parts, a curved or bent shape can give the impression of movement and appear to be alive, which can trigger trout to feed. Hook makers are starting to recognize this; more curved and bent hook shanks are available now than ever before, but you can also bend your own.

When adrift, swimming, or emerging, mayflies often flip up and down like dolphins, making a curved shape, or even better an articulated pattern, more realistic. Caddis pupae are shaped like a half letter C, represented by scud hooks like Tiemco 2457, or some of the new caddis-shaped hooks like Dohiku 644 and the Maruto 206BL. Stoneflies are long and straight, but when moving or scurrying for a hold, they often arch their abdomen upward so their powerful thorax legs can grab. To form this shape, put a 300 or a Mustad R75 in the vise, and with forceps bend the hook upward at the back of the thorax location. Midges are generally so small that hook shape is not of great importance, and I generally use lightweight dry-fly hooks #18 and smaller to match the pupa. The exception is when matching the pupa hanging in a U-shape, attached to the underside of the surface film. Midge pupae do this to establish an anchor so they can break through the surface film, hard to do for their size unless they have an anchor to push against. To imitate this U-shape of the natural, bend a hook into a V, with the mid-shank lower than the bend and the hook eye.

Not all hooks will bend without breaking, though most straight-shank nymph and streamer hooks of standard-wire gauge and heavier can, in a vise with a pair of forceps. This is not true of fine-wire dry-fly hooks. Also, high-carbon steel hooks are often too brittle unless the temper is removed with a lighter, and then bent. The Eagle Claw Lazer Sharp and Mustad nymph and streamer straight-shank hooks shape well, even without being heated.

To bend a hook eye, I heat the eye of the hook for about five seconds with a lighter, and before it cools down, I slowly bend the hook eye up to a straight eye. I then heat it again and slowly bend the eye into an upturned eye. You must bend the eye slowly at the shank, just behind the eye. Allow it to cool, and the hook is ready for use. The steel will only take two heatings and bendings before it becomes too weak and can snap.

## TRANSLUCENCE

Some of the best soft-hackle imitations have translucent bodies that match the real thing. A combination of an underbody material that imitates the inside of the nymph, and an overbody that imitates the shell, will show translucence and depth when wet.

The thread underbody is usually a contrasting color, allowing it to glow through the body material and represent a somewhat translucent appearance like that of a natural

Mayfly nymphs like this *Isonychia* have natural curvature. This shows the undulating shape their abdomens make when swimming. JON RAPP

A hand-bent curved swimming-nymph hook, like that used in the Pond's French Dip Nymph, can represent this shape. Forceps can bend heavy-gauge nymph hooks to shape in the vise, before tying the fly.

This Madison's Caddis (variant) is a pupa tied on a straight nymph hook (#12-16 Eagle Claw L063) bent into a mild curve.

invertebrate. Historically, the combination of a silk-thread underbody and a fur overbody has accomplished this, and it's still deadly. The overbody is applied sparsely to the thread, so that when the dubbing becomes wet, it allows the underbody to show through the dubbing and create the transluscent glow.

Touch dubbing is the best way to create just the right amount of overbody. The underbody can be thread, tinsel, Holographic Tinsel, UV dubbing, or colored wire (for weight). Use your imagination. The two contrasting materials will create the needed overbody/underbody combination. However, more material choices naturally offer more ways to do this. One example is wrapping a clear or transparent material, such as V-Rib, over the underbody (clear, or colored with a marker on the flat inside side). Flash materials like Holographic Tinsel make excellent underbodies, because once the overbody fur is wet, the underbody will appear to glow through the fur. This gives the fly a dynamic effect. However, subtler materials, such as raffia and tying thread, also work well, because the V-Rib will amplify the underbody material.

Design flies as they appear wet. Water will sometimes darken them and make materials meld into each other, giving the fly a totally different appearance when it's in the water. After you remove it from the water, hold it against a contrasting surface in the light. It will then show you the true color possibilities the materials can display when wet.

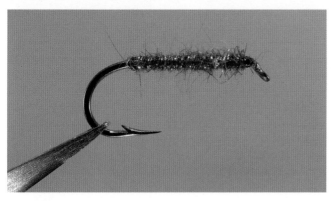

Contrasting tying thread/wire underbody/hare's mask dubbing. This combination gives a complicated appearance to the fly when wet, as the chartreuse wire is wrapped with open sections allowing the black thread to show through, creating contrast. The hare's mask creates contrast as well as life movement, through the undulating fibers and guard hairs.

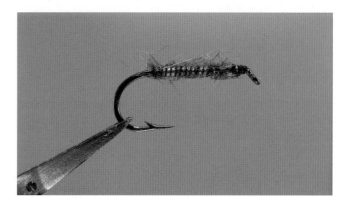

Flashabou underbody/rabbit fur dubbed. Overlap the Flashabou to create a solid color, or leave open to allow the tying thread to show through, to create segmentation and contrast. The soft rabbit-fur fibers will undulate in the current and also provide further contrast to the appearance of the body, for the look of translucence.

## TYING THE GREEN LANTERN

### GREEN LANTERN

| | |
|---|---|
| **Hook:** | #16 White River WR-386 |
| **Thread:** | Rusty dun 8/0 UNI-Thread |
| **Abdomen:** | Chartreuse .010" monofilament |
| **Thorax:** | Rusty brown Orvis Ice Dub |
| **Hackle:** | Brown partridge |

**Note:** This pattern imitates many caddis species pupae for use during caddis hatches or as a prospecting fly. The smooth monofilament body cuts through the water quickly, and also acts as weight. I often use this as middle dropper on a three-fly leader with the point fly heaviest, this fly a little lighter, and the top dropper the lightest fly, to give a three-level drift presentation.

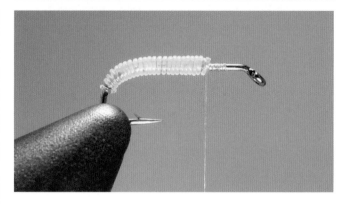

**3** Wrap the monofilament tightly around the hook, up to the thorax; then tie it off with multiple thread wraps and trim closely with nippers. The gray-thread underbody is a neutral color and lets the chartreuse monofilament glow bright and true.

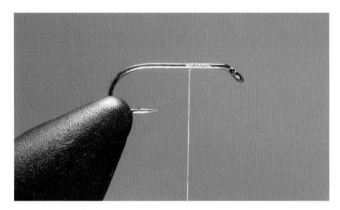

**1** Place the hook in the vise and attach the thread, wrapping it to the back of the thorax.

**4** Dub a thorax.

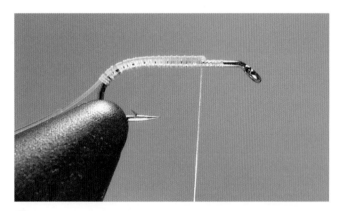

**2** Cut a 5-inch length or so of .010 hi-vis chartreuse monofilament, and tie it in on top of the hook shank, wrapping the thread back to the hook bend and about halfway down the bend. Then wrap the thread back up to the back of the thorax.

**5** Prepare a brownish-gray partridge feather for a tip tie-in using hackle pliers.

**7** Wrap the feather two or three times around the hook, sweeping the fibers back with your free hand with each turn. Tie off and trim the excess fibers. Build a head, treat a small section of the thread with head cement, and whip finish.

**6** Tie in the feather by the tip with the top of the feather facing up. Sweep the fibers back.

**8** This fly will sink at a medium speed, as its sparse body cuts throught the water column quickly. I usually use it for a middle dropper on a three-fly rig because of its medium weight.

# BODY TYPES

Materials such as dubbing, natural furs, threads, and floss can make bodies. However, many materials that not often used for bodies make some of finest bodies—for instance, turkey rounds, marabou, ostrich herl, CDC, wire, monofilament, and V-Rib. All make nice, segmented-looking bodies on wet flies. Ed Story used to like to tell me how he had stopped using dubbing altogether, and used turkey rounds for bodies instead. With a wound material, you can form the body quickly and neatly, and the fly will sink quickly because the body fibers won't trap the air (good and bad) like dubbing. Some of the best bodies combine dubbing and synthetics, herls, or wires. This gives contrast and proportional changes to the shape of the body.

Morning Sulphur. For this fly, I used two bobbins at the same time to wind orange 6/0 Danville Flymaster and light olive 6/0 Danville Flymaster side by side.

Absaroka Nymph. Leaving a bit of a gap between wire wraps on the abdomen allows for the underbody, in this case black thread, to show through, and creates contrast with two colors. You can wrap the wire close if you only want the wire color for the abdomen. Hackle on this fly is hen pheasant, and the head is yellow ostrich.

## Thread Bodies

Tying thread bodies are realistic for small flies and/or slim bodies. You can use a single color of thread, or combine two threads for a mottled and segmented appearance. Use two bobbins with different-color threads, and wind the threads onto the hook by pinching them together with your index finger and thumb. You can also run both threads through one of the bobbins and let the other bobbin hang alongside the main bobbin. As you wrap the threads, they will try to twist together, so you have to spin the bobbins counterclockwise after some wraps to keep the threads separate and lying parallel to each other.

Coats and Clark All Purpose Dual Duty Plus Sewing Machine Thread is another great body material that can be used to make an effective segmented and contrasting body, and comes in a wide array of color choices that match natural mayflies well. The thread stays the same color wet or dry. It's good for low-profile bodies and abdomens on small flies, or as abdomen ribbing in soft-hackle dry flies.

The Bumblebee. In this fly, the body and head are Coats and Clark Sewing Thread #2 Black and #157a Yellow. A strand of DMC #310 and DMC #445 Embroidery Floss can also create the effect. Tip: Since the sewing thread is thicker than tying thread, each color is more distinct in the finished body. Use superglue to finish the head so that the wraps are not twisted, but continue the same segmentation as the body.

## Fur-Dubbed Bodies

Natural fur is still one of the best body dubbings for many wet flies, because it has life-like properties in the water from the fibers that undulate in the current. Muskrat, mole, hare's mask, rabbit, squirrel, and beaver can blend with synthetics like Antron and Ice Dub to give the dubbing some sparkle and draw the attention of fish. I like to brush or pick the dubbing fibers out with a Velcro strip (or use a bodkin if I want more precision), so they stick out from the fly to make it look shaggier and puffier.

Pinch dubbing allows you to fine tune the amount of fur you apply to the thread for a distinct and natural-looking body taper. If you want a smoother body with fur, remove the guard hairs first. Touch dubbing allows the underlying materials to show through. First, cut the dubbing into fine pieces with

Warrior Nymph. Abdomen is hand-mixed rusty brown Hareline Rabbit and rusty brown Orvis Ice Dubbing mixture placed in a red Ultra Wire (extra small) dubbing loop, which builds a little bit of additional weight into the fly.

Caddis green rabbit dubbing, rusty brown rabbit, olive Ice Dub. Use different amounts of each to customize your final shade, being particularly careful with the Ice Dub, as too much of the mixture can become too sparkly and overpower the appearance.

scissors, apply wax to the thread, and then press the chopped dubbing onto the thread. The amount that sticks as you press the fur onto the waxed thread is all you need. I use a stick-type tacky wax like Wapsi Premium Dubbing Wax. It's soft and tacky, and won't dry out. Don't get the wax on your fingers before touch dubbing, as the dubbing fur won't transfer to the thread, mostly sticking to your fingers.

### Layered Dubbing Mixtures

You don't have to premix dubbings before attaching them to the thread. An example is rabbit and Ice Dub. First, direct dub the rabbit onto the thread in the amount you will need to make the whole body. Then, simply pinch some Ice Dub on top of the rabbit, allowing the first dubbing to show through substantially. Next, dub the body and pick out the fibers to rough them up a little and blend them. Leaving a 5-inch tag end of thread at the hook bend, dubbing the rabbit body onto the bobbin thread, attaching the Ice Dub to the tag thread, and loosely dubbing over the first dubbing can also accomplish this effect.

### Pinch and Tear Custom-Blended Dubbing

Hand blending dubbing at the vise is the fastest and easiest way to create a custom-blended dubbing mixture. A custom-blended dubbing will allow you to create the exact color and shade of dubbing, and also to introduce flash into the mixture in varying amounts. I look at packaged dubbing furs and synthetics as an artist looks at paint. For instance, if you want brownish-olive dubbing, you simply take the right proportions of the brown and the olive, and hand mix them by pushing them together and pulling them apart over and over, until they have become uniformly blended into a single dubbing with characteristics of both colors in one overall color. The amount you take from each determines the dominant color shade. You can blend all types of dubbing materials together. I often make just enough for one or two flies at a time.

Hand blend the materials by pushing them together and tearing them apart several times, until they have blended into a uniform mixture. You can add more of each dubbing as you go, to achieve the correct shade balance.

The blended dubbing is ready to use. You can blend natural furs with synthetics in any combination to achieve the correct color, with or without sparkle.

Create a finer dubbing mixture for touch dubbing by cutting the dubbing into finer sections. Cut the sections across the dubbing ball, then gather it up and cut across again.

The finer mixture is ready. This method allows you to make enough for just a single fly or for multiple flies by varying how much material you blend at once.

## TAILING

The choice of whether to use a tail on a fly depends on the species the fly is meant to imitate, or whether you just want it for more action in prospect fishing. To imitate mayflies realistically, you may want to choose a tail. The same goes for stonefly nymphs, but not for stonefly adults, midge adults, or caddis pupae or adults. Sometimes a tail is tied just for the action and movement it makes in the water, like on Softie Buggers or prospecting nymphs. Instead of tailing, which is often so fine as to be unnoticeable on some flies, consider using a trailing shuck on nymphs, emergers, and even dry flies meant to imitate the beginning of a transitional life stage.

Tail for wet flies should exhibit action and movement. For instance, a dubbing trailing shuck, using brown or olive Rabbit Dubbin or Hare's Ear Plus, makes a nice, soft shuck and absorbs water to aid in sinking the fly. Chickabou

### SHUCKED WET SULPHUR

| | |
|---|---|
| **Hook:** | #12-18 Eagle Claw Nymph |
| **Thread:** | Light Cahill 8/0 UNI-Thread |
| **Shuck:** | Brown Hare's Ear Plus Dubbing |
| **Rib:** | Beige 6/0 Danville Flymaster |
| **Body:** | Pale yellow Superfine Dry Fly Dubbing |
| **Wing:** | Swiss Straw (shown) or Hareline Clear Wing |
| **Hackle:** | Bleached partridge |

### THE DOUBLE PLAYER

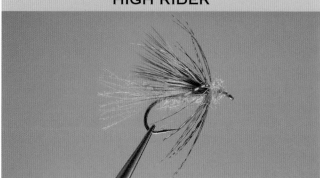

| | |
|---|---|
| **Hook:** | #10-16 Tiemco 5262 |
| **Thread:** | Black 6/0 Danville Flymaster |
| **Abdomen:** | Black thread under pale yellow DMC 25 #745 Embroidery Floss Rib |
| **Thorax:** | Brown grizzly hen cape |
| **Tail and Hackle:** | Olive grizzly marabou |

### HIGH RIDER

| | |
|---|---|
| **Hook:** | #10-16 Mustad R50 Dry Fly |
| **Thread:** | Orange 6/0 Danville Flymaster |
| **Tail:** | Tan CDC |
| **Abdomen:** | Tan Superfine Dry Fly Touch Dubbing |
| **Wing:** | Coastal deer |
| **Hackle:** | Brown partridge |
| **Head:** | Orange and sulphur Spirit River Fine and Dry dry-fly dubbing mixture |

makes a highly active tail. Use a dense tail for a streamer or a sparse tail for an insect. Marabou simulates the action and articulated movement of the thorax of a swimming nymph. Mallard flank has nice segmented mottling like a natural mayfly.

Emerger shucks simulate the shedding nymphal exoskeleton of the invertebrate. Polypropylene yarn makes a great shuck, as it has soft fibers and floats well. Cut to length on the finished fly, Z-Lon also gives the fly the appearance of a shedding nymphal shuck. Finally, Ice Dubbing, Hare's Ear Plus,

and Antron can all give the appearance of a nymphal shuck hanging off an emerger.

In soft-hackle dry flies, the tail can create more flotation, but these materials also offer subsurface drift and movement. Hen cape hackle has stiffer fibers than hen saddles, yet it is pliable. CDC can give the appearance of a floating exoskeleton shuck. Deer hair is a good tail for floating a fly in riffle water. Elk offers strong flotation due to the large diameter of the hair base. Tailor your dry-fly tailing to the turbulence of the water.

## SOFT-HACKLE COLLARS AND METHODS

Most game-bird skins like grouse and partridge contain many feathers suited to hackling #12 and larger flies. It is much harder to find feathers for smaller flies. For small flies, snipe and bobwhite quail are good choices. Both of these skins contain a large amount of soft feathers that will hackle flies from #14 down to #20. When it comes to wild birds like partridge, the younger birds harvested earlier in the year tend to have smaller feather for smaller hooks. Also, pen-raised partridge are smaller than wild birds, with smaller feathers. In general, partridge have neck feathers that will hackle #16-20 flies. Even large feathers like hen pheasant, brown partridge, and Brahma hen can also tie down to #18 if you use the tip fibers, and make only one or two turns of hackle before the fibers get too long farther down the stem.

For partridge, grouse, and other webby game-bird feathers that correspond in size to the fly I am tying, the method I use the most is tying in the soft-hackle collar by the tip of the feather. It allows you to first wrap the thinner, easier-to-wrap part of the stem, and to take closer wraps, using less of the hook shank to make the collar. The shorter fibers at the tip enable you to tie smaller flies.

Hen cape feathers have different fiber characteristics from the tip, down the stem to the base. The tip fibers are shorter and the stem is thinner, but the fibers are often stiffer. As you proceed down the stem, the fibers will lengthen, but also become soft, due to the web extending further out to the tip of the fiber. Just above the afterfeathers at the base are the softest regular fibers on the feather. If you want the softest hackle a hen cape can provide, use the lower stem fibers. They will also sweep back over the fly body better, due to the relaxed fibers on this part of the feather. Usually soft-hackle wraps use both sides of the fiber on the stem when hackling. This lets you take one, one and a half, or two or more turns to achieve the density of the hackle you want on the fly. With some feathers, particularly hen saddles, the fibers are so webby and dense that even one turn looks like too much hackle, and you can't see the body of the fly. If I notice the hen feather becoming too dense, I will strip off the hook side of the fibers. Then I tie in the feather, and wind the hackle using only half of the fibers, creating a sparser collar.

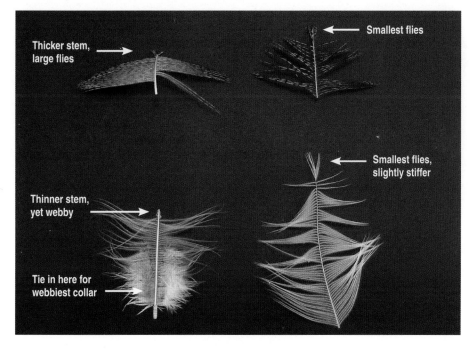

Prepared partridge and hen feathers for both tip tie-in and base feather tie-in. The tip fibers are stiffer than the base fibers, especially on the hen. Use the rest for tailing on the fly.

# HACKLE COLLAR STYLES

The position of the soft-hackle collar on the fly not only affects the amount of action the fly displays, but also the life stage. A short collar imitates immature nymphs with legs, and emphasizes the body; a long collar imitate emergers with more leg movement, antennae, and unfolding wings, or adult wings. The density of the collar will show more or less of the underbody, depending on your design intent. Short-hackle nymphs look realistic, while long hackle has more movement and activity. You can decide which is more important, given water conditions, clarity, insect-hatch density, and depth.

The Grand Caddis has both a rear hackle (Whiting Tan Brahma Hen) and forward hackle (brown hen cape). Different-facing collars give the impression of a swimming caddis with two movements.

The General Practitioner's thorax collar only extends back to the thorax of the fly body, imitating the short legs of the nymph.

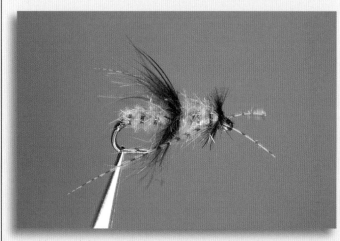

The Mammoth Nymph displays a midshank collar of brown starling. This position on the fly emulates legs or emergence between two stages.

The Skeleton Flymph's full-body hackle collar extends to the back or beyond the back of the hook bend, imitating the full length of caddis wings.

The Copper Basin Flymph shows a midthorax collar. The brown partridge hackle simulates the thorax legs and wing of an insect.

The Beartooth Nymph displays a traditional collar of gray partridge extending back to the hook bend, the most common style, as it copies wings and swept-back legs.

The Elkhorn is a thorax palmered flymph. This fly uses a furnace hen cape for the longer feather length needed, and simulates the wing and three-leg segment of the insect.

The Red Raider is a full palmered fly. The bleached grizzly hen cape holds its form well in faster water currents, and makes for a strong profile.

The Q-Back is a reverse palmered fly. The bleached grizzly hen cape has lots of kick in the water current, resulting in a pulsating action similar to a jig.

The Reflection Nymph displays the fore-and-aft hackle method using brown or gray partridge, one of each color. This fly looks buggy from all angles and has great action in the water.

The Copper Aggressor has a double hackle using the tips of the marabou tail and gray Whiting Brahma Hen to create two different color shades and action.

# HACKLE FEATHERS

The soft-hackle collar is also significant because it expands, contracts, and wavers in the currents. The amount of web in the feather offers the tier the ability to choose stiffer and softer feathers to give the fly different soft-hackle collar characteristics. Generally, the more web a feather has, the softer the fibers are, and the more action it will have in water, particularly slower water.

Hen feathers are more readily available than ever for fly tiers. The wide choice of colors, sizes, contrasts, and webbiness makes them some of the most useful and important soft-hackle feathers.

Feathers are the basis of soft-hackle flies, actually defining them. Soft-hackle collars traditionally are partridge, grouse, snipe, woodcock, quail, or other game birds. In addition to these Brahma hen, genetic hen capes and saddles, marabou, chickabou, and practically any feather that has enough web to make a good soft-hackle collar can be employed using appropriately sized feathers or tying techniques. Whiting, Metz, Collins, Keough, Ewing, and Clearwater genetic hen capes are stiffer than hen saddles, but produce a more delicate collar on the fly. The feather should match the intended useage of the fly. I use hen capes predominantly for soft-hackle dry flies, as the stiffer fibers allow for better flotation, yet can still be pulled under and fished wet. Hen capes also occur in many flies, among them the Silky Emerger, the PMD Lethal Weapon, and the Braided Flycatcher, in which two contrasting colors appear.

## ORANGE CRUSH

**Hook:** #14-18 Mustad S82
**Thread:** Tan 8/0 Orvis
**Body:** Amber and orange Hareline Rabbit mixture
**Tail and Hackle:** Golden straw Whiting Brahma hen saddle

**Note:** This is a Sulphur and Slate Maroon Drake Wingless Wet. Mix the dubbing used for the body by hand. You can use a Mustad R30 dry fly hook, which is lighter, depending on desired sink rate.

Another relatively new material is Brahma hen, available in both capes and saddles. The latter is pretty amazing. Why? Because even though the feathers look large, by using only one turn of the short-tip fibers, you can create a distinctive, mottled hackle collar from hook size 2 down to size 18. It's better than genetic hen capes for webbier collars, because the fibers are denser and require fewer turns of the feather. You want to use India hen capes for soft, webby collar on flymphs.

## GINGER STAR FLYMPH

**Hook:** #14-18 White River WR-396
**Thread:** Tan Orvis 8/0
**Tail:** Mallard flank wood duck
**Body:** Antique gold Hareline Rabbit Dubbin
**Hackle:** Bleached starling

**Note:** First cover the body with 6/0 Danville Flymaster before dubbing over it. Use the tan thread for the dubbing.

I also really like the new dyed starling skins. Starling is commonly used for smaller #16-24 flies, due to the short feather fiber length. They come in many colors and have some of the softest feathers, easily activated by currents. I use these to tie the Picabo Mayfly, the Mammoth Nymph, and the Speckled Caddis (bleached starling).

## THE SPECIALIST

| Hook: | #14-18 Mustad R30 |
|---|---|
| Thread: | Beige 6/0 Danville Flymaster |
| Tail: | Olive hen cape fibers |
| Body: | Olive and tan Superfine Rabbit Dubbin mixture |
| Rib: | Hunter green DMC 25 #3346 Embroidery Floss or Olive 6/0 Danville Flymaster |
| Wing: | Dun hen cape feather tip |
| Hackle: | Olive Woolly Bugger marabou |

**Note:** This pattern can be used for *Baetis*, Green Drake, and Flav imitations.

While marabou and chickabou feathers haven't been commonly used for soft-hackles, they are the softest feathers available. In fact, they are so soft and so sensitive to movement that you can use them for checking drafts around windows. More importantly, they offer an unparalleled fluid, life-like breathing action underwater. The natural action of the feather led me to begin using marabou feather for collars and tails in the first place. I found that they activate in the slightest water hydraulic, more so than any other soft-hackle feather available. In fact, my Minimalist Nymphs are nothing more than bare hook and a marabou hackle collar, and they're deadly. These flies embody the basics of enticement: movement and life. Some of the flies I tie with marabou include the Mossy Creek Nymph and Marabou Soft-Hackle Nymph. It can also be used for bodies and thoraxes on the White Sulphur Soft-Wing and the PMD Transition Flymph.

## MINIMALIST NYMPH

| Hook: | #12-18 WR-396 |
|---|---|
| Thread: | Tobacco brown 6/0 Danville Flymaster |
| Hackle: | Ginger Woolly Bugger marabou |

My fly-tying bench location provides plenty of adjustable lighting, with natural light and daylight color lamps to show true outdoor colors of the materials I'm using. This ensures accurately matching materials to natural bugs.

# USING MARKERS TO COLOR FLY-TYING MATERIALS

Coloring white or light dun materials with a variety of art markers in natural colors allows you to color just enough material for a fly at a time.

Most naturally colored feathers only come in so many colors. Grizzly, dun, brown, ginger variants, black, and white are the most common. This especially applies to chickens, as they have more variations than game birds. For other colors, dying with acid dyes is a popular method to get red, green, yellow, blue, purple, and others. Dying is an effective method, but usually dying the whole pelt changes all the feathers into a single base color. Moreover, the entire feather is colored in one solid manner. Markers allow a variety of color schemes.

A permanent marker with too high an alcohol content can make the feather fibers stick together and become matted and gooey. Too much marker pigment can also make the feather matted. Apply the marker uniformly and quickly to coat the fibers, but don't oversaturate them. This means one or two strokes of the marker over the feather, in one direction from the stem out to the tips.

I use Prismacolor and BIC Mark-It markers. Both of these are alcohol-based permanent inks and, applied correctly, they will allow you to customize feathers and other materials. The Prismacolor is a more muted and natural shade of color, the reason I use it for match-the-hatch shading of the material to simulate the naturals. The BIC Mark-It markers work well for attractor patterns because they offer brighter, more vivid color. Mark the top of the feather on a tissue. Lightly and quickly run the marker from the feather stem out to the tips around the feather. To color white thread another color with the marker, use only one stroke of marker, as more will darken the thread too much. You can tie a fly right away, but marked feathers need about 10 minutes to dry before exposing them to water, or they can bleed.

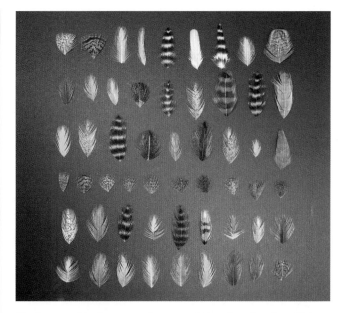

The top row of feathers: gray, brown partridge, American hen, Metz hen cape, Keough hen cape, light dun Whiting hen saddle, Whiting grizzly hen saddle, India hen cape, Brahma hen saddle; art markers can create all the feathers seen below them. This allows you to buy a smaller number of skins, and even create feather color schemes that are otherwise unavailable.

# PRISMACOLOR SPECIES COLORS FOR SINGLE HACKLE COLLAR

**Insect Species**

Quill Gordon • Hendrickson • Sulphur Orange • Light Cahill • Blue-Winged Olive • March Brown • Hexagenia • Mahogany Dun • PMD

**Prismacolor Marker Color**

Walnut • Walnut • Tulip Yellow • Deco Yellow • Dark or Light Olive • Goldenrod • Deco Yellow • Light Tan • Deco Yellow

# PRISMACOLOR MARKER COLORS FOR COMPOUND HACKLE COLLARS ON WHITE HEN CAPE FEATHERS

| Mayfly Dun Wing/Leg Color | Prismacolor Marker on White Hen Feather |
| --- | --- |
| *Baetis* Dun/Olive | 114 Cool Gray/028 Dark Olive Green |
| Sulphur Dun/Yellowish Olive | 114 Cool Gray/017 Sunburst Yellow |
| *Isonychia* Grizzly Dun/Olive Brown | 114 Cool Gray/172 Light Umber |
| March Brown Grizzly/Tan Grizzly | 095 Light Tan |
| Quill Gordon Dun/Olive Grizzly | 114 Cool Gray/028 Dark Olive Green |
| Western Green Drake Dun Grizzly/Olive Grizzly | 114 Cool Gray /028 Dark Olive Green |
| PMD Dun/Yellowish Olive | 114 Cool Gray/017 Sunburst Yellow |
| Mahogany Dun Dun/Reddish Brown | 114 Cool Gray/061 Dark Umber |
| Hendrickson Dark Dun/Yellow Orange | 114 Cool Gray/015 Yellowed Orange |
| Light Cahill Yellow Grizzly/Light Olive Grizzly | 017 Sunburst Yellow/026 Light Olive Green |

**Note:** Use a few stripped fibers from the wing-colored feather for tailing.

## Using Markers to Imitate Protected Bird Feathers

Matching feathers requires consideration of not only the color and size of the feather, but also the web characteristics. It seems simple to take a white hen feather and mark it with a marker, but in many of the game-bird feathers, the individual fiber characteristics make up the appearance and softness of the soft-hackle collar. Sometimes it's necessary to use a substitute to match a bird feather that is protected under the Migratory Bird Act. Here are some recipes for imitating protected game-bird feathers.

A further advantage to coloring your own feathers is the ability to create color schemes not available through dying, such as half-and-half feather color combinations that create contrast in the hackle collar. For example, a light dun hen cape feather marked yellow on only one side of the stem displays both yellow and gray hues using a single feather.

Waterhen Bloa. When waterhen or moorhen is called for, substitute a mallard duck marginal covert wing feather, medium dark dun India hen neck, Whiting medium dun hen saddle, or white hen saddle (shown here) marked with Prismacolor Cool Gray PM-113.

Dark Watchet. Imitate the jackdaw called for in the original recipe with a white hen cape, marked first with BIC Mark-It Tuxedo Black and then BIC Mark-It Playful Purple, as shown here. A jackdaw feather is black at first appearance, but has subtle purple tints when held in the light.

Coot and Purple. Imitate coot feathers with a dark dun India hen cape or, as shown here, with a white genetic hen saddle marked with Prismacolor Cool Gray PM-113. The hen cape feather has the same web density as coot.

Woodcock and Hare's Lug. Imitate woodcock with a blue grouse wing feather (shown here) or a medium dun hen saddle feather, first marked with Prismacolor Goldenrod PM-69 and then crossmarked with Prismacolor Cool Gray 60% PM-113. While smaller, a bobwhite quail wing feather also has similar characteristics.

Snipe and Yellow. Imitate snipe with a ruffed grouse or starling undercovert feather or, as shown here, with a bobwhite quail white belly feather marked first with Prismacolor Light Tan PM-95 and then Prismacolor Cool Gray PM-113 in the center of the feather, leaving the tips cream. This fly appears in works by Leisenring, Pritt, and others as far back as the 1850s. It's good for matching Yellow Sallies and Sulphurs.

Hare's Lug and Plover. Imitate the golden plover called for in the original recipe, with a dun hen saddle feather marked on the edges with a Prismacolor Deco Yellow PM-131, and the center with Prismacolor Cool Gray PM-113. Either color the edge uniform yellow as seen here, or with patches of yellow on the edge to imitate the bird feather. This modern-style fly has a longer body and hackle than the North Country Spider style, where a body only extends to between the hook barb and the point.

## CDC SOFT-HACKLES

CDC mallard duck feathers float naturally due to the preen-gland oils and fiber structure that trap air. A great dry-fly material, they are also useful for a collar hackle on wet flies, because they are soft and move somewhat like marabou in the water. Also, they can capture tiny air bubbles and hold them underwater on the feather, giving the fly sparkle with light reflection on the air bubbles. Used alone or with another soft-hackle feather for contrast, they are particularly useful for tying CDC caddis imitations that can mimic both pupae and diving egg-laying caddis, trapping air hydrofuge as they dive to oviposit. CDC also works for a wing on a soft-hackle dry fly or a soft-hackle collar to imitate a floating stillborn emerger or a spent mayfly spinner. The CDC lets the fly sit flush in the surface film, like these life stages.

Use CDC for a hackle collar. This CDC Soft-Hackle Dry/Wet fly can float in the surface film or be fished wet. The duck fibers also hold shimmering air bubbles as the fly lands.

The CDC Rusty Spinner is a wet fly that can also be fished in the surface film. It imitates both floating spinners and sunken spent spinners.

## Collar Compensation Hackling Methods

One of the issues with soft-hackle collars has to do with finding the right feather size to fit the hook, because the feathers are often too large. By using a compensation soft-hackle method, you can use a larger feather to tie a smaller fly. This applies to soft-hackle bird feathers, including marabou. Using compensation hackle methods allows choosing the right color, mottling, and web characteristics you want on the fly, without the size of the feather limiting you. Obviously this only works for larger feathers on smaller hooks. Also, compensation methods eliminate the issue of too thick a stem, take up less real estate on the hook shank, and relieve you of winding the feather.

Choosing the best compensation hackle depends on the feather. Some feathers like partridge and grouse work well with all compensation methods, while you must usually strip hen feathers off the stem, because notching methods don't produce enough even-length fibers to form a distributed collar.

### *Stripped-Fiber Method*

My favorite compensation soft-hackle method for tying flies, other than with a bead thorax, is the stripped-fiber method. You can sweep back the fibers at different angles, to the same extent you wrap the thread head back into them. It works on all larger feathers and allows you to control the density of the hackle collar. You can use any soft bird feather by evening the fibers first, and stripping them off the stem without disturbing their relative positions. Some other compensation methods need feathers that have even tips while on the stem. You can see if the feather needs to have the fibers stripped and spun, or if you can use it with the fibers on the stem by notching out the stem and pulling the fibers out to the tip. If they are even, they can be left on the stem; if not, they need to be stripped and spun. You can also mix two kinds of feather fibers in the hackle collar. Always keep in mind the wing and body proportions of the natural. For example, caddis wings are usually a hook-gap length longer than the body, while mayfly wings are about the same length or just slightly longer than the body.

You can also use the strip and spin method with a bead-thoraxed nymph, which allows you to create proportions of the larger thorax, weight the fly, and create some flash all together. The somewhat hidden bead is not as prominent as on a bead-head fly, and the hackle collar will disguise it, making it a good choice for spooky fish. Tie in the stripped fibers slightly in front of the bead so that you leave a small gap between the bead and the hackle. When you wrap the thread dam in front of the hackle, the tying thread can sweep the hackle fibers back.

## TYING THE WINGED PMD (STRIPPED FIBER METHOD)

### WINGED PMD

**Hook:** #14-18 Mustad R50
**Thread:** Light Cahill 8/0 UNI-Thread
**Shuck:** Rusty brown Hare's Ear Plus Dubbing
**Abdomen:** Pale yellow DMC 25 #745 Embroidery Floss
**Wing:** Swiss Straw
**Thorax:** Pale yellow Hareline Rabbit Dubbin
**Tail and Hackle:** Gray partridge

**Note:** Mark the partridge with Prismacolor Deco Yellow.

**1** Choose an oversize feather (in this case, Brahma hen saddle) and pull the fibers 90 degrees out from the stem so that the fiber tips are even.

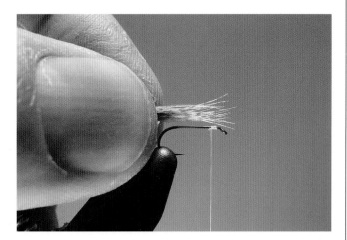

**2** Strip the fibers off the stem with your right hand, transfer them to the left hand, and measure how long the hackle collar will be. The length of fibers coming out between the fingers is the collar length.

**3** Tie the fibers onto the top of the hook with two pinch wraps of thread. Leave about a hook-eye length of space between the front wrap and the hook eye.

**4** Pull down on the thread while manipulating the fibers evenly around the hook shank with your other fingers. Distribute the fibers evenly around the hook.

**5** Cut off the bulk of the fibers, then wind back to the hook bend. Tie in a pinch of Hare's Ear Plus Dubbing tightly twisted into a rope with your thumb and index finger before tying in.

**6** Wind back over the dubbing a few turns to the hook bend, to lock it in and form a shuck. Trim it to about a hook shank in length.

**9** Push the fibers back evenly with a bodkin. Use your left hand to hold the fibers back.

**7** Tie in one strand of DMC 25 pale yellow embroidery thread. Don't trim the tag; leave it for a smooth underbody.

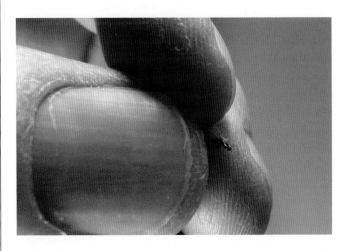

**10** Use a three-finger pinch to hold the fibers swept back, and make a thread dam in front of them. The more you wrap back into them, the more they are swept back.

**8** Wind the thread forward, tie down, and make a thorax with pale yellow rabbit dubbing. Cut out a wing with either Swiss Straw or Medallion Sheeting and tie it on top of the hook. Then finish the thorax.

**11** The finished Winged PMD. PMDs sometimes emerge just under the water's surface instead of on top of the water.

### Rearward Compensation Hackle Collar

The Rearward Soft-Hackle Compensation Method is the fastest way to distribute hackle. Not only is it easy to size the hackle collar, but you get an even and consistent distribution, and the top of the fibers face to the outside of the fly. I credit Blue Ribbon Flies in West Yellowstone for this method. Using this construction method, a dubbed or bead thorax helps flair the fibers. With this versatile technique, you can use two different feather types or colors, stacked and tied in at the same time to create contrast.

To get a denser hackle collar with a single feather, first cut the base fluff off the feather. Then notch the feather the length of the desired hackle collar, so that the collar will contain no stem. Cut the feather at the stem in half. Stack this on top of the base and tie the collar, as outlined in the tying sequence.

## TYING THE CONTRAST NYMPH

### CONTRAST NYMPH

| | |
|---|---|
| **Hook:** | #14 Mustad S82 |
| **Thread:** | Camel 8/0 UNI-Thread |
| **Tail:** | Tan Brahma saddle |
| **Abdomen:** | Golden brown Orvis Hare'E Ice Dub |
| **Rib:** | Copper Holographic Tinsel |
| **Thorax:** | Brown Hareline Rabbit and rusty brown Orvis Ice Dubbing mixture |
| **Hackle:** | Ruffed grouse |

**Note:** This soft-hackle nymph creates contrast by using a light/dark or dark/light abdomen and thorax. This highlights the difference in size and color shades that exists between the two body segments, both visually and physically.

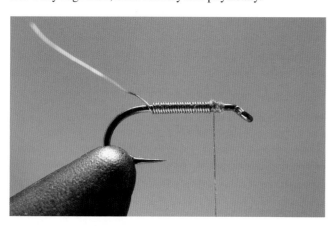

**1** Attach the thread to the hook shank. Tie in a small copper wire. Wrap back to the hook point.

**2** Wrap over the wire to the hook bend and tie in some Brahma saddle fibers for a tail.

**3** Tie in a piece of small Holographic Tinsel and dub an abdomen with a golden brown Ice Dub.

**4** Wrap the ribbing and tie down.

**5** Dub a thorax with a mixture of rabbit and rusty brown Ice Dubbing. Use a Velcro brush to rough up the dubbing.

**6** Notch the stem out of a ruffed grouse feather as deeply as you want the hackle collar to be long.

**7** Hold the feather on top of the hook to where the hackle collar should extend. Make two loose wraps of thread around the feather and the hook. Then pull the thread tight while distribution spinning the fibers around the hook evenly. Use your right-hand fingers to spin it around all sides of the hook.

**8** Cut the loose fibers.

**9** The hackle collar can be swept back or more open, depending on how much of a head you build and how far you wrap into the fibers. Pulling them forward will also open up the hackle collar.

**10** The finished Contrast Nymph. This method works well on larger feathers that have the desired web and mottling, but are too large for a hook if wound. Now you can buy feathers you like, or use ones you already have that can't be wrapped.

A variation of the rearward compensation method is the enveloping hackle method. Instead of spinning the fibers around the hook shank, envelop them around the hook before tying down and flaring. This keeps them straight and lined up better. I often use this method with the downy base fibers on game-bird feathers to create an abdomen collar behind the front collar. The main difference between this and the rearward compensation collar is that the feather is notched and placed around the hook; then the tying thread is distributed around the hook shank before being tightened.

## TYING THE SHUCK NYMPH (ENVELOPING HACKLE METHOD)

### SHUCK NYMPH

| | |
|---|---|
| **Hook:** | #14 Mustad S82 |
| **Thread:** | Tobacco brown 6/0 Danville |
| **Shuck:** | Golden brown Hareline Ice Dub |
| **Abdomen:** | Hare's mask |
| **Thorax:** | ³⁄₃₂" gold bead |
| **Hackle:** | Brown partridge |

**3** Dub hare's mask dubbing and wrap the ribbing. Then build up the wraps and whip finish enough so the bead will be held in place. Cut the thread.

**1** Insert a straight-eye nymph hook in the vise. Attach a gold bead. Attach small gold wire and wrap back to the hook bend, less two wraps. Tie in a tightly twisted strand of golden brown Ice Dub.

**4** Reattach the thread in front of the bead and wind up to just behind the hook eye.

**2** Wrap two turns back to the hook bend to lock the shuck in.

**5** Make a notch in the feather of the length you want the collar.

**6** With your right hand, push the feather against the hook up to the stem.

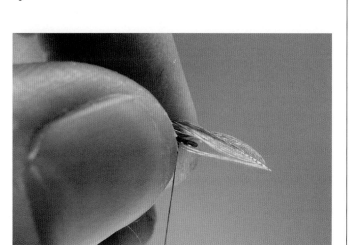

**7** Transfer the feather to your left hand without moving the position.

**8** Make a loose turn of thread around the hook and then a tight turn of thread. Don't spin the fibers; they should be already distributed around the hook evenly. Clip the remaining stem and fibers close with sharp scissors.

**9** Build thread head. Treat about a quarter inch of thread with water-based head cement. Whip finish.

**10** The finished fly.

## Compound Hackle

Sometimes one hackle just isn't enough to make a fly pop. Using two hackle feathers gives the fly depth and complexity. You can either wrap the feathers together at the same time, resulting in a staggered mottling of feathers, or tie one in front of the other for better definition. Both styles create intricate effects, adding to the overall perception of life.

Using two materials, like marabou and partridge, adds different action elements to the fly. On small flies, these differences in action might not be noticeable, and there isn't really enough room on small hooks to fit two hackles anyway, so I generally use compound hackles on size 16 and larger flies.

Mayfly nymphs and dry flies usually have combinations of two primary colors in their makeup. For instance, a Western Green Drake has elements of olive and darker blacks in the body segmentation. A black hen and a grizzly olive hen feather wrapped in front can imitate this impressionistically. My Two-Feather Mayfly Emergers use this premise to create a lineup of flies, using a combination of two feathers to create the primary colors of the mayfly. The back feather represents the wing color and the front feather represents the leg color.

If the feathers you like are too large, use a strip and spin compensation hackle method. This allows you to combine two feathers, like partridge and hen or mallard flank and marabou, to create a new hackle-collar appearance.

Western Green Drake. Olive partridge and black hen cape wrapped together.

Traveling Sedge. Hackle: Olive hen cape and gray partridge wrapped together.

A Back-to-Back Compound Hackle Collar creates more definition between the two hackle collar feathers by separating the hackles, one in front of the other.

Sheepeater. Whiting Furnace Hen Cape behind gray partridge.

Warm Springs PMD. Two hen cape feathers, light dun behind yellow.

## Marabou Compensation Hackle Collar

The Marabou Soft-Hackle UV Caddis in action. In this case, the fish took the heavy bead head tied as a dropper off the tag of the tippet blood knot that acted as weight for the point fly.

Marabou nymphs will work in a variety of stream conditions, tailored to match many natural species. These flies hold water well and sink quickly. They will not ride on the surface, even when swung. You can prime them to sink by holding them underwater and pinching them for a second, after you tie them on the leader. This helps them soak up water and become "weighted." The more you push the thread dam back into the collar, the more swept back it will be. The best angle is about 45 to 90 degrees from the hook shank, as this will allow the fibers to breathe and move in the water current. . For a sparser marabou hackle collar, preen more fibers away before you tie in the feather. For a heavy collar, use more or all the fibers, swept out to the tips before tying it in.

Marabou Soft-Hackle Nymph (brown). This fly uses brown Woolly Bugger marabou for the hackle. I showed Lefty Kreh how to tie this once. He looked at it, rather puzzled at first, and said, "Good *Isonychia!*"

Chickabou Soft-Hackle Nymph (olive). This fly uses olive grizzly marabou for tail and hackle. Fish this as a general-purpose prospecting nymph, or to imitate *Drunella grandis.*

Ballybrado Flymph. This fly uses a green marabou hackle. It's an attractor nymph fished as either dropper or point fly.

Golden Emerger. This fly uses golden brown Brahma chickabou for the tail and hackle. It is good when fished as a prospecting fly, with a contrasting fly like the Ballybrado Flymph to show two colors to fish.

## TYING THE ARCHED CADDIS

### ARCHED CADDIS

| | |
|---|---|
| **Hook:** | #14 Tiemco 206BL |
| **Thread:** | Black Danville Flymaster 6/0 |
| **Abdomen:** | ¼" clear Scud Back, green Flashabou, and chartreuse wire |
| **Thorax:** | Black Hends Spectra Dubbing |
| **Hackle:** | Olive Woolly Bugger marabou in front of brown partridge |

**Note:** This fly demonstrates how to make both a compensated marabou hackle collar and a back-to-back compound collar.

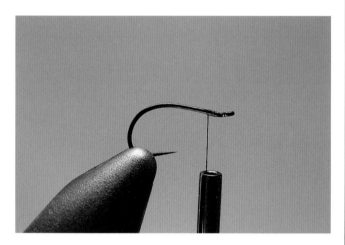

**1** Attach thread to hook. Wrap four times and cut the tag.

**2** Cut the stem out of the tip of a Woolly Bugger marabou feather. Use more fibers for a bulkier hackle collar, and fewer for a sparse collar.

**3** Preen the amount of fibers back to create the hackle density you desire. Also size the hackle for the right length of collar.

**4** Tie in the feather on top of the hook with two pinch wraps of thread. Leave about a hook eye of space between the hackle collar and the hook eye.

**5** Pull down on the thread and use your fingers to spin the fibers evenly around the hook, making the hackle collar uniform.

**6** Cut the bulk off. Wrap the thread back and halfway around the hook bend.

**9** Use black Hends Spectra Dubbing to dub a thorax.

**7** Attach a quarter-inch clear Scud Back, green Flashabou, and chartreuse small wire. Mark the edge of one side of the Scud Back with a black marker. This will create segmentation.

**10** Prepare a brown partridge feather. Tie the feather in by the tip.

**8** Wrap the Flashabou up to the thorax first, then rib the wire and the Scud Back over the abdomen. The Scud Back should show the underbody.

**11** Wrap the partridge with two turns. More or fewer turns can be used for effect.

**12** Push the marabou back with a bodkin. Use your left hand to hold the fibers swept back.

**13** Hold the fibers back with a three-finger pinch. Wrap the thread to in front of the marabou.

**14** For antennae, pull two partridge fibers forward through the marabou hackle collar. Build a small thread head, or just make a five-turn whip finish to keep the head small.

**15** Finished Arched Caddis. This medium-weight fly is a good middle dropper or light point fly on its own.

## MAYFLY WET FLY WINGING METHODS

Winged wets excel at imitating a mayfly emerger crawling out of the nymphal case, one stuck in the shuck, or a fully developed subsurface dun or sunken spinner. Some insects, such as *Baetis* and certain species of caddis, dive underwater to lay their eggs, making winged wet flies good options for imitation. The wing on an emerging soft-hackle pattern may be an important trigger for trout that key in on the mayfly wings' UV reflection. A fly tied with a UVR wing material will look incredibly realistic to a trout. With this in mind, I like wings made from hen hackle tips, Swiss Straw, Medallion Sheeting, UV Ice Dub, and hackle burned with a wing burner, all of which will reflect UV. Other options for wings include stripped feather fibers from a single bird or in combination, or entire feathers such as rooster, hen, or starling, which come to a nice taper such as the Wood River Caddis.

Using two wings on the fly is not necessary; one wing will give the impression of two stuck together, common when they are unfurling from the nymphal shuck wing-case opening, as well as the silhouette and visual trigger that wings provide. Also, there is less buildup on the fly and less chance of twisting the tippet.

*Callibaetis* Winged Wet with a Brahma hen burned wing (top) and a Swiss Straw synthetic wing (bottom). The tier and then the fisherman on stream can choose to use an opaque wing or a translucent wing, as both work.

Sunburst Caddis. Feather-fibers wing from mallard flank dyed wood duck and a yellow grizzly marabou hackle. This pattern incorporates the V-Rib translucent abdomen for weight, and is a good prospecting caddis pupa pattern.

Wood River Caddis (Diving Egg Layer). Feather wing. On this fly, the bleached starling is tied flat on top of the hook. The hackle is also bleached starling.

Double R May-Cad. A small wing burner and hen feather can effectively make caddis pupa winglets. You can make two winglets out of a single feather; just make one near the tip, then cut it off and make another with the remaining feather. The hook on this fly is a Mustad S82 Bent Nymph. Winglets are from two dun hen cape feather tips, and the hackle is speckled brown India hen back. This fly imitates both caddis and mayfly, due to the marabou tail.

Madison Mosquito. The Glanrhos wing uses the hackle collar feather tip to create the wing and then wrap the hackle, all with the same feather. This creates little thread buildup, ideal for smaller flies. The wing and hackle here are starling. Alternatively, mark a light dun hen cape feather, leaving the tip natural to get a light dun wing and colored hackle.

Jupiter Mayfly. Mayflies exhibit ultraviolet reflection in their wings that trout can see and use to target subsurface mayfly emergers. Gray UV Ice Dub tied as an emerging wing can imitate this.

## TYING THE SULPHUR WINGED TRANSITION FLYMPH

### SULPHUR WINGED TRANSITION FLYMPH

| | |
|---|---|
| **Hook:** | #16 Tiemco 3761 |
| **Thread:** | Light Cahill 8/0 UNI-Thread |
| **Shuck:** | Brown Z-Lon |
| **Abdomen:** | Four natural pheasant tail fibers |
| **Rib:** | Copper UNI-Wire (small) |
| **Thorax:** | Pale yellow Hareline Rabbit Dubbin |
| **Wing:** | Dun hen saddle |
| **Hackle:** | Ginger India hen cape |

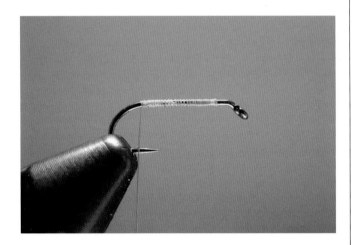

**1** Place a hook in the vise and wrap back to the hook bend with thread. I am using a #16 Tiemco 3761, but you can also use a lighter Tiemco 100, depending on the desired depth of the drift.

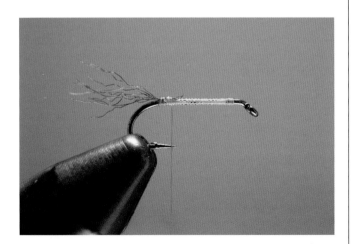

**2** Tie in a brown Z-Lon shuck and trim it to the length of the body or a little shorter.

**3** Tie in four natural pheasant-tail fibers and a section of wire.

**4** Wrap the pheasant tail around the hook, and then wrap the ribbing up to the thorax.

**5** Dub a thorax with pale yellow Hareline Rabbit Dubbin. Newly emerged Sulphurs are bright yellow.

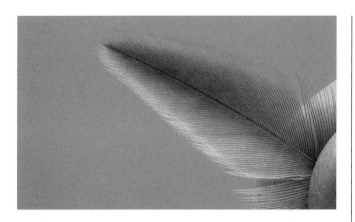

**6** To create wings from almost any feather (I most commonly use hen and rooster), you can use a small or medium wing burner to shape the wing. Select a medium dun hen saddle feather. Saddle feathers work best because the web extends out to the fiber tips and creates a nicer wing appearance.

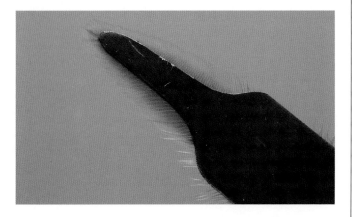

**7** I locate the highest spot on the feather that will be all web in the finished wing, yet with the thinnest part of the stem nearer the tip. This makes the wing more pliable, allowing it to move freely in the water currents. Shape with a wing burner appropriately sized to the hook.

**8** Peel back the fibers to make the wing the same length as the hook shank.

**9** Tie in the wing with three or four thread wraps and cut off extra bulk. Keep a few of the fibers in place to lock the wing securely.

**10** Select a ginger India hen cape feather. Prepare the feather and tie it in by the tip.

**11** Make a two-turn hackle collar and tie down. Trim the extra stem material closely to the hook. For a sparser collar, strip the fibers from one side of the feather.

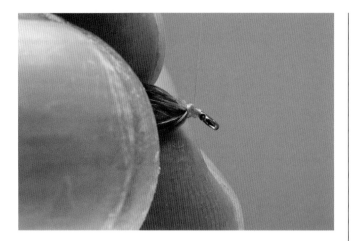

**12** Pull back the hackle collar with a three-finger pinch and form a neat head.

**13** Treat a small section of the thread with water-based head cement, then whip finish the head. This preserves the original color of synthetic thread for the head.

**14** The finished Sulphur Winged Transition Flymph. This pattern can match many different mayfly species by changing the hook size, thread, and thorax color.

## Synthetic Wings

While feather wings give the right profile to the fly, they aren't as translucent as the real thing. A mayfly dun wing has fine venation and is totally translucent. Spinner wings are even clearer. When underwater, the mayfly wing is pliable and moves in the current.

Swiss Straw is a great wing material for wet flies because it doesn't twist your tippet, is readily available and realistic, and waves in the currents like the wing of an emerging mayfly. However, it tears too easily and tends to curl when removed from water. Treating it with Sally Hansen's Hard as Nails solves these issues and also makes it shiny and clear like the natural's wings. Hareline Medallion Sheeting and Hareline Clear Wing also are realistic looking and don't require lacquer. Both of these materials are best cut with a wing cutter or trace cut with sharp scissors around a wing burner. The Medallion Sheeting won't cut or tear easily, and keeps its shape without lacquer, even when removed from the water. It's also available in many colors to match different mayfly wings. For a light-dun style wing, I use the clear color, which is actually opaque.

The Valley Drake incorporates a wing tied with dun Swiss Straw, marked with Prismacolor Cool Gray to create venations, and sealed with Sally Hansen Hard as Nails. The hackle is golden olive Whiting Brahma Hen. It is an excellent imitation for *Baetis* (seen here), Flavs, and Western Green Drakes.

# WORKING WITH SWISS STRAW

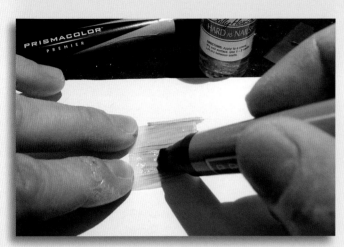

Swiss Straw comes in many colors, but use light dun Swiss Straw and markers to create darker dun wings or different colored wings like olive, yellow, or tan. This lets you match mayfly wings by species. The marker also highlights the venations more pronouncedly.

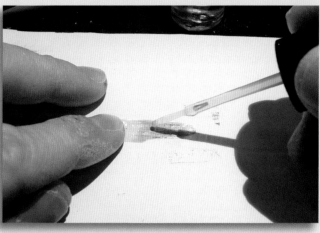

Treat the cut wing on both sides with Sally Hansen's Hard as Nails for a stronger wing that will hold shape better when wet.

Use either a wing cutter or a razor blade to cut the Swiss Straw to shape.

Let the wings dry before tying them in.

Gray Antron or Z-Lon strands tied over the back of the fly also make a nice wing material. They don't dominate the fly's appearance, but suggest the unfurling wing of the mayfly emerger. This captures and reflects light in the crinkly fibers, and gives the same kind of look as the venations of the natural mayfly wing. White Antron colored with a gray marker yields a dun color. A black marker can give the material some barring. Depending upon fishing method design, I keep the wing sparse for a subsurface wet, using only about 10 strands, or thicker if I want to apply floatant to the wing. Then I fish it with the wing riding in the surface, and the rest of the fly just under the surface.

Pearl Krystal Flash can also effectively suggest wings. For a simple impression of wings, two Krystal Flash strands reflect light and will sway in the water. I tie them back over the body at a 45-degree angle like the Z-Lon wing. Krystal Flash is slightly more visible than Z-Lon in the fly; that is why two strands suffice to suggest the wings.

## HOT SULPHUR

| | |
|---|---|
| **Hook:** | #14-16 Mustad R50 |
| **Thread:** | Light Cahill 8/0 UNI-Thread |
| **Abdomen:** | Yellow DMC 25 #744 Embroidery Floss |
| **Thorax:** | Hot Yellow Ultra Wire (extra small) |
| **Wing:** | Medium gray Antron Yarn |
| **Tail and Hackle:** | Gray partridge |

**Note:** Mark the gray partridge with Prismacolor Deco Yellow. This works as mayfly emerger/dun/sunken spinner all in one.

## GREEN CADDY

| | |
|---|---|
| **Hook:** | #10-#16 Tiemco 2457 |
| **Thread:** | Camel 8/0 UNI-Thread |
| **Ribbing:** | Camel 8/0 UNI-Thread lightly dubbed with Hareline Natural Rabbit Dubbin |
| **Abdomen:** | Chartreuse rayon floss |
| **Winglets:** | Two dark dun hen saddle feathers formed with wing burner |
| **Thorax:** | Rusty Brown Hareline Rabbit Dubbin |
| **Wing:** | Two Gold Krystal Flash Strands |
| **Hackle:** | Brown Partridge |

## DRY FLY WINGS

For soft-hackle dry flies, I use either CDC or deer hair for wings to float the fly on the surface, for imitating adult caddis, mayfly, midge, and stoneflies. But when pulled underwater and fished submerged, they imitate the emerger or sunken adult, all in the same fly and presentation. A few false casts between presentations helps soft-hackle dry flies float high before being pulled under for the subsurface presentation. The choice of whether to use deer hair or CDC depends on the water conditions. For slow-moving flat water, either wing will work, but CDC really is buggy, yet delicate. In faster, more turbulent water, a deer-hair wing will float longer between surface and subsurface drifts. After the fly won't float, even after false casting, use a dessicant like Loon Easy Dry to allow the fly to float well again after the subsurface presentation.

Soft-hackle dry flies divide into four basic categories, based on the water current in which they are generally designed to be fished. Use whichever combination you find most effective on a specific stream and hatch. The stiffer the wing and hackle, the better a soft-hackle dry fly will float, but also the worse it will sink on the swing. Just as you choose a weighted nymph for the water conditions and sink depth, so should you choose the right wing-and-hackle combination for the flotation characteristics that will target the intended depth of the trout.

Slowest water: CDC wing/hen cape or partridge hackle
Slow water: CDC wing/hen cape hackle
Medium water: Deer-hair wing/partridge hackle
Fast water: Deer-hair wing/hen cape hackle

The Blue Quill Dun is an example of a CDC wing on a soft-hackle dry mayfly dun. I use this wing in calmer waters.

The Hendrickson Spinner soft-hackle dry/wet uses Sparkle Organza for the spent wing, which sits low in the surface film and sparkles as the light plays off the fibers.

The Apple Caddis is an example of a deer-hair wing on a soft-hackle dry. The deer hair floats well and works in fast, turbulent water, as well as slow water.

A 27-inch wild rainbow caught on a #16 Bead Thorax Pheasant Tail fished just under the surface of the water. Larger trout often feed primarily on the ascending nymphs and pupa under the surface even when smaller fish are rising to adults on the surface during hatches. These larger fish are generally more cautious and, I believe, realize through experience that these life stages cannot escape as quickly.

# Progressive Fly Design Applications

3

A well-designed fly and a presentation that activates the fly are the two factors that, when combined, result in a life-like offering. But to understand how to design our artificial flies to look real, we must first understand how trout use their senses to hunt for food. This will tell us what materials to use and why. The foremost aspect is trout vision and how trout view their food sources.

I remember sitting in a presentation on soft-hackles. When the presenter showed a slide of a fly tied with a gray partridge hackle collar, he told the audience that this fly "isn't tied with the right color feather." He said that it should have been tied with a brown partridge feather. He went on to say that he never used gray partridge feathers, and gave them away. I wanted to stand up and say, "Give them to me," and I should have. A gray partridge feather has tons of ultraviolet reflection (UVR) and

makes a fly pop in the eyes of a trout. It resembles a mayfly wing, which also has UVR. Furthermore, a fly tied with gray partridge is going to have much more visibility, and stand out as more attractive to a fish than one tied with a brown partridge feather, although brown partridge is more natural for imitating caddis with UVR in its body.

Trout see into the UV wavelengths as well as visible light wavelengths. To them, it's all one spectrum, just like we have one color spectrum. But theirs goes into shorter wavelengths that can travel deeper into the water. In lower light, trout use them for predation of insects and forage fish. But it's not all about UVR; it's about nonUVR as well, since this contrast (signature) exists in both insects and baitfish in the trout stream. Trout use this for contrast recognition against backgrounds, to quickly key in on and capture their prey.

The Chattooga River is one of my home rivers. I've developed many patterns here over the years, and I consider it the best freestone trout fishery in the Southeast. The fishing gets better and better the farther upstream you hike.

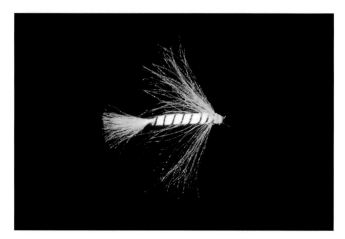

Most adult humans can't see UVR. To design flies with UVR signatures where you want them, you must understand in a general sense what materials reflect UV and what materials don't. The materials in this fly that reflect UV are the white Z-Lon, the clear V-Rib, and the gray UV Ice Dub thorax. The black thread and hen hackle absorb light and don't reflect UV. Since the black thread is under the V-Rib, there will be some UVR from the V-Rib, but the underbody thread will mute the degree. Overall, this fly will have strong contrast between nonUVR and UVR materials.

There are three types of ultraviolet light reactions—ultraviolet fluorescent (UVF), ultraviolet phosphorescence (UVP), and ultraviolet reaction (UVR). Examples of UVF are day-glo chartreuse and orange materials. They reflect light at a different wavelength when exposed to UV light from the sun or an ultraviolet light source like a UV flashlight. We can see this fluorescence to a certain degree, as can fish. This is what you see when you shine a black light on materials. Some materials will react and have bright fluorescence, really not useful for matching insects, because insects have ultraviolet reflection. While not necessarily natural, UVF-reactive materials can appeal to the fish in the same way that sparkle dubbing, bead heads, and bright hot spots can. These UV-reactive materials create fluorescence that can entice a fish to bite. Predatory fish, like trout, can strike to defend their territory when annoyed or angered. A vivid fluorescent fly may annoy the territorial fish enough that it strikes sheerly out of annoyance.

The Dusk til Dawn uses Glo Yarn to display phosphorescence. Try this one for night fishing. It needs a charge before each presentation. Just hold it up to a headlamp for about 5 to 10 seconds, then cast. It also works well in the daytime with UVR. In deeper water where there's less light, it shines.

The White Lie displays contrast between UVR and non-UVR elements. Trout stream invertebrates also exhibit this contrast. The body is peacock here and the hackle is light dun hen cape in front of gray partridge.

Ultraviolet phosphorescence is also known as luminescence. This type of light is delayed fluorescence. UV light activates the material, which can glow in the dark. These materials need light to activate them, but can emanate light for a specific period after being removed from the light. These are your glow-in-the-dark materials.

Finally, the third kind of ultraviolet reaction is ultraviolet reflection, which occurs to varying degrees both in certain parts of insects' bodies and in certain materials we use to tie flies. A subject reflects ultraviolet reflection light in wavelengths below 380 nM. Humans cannot see wavelengths this low, due to the UV lens we develop around age 7. Individuals who have the lens removed with cataract surgery can once again see into the low-wavelength UV spectrum, as can children under 7 years old. Trout-stream invertebrates display UVR signatures differently among species. Both baitfish and insects exhibit degrees of ultraviolet reflection. The deeper in the water that trout and prey are, the more UVR comes into play for trout to use to spot the target. At dawn and dusk, sunlight rays are shorter toward the lower end of the visible spectrum (notice that purple is the first and last light in the sky at these times). This is when trout really use their UV vision to spot their prey against a background. For prospect nymphing, the combination of the UVR and scattering of light catches the eyes of opportunistic trout, and UV Ice Dub bodies, both straight and blended with fur, are effective in nymphs.

Since most human adults can't see UVR, we can't see how trout bugs actually appear to the trout. A trout will see the visible spectrum of colors as we do, but will also see any UVR in the bug's body. With this in mind, here are some basic rules of thumb. Mayflies have a lot of UVR in their wings and head. Caddis wings are not UV reflective, but their bodies are. Terrestrials like crickets and beetles do not have UV reflection, so little or no UVR material should be used when attempting to imitate them. Black and white flies have the ultimate in contrast, and use silver tinsel when there is moonlight, for the reflection it offers. The loss of light at depth also indicates the use of ribbing that can reflect light, like wire ribbing. Remember that soft-hackles also have the advantage of holding air bubbles that catch light and reflect it, giving the fly sparkle and flash wherever light is present.

Contrast can often take on extreme forms, such as in this freshly molted *Heptagenia marginalis* mayfly nymph. Building nymphs with both visible light spectrum contrast and UVR material contrast is the secret of the most effective flies.

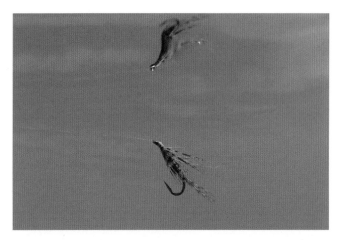

Notice the UV Ice Dub wing lit up by the sunlight in this shallow subsurface wet fly. The surface film reflection that trout also see seems to be even stronger than the fly itself.

Sunlight travelling through the wing creates the blue bands on this March Brown spinner, due to the prism effect of the wing venations. Trout would also expect this UVR signature in a fly.

UVR occurs naturally in many materials, so you don't have to necessarily buy any specially labeled UVR fly-tying materials. Almost all white, cream, gray, yellow, pink, and tan items will have the highest amount of UVR, but feather construction and dyes can affect that. Generally, the darker the feather is, the less UVR. Here is the order of UVR in feathers: white (over 75% UV reflective), blue, yellow/green, red, brown, black (less than 5% UV reflective). UVR is also present in white turkey and goose biots, yarns, threads, tinsels, and wire. Low-UVR materials include ostrich, peacock, dark dubbing, black and brown hen feathers. Furs are generally less UV-reflective because they are high in keratin, which absorbs UV. Natural white marabou has more UVR than most feathers. Gray partridge and light-colored hen are higher in UVR. Using both light and dark contrasting feathers, or a UVR hackle collar with a less reflective body, gives you visible light color contrast and UVR contrast, the best of both worlds.

When I first began studying UV reflection, my biggest obstacle was not knowing exactly how much UV reflection my materials had. In addition, I wanted to see the contrast of nonUV materials and UV reflection in the final fly, and to begin studying the naturals for UVR signatures, all of which would have required a camera. Many ultraviolet cameras are expensive. Reed Curry, who wrote the book *The New Scientific Angling: Trout and Ultraviolet Vision* (Buckram Publishing, 2009), suggested that using a Sony Handycam DCR-HC52 Camcorder and UVR filter would be less expensive. This camcorder isn't made anymore, but it has a feature that is mandatory to be able to bypass the internal UV filter, a mode setting called Nightshot Plus. This setting both turns on the Infrared Lamp and swings the UV/IR cut filter out of the way of the sensor, allowing ultraviolet light to pass through to the sensor. I had Reed make me one of his 30 mm Andrea U filters that filter out visible light and only pass through light in the 370 nm to 400 nm ranges. You can buy the camcorder from eBay and the filter from Reed's website, UVROptics.com. This combination allows me to use the camcorder as a UV scope and recorder. Then you simply need a UV light source (the sun) to scope UVR. Carry it onstream in the back of your vest to study naturals' UVR signatures and flies for accuracy.

Finally, don't overthink this. Even if you choose to use UVR materials or any UV-activated fly-tying material, you still want contrast between light and dark, UV and nonUV materials, shades, colors, and textures of the materials in the design of the fly. Apart from the UV spectrum ability, the human eye is similar to the trout's eye. Don't think that UV is the only trigger for trout to strike a fly; color, shape size, shade, contrast, sparkle, and translucence are all important in fly design. After all, fly tying at its heart is about feeling what is right to do with the hook and materials when you sit down at the vise, and reflect on the water and what does or doesn't work. Look inward, and the right fly comes out through your hands. It's the magic of fly tying and the other half of fly-fishing.

## ONE-FEATHER FLIES

I have always loved a simple, effective fly. By "simple" I mean getting the imitation I want with the least amount of materials. This allows tying the fly more quickly, and applies the principle of "less is more," because you allow the materials to speak for themselves. Any soft-hackle feather can fill the role, but I often use grouse, partridge, and my favorite, Brahma hen. The tip of the Brahma hen saddle back feather that you use to create the hackle collar is thick and webby, and the fibers slowly get longer down the stem, allowing for a larger feather to tie a small fly. Furthermore, the speckled markings of the feather give the fly segmentation; mottling helps the fly take on character. The most important feather consideration is that it will provide enough material to fill the hook shank with body and hackle collar.

One-Feather Nymphs are impressionistic patterns that can imitate many streambed life-forms, such as caddis pupae, mayfly nymphs, stonefly nymphs, crane fly larvae, and small fish like sculpins. They are fast to tie consistently, in under a couple of minutes each. I usually fish a One-Feather Nymph with another one of a different color or shape, or in combination with another soft-hackle nymph or two.

## TYING THE ONE-FEATHER MAYFLY

### ONE-FEATHER MAYFLY

| Hook: | #14-16 Mustad S82 |
|---|---|
| Thread: | Tobacco brown Danville Flymaster 6/0 |
| Rib: | Gold UNI-Wire (small) |
| Tail, Body, and Hackle: | March Brown Brahma saddle |

**1** Place the hook in the vise. Wind the thread from the eye back, tying in the wire as you go. Then select a Whiting March Brown Brahma hen saddle feather.

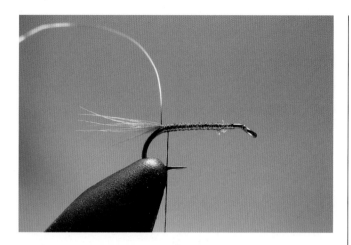

**2** Cut off a section of fibers from the base of the feather where the web fibers meet the marabou, and tie in a tail if you wish.

**3** Notch out the top of the feather in the size of the hackle collar. Pull the fibers together and tie in on the hook at the tail. Pull the fibers through the tie-in thread until they are still just holding. This gives you the fibers for the body of the fly.

**4** Wrap the fibers forward to create an abdomen. Then counter-rib the gold wire up to the thorax. Cut the wire-ribbing excess. Then tie the abdomen and ribbing down, or tie off with a couple of whip finishes to secure.

**5** Cut the fibers to make them smaller. Wrap a thorax. Trim the excess in front of the tie-down point.

**6** Take the collar section that you cut out and prepare. Next, tie it in by the tip.

**7** Wrap the hackle collar forward two or three times. Tie down and strip any excess. Form the head and apply head cement to the thread hanging from the bobbin. Then whip finish. Just like the natural mayflies, the fly is a consistent color with some highlights.

## ARTICULATED SOFT-HACKLE NYMPHS

Real mayflies and stoneflies aren't static in the drift. They move around and contort their body, particularly the abdomen, which they bend quickly up and down vertically when they swim. In comparison, "stiff nymphs" don't have this movement. The ArticuNymph's hollow abdomen can bend and change direction with the current. The body shape will change each time you present the fly, and will always "fit" the water.

Using tying thread to connect gives the abdomen connection nearly neutral buoyancy in the water. This allows for both a more realistic appearance and free action of the abdomen's movement in currents. You can fish this design all the way from the streambed to the top, imitating nymphs to emergers. Reserve it for larger species because of the hook size; it makes excellent prospecting nymphs.

## TYING THE BROWN DRAKE ARTICUNYMPH

### BROWN DRAKE NYMPH

| Hook: | #14 Mustad S82 |
| Thread: | Tobacco brown 6/0 Danville Flymaster |
| Rib and Tail: | Brown ostrich herl |
| Body: | Amber Hareline Rabbit Dubbin |
| Hackle: | Brown partridge |

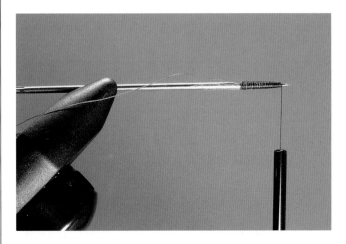

**2** Attach the thread near the point and wrap forward the length of the abdomen. The length you wrap will determine the length of the abdomen, which should be about half the length of the fly.

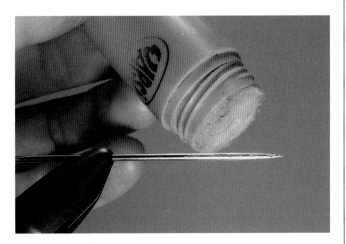

**1** Place a darning needle in the vise and coat the tip with dubbing wax. The needle size will determine the size of the abdomen.

**3** Tie in three brown ostrich herls and divide. Wrap one herl back under the thread for the ribbing. Then wrap the thread forward and back again.

**4** Saturate threads with a water-based head cement.

**5** Dub from the tail forward with rabbit dubbing, then wrap the ostrich herl forward. Tie down the herl and cut the excess. Leave a small section of thread undubbed, then dub a little more rabbit about half an inch on the thread. Coat the undubbed section with a dab of superglue applied with the sewing needle.

**6** Wrap the rest of the thread with the dubbing to hide the threads. Cut the thread, leaving a 2-inch tag, but don't tie off with a knot. The thread tag will be used to make the attachment to the hook. The glue will hold it together for the time being. Work quickly to slide the abdomen off the needle (grasp the abdomen not the tail materials) before the superglue adheres to it.

**7** Apply superglue to the tip with a small sewing needle. The best way is to push the needle down into the superglue tube from the nozzle, with the nozzle loaded with glue. Slide the needle deep into the hollow abdomen and slide out. Let the abdomen dry for a few seconds.

**8** Place a hook in the vise. Attach the thread behind the hook eye and wrap back to the hook bend. Tie in the abdomen with the thread tag on top of the hook. Position the abdomen close to the hook, but with enough space that it can freely move around. Wrap up to the hook eye back to secure the tag.

**9** Tie in a brown ostrich herl at the hook bend, and dub the thorax with amber Hareline Rabbit Dubbin.

**10** Pick out fibers of the dubbing with a bodkin to make a buggier body.

**11** Pull the ostrich herl over the thorax for a wing case and tie down.

**12** Prepare a brown partridge feather.

**13** Tie the partridge feather in by the tip.

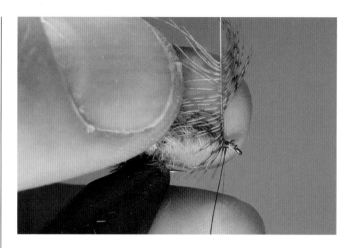

**14** Wrap the partridge two or three turns and tie down. Cut the extra fibers off.

**15** Sweep the hackle back and build a head. Before whip finishing, apply some head cement to the hanging thread with the bottle brush.

**16** The Articulated Soft-Hackle Nymph imitates large mayfly nymphs like Drakes, *Hexagenia*, and stoneflies. You can customize this universal design to imitate other mayfly nymphs and stoneflies by changing only color and size.

# EXTENDED BODY EMERGER

You can see floating mayfly shucks during a hatch because mayflies crawl out of the nymphal shuck horizontally at the surface or on top of the surface. Tied on a hook smaller than the fly length, the Extended Body Soft-Hackle (EBSH) floats well, but will sink if saturated or pulled under. This creates opportunities for two presentation types. You can fish the EBSH on top of the surface to rising fish, with a drag-free dry-fly presentation; or you can fish it underwater with wet-fly tactics. An even more versatile method is to make the first cast and fish the pattern dry on top; then, after it begins to drag, pull the fly underwater and fish out the drift with a wet-fly swing or other line manipulations. This is the Two-Life-Cycle method of fishing soft-hackle dry flies. You can treat the soft-hackle collar with floatant to keep it on the surface during the drift, but it will still sink if pulled under.

This fly grew out of a tying method that Ralph Graves originally introduced me to in Roscoe, New York, many years ago. He made his Green Drake Coffin Fly abdomen with a bodkin, white dubbing, moose hair for tails, and head cement for hold. He showed me how to pinch wrap and twist the dubbing into a tightly bound, yet hollow and light extended body segment. When I look at emerging mayflies, I notice the hanging shuck as the adult dun crawls out of the exoskeleton. The nymphal shuck hangs down at a different angle than the emerging adult, something that straight shank hooks don't simulate. Tying the shuck using the extended-needle method makes a realistic-looking emerger, with the extended shuck free to move, apart from the ridged thorax segment typical of the adult dun. A Swiss Straw wing and a partridge hackle, depicting legs and movement in general, can further accessorize the fly.

## TYING THE GREEN DRAKE EXTENDED BODY EMERGER

### GREEN DRAKE

| | |
|---|---|
| **Hook:** | #14 Tiemco 2487 |
| **Thread:** | Olive 6/0 Danville Flymaster |
| **Tail:** | Olive mallard flank fibers |
| **Exoskeleton:** | Brown Hareline Rabbit Dubbin |
| **Body:** | Green Hareline Rabbit Dubbin |
| **Wing:** | Light dun CDC |
| **Hackle:** | Olive grizzly hen cape |

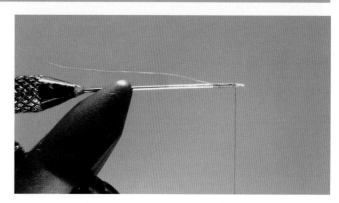

**2** Attach thread and wrap forward, then back to near the point.

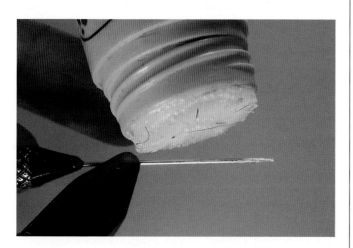

**1** Place a thin bodkin or medium sewing needle in the vise. Coat the end with dubbing wax. These needles are thinner in diameter than darning needles.

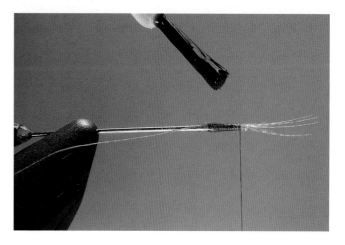

**3** Tie in fibers for the tail. Wrap the thread forward, then back. Coat with water-based head cement.

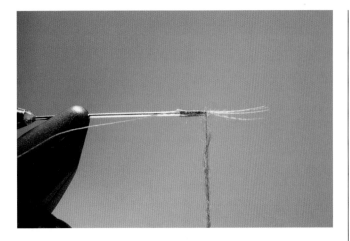

**4** Dub the abdomen with brown Hareline Rabbit Dubbin.

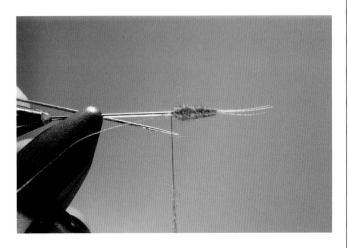

**5** Apply a dab of superglue to the exposed thread. Notice the small section of dubbing on the thread. Wrap this quickly. Cut the thread, but leave a 2-inch tag.

**6** This creates no exposed whip-finish threads. Slide off the needle quickly before the superglue can adhere.

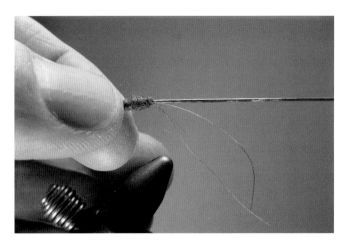

**7** Coat the inside of the hollow abdomen with a drop of superglue on a thin sewing needle. Let the abdomen dry for a few seconds.

**8** Place a hook in the vise and wrap with the same thread.

**9** Attach the abdomen to the hook by wrapping down in the fibers at the end.

**10** Dub to midshank with green Hareline Rabbit Dubbin and tie in a light dun CDC feather on top of the hook shank.

**11** Trim the wing to length and cut off the excess base fibers.

**12** Dub a little bit of Rabbit Dubbin in front of the CDC wing and tie in an olive grizzly hen cape feather by the base of the feather stem.

**13** Make two, three, or four turns of hackle, tie off, trim the excess feather, and treat the hanging thread with head cement so the thread head is not discolored; then whip finish.

## SOFT-HACKLE DRY FLIES

I invented the first soft-hackle dry fly I tied to match the chartreuse Beaverhead midge. I was fishing the river at the Clark Canyon dam, and these midges were drawing some intense surface action from the large brown trout. I didn't have any midges in this color, but I had parked only feet from where I was fishing. I went back to the rental car, took out my fly-tying kit, and got the idea for a dry fly that I could also fish subsurface after it started to drag. I used a #18 hook, chartreuse rabbit dubbing, CDC wing, and a dun hen hackle tied in at the thorax. I fished to rising fish with dry-fly presentations; then, after the fly drifted past the fish, I would let it drag, pulling it under the surface and swinging in front of other fish down and across-stream. The subsurface swing represented the emerging midges. I was able to dry off the CDC wing with a few false casts and repeat. The presentation complemented the fly, and I caught many nice, big fish that afternoon and into the evening. Since that day, I've adapted the soft-hackle dry idea to imitate all species of mayflies, caddis, midges, and stoneflies.

A brown soft-hackle wet/dry that can imitate *Isonychia*, March Brown, and *Paraleptophlebia*, among other species, tied in the right size for each. The tail can be either a Z-Lon shuck imitating emergence, or hen-cape fibers imitating the dun.

# SOFT-HACKLE SPINNERS

Mayfly spinners are often the unseen "hatch." Unless you see mating clouds of them over the stream, they often fall to the water undetected by many anglers, but definitely not by the trout. If you see fish fully rising on the surface, but don't observe upright wings duns, it may be midge pupae or small spinners. This design uses a combination of Sparkle Organza for the wings and a soft-hackle hen cape collar in front. Using dry fly hooks for flotation soft-hackle spinners float well in sizes (#12-18) but for larger species I use the extended body design. The spinner can be fished dead drift only on the surface; underwater for a sunken spinner; or both on the same cast, first dead drift, then pulled under when the fly starts to drag. If you want extra flotation, tie them with a small CDC or deer-hair wing. If you coat the wings, tail, or body with floatant, you won't be able to fish the fly underwater effectively.

The Extended Body Spinner is used to imitate large mayfly species like the Brown Drake, the Green Drake (both East and West), and the *Hexagenia* (seen here). Fish it both dry and subsurface wet when it begins to drag, or at only one level.

## TYING THE SULPHUR SOFT-HACKLE SPINNER

### SULPHUR SOFT-HACKLE DRY/WET SPINNER

| | |
|---|---|
| **Hook:** | #16 Tiemco 101 |
| **Thread:** | Light Cahill 8/0 UNI-Thread |
| **Tail:** | Light dun hen cape |
| **Abdomen:** | Orange/yellow turkey biot |
| **Thorax:** | Amber Superfine dubbing |
| **Wing:** | Sparkle Organza |
| **Hackle:** | Light dun hen cape |

**2** Tie in a light orange/yellow turkey biot at the hook bend on the near side of the hook. The ridged side of the biot should be the leading forward edge when you wrap it, and the thinner smoother edge will be in the back of each wrap. Wrap a smooth tapered underbody up to the thorax.

**1** Place a hook in the vise, attach thread, and tie in some light dun hen cape fibers for the tail. Leave the fibers under the thread so the underbody is smooth and even.

**3** Wrap the turkey biot up to the thorax. Tie it down with thread wraps.

**4** Make two turns of amber Superfine Dry Fly Dubbing.

**5** Tie in a few fibers of Sparkle Organza, leaving them longer than the hook shank on both sides of the hook. Make a Figure-8 wrap with the thread to secure the fibers, but don't use any dubbing here.

**6** Choose a webby light dun hen cape feather. Since this is a soft-hackle dry fly, the hackle collar can be a little stiffer and should be sparse.

**7** Color the top side of the feather on a tissue with a Prismacolor Tulip Yellow marker. The color should match the mayfly's legs. Let it dry for a minute before tying it in.

**8** Pull the fibers 90 degrees out from the stem, leaving just a few at the tip, and then tie in the hen feather by the tip fibers.

**9** Attach hackle pliers to the feather stem and then make two, three, or four turns of hackle around the hook, sweeping the fibers back between each turn. The hackle collar should extend to the hook bend.

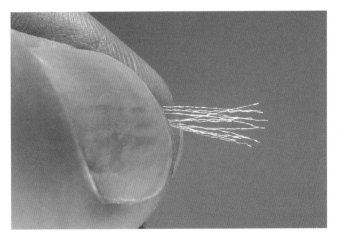

**10** Pull both sides of the hook Sparkle Organza fibers forward and hold them evenly out in front of the hook eye. Trim the wings to the same length as the hook shank, or slightly longer for better definition from the hackle and flotation.

**13** Apply a thin amount of water-based head cement to a short section of the thread. Whip finish to tie off.

**11** The hackle collar should be distinct from the wing, to give the appearance of the legs and the wings of the mayfly.

**14** This fly can be used during Sulphur spinnerfalls or as a searching wet-fly pattern at any time, on water surface with dry-fly floatant on the wings and hackle, underwater, or even both dry/wet on the same presentation. If you want to fish it with better surface flotation, apply a small amount of floatant to first the wing only, then the tail, and then the hackle (in that order) to offer from just a little to maximum flotation. The more segments that have floatant, the less subsurface fishability there is. However, you can still pull the fly underwater, especially in faster water where Sulphur spinners congregate to oviposit.

**12** Finish dubbing the head all the way up to the hook eye. The thread head will be small and inconspicuous.

Vegetated spring creeks are fertile insect factories. I can think of no better place than these environs to prove the effectiveness of soft-hackle design for matching the bugs in both form and life behaviors.

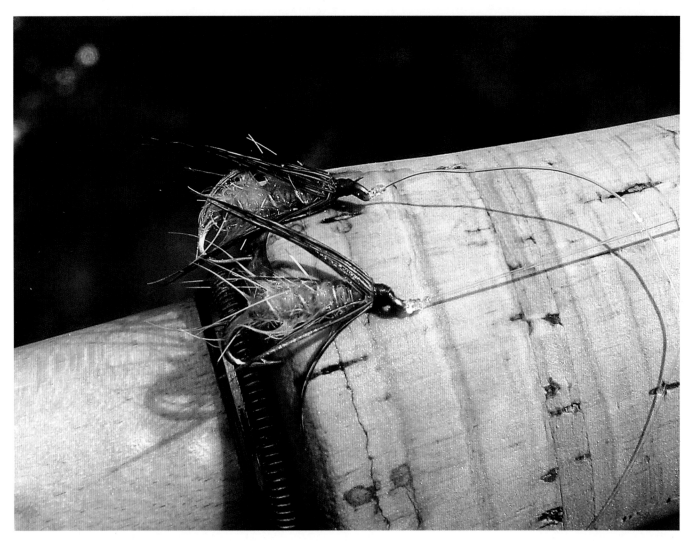

Tying thread can be used to create degrees of translucence by using dubbings of various lighter shades, allowing the thread to shine through when wet, as evident on these two Grouse & Gray wet flies. This effect may not be wholly evident at the vise, but it will be when the fly is wet.

# Match-the-Hatch Soft-Hackles: Mayflies

4

While influenced by traditional flies, the flies I fish now are of my own design, many to match specific species and with region in mind, including water type and fish behavior toward the bugs in a particular river. However, the flies work on any trout stream in any place by fine-tuning color shades and size. Learn the bugs first, then the flies. In both designing flies and fishing them, I keep two factors in mind: matching and behavior.

Matching the size and shape of the natural insect are the first considerations when designing and choosing flies to imitate specific species. I always carry both the true size of the fly and one size smaller. If the fish don't first respond to the match, I've found the smaller size can often work better. Similarly, I carry both buggy and slimmer and sparser designs to see which the fish prefer. Subtle differences in color can also affect performance. Not only are there regional variations, but mayflies change in color through their emergence process.

Mayfly adults often lighten or darken seconds or minutes after emergence. PMDs lighten after emergence, first appearing reddish brown, then a light orange-yellow, and finally a pale yellow with light orange accents. Life-stage flies should reflect this color transformation as well.

The Beaverhead Midge soft-hackle dry fly and the natural. Fished on the surface, this imitates an adult or an egg-laying adult. Fished wet, it imitates both an emerging pupa and a sunken egg layer. To match other species, alter the hook size and color shade to imitate the naturals you encounter in midge hatches.

Another example is the *Isonychia* emerging dun, a light green that quickly darkens to a dark brown after emergence. This color change between life stages doesn't always happen in every species, so it's important to note which mayflies have a lighter emerger color, and what it is. Color transformation also commonly occurs when the dun molts into a spinner, often a shade of rusty brown. But it doesn't end there; regional color of interspecies adults can vary as well.

The behavior, size, and shape of the mayflies may be the same within the species, but color is a differentiating factor and, in my opinion, is important in technical-hatch situations with wary and selective trout. In extreme cases, different regional mayflies can vary wildly enough in color to look like different species. Using hand-blended dubbings allows you to make your flies with markings and color shades similar to the naturals. When tying emergers like the Transition Flymph or other patterns that imitate both the nymphal shuck and the newly emerging dun, make the thorax a shade of dubbing that matches the fresh dun. Also remember that natural fur dubbings will darken when wet. You can test this at home with a cup of water and a small amount of the dubbing you intend to use, to see how much it darkens and how it appears when wet. This will help you become a better angler as well, as you think about how your flies appear in the water to the fish.

A natural PMD (*E. excrucians*) seen alongside a #16 Ascension Flymph. This species hatches on or near the surface, and this wet fly is tied on a wet-fly hook with a rabbit fur body, just heavy enough to sink an inch or two under the surface to target fish holding near the surface during the hatch. Extra fish attention results from the two Pearl Krystal Flash strands that imitate the shimmer of the dun's unfolding wings.

In addition to proper color, the fly needs to have a natural yet eye-catching, appealing behavior about it. This appearance factor is the combination of movement and the correct location of the fly relative to the naturals in the water. Roger Rohrbeck writes, "The emergence behavior of mayflies varies greatly, not only by species, but also by environmental circumstance. For example, a species of mayfly nymph which (under normal circumstances) crawls out of the water to shed its exoskeleton, may do so at the water's surface during flood conditions. While some mayfly species tend to depart their nymphal exoskeleton at or near the bottom, probably the vast majority of species tend to do so at or near the water's surface. Generally speaking, I would expect any given species to have evolved with an emergence strategy which most favors their successful propagation." Trout bugs will hatch often under the conditions that give them an advantage of survival, however trout try to counteract this by keying in on the most vulnerable

life stage and location in the water. Often this is just under the surface film as the insect is ascending or descending. It's also a reason that many hatches and spinnerfalls occur near dusk when light is fading and it is harder for the bugs to be seen. As evening approaches the cones used for color recognition in trout eyes withdraw and the rods that detect light sensitivity increase. This allows them to still feed under low light conditions while the exact color shades of our flies are less important that the visibility of them to the fish. Trout also will often strike a fly that is appearing to be escaping. The movement and behavior of the fly can be increased with line strips or Figure-8 retrieves. When fishing to the most selective trout during a heavy hatch when fish are keying in on a specific species, I will often fish my flies with dead drifts and then increase the amount of movement I impart. Whichever way is more successful will be employed more as this gives me an idea of what the fish want or are seeing in the bugs that day.

I always have a full arsenal of flies in sizes and colors to allow me to imitate life-stages, appearance, and behaviors of the insects I am likely to encounter at different times. These choices of fly design allow me to match them up to presentation methods that I think will work best under the given and changing conditions that I encounter throughout each day of fishing.

While fishing the River Liffey in Ireland, I encountered Large Green Dun (*Ecdyonurus insignis*) spinners and imitated them with a soft-hackle spinner, both dead drifted dry and underwater as a sunken spinner. Armed with pattern and life-cycle knowledge, you can travel the world and confidently catch trout everywhere.

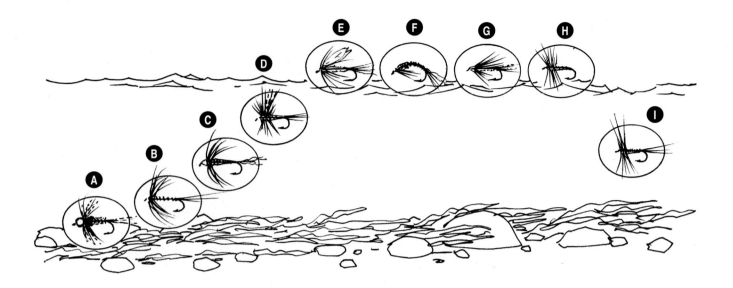

Mayfly Lifecycle. Soft-hackle patterns imitating the complete Pale Morning Dun Lifecycle. This bottom to top approach can be applied to all mayfly species depending on their specific lifecycle behavior.

**A.** Deep Nymph; **B.** Light Nymph; **C.** Transition Flymph; **D.** Winged Transition Flymph; **E.** Winged Wet Fly; **F.** Surface Emerger; **G.** Soft-Hackle Dry/Wet; **H.** Soft-Hackle Spinner; **I.** Sunken Spinner.

# MAYFLIES (EPHEMEROPTERA)

I tie my mayfly nymphs with hyperdefinition of body segments. Proportions largely determine the design: a thin abdomen, the thorax tied like a ball to accentuate the larger thorax of the natural, and a shorter hackle collar to allow visibility of the body and imitate the front legs of the nymph. In the water, materials will meld and there will be a smooth transition between the abdomen and thorax. I like to use straight-shank nymph hooks for mayfly nymphs, sometimes bent into a swimming shape.

Mayflies have two-colored bodies. The dorsal (top) side of the bug is usually darker, often much more so than the ventral (bottom) side of the fly. Most pictures and artificials show and imitate the darker shade of the dorsal side. However, fish often see both sides of the fly, and the dark/light contrast is significant. It's difficult to make a fly that has different top and bottom colors, as most flies are a single material such as dubbing. Making a custom blend of dubbing that incorporates both colors is the easiest way. For example, a Quill Gordon has a brownish-gray dorsal color and a light-olive ventral color. Mixing brown and olive dubbing together gives it a nice shade. Since the fly is tied in the round, it will not have a specific top and bottom color, but the combined dubbing will give it the overall color shade of the fly. Ribbing contributes to the overall segmentation and adds further color contrast to the imitation.

To grab the fish's attention, especially during a heavy hatch, your fly must both look natural and still stand out a little from the others. Remember that you can slightly exaggerate features on the fly. Without making it look noticeably bigger, you want to provide distinction to each element. Materials like winglets may be slightly longer and stand out, hackle collars provide movement, hot spots may appear on the thorax wing case or thread head, and dubbing may increase flash, all in an attempt to make the fly more attractive.

I tie and fish flies that include bits of both impressionism and realism, combined to enhance shape and action in the artificial fly. Nymphs should have life-like behavior built into the fly with materials that will activate in the current. Moreover, fishing them correctly means at the depth the trout are holding, and in ways that make them look most alive, yet natural. With that said, sometimes showing the trout a less realistic fly in the right place, and fished in the right way, causes the fish's brain to fill in the rest. At other times, realism in fly design is more important, especially when a fish has hundreds of naturals with which to compare the artificial, such as during a Sulphur hatch when the trout feed on the drifting, emerging nymphs.

## GILL NYMPH

| Hook: | #10-16 WR-396 |
|---|---|
| Thread: | Camel 8/0 UNI-Thread |
| Abdomen: | Copper Ultra Wire (small) |
| Gills: | Gray rayon floss |
| Thorax: | Rusty brown Hareline Rabbit and rusty brown Orvis Ice Dub mixture |
| Tail and Hackle: | Brown partridge or marked light brown partridge |

**Note:** A combination of realism and impressionism, this soft-hackle nymph has rayon-floss gills that have lots of movement in the water, further giving life to the fly. Hook is bent upward at the thorax.

*Baetidae* (top), *Ephemerella invaria* (middle), *Ephemerella infrequens* (bottom). These color combinations will match most (#14 and smaller) mayfly nymph species. Tie to match size, and then fish with the correct behavior, either for prospecting or to match floating nymphs just under the surface. That can sometimes be more effective than dry flies during hatches of some species.

## MCGEE'S CONTRAST NYMPH

| | |
|---|---|
| **Hook:** | #10-18 WR-396 |
| **Thread:** | Olive, dark brown, or camel 8/0 UNI-Thread |
| **Tail:** | Partridge to match hackle collar |
| **Abdomen:** | Sparkle olive, mahogany, or golden olive Wapsi Superfine dry-fly dubbing |
| **Rib:** | Olive (*Baetis*), hot yellow (Sulphur), copper (*Epeorus*) Ultra Wire (small) |
| **Thorax:** | Green rabbit and Spectra dubbing mix (*Baetis*), brown rabbit and Spectra dubbing mix (Sulphur), rusty brown rabbit and orange Spectra dubbing (*Epeorus*) |
| **Hackle:** | Gray partridge marked with BIC Mark-It Margarita Green, partridge Prismacolor PM-17, BIC Mark-It Tiki Hut Tan |

Mayfly species vary in the ways they emerge. Some hatch out of the nymphal shell on the streambed and travel up the surface as fully formed winged duns. These include Quill Gordons and Slate Maroon Drakes. Most, like Light Cahills and Flavs, hatch in the surface film, while others such as the *Isonychia* nymphs sometime migrate to shore to emerge out of the water and sometimes hatch midstream at the surface. When you see the adult dun on the water or in the air above the stream, you must understand the behavior and the location of the emerging stage of the species to imitate it correctly.

## HENDRICKSON TRANSITION FLYMPH

| | |
|---|---|
| **Hook:** | #12-14 Mustad R50 |
| **Thread:** | Black 12/0 Benecchi |
| **Shuck:** | Brown Z-Lon |
| **Abdomen:** | Brown Wapsi Superfine Dry Dubbing |
| **Rib:** | Brown ostrich |
| **Wing:** | Coastal deer |
| **Hackle:** | Olive Whiting American Hackle |
| **Thorax:** | Pale Evening Dun Superfine Dry Dubbing |

Strangely, most mayflies have an extra stage of molt to become egg layers, even stranger because they have an incomplete metamorphosis, skipping the pupal stage. This molting process turns them into spinners, after which they mate and the females lay eggs. The spinners look different than the duns. Legs and tails become longer, with lighter transparent wings and bodies to help in the midair mating swarms and subsequent spinnerfalls. Minutes to hours after they mate and lay eggs, the spinners die. Understanding species egg-laying behavior is important, as trout may be feeding on spinners you don't even see. Examples are many *Baetis* species that crawl underwater to lay eggs, or the sunken spinners that some spinners become if they aren't eaten on the surface.

A Soft-Hackle Dry Rusty Spinner imitates both *Ephemerella* and *Baetis* well. In fact, it can imitate at least a dozen different and important mayfly species spinner life stages.

## Mayfly Life-Cycle Patterns

When I'm matching life cycles and species, I like to have versatile patterns, adaptable to all species by changing the color and size of the fly; then fishing the fly to best match the natural behavior, movement, and location of the species I'm imitating, by using pattern references. First determine what species and life stage you want to match, depending on the hatch and fish feeding behavior. Then choose the size and color of the life stage. Fish the patterns according to the natural B. A. M. of the species. I've divided mayflies into two categories based on size. Each has life-cycle fly patterns that best suit the size of the natural insect. Soft-hackle patterns can imitate the complete mayfly cycle.

*Small (#14-24) Mayfly Lifecycle Patterns:*
- Nymphs: Deep Nymph, Light Nymph
- Emergers: Transition Flymph, Floating Soft-Hackle Emerger
- Adult Dun: Soft-Hackle Dry Fly, Winged Wet Fly
- Adult Spinner: Soft-Hackle Spinner, Sunken Spinner, Diving Spinner

*Large (#8-12) Mayfly Lifecycle Patterns:*
- Nymphs:
    Deep ArticuNymph
    Light ArticuNymph
    Soft-Hackle Nymph
- Emergers:
    Transition Flymph
    Extended Shuck Emerger
- Adult Dun:
    Soft-Hackle Dry Fly
    Extended Body Soft-Hackle Dry Fly
    Winged Wet Fly
- Adult Spinner:
    Extended Body Soft-Hackle Spinner
    Sunken Spinner

## Quill Gordon (*Epeorus pleuralis*)
### East, hatches April through late May (#12-16)

Nymph is a dark olive clinger that emerges in early spring, starting around mid-April. Duns wait to emerge until the warmest part of the day in the afternoon, as the weather can be cold at this time of year. Adults shed the nymphal husk, emerge underwater, and swim to the surface fully emerged. Fishing a winged wet fly is appropriate. Duns are a light tannish olive with medium dark dun wings. They float on the water's surface until wings are dry. Spinners have light tannish olive bodies and clear wings. Spinners lay eggs when temperatures reach into the 50s at the warmest part of the day. Emergence of duns and spinners can overlap; pay attention to the naturals on water. Fishing an emerger and spinner together can be successful.

**NYMPH**

| | |
|---|---|
| **Hook:** | #12-16 Mustad S82 |
| **Thread:** | Dark brown UNI-Thread |
| **Tail/Hackle:** | Gray partridge |
| **Abdomen:** | Brown Hareline Rabbit Dubbin |
| **Rib:** | Yellow Holographic Tinsel |
| **Thorax:** | Brown Hareline Rabbit and rusty brown Orvis Ice Dub |

**Note:** Mark gray partridge with Goldenrod Prismacolor.

**TRANSITION FLYMPH**

| | |
|---|---|
| **Hook:** | #12-16 Mustad S82 |
| **Thread:** | Camel 8/0 UNI-Thread |
| **Tail and Hackle:** | Brown partridge |
| **Abdomen:** | Brown Hareline Rabbit Dubbin |
| **Rib:** | Light olive 6/0 Danville Flymaster |
| **Thorax:** | Olive Hareline Rabbit Dubbin |
| **Wing:** | Dun Swiss Straw |

## WET FLY

| | |
|---|---|
| **Hook:** | #12-16 Mustad S82 |
| **Thread:** | Light olive 6/0 Danville Flymaster |
| **Tail and Hackle:** | Brown partridge |
| **Body:** | Brown Hareline Rabbit Dubbin |
| **Rib:** | Light olive 6/0 Danville Flymaster |
| **Wing:** | Dun Swiss Straw |

**Note:** Wing marked with Prismacolor Cool Gray Marker and sealed.

## DUN

| | |
|---|---|
| **Hook:** | #12-16 Eagle Claw L059 |
| **Thread:** | Coffee 6/0 Danville Flymaster |
| **Tail:** | Grizzly hen cape |
| **Body:** | Dark tan Wapsi Superfine and a small amount of brown dubbing mixture |
| **Rib:** | Tan Coats and Clark #8120 thread |
| **Wing:** | Coastal deer |
| **Hackle:** | Grizzly hen cape |

**Note:** Tail marked with BIC Tiki Hut Tan; hackle marked half Tiki Hut Tan and half Feather Lime Sorbet.

## SPINNER

| | |
|---|---|
| **Hook:** | #12-16 Eagle Claw L059 |
| **Thread:** | Coffee 6/0 Danville Flymaster |
| **Tail:** | Grizzly hen cape |
| **Body:** | Dark tan Wapsi Superfine and a small amount of brown dubbing mixture |
| **Rib:** | Tan Coats and Clark #8120 thread |
| **Wing:** | Sparkle Organza |
| **Hackle:** | Grizzly hen cape |

**Note:** Tail marked with BIC Tiki Hut Tan; hackle marked half Tiki Hut Tan and half Feather Lime Sorbet.

### Green Drake (*Ephemera guttulata*)
#### East, hatches late May through late June (#6-10)

Nymph is a light-brown burrower that lives in streambed silt, not readily available to fish until emergence. Hatch begins when the sun sets and continues past dark.

The cream and olive dun has yellowish green, mottled wings. The spinner has a white abdomen and black thorax, and clear wings with mottling. The evening spinnerfall is the most important stage of the hatch, because the spent naturals stay on the water longest of all in the life cycle. Trout feed well into the night on the spinners. Fishing a soft-hackle spinner dead drift, and then pulling it underwater and fishing it as a sunken spinner is effective.

## DUN

| | |
|---|---|
| **Hook:** | #6-10 Mustad R43 |
| **Thread:** | Olive 6/0 Danville Flymaster |
| **Tail:** | Moose body fibers |
| **Body:** | Olive and brown Wapsi Superfine Mix |
| **Rib:** | Olive Coats and Clark #6340 thread |
| **Wing:** | Olive mallard flank under natural dun CDC |
| **Hackle:** | Olive CDC |

## SPINNER

| | |
|---|---|
| **Hook:** | #14 Mustad R50 |
| **Thread:** | Black 6/0 Danville Flymaster |
| **Tail:** | Moose body fibers |
| **Abdomen:** | White Wapsi Superfine dubbing |
| **Thorax:** | Black Wapsi Superfine dubbing |
| **Upright Wing:** | Light dun CDC |
| **Spent Wing:** | Sparkle Organza |
| **Hackle:** | Grizzly hen cape |

### Blue Quill (*Paraleptophlebia adoptiva*)
**East, hatches April through early June (#16-18)**

Nymph body is brown, found in medium flow currents. Emergers hatch late morning through afternoon, often emerging on cold days with low sun and snow. Quill Gordon and Hendrickson emergences can overlap. Trout feed on nymphs during hatch, as well as duns. Dun body is dark brown with a medium dun wing. Behavior is characterized by normal drift and flying off water. Spinner body is reddish brown, the wing clear. Spinners fall midday. Females dip abdomens into water to oviposit eggs, then drift spent, eventually sinking. Found in medium-speed currents. Often hatch alongside the larger Hendricksons, and trout will often key in on the smaller, less obvious Blue Quill. Watch closely.

## NYMPH

| | |
|---|---|
| **Hook:** | #16-18 WR-396 |
| **Thread:** | Camel 8/0 UNI-Thread |
| **Tail, Abdomen, Hackle:** | Ginger blood marabou |
| **Rib:** | Copper Ultra Wire (small) |
| **Abdomen:** | Two rusty brown blood marabou fibers |
| **Hackle:** | Brown starling |

## DUN

| | |
|---|---|
| **Hook:** | #16-18 Tiemco 100 |
| **Thread:** | Camel 8/0 UNI-Thread |
| **Tail:** | Light dun hen cape fibers |
| **Body:** | Dark tan and brown Wapsi Superfine dubbing mixture |
| **Rib:** | Tan Coats and Clark thread |
| **Wing:** | Medium dun CDC |
| **Hackle:** | Brown hen cape |

### March Brown (*Maccaffertium vicarium*)
**East, hatches mid-May through early June (#12)**

Nymph body is light brownish amber. Nymphs are clingers that often lose their hold and drift. Found in fast-water habitats when immature, then in shallow, slow-water sections leading up to and during emergence. Fish them deep in riffles earlier in the year, and then deep with ascending lifts in the shallows in late May and early June. Presentation methods include high-stick deep nymphing and the Modified Leisenring Lift. Trout feed heavily on nymphs in the weeks leading up to emergence. Hatches take place late morning into afternoon, and then on hot evenings in May through early July in the East. The hatch lasts about two weeks in each location. They are slow to escape the nymphal shuck, taking up to 30 seconds to emerge, so trout have time to capture them with relative ease. Transition Flymphs imitate this well. Fish the wet fly by mending line and slowing the drift as it reaches the fish. Dun body is shades of yellow, olive, and tan. Wing is mottled olive and yellow. They drift long on the water, as it takes a while for them to dry their wings. Spinner body is olive-yellow. Wing is clear mottled. Spinners fall late evening through dusk a few days after emergence. Spinnerfalls are not predictable, but good when they happen, as many days' worth of insects will mate at one time.

## NYMPH

| | |
|---|---|
| **Hook:** | #12 Mustad S82 |
| **Thread:** | Coffee 6/0 Danville Flymaster |
| **Tail:** | Bleached partridge |
| **Abdomen:** | Golden olive Wapsi Superfine dubbing |
| **Rib:** | Copper Ultra Wire (small) |
| **Thorax:** | Brown Hareline Rabbit Dubbin and golden brown Hareline Ice Dub mixture |
| **Hackle:** | Brown partridge |

## WINGED WET FLY/FLOATING FLYMPH

| | |
|---|---|
| **Hook:** | #12 Mustad R50 |
| **Thread:** | Coffee 6/0 Danville Flymaster |
| **Body:** | Hareline light olive and a small amount of March Brown dubbing mixture |
| **Rib:** | Hay Ride Coats and Clark #7430 thread |
| **Wing:** | Dun Z-Lon |
| **Tail and Hackle:** | Brown partridge |

**Note:** (Optional) Apply floatant to wing to ride in surface film; leave untreated for a wet-fly-only presentation.

## TRANSITION FLYMPH

| | |
|---|---|
| **Hook:** | #12 Tiemco 5262 |
| **Thread:** | Coffee 6/0 Danville Flymaster |
| **Shuck:** | Brown Z-Lon |
| **Abdomen:** | Pheasant tail |
| **Rib:** | Copper Ultra Wire (small) |
| **Thorax:** | Natural Hareline Rabbit Dubbin |
| **Wing:** | Dun Swiss Straw |
| **Hackle:** | Brown partridge |

## SHUCKED DUN

| | |
|---|---|
| **Hook:** | #12 Tiemco 100 |
| **Thread:** | Coffee 6/0 Danville Flymaster |
| **Shuck:** | Brown Z-Lon |
| **Body:** | Brown Wapsi with a small amount of tan Superfine dubbing |
| **Rib:** | Coffee 6/0 Danville Flymaster |
| **Wing:** | Coastal deer |
| **Hackle:** | Light brown hen cape |

## Hendrickson (*Ephemerella subvaria*)
### East, hatches April through May (#12-14)

The Hendrickson is synonymous with the famous fly-fishing water of the Northeast. This marks the beginning of the classic mayfly hatches, and fish will feed heavily and often selectively on them. Nymph body is dark brown though colors vary from one body of water to the next. Found in riffles with medium-to-fast currents. The nymphs will become more active before the hatch, when the water reaches about 50 degrees in April. Even though they are crawler nymphs, these good swimmers attract trout as they swim to the surface to emerge. Nymphs are strong swimmers with undulating dolphin kicks of the abdomen in slow water. In fast water, they dead drift. Soft-Hackle ArticuNymphs reflect the kicking motion well. Nymphs often make practice runs to the surface in the days leading up to the hatch, and trout key in on this; thus the Practice-Run Method is realistic and effective. Other presentation methods include the Leisenring Lift, dead drift, and small line strips.

Emergers in the surface film in mid-afternoon often are stuck in the shuck, making Transition Flymphs effective. The emerging dun is olive-tan, but soon darkens to an amber color after emerging. Soft-hackle emergers should be tied with the natural olive-tan color body. Dun body is yellowish tan, and wing is medium dun. Characterized by long drifts as they dry their wings in the cool spring weather. A soft-hackle dry fly fished dead drift, then pulled underwater at the end of the drift and swung (with or without stripping line) is deadly before, during, and just after a hatch. Spinner body is reddish brown, the wing is clear. They become active when air temperatures reach 65 to 70 degrees. The spinnerfall is important. They often drop eggs to the water from in-flight, but sometimes land on the surface to finish egg laying. In this case, a spinner with a bright-yellow butt will imitate the egg sack. Egg laying usually happens in the late afternoon and evening, unless it's cold; then it will occur the next morning.

### TRANSITION FLYMPH

| | |
|---|---|
| **Hook:** | #12-14 Mustad S82 |
| **Thread:** | Coffee 6/0 Danville Flymaster |
| **Shuck:** | Brown Z-Lon |
| **Abdomen:** | Brown turkey rounds |
| **Rib:** | Copper Ultra Wire (extra-fine) |
| **Thorax:** | Natural Hareline Rabbit |
| **Wing:** | Light dun Swiss Straw |
| **Hackle:** | Brown partridge |

### DUN

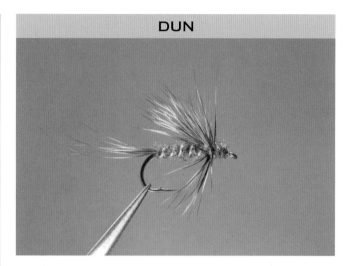

| | |
|---|---|
| **Hook:** | #12-14 Mustad R50 |
| **Thread:** | Camel 8/0 UNI-Thread |
| **Body:** | Brown and tan Hareline Superfine Dubbing Mixture |
| **Rib:** | Golden tan Coats and Clark #8140 thread |
| **Wing:** | Coastal deer |
| **Tail and Hackle:** | Grizzly hen cape marked BIC Tiki Hut Tan |

### SPINNER

| | |
|---|---|
| **Hook:** | #12-14 Tiemco 100 |
| **Thread:** | Camel 8/0 UNI-Thread |
| **Tail and Hackle:** | Grizzly hen cape |
| **Body:** | Brown and tan Hareline Superfine Dubbing Mixture |
| **Rib:** | Golden tan Coats and Clark #8140 thread |
| **Wing:** | Sparkle Organza |

## Small Blue-Winged Olive (*Drunella lata*)
### East and Midwest, hatches June through August (#16-18)

Nymph body is dark olive to grayish or reddish brown. Found in medium-speed current with weedy streambeds, fishing a rising nymph before and during a hatch is effective. Hatches in the morning in late June through August, in medium-to-slow flat-water river sections. Adults emerge under or at the surface. This is an important hatch on midwestern trout streams. Dun body freshly emerged is light olive, and darkens to olive gray. They drift on top of the water until their wings are dry. Spinner body is dark olive, egg sack is the same color. Wing is clear. Spinners fall over riffles and get trout moving the best, as the falls are more intense than the hatches, which can be more spread out in duration. Females drop their eggs from the air and fall spent onto the surface.

## TRANSITION FLYMPH

| **Hook:** | #16-18 WR-396 |
| **Thread:** | Olive 12/0 Benecchi |
| **Shuck:** | Brown Z-Lon |
| **Abdomen:** | Stripped peacock quill |
| **Thorax:** | Olive Superfine dry-fly dubbing |
| **Hackle:** | Dun hen cape |

## WINGLESS WET

| **Hook:** | #16-18 Dai-Riki #070 |
| **Thread:** | Olive 12/0 Benecchi |
| **Body:** | Green Flashabou under Superfine olive |
| **Hackle:** | Light dun hen cape |

**Note:** For body, dubbing is scissors-diced into a finer dry-fly touch dubbing. For hackle, tie in by the base of the stem to get the fuzziest fibers

## Large Blue-Winged Olive (*Drunella cornuta*)
### East and Midwest, hatches Mid-May through Mid-June (#12-14)

Nymph body is olive brown. This crawler mayfly is found in medium and fast riffles. Hatches in moderate-speed current riffles and runs in the morning, later if it's cold. The duns emerge from the nymphal shuck about 12 inches underwater, and arrive at the surface as adults. Some may get stuck in the shuck or be stillborn, making both Winged Flymphs and Transition Flymphs effective. Dun body is light olive newly emerged, then darkens to medium brown-olive with a dark dun wing. They drift to dry their wings, then fly off the water. Spinner body is dark olive with a clear wing. Spinners mate over riffles and fall spent in the evening. These eastern and midwestern blue-winged olives are an important hatch. It occurs during the season when Sulphurs, Green Drakes, and *Isonychia* are emerging, but since they hatch in the morning while these other hatches come off in the evening, trout often key in on the *Drunella* duns. However, spinnerfalls of this species do happen in the evening while trout may be keying in on other species.

When there are overlapping hatches and spinnerfalls, and fish are surface feeding, you have to be able to change flies until you identify the target species. This is a good situation in which to fish two soft-hackle dry flies of different species at the same time, with the dropper tied off the hook eye of the point fly, to determine a preference. It may be one fish is keying in on one species, and another fish on the other.

## WET EMERGER

| **Hook:** | #12-14 Eagle Claw L063S |
| **Thread:** | Olive 8/0 Orvis |
| **Shuck:** | Brown Hare's Ear Plus Dubbing |
| **Body:** | Olive Hare's Ear Plus Dubbing |
| **Wing:** | Light dun Swiss Straw |
| **Hackle:** | Olive partridge |

**Note:** You can use the lighter Eagle Claw L059 (shown), depending on desired weight.

## WINGED WET

| | |
|---|---|
| **Hook:** | #12-14 Mustad R50 |
| **Thread:** | Olive 8/0 Orvis |
| **Tail and Hackle:** | Bleached ginger |
| **Body:** | Olive Hareline Rabbit Dubbin |
| **Rib:** | Green Danville rayon floss |
| **Wing:** | Dun Swiss Straw |

## DUN

| | |
|---|---|
| **Hook:** | #12-14 Mustad R50 |
| **Thread:** | Black 12/0 Benecchi |
| **Tail:** | Olive grizzly hen cape |
| **Body:** | Golden olive Superfine with a touch of tan dry-fly mixture |
| **Rib:** | Light olive 6/0 Danville thread |
| **Wing:** | Coastal deer |
| **Hackle:** | Olive hen cape |

## CRIPPLED DUN

| | |
|---|---|
| **Hook:** | #12-14 Eagle Claw L059 |
| **Thread:** | Olive 6/0 Danville Flymaster |
| **Shuck:** | Brown Z-Lon |
| **Body:** | Olive Superfine with a touch of brown dry-fly dubbing mixture |
| **Wing:** | Dun CDC |
| **Hackle:** | Olive green hen cape |

## Orange Sulphur, Little Marryatt or Pink Cahill (*Epeorus vitreus*)

### East and Midwest, late-May through mid-June (#14)

Nymph body is pale tannish-olive. Clinger nymphs are found in fast riffles. Fish deep with high-sticking methods and weight in faster riffles. Other presentation methods include high-stick nymphing and the mend-and-swing wet-fly method. Nymphs emerge to duns in late afternoon and evening, with a peak at sundown. These mayflies emerge underwater, exiting their nymphal shucks while rising before they reach the surface. Wet flies that imitate the dun underwater are natural and effective. The male dun body is pale olive, the female is olive-orange. Wing is light dun. They quickly fly off the water, as they arrive at the surface already emerged. The male spinner body is pale creamy olive, the female bright orange/yellow, and the spinner wing is clear. Spinnerfalls occur in the evening, or earlier if the weather is warm. Females fly low over the water, dipping their abdomens to lay eggs in the water. After they are finished, they fall spent with the males. Dead drifting a spent spinner on the surface or a sunken spinner underwater works well. These mayflies are sensitive to pollution and multibrooded. Males are a size smaller than females and are light yellowish olive, while females are pale yellow with an orange middle abdomen.

## WINGED WET

| Hook: | #14 Daiichi 1530 |
|---|---|
| Thread: | Orange 6/0 Danville Flymaster |
| Tail: | Light dun hen cape |
| **Abdomen** | |
| Underbody: | Orange 6/0 Danville Flymaster |
| Rib: | Yellow DMC 25 #3822 |
| Thorax: | Sulphur orange Nature's Spirit Hare's Mask Dubbing |
| Wing: | Light dun hen tip |
| Hackle: | Hen cape marked Prismacolor Deco Yellow |

## Sulphur (*Ephemerella invaria*)
### East and Midwest, hatches May and June (#14-16)

Nymph body is dark brown with yellow highlights. A crawler mayfly that lives in riffle water, nymphs often make practice runs to the surface before the hatch, and are available to trout.

The Sulphur dun exhibits a yellowish-orange body and medium dun wing.

The spinner is more amber in color, with a clear wing. Color is important in matching mayfly adults, but not as important as size and correct presentation. You could arguably use the same-color body for dun and spinner to match this species, if the size and behavior are spot on.

Hatches are in the afternoon and evening. Nymphs drift under the surface film for a long distance before the dun is able to escape the nymphal husk, which takes some time. Trout feed heavily on these floating nymphs, especially during hatches. Floating nymphs that drift just under the surface are common with *invaria* hatches. Trout will feed on them, and it can be difficult to see what they are eating unless the hatch is heavy and you look at the water for nymphs. An unweighted Transition Flymph (no wire ribbing) or Contrast Nymph imitates this appearance well. Fish these floating nymphs with a downstream parachute cast dead drift just under the surface, into the mouths of rising fish. The nymphs are more vulnerable than the duns. Another method is to use a soft-hackle dry fly and drop the flymph off the hook bend with 10 inches of 5X tippet. *Invaria* hatch in mid-afternoon through evening, when the water is 52 to 60 degrees. The newly emerged dun is bright yellow and soon darkens to yellowish-orange.

The dun's body is pale yellow, with a light dun wing. Once emerged, Sulphurs are quick to fly off the water, further emphasizing the importance of the floating nymph, emerger, and stuck-in-the-shuck cripples. Spinner bodies are amber with a clear wing. Duns molt and return to the water to lay eggs at dusk or morning. They mate over shallow riffles, and the females lay eggs on the surface and eventually sink, making both floating and sunken spinners fished just under the surface important. Males fly off and are often found on slower water below the riffle.

These legendary bugs are arguably the best hatches in the Northeast and Upper Midwest, as far as predictability and food source for trout go. *Ephemerella invaria* are the larger Sulphurs that now include *Ephemerella rotunda* as a single species, which have a wide range of slight color and size variations. The smaller Sulphurs are *Ephemerella dorothea* and remain a different species. Trout can feed selectively on these bugs, but fishing floating nymphs often is the key to the hatch.

## TRANSITION FLYMPH

| | |
|---|---|
| **Hook:** | #14-16 Tiemco 101 |
| **Thread:** | Light Cahill 8/0 UNI-Thread |
| **Tail and Abdomen:** | Pheasant tail |
| **Thorax:** | Pale yellow Superfine dry-fly dubbing |
| **Hackle:** | Partridge marginal covert |

## FLOATING EMERGER

| | |
|---|---|
| **Hook:** | #14-16 Tiemco 2488 |
| **Thread:** | Light Cahill 8/0 UNI-Thread |
| **Tail:** | Brown hen cape |
| **Abdomen:** | Brown Superfine Rabbit Dubbin |
| **Rib:** | Yellow Hends Body Quill |
| **Thorax:** | Pale yellow Superfine dry-fly dubbing |
| **Wing:** | Dun CDC |
| **Hackle:** | Yellow hen cape |

## WINGED EMERGER

| | |
|---|---|
| **Hook:** | #14-16 Tiemco 3761 |
| **Thread:** | Light Cahill 8/0 UNI-Thread |
| **Shuck:** | Brown Z-Lon |
| **Abdomen:** | Brown turkey biot |
| **Thorax:** | Pale yellow Hareline Rabbit Dubbin |
| **Wing:** | Dun hen feather tip |
| **Hackle:** | Hen cape marked Prismacolor Deco Yellow |

## WINGED WET

| | |
|---|---|
| **Hook:** | #14-16 Mustad R50 |
| **Thread:** | Light Cahill 8/0 UNI-Thread |
| **Shuck:** | Brown Z-Lon |
| **Abdomen:** | Sulphur turkey biot |
| **Thorax:** | Superfine Pale Morning Dun |
| **Wing:** | Clear Medallion Sheeting |
| **Hackle:** | Light dun hen cape |

**Note:** For thorax, mix with a small amount of amber dry-fly dubbing mixture. Form Medallion Sheeting with a wing cutter.

## FLOATING EMERGER

**Hook:**      #14-16 Tiemco 2488
**Thread:**    Light Cahill 8/0 UNI-Thread
**Shuck:**     Brown Hare's Ear Plus
**Abdomen:**   Brown Hends Body Quill
**Thorax:**    Superfine Pale Morning Dun dry-fly
               dubbing
**Wing:**      Dun CDC
**Hackle:**    Yellow hen cape

## DUN

**Hook:**      #14-16 Mustad R50
**Thread:**    Light Cahill 8/0 UNI-Thread
**Shuck:**     Golden tan Wapsi Antron March Brown
               dubbing mixture
**Abdomen:**   Yellow turkey biot
**Wing:**      Dun CDC
**Thorax:**    Superfine Pale Morning Dun
**Hackle:**    Yellow hen cape

**Note:** For thorax, mix with a small amount of amber dry-fly dubbing mixture.

## SURFACE EMERGER

**Hook:**      #14-16 Tiemco 2488
**Thread:**    Light Cahill 8/0 UNI-Thread
**Shuck:**     Brown Hare's Ear Plus
**Abdomen:**   Yellow Hends Body Quill
**Thorax:**    Pale yellow Superfine dry dubbing
**Wing:**      Dun CDC
**Hackle:**    Dun hen cape

## WET FLY

**Hook:**      #14-16 Tiemco 3761
**Thread:**    Light Cahill 8/0 UNI-Thread
**Tail:**      Mallard flank wood duck
**Abdomen:**   Yellow DMC 25 #3822
**Thorax:**    Amber and pale yellow Hareline Rabbit
               Dubbin mixture
**Hackle:**    Gray hen cape marked BIC Yellow

## WINGED WET

| | |
|---|---|
| **Hook:** | #14-16 Eagle Claw L063S |
| **Thread:** | Orange 6/0 Danville Flymaster |
| **Tail:** | Mallard flank wood duck |
| **Body:** | Pale yellow Hareline Rabbit touch dubbing over thread |
| **Wing:** | Dun Swiss Straw |
| **Hackle:** | Honey dun Whiting Hebert-Miner hen cape |

## SPINNER

| | |
|---|---|
| **Hook:** | #14-16 Eagle Claw L059 |
| **Thread:** | Light Cahill 8/0 UNI-Thread |
| **Tail:** | Light dun hen cape |
| **Abdomen:** | Yellow turkey biot |
| **Thorax:** | Pale yellow Superfine dry-fly dubbing |
| **Wing:** | Sparkle Organza |
| **Hackle:** | Yellow hen cape |

## SPINNER

| | |
|---|---|
| **Hook:** | #14-16 Mustad R50 |
| **Thread:** | Light Cahill 8/0 UNI-Thread |
| **Abdomen:** | Yellow DMC 25 #3822 |
| **Thorax:** | Hareline Green Damsel Rabbit Dubbin |
| **Hackle:** | Dun CDC |

**Note:** Dun CDC cut to length on the stem and wound.

## Little Sulphur (*Ephemerella dorothea dorothea*)
### East and Midwest, hatches May through July (#18-20)

Nymph body is dark brown. Found in many places in the stream, from riffles and runs to the slower pools. Like *Ephemerella invaria*, these sulphur nymphs are active leading up to the hatch, and trout feed on the nymphs even when there aren't signs of rises. Emergers usually hatch late afternoon into late evening. On tailwaters and spring creeks where the flow is consistent and water temperature stable, they may hatch all summer. The nymphs float in the surface for a long time, trying to break out of their nymphal shuck. Many are crippled and stillborn. Trout feed on the emergers heavily, and dead-drifted Transition Flymphs and Floating Flymphs are effective.

Little Sulphur. JON RAPP

Emergence is usually in the evening in 60-to-65-degree slow-water sections, especially in spring creeks. The dun has a pale yellow abdomen and orange thorax, with a light dun wing. Many duns are crippled and offer trout an easy meal; use a shuck dun. Spinner body is rusty brown and the wing is clear. Spinnerfalls occur in the morning and at dusk. Egg laying is typically near dusk in the broken-water riffles of streams. Female spinners fly over the water laying eggs, and fall spent. Some females fall to the surface before releasing their eggs, making a spinner with a bright yellow egg sack butt effective.

Spinnerfalls and dun hatches may overlap, making it effective to fish a floating Soft-Hackle Spinner with a Transition Flymph, or other soft-hackle emerger on a 10-inch 5X dropper off the hook bend. See which is taking more fish; it may be both. This hatch commonly occurs alongside the larger sulphur *Ephemerella invaria*, further complicating this hatch. You may have Sulphurs in sizes 14 through 20 hatching simultaneously with spinners. I like to fish the smaller flies, as fish often will key in on them, then figure out if it is spinners (a rusty-spinner colored pattern) or emergers. Try both, at the same time if you want.

## TRANSITION FLYMPH

| | |
|---|---|
| **Hook:** | #18-20 Eagle Claw L059S |
| **Thread:** | Orange 6/0 Danville Flymaster |
| **Tail and Abdomen:** | Pheasant tail |
| **Rib:** | Fluorescent orange Ultra Wire (small) |
| **Thorax:** | Orange Hareline Rabbit Dubbin |
| **Hackle:** | Brown partridge |

## NYMPH

| | |
|---|---|
| **Hook:** | #18-20 WR-396 |
| **Thread:** | Tobacco brown 6/0 Danville Flymaster |
| **Tail and Hackle:** | Partridge marginal covert |
| **Abdomen:** | Amber Hareline Rabbit Dubbin |
| **Rib:** | Fluorescent orange Ultra Wire (small) |
| **Thorax:** | Rusty Hareline Rabbit Dubbin |

## WINGED WET

| | |
|---|---|
| **Hook:** | #18-20 Eagle Claw L059S |
| **Thread:** | Orange 6/0 Danville Flymaster |
| **Tail:** | Mallard flank wood duck |
| **Abdomen:** | Yellow DMC 25 #3078 Embroidery Floss |
| **Thorax:** | Yellow and fluorescent orange Hareline Rabbit Dubbin |
| **Wing:** | Dark dun hen cape tip |
| **Hackle:** | Yellow hen cape |

## EMERGER DUN

| Hook: | #16-18 Eagle Claw L055 |
|---|---|
| Thread: | Light Cahill 8/0 UNI-Thread |
| Shuck: | Brown Hare's Ear Plus Dubbing |
| Body: | Brown Hareline Rabbit and pale yellow Superfine dry-fly dubbing |
| Wing: | Dun CDC |
| Hackle: | Yellow hen cape |

## DUN

| Hook: | #18-20 Tiemco 100 |
|---|---|
| Thread: | Orange 12/0 Benecchi |
| Tail and Hackle: | Medium dun hen cape |
| Abdomen: | Yellow turkey biot |
| Thorax: | Orange Nature's Spirit Fine Natural Dubbing |

## SPINNER

| Hook: | #18-20 Tiemco 100 |
|---|---|
| Thread: | Rusty brown UTC 70-denier Ultra Thread |
| Tail: | Dun hen cape |
| Abdomen: | Rusty brown turkey rounds |
| Thorax: | Mahogany Nature's Spirit Fine Natural Dubbing |
| Hackle: | Dun CDC |

**Note:** Hackle is clipped to length on stem and wound around the hook.

*Isonychia* dun. JON RAPP

## Slate Drake, White Gloved Howdy (*Isonychia bicolor*)
### East and Midwest, hatches late May through September (#12)

Nymph body is dark reddish brown with cream stripe along the back. These are strong swimmers with lots of abdominal dolphin-like kicks. They live in fast riffle water where they swim, even in the fast water. Nymphs often move to the stream backs or in-stream structure that protrudes out of the water. They climb out of the water to hatch. You will see evidence of this from the empty nymphal husks they leave behind. At other times, they hatch in the surface film. Hatches begin in mid-June, and the peak lasts through early July, though they can still be seen into October. While the duns are olive brown, the emergers first appear a shade of light green. If you tie an emerger such as the Transition Flymph, make the thorax with light-green dubbing to match that of the natural emerger. The dun has an olive-brown body, with a dark dun wing. They hatch in the afternoon and evening, in or out of the water. Spinners are rusty brown with clear wings. Egg laying occurs at dusk in the air above riffles. Females and males fall spent afterwards.

Leadwing Coachmen are an important hatch that is relatively sparse but enduring, lasting from early June through October on many eastern streams. They are large mayflies that trout can focus in on, and may lead trout to feed selectively because they provide a lot of nutrition. Trout seem to expect them during the season on fertile eastern streams, and will take artificial flies even when the naturals aren't hatching. When *Isonychia* duns first hatch out of their nymphal shuck, they are a bright green, but darken to a reddish purple/grayish pink soon after. In this respect, a Transition Flymph should have a green thorax segment to simulate the freshly emerging dun.

To realistically imitate the natural behaviors and movements of the nymphs, use down and across deep drift with rod-tip twitches. The *Isonychia* has a lot of movement in the abdomen while swimming, and a presentation that accentuates this movement with a rise and fall is natural. After the fly has been fished out and is directly downstream, pause and hold it in the current, then strip it back toward you. Many strikes will happen when the fly is downstream on a tight line. More presentation methods include the dead drift, hand twist, and rod-tip jigging. *Isonychia* are strong swimmers and risers, so stripping or twitching a soft-hackle wet fly is a natural presentation for the emerging flymph. The spinnerfall can be of particular importance in late May and early June on northeastern trout streams. In late May at dusk, the East Branch of the Delaware River sees swarms of these mayflies fall, and trout feed heavily on them in the surface film. Don't forget the opportunity to fish a rusty sunken spinner in the tailouts of pools and the heads of riffles below them.

### NYMPH

| Hook: | #12 Tiemco 5262 |
|---|---|
| Thread: | Rusty brown UTC 70-denier Ultra Thread |
| Tail and Hackle: | Partridge body side feather |
| Abdomen: | Amber Hareline Rabbit Dubbin |
| Rib: | Brown ostrich herl |
| Thorax: | Rusty brown Hare's Ear Plus Dubbing |
| Wing case: | Three tan blood marabou fibers |

**Note:** Pull wing-case fibers over thorax.

### DUN

| Hook: | #12 Mustad R50 |
|---|---|
| Thread: | Coffee 6/0 Danville Flymaster |
| Tail and Hackle: | Grizzly hen cape marked with BIC Mark-It Tiki Hut Tan |
| Rib: | Tan Coats and Clark #8120 thread |
| Body: | Superfine dark tan, tan, and *Callibaetis* dubbing mixture |
| Wing: | Coastal deer |

### SPINNER

| Hook: | #12 Tiemco 100 |
|---|---|
| Thread: | Burnt orange UTC 70-denier Ultra Thread |
| Tail and Hackle: | Olive grizzly hen cape |
| Abdomen: | Rusty brown turkey biot |
| Thorax: | Mahogany Nature's Spirit Fine Natural Dubbing |
| Wing: | Sparkle Organza |

## SUNKEN SPINNER

| | |
|---|---|
| **Hook:** | #12 Mustad R50 |
| **Thread:** | Coffee 6/0 Danville Flymaster |
| **Tail:** | Mallard flank wood duck |
| **Abdomen:** | Rusty brown turkey rounds |
| **Thorax:** | Brown ostrich herl |
| **Hackle:** | Brown partridge behind black hen cape |

## Brown Drake (*Ephemera simulans*)
### East to West, hatches late May through early October (#10-12)

The nymph body is light yellow-brown. Nymphs take one or two years to mature. They are burrowers that live in sand, fine gravel, and silt in medium and slow currents, so nymphs are not generally available to trout until the days before the hatch. Although fish will eat nymph imitations almost anytime if fished effectively, articulated nymphs are great for matching the natural's movements. Some presentation methods include high-stick nymphing, swimming-nymph method, Figure-8 Retrieve, rod-tip jigging, and small line strips. Hatches occur at dusk. Emergence is fast and usually lasts three to five days before moving upriver. They rise and pop out of the nymphal shuck almost immediately. Since the transitional phase is so fast, trout key in on the nymphs even during hatches. These mayflies actually hatch underwater just under the surface, with the dun emerging from the nymphal shuck and arriving at the surface fully hatched. Sometimes they get stuck in the shuck or are stillborn, and Floating Flymphs imitate these. Hatches occur in the evening when the water reaches 50 degrees. They prefer to hatch in smoother water. The dun body is yellowish-brown with a wing that is mottled dun with yellow markings. Duns are not important because they are fast to fly off water. Spinners are yellowish-brown with a clear mottled wing. Spinnerfalls occur from dusk until after dark. Found in smooth-water river sections, spinnerfalls are the most important stage; when they fall on the water spent, these large mayflies are a big, easy meal for trout. Midwestern peak is in June. Western rivers see this hatch in June into mid-July.

## NYMPH

| | |
|---|---|
| **Hook:** | #14-16 Eagle Claw L0 |
| **Thread:** | Rusty brown UTC 70-denier Ultra Thread |
| **Tail:** | Brown ostrich herl |
| **Abdomen:** | Amber Hareline Rabbit Dubbin and golden stone Antron mixture |
| **Rib:** | Brown ostrich herl |
| **Thorax:** | Amber Hareline Rabbit Dubbin |
| **Wing case:** | Brown ostrich herl |
| **Hackle:** | March Brown Whiting Brahma hen saddle |

## WINGED WET/FLOATING EMERGER

| | |
|---|---|
| **Hook:** | #10-12 Tiemco 200R |
| **Thread:** | 6/0 Danville Flymaster Black |
| **Tail and Hackle:** | Brown Partridge |
| **Abdomen:** | Reddish-brown DMC 25 #300 Embroidery Floss |
| **Rib:** | Golden brown ostrich herl |
| **Thorax:** | Brown Hareline Rabbit and rusty brown Hareline Ice Dub mixture |
| **Wing:** | Gray Hareline UV Ice Dub |

## WINGED BROWN DRAKE EMERGER

| | |
|---|---|
| **Hook:** | #10-12 Mustad R43 |
| **Thread:** | Coffee 6/0 Danville Flymaster |
| **Abdomen:** | Brown Hareline Rabbit Dubbin |
| **Rib:** | Coffee 6/0 Danville Flymaster |
| **Thorax:** | Olive-brown hare's mask |
| **Wing:** | Tan Swiss Straw |
| **Tail and Hackle:** | Brown partridge |

## DUN

| | |
|---|---|
| **Hook:** | #16 Tiemco 200R |
| **Thread:** | Coffee 6/0 Danville Flymaster |
| **Tail:** | Moose body fibers |
| **Body:** | Brown, light olive, and tan Superfine dry-fly dubbing mixture |
| **Wing:** | Coastal deer |
| **Hackle:** | Grizzly hen cape marked with BIC Tiki Hut Tan |

## SURFACE EMERGER

| | |
|---|---|
| **Hook:** | #10-12 Tiemco 2487 |
| **Thread:** | Rusty brown UTC 70-denier Ultra Thread |
| **Shuck:** | Amber Z-Lon |
| **Abdomen:** | Brown Hareline Rabbit Dubbin |
| **Mid-Thorax:** | Amber ostrich herl |
| **Thorax:** | Dark tan, tan, *Callibaetis*, and a small amount of brown Superfine Dubbing Mix |
| **Wing:** | Natural dun CDC |
| **Hackle:** | Grizzly hen cape marked with BIC Tiki Hut Tan |

## DUN

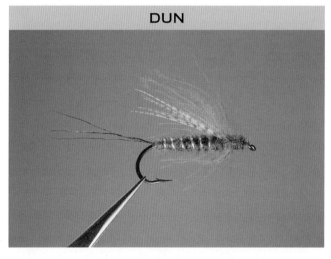

| | |
|---|---|
| **Hook:** | #10-12 Mustad R43 |
| **Thread:** | Coffee 6/0 Danville Flymaster |
| **Tail:** | Moose body fibers |
| **Body:** | Brown, light olive, and tan Superfine dry-fly dubbing mixture |
| **Rib:** | Tan Coats and Clark #8120 thread |
| **Wing:** | Mallard dyed wood duckunder natural dun CDC |
| **Hackle:** | Natural dun CDC |

**SPINNER**

| | |
|---|---|
| **Hook:** | #14 Tiemco 100 |
| **Thread:** | Coffee 6/0 Danville Flymaster |
| **Tail:** | Moose body fibers |
| **Body:** | Brown, light olive, and tan Superfine dry-fly dubbing mixture |
| **Rib:** | Tan Coats and Clark #8120 thread |
| **Wing:** | Natural dun CDC |
| **Spent Wing:** | Sparkle Organza |
| **Hackle:** | Grizzly hen cape marked with BIC Tiki Hut Tan |

Hex. JON RAPP

## Hex (*Hexagenia limbata*)
### East and Midwest, hatches late June and early July (#8-10)

Nymph body is yellowish brown. These large mayfly nymphs are a burrower species that need silt soft enough into which they can dig easily, yet hard enough that it won't collapse. They are found in slower-water sections of river, mainly in the Midwest, but they are transcontinental, found in many states. They molt at night, and the heavy concentration of the dense nymphs, sometimes up to 2,000 nymphs available per day to trout that take two to three years to mature, results in a major food source for trout in these river sections. These mayflies usually hatch at dusk and throughout the night. The nymphs are a major food source during the hatch, as are duns. But since it's harder to see at night, fishing an emerging nymph with lifts and drops, and lift of the fly and rod tip, will be more effective than a dry fly, as you will feel the strike of the trout and won't have to worry about drag-free drifts. Other presentation methods are high-stick nymphing and the Leisenring Lift.

These mayflies emerge at twilight from June through September, concentrating in late June and early July, and will bring up some of the largest trout. On calm, humid, warm, and dark evenings in summer, the hatches are concentrated in certain river sections that the best local fly fishermen hold close to the vest. The nymphs swim to the surface where they attempt to break through the surface film. The commotion is obvious to the trout, which can detect the large food source and feed on vibration, even at night. Dun bodies are yellow to light tan, with yellow dun wings. These large mayflies drift for a long distance, and fishing extended-body soft-hackle dries to them is effective, as long as you can approach the trout closely enough to fish in low-light conditions. Get close without spooking these fish during a hatch, and half the battle is won, making more accurate casts and detecting a strike even if you can't see the fly. Spinner have a light tan body and clear wing. Spinnerfalls are an important part of the hatch to match if you target trout. The males and females mate 5 to 20 feet above the river, then fall spent, making themselves available to the trout either on the surface or sunken. These mating flights occur right after dark, in the same habitat as the nymphs and duns. The spent spinners can float for long distances due to their size.

The best of these hatches occur in Wisconsin. Michigan, Oregon, and California. These are the largest or second largest mayfly in the United States, depending on where the hatch is. In some places, they are second only to Large Green Drake (*Litobrancha recurvata*), except when they exceed 40 mm and outsize the Large Green Drake. Early in the season, fish may feed on all life stages of the bug, nymph, emerger, dun, and spinner, although as the season progresses they may focus on one. It may be that they are feeding heavily on nymphs and not rising at all, or they could be rising only to emergers and duns. Female duns are larger than the males. Since the hatch occurs at dark and through the night, many anglers will find suitable habitat in the day and wait for the hatch to occur. Then they will fish nymphs, duns, or spinners, depending on what the trout seem to key in on.

## NYMPH

| | |
|---|---|
| **Hook:** | #12-14 Eagle Claw L063S |
| **Thread:** | Tobacco brown 6/0 Danville Flymaster |
| **Tail:** | Brown ostrich herl |
| **Abdomen:** | Amber Hareline Rabbit Dubbin and golden stone Wapsi Antron Dubbing Mixture |
| **Rib:** | Brown ostrich herl |
| **Thorax:** | Amber Hareline Rabbit Dubbin |
| **Wing case:** | Brown ostrich herl |
| **Hackle:** | Ruffed grouse |

## WINGED WET/FLOATING EMERGER

| | |
|---|---|
| **Hook:** | #12-14 Tiemco 2487 |
| **Thread:** | Light Cahill 8/0 UNI-Thread |
| **Tail:** | Pheasant tail |
| **Abdomen:** | Hareline Rusty Rabbit Dubbin |
| **Thorax:** | Pale yellow Superfine dry-fly dubbing |
| **Wing:** | Light dun CDC |
| **Hackle:** | Bleached partridge |

## SPINNER

| | |
|---|---|
| **Hook:** | #12-14 Tiemco 100 |
| **Thread:** | Light olive 6/0 Danville Flymaster |
| **Tail:** | Mallard flank wood duck |
| **Body:** | Amber, tan, olive and a small amount of dark tan Superfine dry-fly dubbing mixture |
| **Wing:** | Sparkle Organza marked with Prismacolor Deco Yellow |
| **Hackle:** | Grizzly hen cape marked Prismacolor Tulip Yellow |

## Yellow Drake (*Ephemera varia*)
### East and Midwest, hatches mid-June to mid-August (#8)

The nymph body is amber brown. The nymphs are found in slower waters with fine gravel, sand, and silty streambeds, as they are burrowers. They live one to two years in the nymphal stage. When the hatch begins, trout will feed heavily on the subsurface nymphs. The hatch occurs at dusk on cloudy, dry, and cooler days. They take a while to break out of the nymphal shuck, making Transition Flymph-type flies effective, both floating and just under the surface film, with a little rod-tip action to imitate the struggling dun trying to free itself from the shuck. Hatches can be sparse, but trout will still feed on the emergers and dun because it's late in the season and there is less food on the surface. Duns are pale creamy white-yellow, with mottled creamy yellow light dun wings. Once free from the nymphal shuck, these mayflies will drift on the surface until they are able to dry their wings and fly off the water. Spinners have a pale creamy whitish yellow body and a mottled clear wing. Spinnersfalls often happen over riffles at dusk. Females may deposit eggs either by dipping their abdomens into the water and rising, or by floating dead drift in the current. If you see this mayfly on the surface, fish a nymph just under the surface, as trout will often key in on the emerging nymph, leaving duns alone. Only if I saw rising trout taking floating duns would I tie on an Extended Body Soft-Hackle Dry Fly or floating Extended Body Soft-Hackle Emerger.

## NYMPH

| Hook: | #12-14 Tiemco 3761 |
| Thread: | Camel 8/0 UNI-Thread |
| Tail: | Pheasant tail |
| Abdomen: | Amber Hareline Rabbit Dubbin |
| Rib: | Brown ostrich herl |
| Rear-Thorax: | Amber ostrich herl |
| Thorax: | Amber Hareline Rabbit Dubbin |
| Wing case: | Brown ostrich herl |
| Hackle: | Tan Whiting Brahma hen saddle |

## WINGED HEAVY FLYMPH

| Hook: | #8 Eagle Claw L063S |
| Thread: | Light Cahill 8/0 UNI-Thread |
| Tail: | English grouse |
| Abdomen: | Brown Ultra Wire (small) |
| Rib: | Hot yellow Ultra Wire (small) |
| Thorax: | Pale yellow Hareline Rabbit Dubbin |
| Wing: | Light dun poly yarn |
| Hackle: | Gray partridge marked Prismacolor Deco Yellow |

## WINGED WET EMERGER

| Hook: | #8 Mustad R50 |
| Thread: | Light Cahill 8/0 UNI-Thread |
| Tail: | Brown grizzly marabou over brown Z-Lon |
| Body: | Yellow Flashabou under pale yellow Hareline Rabbit Dubbin |
| Wing: | Dun Swiss Straw |
| Hackle: | Bleached partridge |

Light Cahill. JON RAPP

### Light Cahill or Orange Cahill (*Stenacron interpunctatum*)
**East and Midwest, hatches late June through early July (#14)**

Nymph body is light brown and amber. Clinger mayflies that prefer riffles as a nymph, they migrate to slow water to emerge, and emergers are often the focus of trout just under the surface. Dun bodies are light yellow with an orange-yellow thorax, with wings that are mottled pale yellow dun. Typical behavior includes classic long mayfly dun surface drifts. A mayfly Soft-Hackle Dry fished dead drift imitates this perfectly. Spinner males are pale yellow, and females have a bright orange abdomen with a yellow-orange thorax. Wings are mottled clear. Spinners return a couple of days after hatching, and egg-laying spinners congregate over riffles, and fall at dusk and after dark. Female spinners oviposit lying on the water. The spinner can be important, as it's an easy meal that won't fly away.

This is one of two species often called the Light Cahill. Their hatches are not usually heavy, but they draw the attention of trout because they occur later in the season when not much else is hatching. This mayfly is easy to distinguish from *Ephemerella invaria* Sulphur, as the Cahill is larger and has two tails. It also hatches later in the season than most Sulphurs. The red spinner phase of the *Stenacron interpunctatum* is sometimes confused with the Pink Cahill *Epeorus vitreus*, because they have the same size, color, and two tails. However, the *Stenacron interpunctatum* spinner is found in more abundance in July and August, later than *Epeorus*. The Pink Cahill *Epeorus vitreus* doesn't have the same amount of mottling on its wings, and its body is thicker. Nonetheless, the same soft-hackle spinner patterns can be used to imitate both species.

### SUNKEN SPINNER

| | |
|---|---|
| **Hook:** | #14 Eagle Claw L063S |
| **Thread:** | Yellow 12/0 Benecchi |
| **Tail:** | Mallard flank wood duck |
| **Abdomen:** | Light yellow DMC 25 #3078 embroidery floss |
| **Thorax:** | ³⁄₃₂" gold bead |
| **Wing:** | Sparkle Organza |
| **Hackle:** | Light dun hen cape |

**Note:** Hook can be L060, depending on desired weight.

## Light Cahill (*Maccaffertium ithaca*)
### East and Midwest, hatches June through September (#12)

Nymphs have brown-amber bodies. This clinger mayfly is found in riffles. It emerges on the surface, and can hatch any time of day, but if the weather is hot, the hatch is usually in the evening. Duns are creamy yellow with mottled pale yellow dun wings. These mayflies drift a long way emerging out of their nymphal shucks. Trout focus on the surface dun, making a dead-drift Soft-Hackle Dry Fly the best choice when these are on the water. Spinners have an orange-yellow body with a clear wing. Spinners fall at dusk, and imitating spinnerfalls with a floating Soft-Hackle Spinner or Sunken Spinner is effective.

The Yellow Light Cahill begins showing in late May, and peaks in late June through early July in the East, about a month later in the Midwest. Often a sparser hatch, but important because the duns are not overwhelmingly dense, your fly has a better chance of being targeted by trout. Look for cahills in the late afternoons and evenings on flat-water sections, frequently between riffles.

### SHUCKED WINGED WET

| | |
|---|---|
| **Hook:** | #14 WR-396 |
| **Thread:** | Light Cahill 8/0 UNI-Thread |
| **Shuck:** | Rusty brown Hare's Ear Plus |
| **Abdomen:** | Yellow turkey biot |
| **Thorax:** | Pale yellow Superfine dry-fly dubbing |
| **Wing:** | Clear Medallion Sheeting |
| **Hackle:** | Light dun feather |

**Note:** Medallion sheeting is formed with wing cutter. The hackle feather is half marked with Prismacolor Deco Yellow.

### SHUCK DUN

| | |
|---|---|
| **Hook:** | #14 Tiemco 100BL |
| **Thread:** | Yellow 12/0 Benecchi |
| **Shuck:** | Brown Z-Lon |
| **Body:** | Pale yellow Superfine dry-fly dubbing |
| **Wing:** | Dun CDC |
| **Hackle:** | Light dun hen cape marked BIC Yellow Blaze |

## WINGED WET/SURFACE EMERGER

| Hook: | #12 Tiemco 100 |
|---|---|
| **Thread:** | Yellow 12/0 Benecchi |
| **Shuck:** | Brown Z-Lon |
| **Abdomen:** | Brown turkey rounds |
| **Rib:** | Copper Ultra Wire (small) |
| **Wing:** | Light Dun Z-Lon |
| **Thorax:** | Pale yellow Hareline Rabbit Dubbin |
| **Hackle:** | Gray partridge (shown) or gray partridge marked Prismacolor Deco Yellow |

**Note:** You can apply floatant to the wing for the surface emerger.

## WINGED WET

| Hook: | #12 Eagle Claw L063S |
|---|---|
| **Thread:** | Pale yellow 6/0 Danville Flymaster |
| **Tail:** | Mallard flank wood duck |
| **Abdomen:** | Yellow turkey biot |
| **Thorax:** | Pale yellow Superfine dry-fly dubbing |
| **Wing:** | Light dun hen cape fibers on stem |
| **Hackle:** | Light dun hen cape |

**Note:** Hen cape is marked with Prismacolor Deco Yellow on the center stem fibers and the tip fibers, leaving the middle fibers a light dun shade.

## DUN

| Hook: | #14 Eagle Claw L059 |
|---|---|
| **Thread:** | Pale yellow 6/0 Danville Flymaster |
| **Tail:** | Mallard flank wood duck |
| **Body:** | Pale yellow Superfine dry-fly dubbing |
| **Rib:** | Yellow 6/0 Danville Flymaster |
| **Wing:** | Coastal deer |
| **Hackle:** | Light dun hen cape |

Little Black Quill.

## Little Black Quill (*Teloganopsis deficiens*)
### East and Midwest, hatches mid-July through early September (#20-22)

Nymph has a dark brown body. This crawler mayfly emerges in surface film morning, afternoon, and evening, depending on location and water temperature. This hatch can be particularly important on spring creeks and tail waters. The male dun's body is reddish dark brown, the female olive brown, and both have dark dun wings. Previously known as *Serratella deficians*, some call this species the Darth Vader, due to the color of the body and wing. This fly is often mistaken for a small Blue-Winged Olive by anglers, but the size is similar to *Acentrella turbida* and some small olives. Long drifts on the surface before flying off make this the most effective life stage to match. Use a CDC dark dun wing soft-hackle dry fly fished dead drift to risers. Spinners have brown bodies and clear wings. They fall in the evening and can overlap hatches.

and spinnerfalls occur at dusk and after dark, night fishing is both effective and necessary. Carrying a headlamp during the summer months and fishing late can pay off.

## WINGED WET

| | |
|---|---|
| **Hook:** | #20-22 Tiemco 2487 |
| **Thread:** | Camel 8/0 UNI-Thread |
| **Tail:** | Pheasant tail |
| **Abdomen:** | Olive Hare's Ear Plus |
| **Wing:** | Black blood marabou |
| **Thorax:** | Medium hare's mask dubbing |
| **Hackle:** | Welsummer hen saddle patch |

**Note:** Hook shank and eye are straightened.

## NYMPH

| | |
|---|---|
| **Hook:** | #12-14 Dai-Riki #070 |
| **Thread:** | Black 8/0 UNI-Thread |
| **Tail:** | Light gray Whiting Brahma Hen Chickabou |
| **Body:** | Light gray Hareline Rabbit Dubbin |
| **Rib:** | Gray ostrich herl |
| **Hackle:** | Light gray Whiting Brahma Hen Chickabou |

## White Mayfly (*Ephoron leukon*)
### East and Midwest, hatches late August through September (#12-14)

Nymph bodies are cream and brown. Nymphs are burrower-type mayflies. A couple of hours before emerging, the nymphs leave their burrows and prepare to rise to the surface to emerge. During this time, trout feed heavily on the nymphs on the streambed and just under the surface. Use a white-abdomen soft-hackle nymph with a brown thorax and gray partridge feather to imitate the nymph. Emergers hatch at dusk, with a quick emergence at the surface. The body of the dun is cream, with a light dun wing. Males hatch first, and when the females emerge, mating soon follows. Use a white soft-hackle dry fly to match the hatch. Spinners are cream with light dun wings. As the females don't molt into spinners, mating can often take place on the water right after the females emerge. This makes hatching and egg laying overlapping events. The emergence, molting, and egg laying all take place in a couple of hours. After mating, the males fall spent, but the females fly upriver to lay eggs, then fall spent. Use a white soft-hackle spinner. The spinner is usually the most important life stage, with trout feeding on the spent mayflies on the surface after the sun sets.

These large mayflies make a lot of movement, and mating is a chaotic scene. A soft-hackle dry fly skittered over the surface can imitate the activity. The hatch can be heavy and occur over long stretches of river. Since this and other hatches

## EMERGER DUN/WET SPINNER

| | |
|---|---|
| **Hook:** | #12-14 Dai-Riki #070 |
| **Thread:** | Iron gray 8/0 UNI-Thread |
| **Tail:** | Gray partridge |
| **Abdomen:** | Cream Hareline Rabbit Dubbin |
| **Rib:** | Iron gray 8/0 UNI-Thread |
| **Wing:** | Dun hen cape feather tip |
| **Hackle:** | Brownish-gray partridge |

Blue-Winged Olive dun

## Blue-Winged Olive (*Baetis tricaudatus*)
**East to West, hatches late March through April, June, and September through October (#14-20)**

The nymph body is pale tannish olive. They are often found in riffles and broken water, where they feed on streambed vegetation. They are a swimmer species and swim well due to their long legs and thin abdomens. They emerge on or just under the surface. Adults dehydrate in the hot sun, making cool and damp days their preference, and the fishing can be good because it takes their wings longer to dry before they can fly off the water. On many fertile spring creeks and tail waters with stable temperatures, they can hatch anytime. The dun body is grayish olive, the wing medium dun. Nymphs often ride the surface currents for a long time before flying off as they try to dry their wings, due to the weather in which they emerge. The spinner body is olive-brown to reddish brown, with a clear wing. Female spinners will dive underwater to lay eggs on rocks, logs, or other structures.

*Baetis tricaudatus* is the most important mayfly species because of the wide variety of water in which it hatches and its transcontinental distribution. It is also the most common species of blue-winged olive mayfly in the United States. They can hatch in any month of the year because they are a multibrooded species, meaning the hatches are born from eggs laid the same year, not the previous year. This creates many life cycles of the species in a year, all year round on certain waters, so trout feed more on them than on any mayfly. They can have three broods a year, with egg laying and hatching overlapping throughout the season. These used to be known as *Baetis vagans* in the East, but now we consider them the same as the western species. Eastern flies are #16-20, but western species can be as large as #14. The nymphs are swimmers, and some nymphing presentation methods include a dead drift, hand twist, or rod-tip jigging. As these flies are multibrooded, hatches and spinnerfalls can overlap, adding to the complexity of matching the hatch. Therefore, fishing a sunken spinner and an emerger dropper could be appropriate if you see both duns and spinners on the water. The duns hatch in smooth, flat water, and often ride the current for a long distance. Spinners

will be found here too. Look closely at the fish rise forms. Duns are gulped and spinners are sipped because they won't fly off the water. The blue-winged olive hatch is the most important hatch to master, because it's common, the fish love it, the flies are small, and often the fish will be selective. It lasts for long segments of the year, and the flies drift in flat water, making for long inspection periods by the trout. When you can fish this hatch successfully, you can fish any other hatch easily. Work on it and it will pay dividends.

### WINGLESS WET

| | |
|---|---|
| **Hook:** | #14-20 Mustad S80 |
| **Thread:** | Olive 12/0 Benecchi |
| **Tail:** | Olive partridge |
| **Body:** | Olive hare's mask touch dubbing |
| **Hackle:** | Olive starling |

### WINGLESS WET

| | |
|---|---|
| **Hook:** | #14-20 Mustad S80 |
| **Thread:** | Olive 12/0 Benecchi |
| **Abdomen:** | Golden olive and dark olive Antron dubbing mix |
| **Hackle:** | Dark dun hen cape |

## TRANSITION FLYMPH

**Hook:** #14-20 Tiemco 100
**Thread:** Olive 12/0 Benecchi
**Shuck:** Olive brown Z-Lon
**Abdomen:** Stripped peacock herl quill
**Thorax:** Olive Superfine dubbing
**Hackle:** Light dun hen cape

## EMERGER DUN

**Hook:** #14-20 Tiemco 2487
**Thread:** Olive 12/0 Benecchi
**Shuck:** Brown Hareline Rabbit Dubbin
**Abdomen:** Brown Hareline Rabbit Dubbin
**Thorax:** Olive Superfine dry-fly dubbing
**Wing:** Dun CDC
**Hackle:** Olive hen cape

## WINGED WET EMERGER

**Hook:** #14-20 Mustad R50
**Thread:** Light olive UTC 70-denier Ultra Thread
**Shuck:** Olive and brown Z-Lon mix
**Abdomen:** Olive turkey biot
**Thorax:** Olive Hare's Ear Plus Dubbing
**Wing:** Clear Medallion Sheeting
**Hackle:** Light dun hen cape

## WINGLESS WET

**Hook:** #14-20 Tiemco 101
**Body:** Olive DMC 25 #937 embroidery floss
**Thorax:** Olive Hareline Rabbit Dubbin
**Tail and Hackle:** Light dun hen cape

## DUN

**Hook:**  #14-20 Tiemco 100
**Thread:** Olive 12/0 Benecchi
**Tail:**  Dun hen cape
**Body:**  Olive Superfine dry-fly dubbing
**Wing:**  Dun CDC
**Hackle:** Olive hen cape

## WINGED WET

**Hook:**  #14-20 Mustad R50
**Thread:** Olive 6/0 Danville Flymaster
**Tail:**  Medium dun hen cape
**Abdomen:** Insect green Danville rayon floss
**Rib:**  Metallic Green Wire (small)
**Thorax:** Green Hareline Rabbit Dubbin
**Wing:**  Dun Z-Lon
**Hackle:** Olive Brahma hen saddle,

**Note:** Strip one side of hackle feather fibers.

## WET SPINNER

**Hook:**  #14-20 Mustad R50
**Thread:** Tobacco brown 6/0 Danville Flymaster
**Tail:**  Mallard flank wood duck
**Abdomen:** Rusty brown DMC 25 #355 embroidery floss
**Thorax:** Rusty Hareline Rabbit Dubbin
**Hackle:** Light dun hen cape

**Note:** Options are to apply floatant to the hackle for surface presentation, or leave untreated and fish as a sunken spinner.

Blue-Winged Olive dun.

## Blue-Winged Olive (*Acentrella turbida*)
**East to West, hatches May through June, August through September, and October (#22-26)**

Nymph body is light olive-tan. This is a swimmer-type mayfly that emerges just under the surface or in the surface film. In tailwaters they can hatch anytime year-round. The dun's body is light olive to dark brown-olive, with a medium and dark dun wing. When they hatch in cool or rainy weather, they can ride long distances on the surface while drying wings. Spinner bodies are light olive-brown, and the wing clear. Duns often molt quickly, and morning hatches fall as spinners that evening. They crawl underwater or deposit eggs while floating on the surface.

These are the tiny blue-winged olives. In the East, they used to be known as *Pseudocloeon Carolina*, and *Pseudocloeon turbidum* out West. Now classified as *Acentrella turbida*, they are found across the country in various sizes and colors. Often they hatch at the same time as other large *Baetis* species, which makes for a challenging, complex hatch. These olives often hatch on smooth spring creeks and tailwaters. Like *Baetis*, they are multibrooded and can hatch throughout the entire year. Rainy, cool weather helps create ideal hatch conditions. Spring and fall are often the peak times. Watch the naturals on the water closely to determine if they are duns or spinners, and match appropriately. A wingless olive wet fly is often the only choice you need, as it imitates both dun and sunken/diving spinner. You can identify *Acentrella* because they have no hind wing, while *Baetis* do.

## DUN

| | |
|---|---|
| **Hook:** | #22-26 Tiemco 100 |
| **Thread:** | Olive 12/0 Benecchi |
| **Body:** | Olive Superfine dubbing |
| **Wing:** | Dun CDC |
| **Tail and Hackle:** | Medium dun hen cape |

## WET FLY

| | |
|---|---|
| **Hook:** | #22-26 Tiemco 100 |
| **Thread:** | Light olive 8/0 UNI-Thread |
| **Body:** | Olive turkey rounds |
| **Hackle:** | Starling |

## EMERGER/DIVING EGG LAYER

| | |
|---|---|
| **Hook:** | #22-26 Tiemco 100 |
| **Body:** | Olive 12/0 Benecchi |
| **Thorax:** | Green metallic Ultra Wire (extra small) |
| **Tail and Hackle:** | Light olive partridge |

Trico dun.

## Trico (*Tricorythodes*)

**East to West, hatches late July through early September (#22-24)**

The body of the nymph is dark grayish-black. A crawler-type mayfly, Tricos are poor swimmers, easily targeted as they ascend to the surface to emerge. Trout key in on this first, but soon turn their attention to the dun and spinner. Males hatch at night, and females hatch around seven thirty to eight thirty the next morning. Female nymphs swimming to the surface in the morning can be important to match. Male dun bodies are black while females are olive, both with clear wings. Female duns can be important to match. Male spinners have black bodies, females a white abdomen and black thorax; both have clear wings. Mating and spinnerfalls occur soon after the females emerge. The spinnerfalls are the most important part of the hatch. I've had more success with black-bodied Tricos; however, both can work. Perhaps the reason the males have provided me with more action for trout is that they fall first to the water after mating, making them the first spinners available to the trout. After mating, the females fly to streamside vegetation to produce the external egg ball on their abdomens, before returning to the water to lay eggs and fall spent.

Tackle tips: use at least a 12-foot, 7X fluorocarbon tippet leader for stealth and strength. Downstream presentations work best for stealth, as the fly gets to the fish first and there is no spray, "lining," or "leadering" of the fish that would cause them to spook and refuse the fly. Trico are multibrooded and hatches can last many weeks. On small flies like these and other #20 and smaller, I use forceps to carefully offset the hook point slightly from the hook shank on my finished flies, to allow it to penetrate the lip tissue of the fish. It not only helps in the initial hookup, but if the fish is large, it can mean the difference between landing the fish or not.

### MALE SPINNER

| | |
|---|---|
| **Hook:** | #22-24 Tiemco 100 |
| **Thread:** | Black 12/0 Benecchi |
| **Tail:** | Dun hen cape |
| **Abdomen:** | Black thread or Superfine dubbing |
| **Thorax:** | Black Superfine dry-fly dubbing |
| **Wing:** | Sparkle Organza |
| **Hackle:** | Black hen cape |

## Pale Morning Dun (*Ephemerella excrucians*)
**East to West, hatches April through October (#14-18)**

Nymph body color varies, depending on region, to include olive, brown, or reddish brown, This crawler mayfly lives in riffles and makes practice runs for emergence, making presentations like the Rising Swing and Practice-Run Method effective. This is a surface emerger similar to *E. dorothea infrequens*, except that, due to their smaller size, they take longer to break through the surface film, making Floating Flymphs and subsurface Transition Flymphs effective. The dun's body also varies by region, and can be pale yellow, creamy orange, olive green, or reddish brown. Their wing is medium dun. They drift to dry their wings, but fly off the water faster than *E. dorothea infrequens*, emphasizing the emerger's importance.

If you see duns being taken, fish a Soft-Hackle Dry Fly, then pull it under, and fish it on the swing as an emerger. Dry the fly with a few false casts, and cast again. Like the other life stages, spinner color depends on region, so bodies can be pale yellowish olive, pale yellow, rusty brown, with clear wings. Spinnerfalls can be important near riffles. Use a soft-hackle surface spinner or sunken spinner wet fly, or both together to target feeding fish.

This species includes many sizes and shades of mayflies, but they are all considered *Ephemerella excrucians*. The species now includes the Little Red Quill of the Midwest, the PMD formerly known as *E. inermis*, and the lake PMD of Yellowstone, formerly *E. lacustris*. The bugs of this species vary depending on the water where they are found. Eastern species are less important than Western, with respect to duration, intensity, and ultimately importance to the trout. They last from days or weeks in the East up to months in the West. This hatch follows behind the other PMD *Ephemerella dorothea infrequens* in the West. They are found in all water types, including spring creeks, freestone streams, lakes, and tailwaters.

### TRANSITION FLYMPH

| | |
|---|---|
| **Hook:** | #14-18 Tiemco 3761 (heavy, shown) |
| **Thread:** | Light olive 6/0 Danville Flymaster |
| **Shuck:** | Brown Z-Lon |
| **Abdomen:** | Pheasant tail |
| **Rib:** | Copper Ultra Wire (extra small) |
| **Thorax:** | Pale yellow Superfine dry-fly dubbing |
| **Wing:** | Two strands of Pearl Krystal Flash |
| **Hackle:** | Light dun hen dape |

**Note:** The lighter Tiemco 100 can be used, depending on desired sink rate.

## TRANSITION FLYMPH

| | |
|---|---|
| **Hook:** | #14-18 WR-396 |
| **Thread:** | Light Cahill 8/0 UNI-Thread |
| **Tail and Abdomen:** | Rusty brown Woolly Bugger marabou |
| **Rib:** | Copper Ultra Wire (small) |
| **Thorax:** | Amber Hareline Rabbit Dubbin |
| **Wing:** | Light dun hen cape tip |
| **Hackle:** | Medium dun hen cape marked BIC Yellow Blaze |

## WINGED WET FLY

| | |
|---|---|
| **Hook:** | #14-18 Dohiku 302 (heavy, shown) or Dohiku 301 (light), depending on sink rate |
| **Thread:** | Light Cahill 8/0 UNI-Thread |
| **Abdomen:** | Orange-yellow turkey biot |
| **Thorax:** | Superfine Pale Morning Dun dry-fly dubbing |
| **Wing:** | Medium Dun hen cape feather tip |
| **Tail and Hackle:** | Medium dun hen cape |

## EMERGER

| | |
|---|---|
| **Hook:** | #14-18 Mustad C49S |
| **Thread:** | Rusty dun 8/0 UNI-Thread |
| **Shuck:** | Dun Z-Lon |
| **Abdomen:** | Yellow-olive turkey biot |
| **Thorax:** | Natural Hareline Rabbit Dubbin and Wapsi golden light olive Antron dubbing mixture |
| **Hackle:** | Bobwhite quail |

## SHUCK DUN

| | |
|---|---|
| **Hook:** | #14-18 Tiemco 100 |
| **Thread:** | Light Cahill 8/0 UNI-Thread |
| **Shuck:** | Brown Z-Lon |
| **Body:** | Superfine Pale Morning Dun dry-fly dubbing |
| **Wing:** | Dun CDC |
| **Hackle:** | Medium dun hen cape |

## SPINNER

| | |
|---|---|
| **Hook:** | #14-18 Eagle Claw L059 |
| **Thread:** | Black 8/0 UNI-Thread |
| **Tail:** | Brown-olive grizzly hen cape |
| **Body:** | Superfine brown and olive dry-fly dubbing mixture |
| **Rib:** | Light olive 6/0 Danville Flymaster |
| **Wing:** | Sparkle Organza |
| **Tail and Hackle:** | Medium dun hen cape |

## NYMPH

| | |
|---|---|
| **Hook:** | #12-18 WR-396 |
| **Thread:** | Camel 8/0 UNI-Thread |
| **Tail:** | English grouse |
| **Abdomen:** | Olive Flashabou under Midge V-Rib |
| **Thorax:** | Amber Hareline Rabbit Dubbin |
| **Wing Case:** | Pheasant tail |
| **Hackle:** | Light brown grizzly marabou |

## Speckled Wing Quill (*Callibaetis*)
### East to West, hatches May through September (#12-18)

The nymph's body is olive-tan. This is a swimmer mayfly found in slow, flat-water sections of rivers and lakes. Like *Ephemerella*, these mayflies make practice runs to the surface before emerging, thus exposing themselves to trout before they hatch. Hatches occur in slow water in midmorning or early afternoon., with emergence on the surface or just under the surface. Trout feed heavily on nymphs both before and during the hatch. Methods that display the swimming and ascending runs that these nymphs make are most effective, like small, short strips, and lifts and drops (i.e., jigging of the nymph), behaviors irresistible to trout. Dun are brownish tan with mottled brown wings. Sometimes they take off quickly; at other times, they drift for a long distance trying to dry their wings. Spinners are also brownish tan, but their wings are clear. They fall throughout the day, usually in batches during periods of calm conditions. Trout sip these spinners, and since they oviposit and fall in slow water, the fish can inspect flies closely and at length. Dead free drifts with soft-hackle spinners are important.

This species is multibrooded like other *Baetidae*, able to hatch for many months with two or three broods per season in western waters. They get smaller in size and darker in color with each brood. The term "gulpers" describes the trout that eat these mayflies, because in the quiet, slow water in which they are found, you can hear the trout feeding on them in the surface film.

## DUN

| | |
|---|---|
| **Hook:** | #12-18 Mustad R50 |
| **Thread:** | Beige 6/0 Danville Flymaster |
| **Tail:** | Light dun hen cape |
| **Body:** | Tan and dark tan Superfine dubbing mixure |
| **Rib:** | Golden olive Coats and Clark #6940 thread |
| **Wing:** | Dun CDC |
| **Hackle:** | Grizzly hen cape |

## SPINNER

| | |
|---|---|
| **Hook:** | #12-18 Mustad R50 |
| **Thread:** | Coffee 6/0 Danville Flymaster |
| **Body:** | Brown, dark tan, and tan Superfine dubbing mixture |
| **Rib:** | Golden tan Coats and Clark #8140 thread |
| **Wing:** | Sparkle Organza |
| **Tail and Hackle:** | Grizzly hen cape |

## Tiny Blue Quill (*Diphetor hageni*)
### East to West, hatches mid-August through October (#22)

A hindless wing mayfly, formerly known as *Baetis parvus* on western waters and *Baetis devinctus* in the East, especially important in the Rockies. Nymph has an olive-brown body. This swimmer mayfly is found in medium currents, emerging in the early afternoon in moderate to slow current flats, especially on tailwaters and spring creeks. They drift for a long distance trying to dry their wings. Duns have a pale gray-olive abdomen, light tan thorax, and light dun wings, while spinners have a rusty brown body and clear wings. Spinnerfalls at dusk are important to fish and anglers. The small size of the fallen spinners makes them hard to see, but the trout riseforms indicate they are sipping spinners. Fish either a floating soft-hackle spinner dead drift, or a sunken soft-hackle spinner with a subsurface dead drift or mends and slow swing.

## DUN

| | |
|---|---|
| **Hook:** | #22 Tiemco 100 |
| **Body:** | Olive 6/0 Danville Flymaster |
| **Wing:** | Medium dun CDC |
| **Tail and Hackle:** | Light dun hen cape |

## Tiny Blue-Winged Olive (*Iswaeon anoka*)
### Midwest and West, hatches June through July and August through October (#22)

Nymphs are bright green with brown contrasts, and they are found in medium currents and spring creeks. This is a surface emerger, emerging in the afternoon; fish flymphs and Floating Flymphs near the surface. Duns are bright green and medium dun, and drift while drying wings. Spinners have rusty brown bodies and clear wings, and fall in the evening. This mayfly was formerly known as *Pseudocloeon anoka* (Midwest) and *Pseudocleon edmundsi* (West). It's an important small olive on many western streams. The hindless wing mayfly doesn't have the small hind wing found on the majority of mayflies.

## WET EMERGING DUN

| | |
|---|---|
| **Hook:** | #22 Dai-Riki #060 |
| **Thread:** | Olive 12/0 Benecchi |
| **Tail:** | Light olive mallard flank |
| **Body:** | Olive Hare's Ear Plus Touch Dubbing |
| **Hackle:** | Olive starling |

## WINGLESS WET

| | |
|---|---|
| **Hook:** | #22 Dai-Riki #060 |
| **Thread:** | Olive 12/0 Benecchi |
| **Body:** | Olive Superfine dry-fly dubbing |
| **Hackle:** | Dun hen cape |

**Note:** Body dubbing should be dubbed fluffy and loose on thread.

## Western March Brown (*Rhithrogena morrisoni*)
**West, hatches March through May (#10-14)**

The first large mayfly of the western season, the nymph's body is olive-brown. This clinger mayfly is found in medium depth, flow, and rocky water. It hatches in the warmest part of the late morning to midafternoon, in medium-fast flows with cobblestone streambeds. Nymphs migrate to slightly slower water than they live in to emerge into adults. Duns, with their brown and tan bodies and mottled dun wings, then emerge on the streambed and rise to the surface fully emerged. They drift for a long distance trying to dry wings. Winged wet flies mended to sink and then fished with a dead drift, followed by a rising swing, imitate this behavior and life stage well. Fish a soft-hackle nymph near the bottom at a rate slower than the surface speed, with weight if needed. Spinners are brown and tan, with mottled clear wings. Egg layers return to the nymphal riffle water to lay eggs, then fall spent and eventually sink.

### EMERGER

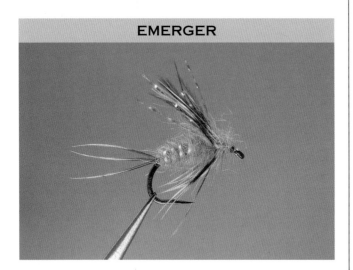

| | |
|---|---|
| **Hook:** | #10-14 Eagle Claw L063S (hand-bent) |
| **Thread:** | Dark brown 70-denier Ultra Thread |
| **Tail and Hackle:** | Welsummer hen saddle |
| **Wing:** | Black Woolly Bugger marabou and three strands Pearl Krystal Flash |
| **Body:** | Olive and golden brown Hareline Rabbit Dubbin blend |
| **Rib:** | Beige Coats and Clark #8040 thread |

### TRANSITION FLYMPH

| | |
|---|---|
| **Hook:** | #10-14 WR-396 |
| **Thread:** | Camel 8/0 UNI-Thread |
| **Shuck:** | Brown Z-Lon |
| **Abdomen:** | Pheasant tail |
| **Rib:** | Copper Ultra Wire (small) |
| **Wing:** | Dun Swiss Straw |
| **Thorax:** | Dark olive Hareline Rabbit Dubbin |
| **Hackle:** | Brown partridge |

**Note:** The wing is marked with Prismacolor Cool Gray and sealed.

### WINGED WET EMERGER

| | |
|---|---|
| **Hook:** | #10-14 Mustad S82 |
| **Thread:** | Camel 8/0 UNI-Thread |
| **Shuck:** | Brown Z-Lon |
| **Abdomen:** | Rust brown turkey rounds |
| **Rib:** | Copper Ultra Wire (extra small) |
| **Thorax:** | Mahogany Superfine dry-fly dubbing |
| **Wing:** | Dun Z-Lon |
| **Hackle:** | Partridge marginal covert |

## WINGED WET FLY

| Hook: | #10-14 Eagle Claw L063S |
|---|---|
| Thread: | Camel 8/0 UNI-Thread |
| Tail and Hackle: | Tan Whiting Brahma Hen Chickabou |
| Body: | Medium hare's mask dubbing |
| Wing: | Brown furnace hen cape feather tip |

## WINGLESS WET

| Hook: | #10-14 Eagle Claw L063S |
|---|---|
| Thread: | Coffee 6/0 Danville Flymaster |
| Tail: | Mallard flank wood duck |
| Abdomen: | Tan Superfine dry-fly dubbing |
| Rib: | Coffee 6/0 Danville Flymaster |
| Hackle: | Brown India hen saddle |
| Head: | Chocolate brown Hare's Ear Plus Dubbing |

**Note:** The Eagle Claw hook is bent into an upturned hook eye; other options are Mustad (heavy, shown) or Mustad R50U (light).

Pale Morning Dun (PMD) dun.

## Pale Morning Dun (*Ephemerella dorothea infrequens*)
**West, hatches May through June in coastal states, July through August in the Rocky Mountains (#14-16)**

Nymphs have a reddish orange-brown body. This crawler mayfly actively moves leading up to the hatch, allowing trout to feed on them in the drift. Their behavioral drift occurs in the evening, and using a soft-hackle nymph in the evenings on days before the hatch for prospect nymphing can be effective. They live on rocks in vegetated environments such as alkaline spring creeks. Like some other mayflies, PMDs make practice runs, ascending a little to the surface and dropping back down to the streambed. A jig-nymph presentation represents this closely.

Hatches can occur morning and evening, with emergences occurring sometimes at the surface and other times as they are ascending to the surface, arriving as fresh duns that will drift on the surface until their wings are dry. The duns are pale yellow with medium dun wings and three tails. Spinners also have three tails, but on rusty brown bodies with clear wings. Spinners return to mate and lay eggs a couple of days after hatching. The spinners fall after dropping their eggs from the air. Some females fall without releasing all their eggs, and a rusty spinner with a yellow egg sack at the end of the abdomen can be effective, as fish will key in on these spinners. Females that haven't laid their eggs, but fall on the water, have upright wings, as they aren't spent. A rusty-colored soft-hackle dry fly with a CDC wing and yellow egg sack imitates these egg-laying females. The morning spinnerfalls are easy to see, but at dusk the spinners and trout feeding on them occur in low light. It's then that soft-hackle spinners are effective, as they can be both dead drifted and fished subsurface. When fished underwater, you don't have to see the take to set the hook. Just cast above the fish to allow the fly to penetrate the surface, and let a semitight line dead drift in front of the trout,with the fly just under the surface. You will feel the take, and the hook will set itself with only the tension of the line and the friction of it running through the rod line guides with the lift of the rod-tip. Use a Rusty Spinner Soft-Hackle Dry or Sunken Spinner.

Found in freestone streams, but most important on tailwaters and spring creeks, these mayflies, along with *Baetis*, are the two most important mayflies for trout and fly anglers. PMDs like *Baetis* can have long hatch cycles, and fish will eat a lot of the nymphs, emergers, duns, and spinners. Watch the surface for rising trout. If you see many rises, but not to the drifting duns, they are probably taking the emergers or rusty spent spinners. PMD soft-hackle nymphs and flymphs also make great searching patterns, even when there isn't a hatch, as the fish still recognize them and will feed on them, especially subsurface.

### NYMPH

| | |
|---|---|
| **Hook:** | #14-16 Mustad S82 |
| **Thread:** | Tobacco brown 6/0 Danville Flymaster |
| **Tail and Hackle:** | Partridge Marginal Covert Feather and Fibers |
| **Abdomen:** | Amber Hareline Rabbit Dubbin |
| **Rib:** | Hot yellow Ultra Wire (small) |
| **Thorax:** | Rusty brown Hareline Rabbit Dubbin |
| **Head:** | Brown ostrich herl |

### TRANSITION FLYMPH

| | |
|---|---|
| **Hook:** | #14-16 Mustad S82 |
| **Thread:** | Light Cahill 8/0 UNI-Thread |
| **Shuck:** | Reddish brown Hare's Ear Plus Dubbing |
| **Abdomen:** | Pheasant tail |
| **Rib:** | Copper Ultra Wire (small) |
| **Thorax:** | Pale yellow Hareline Rabbit Dubbin |
| **Wing:** | Gray Wapsi UV Ice Dub |
| **Hackle:** | Gray partridge feather marked with Prismacolor Deco Yellow |

### TRANSITION FLYMPH

| | |
|---|---|
| **Hook:** | #14-16 Mustad S82 (heavy, shown) |
| **Thread:** | Light Cahill 8/0 UNI-Thread |
| **Shuck:** | Sand and golden tan Wapsi Antron dubbing mixture |
| **Abdomen:** | Brown Hends Body Quill |
| **Thorax Hackle:** | Rust Woolly Bugger marabou |
| **Thorax:** | Hareline Gold Rabbit Dubbin |
| **Hackle:** | Pale yellow Brahma hen saddle |

**Note:** Lighter hook option, depending on weight needed, is Mustad R50.

### WINGLESS WET

| | |
|---|---|
| **Hook:** | #14-16 WR-002 bent to shape |
| **Thread and Abdomen:** | Pale yellow 6/0 Danville Flymaster |
| **Thorax:** | Pale Morning Dun Superfine dry-fly dubbing |
| **Tail and Hackle:** | Gray partridge marked with BIC Yellow Blaze |

## WINGLESS WET

| | |
|---|---|
| **Hook:** | #14-16 Tiemco 100BL |
| **Thread:** | Light Cahill 8/0 UNI-Thread |
| **Tail:** | Mallard flank wood duck |
| **Abdomen:** | Yellow DMC 25 #3078 embroidery floss |
| **Thorax:** | Pale Morning Dun Superfine and amber dry-fly blend |
| **Hackle:** | Honey dun hen cape |

## DUN

| | |
|---|---|
| **Hook:** | #14-16 Mustad R50 |
| **Thread:** | Light Cahill 8/0 UNI-Thread |
| **Tail:** | Dun hen cape |
| **Body:** | Pale Morning Dun Superfine with a small amount of golden olive dry-fly dubbing blend |
| **Rib:** | Yellow #3078 DMC 25 embroidery floss |
| **Wing:** | Dun CDC |
| **Hackle:** | Yellow hen cape, light dun marked with Prismacolor Deco Yellow |

## SPINNER

| | |
|---|---|
| **Hook:** | #14-16 Tiemco 100 |
| **Thread:** | Rusty brown UTC 70-denier Ultra Thread |
| **Tail:** | Mallard flank |
| **Abdomen:** | Rusty brown turkey biot |
| **Thorax:** | Rusty brown Superfine dry dubbing |
| **Wing:** | Sparkle Organza |
| **Hackle:** | Light dun hen cape |

## Western Green Drake (*Drunella grandis*)
### West, hatches mid-June through August, some locations into September (#8-12)

Nymph body is olive-brown. This crawler mayfly is found in both medium and fast water. Nymphs will make several practice runs to the surface leading up to emergence, making a jig-nymph technique effective. Hatches occur in the morning early on, but then, as the days progress, occur in the afternoon and evening. Emerging in the slow-water sections near the fast water where they live, duns often fully emerge underwater and arrive at the surface, drifting for a long distance trying to dry their wings. Wet flies imitate this life stage and behavior perfectly. Freshly emerged duns are a bright green, and darken into olive-brown with yellow ribbing and a mottled dun wing after they are exposed to air. Imitate the brighter green color in flymphs and ermergers. Hatches occur on spring creeks a few weeks earlier than on the freestone rivers where they are also found. Spinners have the same yellow rib with a reddish brown body and mottled clear wings. Female spinners oviposit late at night into the early morning, and fall spent. Some sparse spinner activity may be seen in the daytime from midmorning through dusk, but the majority of mating, egg laying, and spinnerfalls occur late at night and into the early morning hours.

Along with *Baetis*, PMDs, and Brown Drakes, the Western Green Drakes are one of the great mayfly hatches of the West. The protein provided by these fat bugs has trout focused and looking for them when they are in season.

## EMERGER

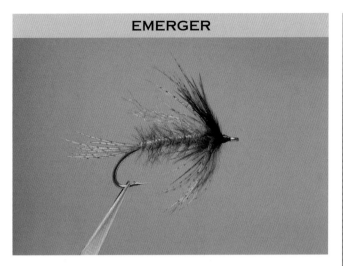

| | |
|---|---|
| **Hook:** | #8-12 Tiemco 200R |
| **Thread:** | Black 6/0 Danville Flymaster |
| **Abdomen:** | Light olive DMC 25 #907 embroidery floss |
| **Rib:** | Green ostrich herl |
| **Thorax:** | Green Hareline Rabbit Dubbin |
| **Wing:** | Olive and dun Z-Lon mix |
| **Tail and Hackle:** | Gray partridge marked with Prismacolor Avocado |
| **Front Hackle:** | Black Woolly Bugger marabou |

## WINGLESS WET

| | |
|---|---|
| **Hook:** | #8-12 Mustad R50 |
| **Thread:** | Black 6/0 Danville Flymaster |
| **Tail:** | Mallard flank wood duck |
| **Abdomen:** | Olive turkey biot |
| **Thorax:** | Dark green ostrich |
| **Hackle:** | Olive partridge wrapped with black hen cape |

## WINGED WET

| | |
|---|---|
| **Hook:** | #8-12 Mustad R43 |
| **Thread:** | Olive 8/0 Orvis |
| **Abdomen:** | Olive turkey biot |
| **Thorax:** | Green Hareline Rabbit Dubbin |
| **Tail and Hackle:** | Light olive grizzly hen cape |
| **Wing:** | Grizzly hen cape |

## DUN

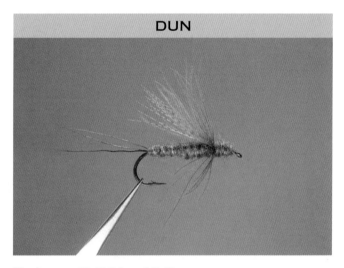

| | |
|---|---|
| **Hook:** | #8-12 Mustad R43 |
| **Thread:** | Olive 6/0 Danville Flymaster |
| **Tail:** | Moose body |
| **Body:** | Dark tan, olive, and *Callibaetis* Superfine dubbing mixture |
| **Rib:** | Olive Coats and Clark #6340 thread |
| **Wing:** | Mallard dyed wood duckunder natural dun CDC |
| **Hackle:** | Olive CDC |

## Small Western Drake, Flav (*Drunella flavilinea*)
**West, hatches July and August (#12-16)**

Nymph body is brown and olive. This crawler mayfly, similar to *Drunella grandis*, is found in moderate-to-fast water, and moves to slower water to hatch. It emerges in the afternoon and evening on the surface, in slower water near the riffle water of their nymphal home, where trout can inspect them carefully. Newly emerged duns are a light olive and should be so imitated with flies. They darken to their yellow-olive shade soon after emergence, with a dark dun wing, and they drift for a long distance, trying to dry wings. Spinners have olive-brown bodies and clear wings. Spinnerfalls occur in the morning or at dusk, over riffles where the nymphs reside. Spinners drop eggs from the air over riffle water, then fall and drift spent before eventually sinking. A sunken spinner fished during spinnerfalls in riffle water is effective.

Flavs start hatching about a week after the larger *Drunella grandis* Western Green Drakes are done. You find these mayflies at higher western elevations between 4,000 and 6,000 feet, mainly in July and August. Trout often key in on a #14 spinner at dusk.

### TRANSITION FLYMPH

| | |
|---|---|
| **Hook:** | #12-16 Eagle Claw L063S |
| **Thread:** | Black 6/0 Danville Flymaster |
| **Shuck:** | Brown Z-Lon |
| **Abdomen:** | Pheasant tail |
| **Rib:** | Copper Ultra Wire (small) |
| **Thorax:** | Olive Hareline Rabbit Dubbin |
| **Wing:** | Dun Swiss Straw |
| **Hackle:** | Brown partridge |

### NYMPH/EMERGER

| | |
|---|---|
| **Hook:** | #12-16 Tiemco 100 |
| **Thread:** | Black 6/0 Danville Flymaster |
| **Tail:** | Mallard flank wood duck |
| **Abdomen:** | Olive Danville rayon floss |
| **Rib:** | Green ostrich herl |
| **Thorax:** | Green and peacock Hareline Rabbit Ice Dub mixture |
| **Hackle:** | Olive partridge and black hen cape |

**Note:** Wind partridge and hen cape for hackle together.

### CRIPPLE DUN/EMERGER

| | |
|---|---|
| **Hook:** | #12-16 Mustad R50 |
| **Thread:** | Black 6/0 Danville Flymaster |
| **Tail:** | Brown hen cape |
| **Abdomen:** | Mahogany Superfine dry-fly dubbing |
| **Rib:** | Coffee 6/0 Danville Flymaster |
| **Thorax:** | Black Superfine dry-fly dubbing |
| **Wing:** | Coastal deer |
| **Hackle:** | Olive Whiting Brahma hen saddle |
| **Head:** | Olive and tan Superfine dubbing blend |

## SHUCK DUN

| | |
|---|---|
| **Hook:** | #12-16 Tiemco 100 |
| **Thread:** | Olive 6/0 Danville Flymaster |
| **Shuck:** | Amber and brown Z-Lon |
| **Body:** | Olive with a small amount of tan Superfine dubbing mixture |
| **Rib:** | Black Coats and Clark #0900 thread |
| **Wing:** | Olive mallard flank under dun CDC |
| **Hackle:** | Grizzly hen cape marked with Prismacolor Avocado |

## DUN

| | |
|---|---|
| **Hook:** | #12-16 Tiemco 100 |
| **Thread:** | Olive 6/0 Danville Flymaster |
| **Tail:** | Dun hen cape |
| **Body:** | Olive with a small amount of tan Superfine dubbing mixture |
| **Rib:** | Black Coats and Clark #0900 thread |
| **Wing:** | Olive mallard flank under dun CDC |
| **Hackle:** | Grizzly hen cape marked with Prismacolor Avocado |

## Black Quill (*Leptophlebia cupida*)
### East to West, hatches late April through May in the East, late May through July in the West (#10)

Nymphs have a light brown underbelly, medium brown back. These nymphs live in slower water sections. They are good swimmers, and hatch sporadically from midday through evening in slow water. When they are ready to emerge, the nymphs gather in schools and make a group migration through the slow water for up to a mile, before ascending to the surface. They emerge with commotion and effort in the surface film and, due to their large size, are noticeable to trout. Duns, with their black back, dark tannish gray underbelly, and medium dun wing, drift on the surface until their wings are dry, then fly off the water. These mayflies are large, but don't hatch in heavy concentrations. When they do hatch, especially in the evening, they can draw the attention of trout, and fishing the hatch can be good. Spinners have a rusty brown back, dark tannish gray underbelly, and clear mottled wings. Spinners fall in afternoon and evening. The females rise and fall over medium and fast water, laying eggs each time they drop to the surface. After laying eggs, they fall spent and eventually sink. Spinnerfalls can be important, but not heavy.

## BIRD'S BLACK QUILL EMERGER

| | |
|---|---|
| **Hook:** | #10 Tiemco 200R |
| **Thread:** | Tobacco brown 6/0 Danville Flymaster |
| **Tail:** | Three brown goose biots |
| **Abdomen:** | Rusty brown Hareline Rabbit Dubbin |
| **Rib:** | Yellow Coats and Clark #7330 thread |
| **Thorax:** | Medium hare's mask dubbing |
| **Wing:** | Black Hareline Rabbit Dubbin |
| **Hackle:** | Reddish brown hen back |

## CRIPPLED DUN

| | |
|---|---|
| **Hook:** | #14 Tiemco 2487 |
| **Thread:** | Camel 8/0 UNI-Thread |
| **Tail:** | Pheasant tail |
| **Abdomen:** | Rusty Hareline Rabbit Dubbin |
| **Thorax:** | Tan and brown Superfine dry-fly dubbing mixture |
| **Wing:** | Coastal deer |
| **Hackle:** | Light brown partridge |

## Slate Maroon Drake (*Ironodes nitidus*)
### West, hatches June through mid-July (#14)

Nymph bodies are light brown, and they live in fast water, where they hatch midday. Duns emerge on the streambed and rise to the surface as adults. They have a tannish-orange thorax with a maroon abdomen and yellow mottled wings. Once emerged, they drift for a moment, then fly off quickly. Spinners are not important with regard to matching and fishing.

Formerly *Epeorus*, these are related to the eastern Quill Gordon. They are a relatively rare far-western mayfly that, when it hatches, is best imitated with a winged wet fly or flymph as the duns emerge underwater.

**WINGED WET**

| | |
|---|---|
| **Hook:** | #14 Tiemco 3761 |
| **Thread:** | Orange 6/0 Danville Flymaster |
| **Abdomen:** | Pale yellow DMC 25 #3078 embroidery floss over orange 6/0 Danville Flymaster |
| **Thorax:** | Golden stone Nature's Spirit dry-fly dubbing |
| **Wing:** | Dun hen cape tip |
| **Tail and Hackle:** | Pale yellow Whiting Brahma hen saddle |

The Western Gray Drake Spinner is a common sight in July on many trout streams in southwestern Montana. They fall over riffle water, and fishing a wet spinner is a great way to match this lifecycle.

## Western Gray Drake (*Siphlonurus occidentalis*)
### West, hatches August through October (#12)

The light brown nymphs often migrate to shore or structure to hatch. Fishing them near these locations during the time they are active is an effective way to fish this hatch. The nymphs migrate to the shore in calm water and crawl out of the water to hatch, or they hatch on the water surface. In-stream emergence is fast, making duns mostly unavailable to fish. Duns are not important to feeding trout, as they emerge fast or sometimes even on structure out of the water, before molting and returning to the water as spinners to mate. Spinners are rusty brown with clear wings. Spinnerfalls happen in midmorning or evening, in faster water than the emergence migration. Imitate nymphs near shore during hatches, and spent and sunken spinners in faster-water sections when spinners are falling. The nymph, and especially the spinner, are the most important life stages to imitate.

**NYMPH**

| | |
|---|---|
| **Hook:** | #12 Eagle Claw L063 |
| **Thread:** | Camel 8/0 UNI-Thread |
| **Abdomen:** | Copper Ultra Wire (small) |
| **Gills:** | Amber rayon floss |
| **Thorax:** | Brown Hareline Rabbit Dubbin and golden brown Hareline Ice Dub Blend |
| **Tail and Hackle:** | Gray partridge marked with Prismacolor Goldenrod |

## SPINNER

| | |
|---|---|
| **Hook:** | #12 Tiemco 100 |
| **Thread:** | Coffee 6/0 Danville Flymaster |
| **Body:** | Mahogany Superfine dry-fly dubbing |
| **Rib:** | Golden tan Coats and Clark #8140 thread |
| **Wing:** | Sparkle Organza |
| **Tail and Hackle:** | Light brown hen cape |

## Mahogany Dun (*Paraleptophlebia bicornuta*)
### West, hatches August through October (#12-16)

Nymphs are olive-brown and found in medium and fast-water riffles. These mayflies have the undulating dolphin-kick movement that allows them to swim relatively strongly. When fishing the nymph, this movement can be imitated with soft-hackle nymphs and articulated soft-hackle nymphs. They can be effectively fished with the Practice-Run Method to allow the current to activate the soft-hackle collar and body, or with more aggressive fishing methods like stripping, swimming, line retrieving, swinging, or a combination of these elements in a single presentation. Also, mending and lifting of the rod tip can imitate the rising nymphs. Hatches occur in flats and gentle runs in morning. Emergence is either below or on the surface. Fish a wet fly like a Transition Flymph to imitate an emerging dun, or a Floating Flymph or Extended Shuck Emerger to imitate a cripple or stuck-in-the-shuck mayfly dun. The brown duns drift for a long distance trying to dry their wings. Spinners are rusty brown with clear wings. Spinnerfalls occur in the late afternoon and evening. Spinners hold their wings upright like duns on the water, not in the spread spent-spinner position of most other mayflies. The dun and the spinner with an upright wing apply to both life stages, so use a rusty-brown soft-hackle spinner fished dead drift to rising trout for this.

Since these emerge in slow, flat water, especially on spring creeks, trout can drift downstream inspecting them before choosing to rise and strike. A long, 12-foot or longer leader, tapered out to 7X fluorocarbon and presented either downstream or up-and-across stream with an S-cast, can help achieve a longer dead drift.

## NYMPH

| | |
|---|---|
| **Hook:** | #12-16 Eagle Claw L063 |
| **Thread:** | Camel 8/0 UNI-Thread |
| **Tail:** | Brown partridge marginal covert |
| **Body:** | Brownish-yellow rayon floss |
| **Gills:** | Light dun rayon floss |
| **Wing Case:** | Brown Thin Skin |
| **Legs:** | Gray partridge |
| **Hackle:** | Brown partridge marginal covert |

## WINGED TRANSITION FLYMPH

| | |
|---|---|
| **Hook:** | #12-16 Tiemco 3761 |
| **Thread:** | Camel 8/0 UNI-Thread |
| **Shuck:** | Brown Z-Lon |
| **Abdomen:** | Pheasant tail |
| **Rib:** | Copper Ultra Wire (small) |
| **Thorax:** | Natural Hareline Rabbit Dubbin |
| **Wing:** | Dun Swiss Straw |
| **Hackle:** | Gray partridge marked with Prismacolor BIC Tiki Hut Tan |

**Note:** Hook can also be Tiemco 100, depending on desired sink rate.

## DUN

| | |
|---|---|
| **Hook:** | #12-16 Mustad R50 |
| **Thread:** | Coffee 6/0 Danville Flymaster |
| **Tail:** | Brown hen cape |
| **Abdomen:** | Dark tan Superfine dry-fly dubbing |
| **Rib:** | Coffee 6/0 Danville Flymaster or summer brown Coats and Clark #8360 thread |
| **Wing:** | Coastal deer |
| **Hackle:** | Brown hen cape behind ginger hen cape |
| **Head:** | Brown Superfine dry-fly dubbing |

## WET/DRY DUN

| | |
|---|---|
| **Hook:** | #12-16 Mustad R50 |
| **Thread:** | Coffee 6/0 Danville Flymaster |
| **Tail:** | Mallard flank wood duck |
| **Abdomen:** | Rusty brown turkey biot |
| **Thorax:** | Brown rabbit |
| **Wing:** | Tan CDC |
| **Hackle:** | Brown partridge |

## WINGED WET

| | |
|---|---|
| **Hook:** | #12-16 Mustad S82 |
| **Thread:** | Tobacco brown 6/0 Danville Flymaster |
| **Abdomen:** | Tobacco Brown 6/0 Danville Flymaster |
| **Ribbing:** | Gold Ultra Wire (small) |
| **Thorax:** | Red Hends Spectra Dubbing |
| **Wing:** | Gray Hareline UV Ice Dub |
| **Tail and Hackle:** | Brown partridge |

Pink Lady.

## Pink Lady (*Epeorus albertae*)
### West, hatches July through August (#14-16)

The brown clinger nymphs, found on rocks in riffle water, hold tight and are seldom dislodged into the drift. *Epeorus* are the only mayfly nymphs with two tails. They emerge in the afternoon in the fast-water habitat in which they live, and the hatch into duns occurs on the streambed rocks. The dun, with yellow body and dun wings, emerges from the nymphal shuck on the bottom and rises to the surface with a gas bubble under the wings and legs, drifting for a long distance trying to dry its wings. This is imitated with a rising swing or lift of a Winged or Wingless Wet Fly. Spinners are creamy pink with clear wings. Spinnerfalls occur in the early morning or late afternoon and evening over riffle water. Some may sink in the fast water, so try fishing a sunken spinner here. Trout will target those that float down in slower runs and pools on the surface. Some spinners will gather in eddies, where trout will feed leisurely and heavily.

*Epeorus* indicate clean water; they don't tolerate pollution and are only found in the most pristine streams. Pink Ladies are not abundant throughout the West, occuring in specific waters.

## WINGLESS WET

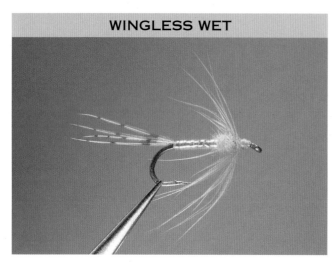

| | |
|---|---|
| **Hook:** | #14-16 Mustad S82 (shown) |
| **Thread:** | Light olive 6/0 Danville Flymaster |
| **Tail:** | Light gray partridge |
| **Abdomen:** | Yellow Flashabou |
| **Thorax:** | Amber Hareline Rabbit Dubbin |
| **Hackle:** | Light dun hen cape |

**Note:** Alternative hook is Mustad R50, depending on sink rate desired. For abdomen, leave spaces between wraps to let the underbody thread show through.

## DUN

| | |
|---|---|
| **Hook:** | #14-16 Mustad R50 |
| **Thread:** | Light Cahill 8/0 UNI-Thread |
| **Body:** | Amber and pale yellow Superfine dry-fly dubbing |
| **Rib:** | Fawn Coats and Clark #8439 thread |
| **Wing:** | Coastal deer |
| **Tail and Hackle:** | Honey dun hen cape |

## WET/DRY SPINNER

| | |
|---|---|
| **Hook:** | #14-16 Eagle Claw L-059 |
| **Thread:** | Camel 8/0 UNI-Thread |
| **Tail:** | English grouse |
| **Body:** | Medium hare's mask Touch Dubbing |
| **Hackle:** | India hen cape |

**Note:** Touch dubbing for body is ribbed over Fluorescent Pink 6/0 Danville Flymaster.

## Western Red Quill (*Timpanoga hecuba*)
### West, hatches July to late October (#8-12)

The nymph has a reddish-brown body. The spiny crawler mayfly can be found in moderate currents. Duns, with olive-brown bodies and dark dun wings, emerge just under the surface in the afternoon to evening, in medium-speed runs and riffles. They are best matched with a Transition Flymph, Ascension Flymph, or Winged Wet Fly, swung slowly rising in front of the fish. This and the subsurface emerger are the most important stages to match when *Timpanoga hecuba* are found hatching. They drift for a long distance trying to dry their wings, often in the middle of the river in moderate currents, bouncing downstream. Trout often stack up at the tailouts of the run or head of the next pool, to wait in the flatter water for the duns. With olive-brown bodies and clear wings, spinners are similar in size and appearance to the Western Green Drake (*Drunella grandis*). However, they occur much later in the season when mostly small mayflies like Trico and *Baetis* are hatching. These mayflies are found where silt is present, and their populations can decrease or increase from year to year, depending on the silt load in their preferred habitat. Spinners return several days after the duns hatch. Oviposit occurs over the moderate-speed currents the nymphs live in. Spinnerfalls are not especially important.

Fishing a high-floating deer-hair wing Soft-Hackle Dry Fly is effective, even if fish aren't rising in a predictable manner. These flies don't hatch heavily, but are so big and filling that trout look up for them and will feed opportunistically when they are emerging.

## NYMPH

| | |
|---|---|
| **Hook:** | #14-16 Tiemco 3761 |
| **Thread:** | Tobacco brown 6/0 Danville Flymaster |
| **Tail:** | Rusty brown Woolly Bugger marabou |
| **Abdomen:** | Hareline Natural Rabbit Dubbin |
| **Rib:** | Brown ostrich |
| **Thorax:** | Rusty brown Hareline Rabbit Dubbin |
| **Wing case:** | Brown ostrich |
| **Hackle:** | Tan Brahma saddle |

## CRIPPLED EMERGER

| | |
|---|---|
| **Hook:** | #10-12 Tiemco 2487 |
| **Thread:** | Coffee 6/0 Danville Flymaster |
| **Shuck:** | Amber Z-Lon |
| **Abdomen:** | Rusty brown Hareline Rabbit Dubbin |
| **Thorax:** | Amber ostrich herl and brown, olive, and tan Hareline Rabbit Dubbin mixture |
| **Wing:** | Natural dun CDC |
| **Hackle:** | Grizzly hen cape marked with Prismacolor Goldenrod |

## WET/DRY-DUN/SPINNER

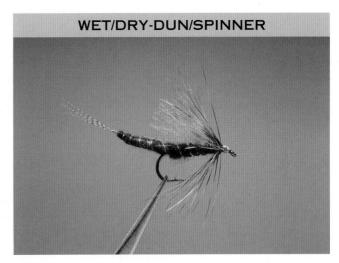

| | |
|---|---|
| **Hook:** | #8-12 Mustad R50 |
| **Thread:** | Tan 8/0 Orvis |
| **Tail:** | Mallard flank wood duck |
| **Body:** | Brown and rusty brown Superfine dry-fly dubbing blend |
| **Rib:** | Tan 8/0 Orvis |
| **Wing:** | Natural dun CDC |
| **Hackle:** | Grizzly hen cape, Prismacolor Goldenrod |

## Pale Evening Dun (*Heptagenia elegantula*)
**West, hatches June through July (#10-16)**

The nymph's body is medium brown. This clinger mayfly is found in moderate-to-fast water with fine gravel and silt. Trout don't typically have the chance to feed on clingers until just before and during a hatch, when they become more active and may be dislodged, or when they migrate to slower water near shore to hatch. Duns subsurface from the nymphal shuck in the morning. Transition Flymphs and Ascension Flymphs work well just under the surface. The emergers work better than dry flies, because the duns don't drift on the water surface for long. After emergence, adult duns fly off the water quickly. They have a creamy pale yellow abdomen, orange-yellow thorax, and yellow-dun wing. Spinner bodies are light tan with yellow rib abdomen, orange-tan thorax, and clear wings. Spinners mate over riffles where the nymphs live. After the females oviposit by dipping their abdomens into the water, they fall spent. Trout will rise wherever they are, but the lower waters downstream of their egg laying, and back eddies downstream, are the easiest places for trout to find these spinners gathered after they have drifted downstream. Don't forget about the ones that sink. Fishing a sunken spinner just under the surface, particularly in fast water where they lay eggs, is both realistic and effective. Strikes are often violent and quick, compared to the common sipping of floating spinners off the surface.

Like other *Heptagenia*, the emergence and dun stage is so fast that trout often don't bother with them. However, the spinners are often the most important life stage to match, because they are easily available for trout when spent and drifting on or under the surface.

## WINGED TRANSITION FLYMPH

| | |
|---|---|
| **Hook:** | #10-16 Tiemco 3761 |
| **Thread:** | Light Cahill 8/0 UNI-Thread |
| **Shuck:** | Brown Z-Lon |
| **Abdomen:** | Brown turkey rounds |
| **Rib:** | Copper Ultra Wire (small) |
| **Thorax:** | Pale yellow Hareline Rabbit Dubbin |
| **Wing:** | Dun hen cape feather tip |
| **Hackle:** | Gray partridge marked with Prismacolor Tulip Yellow |

## WET FLY DUN/SUNKEN SPINNER

| | |
|---|---|
| **Hook:** | #10-16 Eagle Claw L059 (light, shown) |
| **Thread:** | Light Cahill 8/0 UNI-Thread |
| **Tail:** | Mallard flank wood duck |
| **Body:** | Pale yellow Hareline Rabbit Dubbin |
| **Rib:** | Beige 6/0 Danville Flymaster |
| **Wing:** | Dun Swiss Straw |
| **Hackle:** | Bleached partridge |

**Note:** Alternative hook is #10-16 Eagle Claw L059 (light-weight/dry fly hook, shown here) or a L063 (heavy nymph hook), depending on the desired sink rate.

## WINGED TRANSITION FLYMPH

| | |
|---|---|
| **Hook:** | #10-16 Tiemco 3761 |
| **Thread:** | Light Cahill 8/0 UNI-Thread |
| **Shuck:** | Brown Z-Lon |
| **Abdomen:** | Copper Flashabou |
| **Rib:** | Brown ostrich herl and copper Ultra Wire (small) |
| **Thorax:** | Amber Hareline Rabbit Dubbin |
| **Wing:** | Dun hen cape feather tip |
| **Hackle:** | Yellow starling |

The Yellowstone River at Sulphur Caldron on opening day in July is a great place to find large and extremely strong Yellowstone cutthroat trout. The brown shape on the hill just across stream on the right side of the hill is a grizzly bear.

The Orange Hare Thorax Nymph has a Brahma hen tail and collar, and the Starling & Marabou uses a tail/abdomen and thorax of contrasting marabou feathers and a dyed brown starling collar. These are active and productive nymphing patterns that I often fish together in deeper or faster water when the fish are holding near the streambed. The bead heads, while already heavy, will further act as counterweight to each other, similar to using split shot but with the added advantage of the greater-odds two flies and a direct connection for detecting strikes.

# Match-the-Hatch Soft-Hackles: Caddis, Stoneflies, and Midges

### *Trichoptera* (Caddisflies)

In my opinion, caddisflies are the most exciting and fun "hatch" to fish. This includes emerging adults, and surface and diving egg layers. The bugs are strong swimmers, explosively emerging out of the water or swimming underneath to lay eggs. In turn, trout respond with similar behavior. Instead of the delicate rise behavior of sips and gulps when feeding on midges and mayflies, they exhibit the take-no-prisoners attitude of a great white shark breaching the water for a seal. Heavy caddis

hatches and surface feeding remind me of a battle, with sheer pandemonium everywhere you look, due to the fact that trout chase the fast pupae as they swim below and up to the surface. Adults on the surface, trying to get off the water, make a commotion flopping around, and if the fish are feeding on the skittering egg-laying adults, they have to attack swiftly or the fly will move away. All of this adds up to adrenaline-producing fishing events for every character involved on the water and in the moment.

The Madison River has some of the greatest sedge water in the world, with hatches of *Hydropsyche*, *Cheumatopsyche*, *Nectopsyche*, *Rhyacophila*, *Lepidostoma*, *Glossosoma*, and *Brachycentrus*, the famous Mother's Day Grannom hatch. This was in late July, and the caddis came off heavy from about eight o'clock until ten o'clock at night. It was still light enough to fish without a headlamp until nearly eleven o'clock.

Caddisflies are every bit as important as mayflies overall. In fact, on some waters, they are much more important. I've often felt that trout have more of a proclivity for caddis, because I've seen them react and rise to sparser hatches of caddis than sparse hatches of mayflies. Caddis hatching behavior is as complicated as mayflies', and needs to be understood for an angler to catch selective fish when caddisflies are hatching or laying eggs. Caddis species are more numerous than mayfly species, yet fewer species-specific patterns will match them. The important hatches boil down to about four genera producing about 75% of the fishable hatches in the United States. Several more, not as important as the main ones, constitute over 1,000 species of caddis. The main species life cycles, once understood, can be matched with patterns that imitate larvae, pupae, adults, or egg-layers. The size, shape, and color can then be imitated in the fly.

Finally, the angler will imitate the behavior of the natural with presentation, location, and depth. The behavior of the caddis needs to be understood to know whether adults on water or in the air are emergers or egg layers. The nice thing about soft-hackle wet flies is that sometimes you can be wrong and still catch a lot of fish. Many soft-hackle caddis pupa patterns can come off looking like a diving egg-laying caddis; and many egg-laying caddis soft-hackles can imitate pupae emerging into adults. The soft-hackle collar imitates legs, antennae, and general motion and life. With this in mind, it still pays to understand species-specific behaviors and be able to identify caddis species while on the water. Then you will know where in the waterway to fish the artificials, and with what kind of behavior.

There are literally hundreds of caddisfly species, but also times and places that obscure species are important. An angler really needs to be familiar with four important caddis families in North America that produce over 75% of fishable hatches. In order they are:

1. *Hydropsychidae* (Cinnamon Caddis #14-16, and Little Olive Caddis/Little Sister Sedge #18)
2. *Brachycentridae* (Grannom, Mother's Day Caddis, Black Caddis, Apple Caddis #14-16.)
3. *Glossosomatidae* (Little Brown Short-horned Caddis #18)
4. *Rhyacophilidae* (Green Rock Worm, Green Sedge #14-16)

Cinnamon Caddis and Little Olive Caddis (*Hydropsychidae*) make up 40 to 50 percent of the fishable caddis. The pupae emerge midstream. Egg layers dive underwater more than half the time. The rest lay eggs by bouncing across the stream surface. If you carry this caddis family's life-cycle patterns in appropriate sizes and colors, and fish them realistically, you can fish most of the country at both nonhatch and hatch times throughout the season. Check streambed rocks for larvae, water for adults, and the water, air, and streambank foliage for egg-laying adults, to know the species you need to fish, and when and where to fish them.

*Hydropsyche* and *Cheumatopsyche* larvae are the most common caddis species, easily distinguishable by the three dark plates behind the head.

If you carry the four caddis stages in basic the following sizes and color combinations, you will be prepared to match all the species, even if identification of the exact species by name is not possible. This will simplify what you need to tie to prepare for hatches wherever you fish. You only need to present them properly and choose based on any observed caddis activity, or stream-bug surveying of rocks or drift with a seine net. This list covers both eastern and western caddisflies.

Soft-Hackle Larva
    Green body, brown head #12, #14, #16, #18
    Cream body, brown head #8, #12, #14
    Orange body, brown head #12, #14, #16, #18

Soft-Hackle Pupa
    Green body, tan thorax #14-18
    Tan body, tan thorax #14-18
    Brown body, brown thorax #14-22
    Orange body, brown thorax #8

Soft-Hackle Dry (the wing is 1.5x to 2x body length)
    Green body, tan wing #14-18
    Olive body, tan wing #14-18
    Tan body, tan wing #12-20
    Black body, gray wing #16-22
    Light orange body, tan wing #8

The behavior of larvae varies among caddis species. Some are free-living predators that scourge the bottom without a case. Some build cases for protection on streambed rocks, out of gravel, sticks, or detritus, while others build nets to catch small food particles, but otherwise live without a case. Larva cases on streambed rocks are a great way to identify stream populations and get an idea of the species you need to imitate. Case-building caddis larvae go through instars of growth that require them to leave their cases and build new ones. At this time, even cased caddis larvae are vulnerable to trout. Some caddis larvae move from rock to rock during dusk or dawn, migrating to new homes, called behavioral drift. A time that instars find and build new homes, it also helps to disperse the species throughout the river ecosystem, in an effort to ensure long-term survival. Another behavior unique to net-spinner species, the larva can attach a white silk line and use it to rappel from structure to suspend in the current and catch prey. Holding a soft-hackle caddis larvae suspended downstream in the current simulates this behavior.

Pupae can be fished throughout the year as prospecting patterns, and fish will eat them. Particularly important during a caddisfly hatch, they become essential when trout are holding just under the surface film, feeding on the pupae before they reach the surface. Pupae are a more dependable exertion by the trout, because pupae can't fly off the water to avoid capture. Also, fish don't have to expose themselves to the surface world, and can happily feed underwater more safely and securely, even if only inches under the surface.

Caddis pupae swim using their middle set of legs, rising upwards to the surface in a rowing motion. They are powerful swimmers and create a lot of noticeable movement. Once the pupae reach the water surface, they will drift 5 to 30 feet trying to break out of the pupal shell. Trout feed heavily on these drifting, vulnerable pupae. Caddis pupae either swim to the surface and emerge in the surface film, or across the water surface to shore or structure, where they emerge out of the water. In that case, the adults aren't available until they return to lay eggs.

Often when I fish caddis hatches and/or overlapping egg-laying events, I like to fish both a dry fly and a pupa dropper 8 inches off the dry, with 6-inch fluorocarbon, close enough to the dry fly that I can target the same fish. This fly setup imitates both the egg-laying adult and the emerging pupa, covering the two most important stages of a caddis hatch, as the emergence and egg-laying flights can sometimes overlap. This way, you give each and every fish the fly it wants.

After emergence, it doesn't take caddis too long to escape, unlike many mayfly duns that drift on top of the water for long stretches, waiting for their wings to dry before they can fly off. This makes surface-drifting caddis less important, as trout will usually focus on subsurface or floating pupal emergers, an easier meal. But soft-hackle dries can catch fish at times, and make good depth suspenders for a dead-drifted pupa.

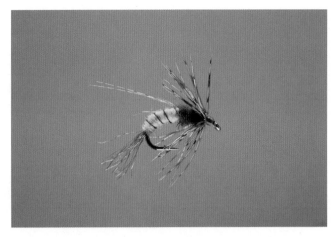

Z-Lon or Antron dubbing tied on the back of a *Hydropsyche* pupa imitates the pupal shuck beginning to shed. This pattern can be fished during hatches or as a searching pattern.

This *Hydropsyche* Soft-Hackle Dry has a somewhat sparse natural dun CDC wing, enough to allow it to float, but also to be fished wet.

The deep caddis larva is the first life stage to imitate in the caddis lifecycle. Seen here is the *Hydropsyche* larva. Change colors and size based on naturals.

The *Hydropsyche* Diver imitates a diving egg-laying caddis. Another option is to grease the hackle with floatant and fish this to rising fish as surface ovipositing egg layer.

Diving caddis become hydrofuge, capturing air and glistening as they dive underwater to lay eggs, making them highly visible to trout. Fur-bodied egg-laying caddisfly patterns imitate this by capturing and holding air bubbles between the fur fibers. Some synthetics, like Ice Dub or sparkle dubbing, can imitate the glistening effect as well. Surface dead drifts or skittering, or even using the wind to move the fly line on and off the water surface by dapping the fly on top of the water, can imitate surface egg laying. Divers can be imitated by subsurface dead drifting or by swimming adult caddis soft-hackles underwater, with or without fly-line strips and rod-tip twitches and animation. After the divers and surface egg layers die, they drift spent on the surface and eventually sink, with both levels providing further opportunity for trout to feed and anglers to fish flies.

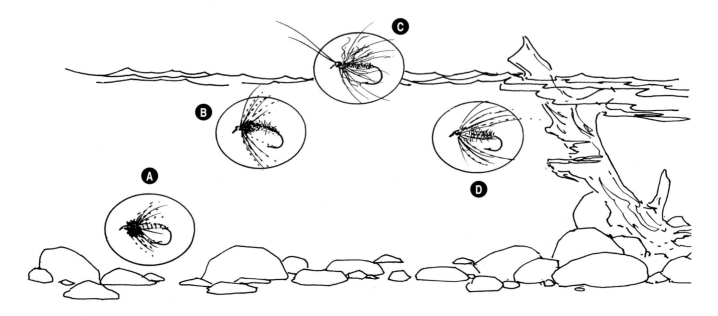

**Caddisfly Life Cycle.** The pupa and diving caddis are the most important stages to match, because many species of caddis larvae are often encased on rocks until they are mature, and the adults fly off the water quickly after emergence. The pupa and diving caddis, though, are vulnerable just under the surface film, highly visible to the trout and easy prey. Caddisfly life cycle patterns: Soft-Hackle Larva, Soft-Hackle Pupa, Soft-Hackle Emerger, Soft-Hackle Dry with Shuck, Soft-Hackle Dry, Floating Egg Layer, Diving Egg Layer, Spent Surface Egg Layer.

**A.** Larva; **B.** Pupa; **C.** Soft-Hackle Dry/Wet; **D.** Diving Caddis.

Grannom.

## Grannom (*Brachycentrus appalachia, B. occidentalis, B. americanus*)

**East to West, hatches April through June, and again in the fall (#14-18)**

Males are one size smaller than females. Larvae have a chartreuse abdomen and tannish-brown thorax. These casemakers use wood and plant matter. Pupae have the same coloring, and hatches occur midday through late afternoon. Fishing a deep pupa dead drift, or with occasional lifts and drops to animate the soft-hackle collar, in the hours leading up to the surface emergence is important. Fish will feed on the streambed pupae even before they ascend to emerge. Then, fish the pupae from streambed all the way up to the surface, with a smooth swing, rod-tip twitches, short one-to-two-inch strips, or lifted and dropped and lifted until reaching the surface.

Adult bodies have varying appearances. *B. appalachia* have a newly hatched bright green body, then dark green with a tan thorax. *B. occidentalis* and *B. americanus* are dark brownish-olive, with a tan wing. They fly off the water quickly, but trout will still feed on the surface caddis when opportunities exist. Some females dive or crawl underwater to lay eggs, others will drift or skitter on the surface, dropping eggs. After they finish, they drift spent. Once the diving egg layers are finished oviposting underwater, they allow the current to carry them back up to the surface, all the while susceptible to trout, underwater and once on the surface drifting spent. They also sometimes lay eggs on the surface by skittering and dipping their abdomens into the water. Fish the diving egg layer, or apply floatant to the wing for a surface spent egg layer. Subsurface, rod-tip twitches either up and down or left and right will represent egg laying. Also, quick vertical rod-tip lifts will skitter the fly across the surface, especially useful in windy conditions when the wind will blow the line in addition to the rod-tip lifts, resulting in a life-like appearance. Watch the water for signs of skittering egg layers if you see mating flights over the water. If you don't see surface activity, try fishing a diving or spent egg-laying caddis.

## PUPA

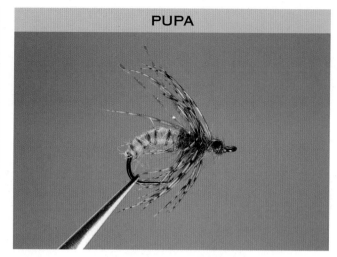

| | |
|---|---|
| **Hook:** | #14-18 Tiemco 206BL |
| **Thread:** | Camel 8/0 UNI-Thread |
| **Abdomen:** | Fluorescent green Wapsi Antron Yarn |
| **Rib:** | Olive Hends Body Quill |
| **Thorax:** | Dark Dun Hareline Rabbit Dubbin |
| **Wing:** | Two strands of Pearl Krystal Flash |
| **Hackle:** | Brown partridge |
| **Eyes:** | Chameleon .010 Maxima |

**Note:** Eyes are burnt and flattened with a lighter.

## LARVA

| | |
|---|---|
| **Hook:** | #14-18 Tiemco 2457 |
| **Thread:** | Chartreuse 8/0 UNI-Thread |
| **Body:** | Green Flashabou |
| **Thorax:** | Olive Hareline Rabbit Dubbin |
| **Hackle:** | Olive partridge |
| **Head:** | Black Bead (³⁄₃₂" #14), (⁵⁄₆₄" #16-18) |

**Note:** Body Flashabou is ribbed with black 6/0 Danville Flymaster and chartreuse Ultra Wire (small) under Scud Back.

## EMERGER

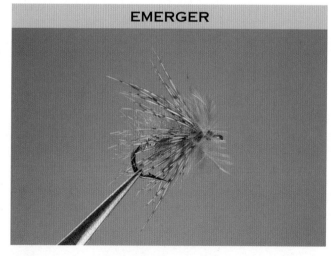

| | |
|---|---|
| **Hook:** | #14-18 Eagle Claw L063 bent to shape |
| **Thread:** | Black 8/0 UNI-Thread |
| **Abdomen:** | Ostrich herl marked with BIC Key Lime |
| **Rib:** | Gold Ultra Wire (small) |
| **Hackle:** | Brown partridge |
| **Head:** | Partridge aftershaft feather |

## PUPA

**Hook:** #14-18 Tiemco 200R
**Thread:** Black 12/0 Benecchi
**Body:** Rust Ultra Wire (small) under green Hareline Rabbit Touch Dubbing.
**Winglets:** Two furnace hen cape tips
**Thorax:** Green Hareline Rabbit Dubbinwith a small amount of Hareline peacock dub
**Hackle:** Starling

**Note:** Leave space between the wire wraps and dubbing wraps to allow the thread to show. Winglet hen cape tips are tied facing outward from each other.

## ADULT

**Hook:** #14-18 Tiemco 200R
**Thread:** Iron gray 8/0 UNI-Thread
**Body:** Gray Spirit River Adams Dry-Fly Dubbing
**Wing:** Tan CDC
**Hackle:** Brown Whiting Furnace Hen Cape

## ADULT

**Hook:** #14-18 Tiemco 200R
**Thread:** Tobacco 12/ Benecchi
**Abdomen:** Olive Hareline Rabbit Dubbin
**Wing:** Tan Swiss Straw under natural dun CDC
**Thorax:** Natural Hareline Rabbit Dubbin
**Hackle:** March Brown Whiting Brahma Hen Cape

**Note:** Hook with thorax bent upwards. For hackle, pull two fibers forward for antennae and whip finish head.

## DIVING EGG LAYER

**Hook:** #14-18 Tiemco 200R
**Thread:** Black 8/0 UNI-Thread
**Abdomen:** Olive Hareline Rabbit Dubbin
**Thorax:** Gray Hareline Rabbit Dubbin
**Wing:** Brown grizzly marabou fibers
**Hackle:** Gray partridge marked with BIC Tiki Hut Tan

**Note:** Hook opened up slightly.

## SPENT CADDIS

| Hook: | #14-18 Tiemco 100 |
|---|---|
| **Thread:** | Black 12/0 Benecchi |
| **Body:** | Copper Holographic Tinsel under Gray Spirit River Adams Dry Touch Dubbing |
| **Hackle:** | Brown starling |

**Note:** For body, leave some space between the wraps of tinsel to allow the thread to create contrast. For hackle, apply floatant to wing for spent caddis surface drift.

## Spotted Sedge (*Hydropsyche*)

**East to West, hatches mid-May through mid-June (#10-14)**

This species is the most widely found trout-stream caddisfly, making it the most important for trout as well. Larvae have a chartreuse body and brown head. This is a net-spinner, a caseless, free-living larva that uses silk net for shelter and to gather small insects and plant material for food. Larvae secrete a white silk line that they use to rappel between rocks and move around. The pupa's body is a chartreuse abdomen and a light-brown thorax. Pupae are important; they drift underwater, either near the bottom or under the surface, for minutes up to a few hours. They can have difficulty breaking through the surface tension to crawl up onto the top of the water and emerge. Trout take advantage of this vulnerable behavior and target the pupae just under the surface. Wet flies imitate this life stage and behavior perfectly. Fishing a deep pupa dead drift, or with occasional lifts and drops to animate the soft-hackle collar in the hours leading up to the surface emergence, is important. Fish will feed on the streambed pupae even before they ascend to emerge. Then, fishing the pupae from streambed all the way up to the surface is effective during hatches, fished with a smooth swing, rod-tip twitches, short one-to-two-inch strips, or lifted and dropped and lifted until reaching the surface. The adult is tan bodied; the freshly emerged adult is a light olive that darkens and turns dark tan with a mottled brown wing relatively quickly. They drift on the surface for longer on cool, rainy days, and take off quickly on warm and sunny days to dry their wings faster. Females dive or crawl underwater to lay eggs, then allow the current to carry them back up to the surface. All the while they are susceptible to being eaten by trout, both underwater and once on the surface, drifting spent. They also sometimes lay eggs on the surface by skittering and dipping their abdomens into the water.

## TRANSITIONING LARVA

| Hook: | #10-14 Tiemco 3761 |
|---|---|
| **Thread:** | Olive 6/0 Danville Flymaster |
| **Shuck:** | Peach blood marabou |
| **Abdomen:** | Tying thread under medium UTC vinyl rib |
| **Head:** | Brown Hareline Rabbit Dubbin |
| **Hackle:** | Gray partridge marked with Prismacolor Goldenrod |

## DEEP PUPA

| Hook: | #10-14 Tiemco 2457 |
|---|---|
| **Thread:** | Black 8/0 UNI-Thread |
| **Abdomen:** | Olive Flashabou |
| **Thorax:** | Black Hareline Rabbit Dubbin |
| **Antennae:** | Olive mallard flank fibers |
| **Hackle:** | Light olive chickabou |
| **Thorax:** | Olive ostrich herl |
| **Head:** | Black 3/32" Bead |

**Note:** For the abdomen, Flashabou is ribbed with small chartreuse Ultra Wire under Scud Back. Leave spaces between the Flashabou to allow the thread to show through slightly.

## EMERGER

| Hook: | #10-14 Tiemco 200R |
|---|---|
| **Thread:** | Black 6/0 Benecchi |
| **Abdomen:** | Ostrich herl marked with BIC Key Lime |
| **Thorax:** | Ostrich herl marked with BIC Forest Green |
| **Wing:** | Brown partridge |
| **Hackle:** | Brown starling |

## ADULT

| Hook: | #10-14 Mustad R50 |
|---|---|
| **Thread:** | Coffee 6/0 Danville Flymaster |
| **Shuck:** | White Z-Lon marked with BIC Tiki Hut Tan |
| **Body:** | Brown and tan Superfine dry-fly dubbing mixture |
| **Rib:** | Café Beige Coats and Clark #8180 thread |
| **Wing:** | Coastal deer |
| **Hackle:** | Brown hen cape |

## PUPA

| Hook: | #10-14 Tiemco 2487 |
|---|---|
| **Thread:** | Tobacco brown 6/0 Danville Flymaster |
| **Abdomen:** | Green Hareline Rabbit Dubbin |
| **Rib:** | Brown ostrich |
| **Thorax:** | Ginger Hareline Rabbit Dubbin |
| **Hackle and Antennae:** | March Brown Whiting Brahma hen saddle |

## ADULT

| Hook: | #10-14 Eagle Claw L059 |
|---|---|
| **Thread:** | Coffee 6/0 Danville Flymaster |
| **Shuck:** | Golden tan and black Wapsi Antron dubbing mixture |
| **Body:** | Hareline Natural Rabbit Dubbin |
| **Rib:** | Tobacco brown 6/0 Danville Flymaster |
| **Wing:** | Natural dun CDC |
| **Hackle and Antennae:** | Whiting Furnace Hen Cape |

## SURFACE EMERGER

| | |
|---|---|
| **Hook:** | #10-14 Mustad C49S |
| **Thread:** | Beige 6/0 Danville Fymaster |
| **Shuck:** | Ginger Z-Lon |
| **Abdomen:** | March Brown Hareline Rabbit Dubbin |
| **Wing:** | Natural dun CDC |
| **Thorax:** | Caddis green Superfine dry-fly dubbing |
| **Hackle:** | Brown India hen cape |

## ADULT

| | |
|---|---|
| **Hook:** | #10-14 Mustad R50 |
| **Thread:** | Coffee 6/0 Danville Flymaster |
| **Body:** | Brown and tan Superfine dry-fly dubbing mixture |
| **Rib:** | Spanish Tile Coats and Clark #8860 thread |
| **Wing:** | Coastal deer |
| **Hackle:** | Light brown India hen cape |

## ADULT

| | |
|---|---|
| **Hook:** | #10-14 Mustad R50 |
| **Thread:** | Coffee 6/0 Danville Flymaster |
| **Abdomen:** | Tan Superfine dry-fly dubbing |
| **Rib:** | London tan Coats and Clark #8770 thread |
| **Wing:** | Natural dun CDC |
| **Thorax:** | Dark tan Superfine dry-fly dubbing |
| **Hackle:** | Light brown India hen cape |

## WET/DRY ADULT/DIVING EGG-LAYER

| | |
|---|---|
| **Hook:** | #14 Dai-Riki #070 |
| **Thread:** | Tobacco Brown 6/0 Danville Flymaster |
| **Body:** | Light hare's mask fur |
| **Rib:** | Copper Holographic Tinsel (small) |
| **Wing:** | Brown partridge |
| **Hackle:** | Brown dyed starling |

## Smokey Wing Sedge (*Apatania incerta*)
### East to West, hatches mid-April through late May (#20-22)

Larvae have a chartreuse body and dark-brown thorax. Trout feed on the streamed larvae of this northern casemaker as they become active before changing into pupae, which have a chartreuse body and brown thorax. Fish a deep pupa dead drift, or with occasional lifts and drops to animate the soft-hackle collar in the hours leading up to the hatch. Then fish the pupa from streamed all the way up to the surface as hatch begins, with a smooth swing, rod-tip twitches, short one-to-two-inch strips, or lifted and dropped and lifted until reaching the surface. At the time of emergence, the trout feed on pupae just under the surface. Adults are dark brown with a tan lateral line, and egg layers have a chartreuse egg sack and dark dun wings. They dead drift on surface, and lay eggs skittering over water.

### PUPA/ADULT EGG LAYER

| | |
|---|---|
| **Hook:** | #16 Eagle Claw L063. |
| **Thread:** | Black 12/0 Benecchi |
| **Abdomen:** | Green ostrich herl |
| **Thorax:** | Black Hareline Rabbit Dubbin |
| **Hackle:** | Hen pheasant or brown India hen saddle. |

**Note:** The natural is a #18 or #20, but tied here on a #16. Using a slightly oversized hook, and tying a body tied short to the size of a #20, is a good way to create heavier weight and better hooking ability, and still have the fly look natural to size. Feather is wound with one turn of hackle.

## Micro Caddis (*Hydroptilidae*)
### East to West, hatches March through October (#22-28)

Small in size, these can hatch in large numbers. Sometimes this is a hidden hatch, as fish are rising taking pupae or adults that aren't immediately apparent. Larvae have a cream body with a brown head. They live as free swimmers until their fifth instar, then build silk cases as they begin the process of turning into pupae. Tannish cream pupae emerge on the surface, but can take a long time to break through due to their small size. Fishing a deep pupa dead drift, or with occasional lifts and drops all the way up to the surface, is effective with a smooth swing, rod-tip twitches, short one-to-two-inch strips, or lifted

and dropped and lifted until reaching the surface. Adults have a dark tan body and medium dun wing. They drift on the surface drying their wings, and fly off the water. Egg layers dive underwater to the bottom or structure to lay eggs.

### ADULT

| | |
|---|---|
| **Hook:** | #22 Dai-Riki #305 |
| **Thread:** | Tan 8/0 Orvis |
| **Body:** | Cinnamon CDC |
| **Wing:** | Natural dun CDC puff feather |
| **Hackle:** | Hareline India hen cape variant |

**Note:** Body feather fibers are pulled together and tied in by the tips at the hook bend, and wound forward like dubbing

## Longhorn Sedge (*Oecetis*)
### East to West, hatches June through August (#16-18)

Larva body is cream with a tan head. These case-builder caddis build homes out of small rocks and gravel on streambed rocks in slow water. As they grow, they must rebuild the homes, and during this time the highly visible larvae may become dislodged or otherwise end up in the current drift, and become available to trout. Pupa bodies are cream with a tan head and wings, and yellowish creamy antennae and legs. Hatches happen midstream in the afternoon and evening, and emerge under the surface. Fishing a pupa dead drift or with occasional lifts and drops all the way up to the surface is effective with a smooth swing, rod-tip twitches, short one-to-two-inch strips, or lifted and dropped and lifted until reaching the surface. The male adult body is bright green, the female yellow, with gray wings. They drift a short distance on the surface, then fly off quickly. Eggs are laid on the surface.

An important species for anglers on some western rivers, where they exist in large numbers, these caddis, like other long-horned caddis species, have antennae that are more than twice the length of their bodies. Also, their wings are one and a half times the length of the body, whereas other caddis species average a wing one and a quarter times the length of the body. These caddis hatch in the West in summer, when Green Drakes and PMDs are also hatching. Trout will sometimes concentrate on the caddis. Watch for the behavior of rising fish to tell if they are taking caddis pupae, or adults emerging or egg laying on the surface. If you see splashy takes, it's usually trout taking caddis pupae just under the surface. Also, watch the adults on the surface to see if fish rise to them. The smaller species, *Oecetis avara* #18, has the same behavior as *Oecetis disjuncta*, but has a tannish wing and is less common. Both species may overlap hatching.

### PUPA

| | |
|---|---|
| **Hook:** | #16-18 Tiemco 2487 |
| **Thread:** | Brown 12/0 Benecchi |
| **Abdomen:** | March Brown Hareline Rabbit Dubbin |
| **Rib:** | Rust brown Ultra Wire (small) |
| **Thorax:** | Brown Hareline Rabbit Dubbin and rusty brown Hareline Ice Dub mixture |
| **Hackle:** | Tan CDC |

**Note:** Hackle feather is tied in by the tip fibers and wound one or two turns.

### ADULT

| | |
|---|---|
| **Hook:** | #16-18 Tiemco 200R |
| **Thread:** | Tan 8/0 Orvis |
| **Body:** | Caddis green Superfine dry-fly dubbing |
| **Wing:** | Natural dun CDC |
| **Hackle:** | Brown India hen back |

**Note:** For hackle, strip one side of fibers off the stem.

## Little Tan Shorthorn Sedge/Igloo Caddis (*Glossosoma*)
### East to West, hatches May through September (#18-20)

These case-builder caddis build homes out of small rocks and gravel on streambed rocks in riffle water. As they grow, the homes must be rebuilt, and the highly visible cream larvae are available to trout during this time, when they may become dislodged or otherwise end up in the current drift. The behavioral drift of this larva often occurs in the morning, but is not predictable. However, this drift is coordinated with the population of the stream species, and many larvae will be available at one time in the drift. Pupae are also cream colored, and emerge in the afternoon under the surface, but not in a well-synchronized effort, making this stage less important than the larvae and egg layers. Fishing a deep pupa dead drift, or with occasional lifts and drops to animate the soft-hackle collar leading up to the surface emergence, and then all the way up to the surface, is effective during hatches. Fish at this time with a smooth swing, rod-tip twitches, short one-to-two-inch strips, or lifted and dropped and lifted until reaching the surface. Tannish brown adults have brown wings in western species, dark tannish gray in eastern species. They tend to drift on the surface, but not in great numbers, making this a less important stage. At dusk, egg layers dive underwater to lay eggs. This is an important life stage to imitate, as the mating flights can be heavy and egg laying predictable, with many naturals available to the trout at one time.

The saddle-case makers are one of the oldest species of caddis to build cases. The only time they are exposed is when they must leave the case to build a new one, and sometimes get washed into the drift. They are an important species for anglers, particularly on some western rivers where they exist in large numbers.

### EMERGER

| | |
|---|---|
| **Hook:** | #18 Eagle Claw L063 (hand-bent) |
| **Thread:** | Tan 8/0 Orvis |
| **Abdomen:** | March Brown Hareline Rabbit Dubbin |
| **Rib:** | Copper Ultra Wire (extra small) |
| **Thorax Hackle:** | March Brown Whiting Brahma hen saddle aftershaft |
| **Thorax:** | Brown Hareline Rabbit and golden brown Hareline Ice Dub mix |
| **Hackle:** | March Brown Whiting Brahma hen saddle |

**Note:** Dubbing for abdomen should be roughed with a Velcro strip.

## Little Black Sedge (*Chimarra aterrima*)
### East and Midwest, hatches Mid-May through June (#18-20)

Larvae have an orange-yellow body and a bright orange head. This net spinner is a free-living caddis and lives in fast-riffle water. Dark gray pupae hatch in the morning through afternoon. Pupae migrate to shore and emerge into adults on land. The dark gray, black-winged adults are not available to trout until the females oviposit in the afternoon. Females dive underwater to oviposit on structure, after which they resurface and drift spent. This can be imitated with a soft-hackle egg-laying caddis fished first dead drift, then pulled underwater and fished on a swing, or dead drift as the ascending egg-laying female.

### TRANSITIONING LARVA

| | |
|---|---|
| **Hook:** | #18 Tiemco 3761 |
| **Thread:** | Tan 8/0 Orvis |
| **Shuck:** | Peach blood marabou |
| **Abdomen:** | UTC Midge Vinyl Rib |
| **Hackle:** | Bleached partridge |
| **Head:** | Hot orange mixed with a small amount of pale yellow Hareline Rabbit Dubbin |

### PUPA

| | |
|---|---|
| **Hook:** | #18 Tiemco 2487 |
| **Thread:** | Camel 8/0 UNI-Thread |
| **Abdomen:** | Black Danville Rayon Floss |
| **Rib:** | Silver Ultra Wire (extra small) |
| **Hackle:** | Brown partridge |
| **Head:** | Seal brown Hareline Rabbit Dubbin and Hareline rusty brown Ice Dub blend |

### PUPA

| | |
|---|---|
| **Hook:** | #18 Tiemco 2487 |
| **Thread:** | Black 8/0 UNI-Thread |
| **Shuck:** | Light dun and dark dun Z-Lon Mixture |
| **Abdomen:** | UTC Midge Vinyl Rib over tying thread |
| **Thorax:** | Gray Hareline UV Ice Dub |
| **Wing:** | Brown India hen back fibers |
| **Hackle:** | Grizzly hen cape |

### ADULT

| | |
|---|---|
| **Hook:** | #18 Mustad R50 |
| **Thread:** | Iron gray 8/0 UNI-Thread |
| **Body:** | Adams gray Hareline Rabbit Dubbin blended with a small amount of Hareline Green Ice Dub |
| **Wing:** | Tan CDC |
| **Hackle:** | Black hen cape |

## Dark Blue Sedge, Black Caddis (*Psilotreta labida*)
### East, hatches mid-June through late July (#14)

This is a stone-cased caddis builder on riverbed stones. The larva has a chartreuse abdomen and dark brown head, and a gravel-bottom habitat in medium-to-fast riffles. The larvae stack up and congregate on rocks, making a large population on single rocks throughout certain river sections. Pupae bodies have chartreuse abdomens and a dark brown thorax. Since the pupae congregate, emergence areas are narrow, and fish will stack up downstream of the rocks from which the pupae ascend to the surface. An angler needs to focus on the zones of emergence. Adults with dark gray body and brownish gray wings hatch in the evening, drift on the surface, then fly off when their wings are dry. Egg layers oviposit in the evening by dropping them from the surface of the water. The ovipositing females are active, and skip, skitter, and flap their wings while egg laying, causing commotion on which trout key in. After they are spent, they will float dead drift on the surface and eventually sink. Use active skittering presentations with soft-hackle egg-laying patterns, or surface dead drift and then underwater dead drift with sunken egg-laying caddisflies. This hatch occurs on the East Coast, is important for trout and anglers, and can be a heavy hatch that prompts aggressive feeding by trout. Egg-laying flights and hatching can overlap.

### PUPA

| | |
|---|---|
| **Hook:** | #14 Tiemco 200R |
| **Thread:** | Black 8/0 UNI-Thread |
| **Abdomen:** | Medium clear UTC vinyl rib over fluorescent green 6/0 Danville Flymaster |
| **Thorax:** | Hareline Hare's Ear Rabbit Dubbin mixed with a small amount of golden brown Hareline Ice Dub |
| **Winglets:** | Two strands of gold Krystal Flash |
| **Hackle:** | Black hen cape |

### PUPA

| | |
|---|---|
| **Hook:** | #14 Eagle Claw L055 |
| **Thread:** | Black 12/0 Benecchi |
| **Abdomen:** | Green UNI-Stretch |
| **Rib:** | Orvis Hare' E Ice Dub Hare's Ear on tying thread |
| **Rear Thorax:** | Rusty brown Hareline Ice Dub mixture |
| **Front Thorax:** | Seal brown Hareline Rabbit Dubbin |
| **Antennae:** | Mallard flank wood duck |
| **Rearward Facing Hackle:** | Speckled India hen back |
| **Forward Facing Hackle:** | Rusty brown India hen neck |

### ADULT

| | |
|---|---|
| **Hook:** | #14 Mustad R50 |
| **Thread:** | Iron gray 8/0 UNI-Thread |
| **Body:** | Black gnat and charcoal gray Antron dubbing mixture |
| **Rib:** | Hemp Coats and Clark #8240 thread |
| **Wing:** | Natural dun CDC |
| **Hackle:** | Ginger hen cape |
| **Antennae:** | Tan mallard flank |

## Little Sister Sedge (*Cheumatopsyche campyla*)
**East to West, hatches April through July and again in the fall (#20-24)**

Larvae body is light green with a brown head. This net-spinner caddis has no case; nets collect insects and plant material for food. Small dens are built out of small gravel and plant debris for shelter. Pupae have a light green abdomen with a brown thorax. Emergence is at the surface in the morning and evening. This is an important life stage to imitate during hatches. Fish a deep pupa dead drift or with occasional lifts and drops, then fish the pupa from streambed all the way up to the surface during the hatch. Adults have a light green abdomen with a tan thorax and medium dun wings. They drift, but fly off water quickly. Oviposit occurs at dusk, when the females dive or crawl underwater to lay eggs. They also sometimes lay eggs on the surface by skittering and dipping their abdomens into the water.

This species is a bit unusual, in that the body color can vary within the species relatively dramatically. The brown types are smaller, #24, while the green types are larger, #20 and #22. These flies are important and, for the most part, fish seem to target the pupae and egg layers.

### SUIR CADDIS

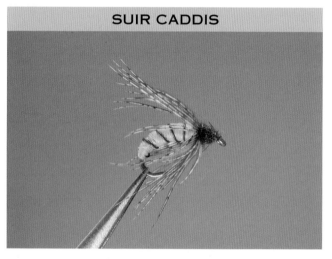

| | |
|---|---|
| **Hook:** | #20 Eagle Claw L055 |
| **Thread:** | Coffee 6/0 Danville Flymaster |
| **Abdomen:** | Fluorescent green Wapsi Antron Yarn |
| **Rib:** | Rusty brown Ultra Wire (small) |
| **Hackle:** | Brown partridge |
| **Head:** | Seal brown Hareline Rabbit Dubbin |

### ADULT

| | |
|---|---|
| **Hook:** | #20 Mustad R50 |
| **Thread:** | Brown 12/0 Benecchi |
| **Abdomen:** | Caddis green Hareline Dry-Fly Dubbing |
| **Rib:** | Bronze green Coats and Clark #6340 thread |
| **Wing:** | Natural dun CDC |
| **Head:** | Brown dry Superfine dubbing |
| **Hackle:** | Brown India hen cape |

## Little Brown Sedge (*Lepidostoma togatum*)
**East and Midwest, hatches August through September (#18-22)**

Larvae are case-makers with yellow, cream, and green bodies. Pupa body has a light green abdomen with a brown thorax. They emerge on or just under the surface in the evening. Fish the pupa from the streambed all the way up to the surface. Adult bodies are a pale tan abdomen with a tan thorax and a medium dun wing. Egg layers have a green egg sack. After emergence, the adults drift for a long time, about 10 to 20 seconds, before taking off from the water. This long period allows trout to feed on the adults more easily, and using a soft-hackle caddis dry fly is effective. Oviposit happens in the evening. Both males and females fall on the water after mating. The females lay eggs as they drift, eventually becoming spent, and drifting before sinking.

## PUPA

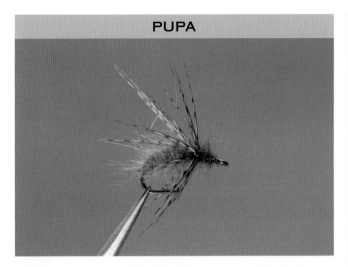

| Hook: | 18 Mustad C49S (shown) or #20-22 Tiemco 2487 |
|---|---|
| Thread: | Rust brown 8/0 UNI-Thread |
| Abdomen: | Caddis green Hareline Rabbit Dubbin |
| Antennae: | Mallard dyed wood duck |
| Hackle: | Brown partridge |
| Head: | Rusty brown Hareline Rabbit Dubbin |

Note: This pupa can be used to match many species in appropriate sizes.

## DRY

| Hook: | #18-22 Tiemco 100 |
|---|---|
| Thread: | Rusty brown 70-denier Ultra Thread |
| Body: | Orvis Hare' E Ice Dub Hare's Ear |
| Wing: | Natural dun CDC |
| Hackle and Antennae: | India speckled hen back |

Note: Body should be dubbed shaggy.

## EGG LAYER

| Hook: | #18-22 Dai-Riki #135 |
|---|---|
| Thread: | Camel 8/0 UNI-Thread |
| Eggsack: | Fluorescent green 6/0 Danville Flymaster |
| Body: | Natural Hareline Rabbit Dubbin |
| Wing: | Tan mallard flank |
| Hackle: | Bleached starling |

## Black Dancer (*Mystacides sepulchralis*)
### East to West, hatches June through July (#18-20)

Larvae have a chartreuse abdomen and a black head, and are tube casemakers. Pupae also have a chartreuse abdomen, with a dark gray thorax. Hatches occur in shallow, slower water in the afternoon through evening. Fishing a pupa from the streambed all the way up to the surface is effective during hatches, with a smooth swing, rod-tip twitches, short one-to-two-inch strips, or lifted and dropped and lifted until reaching the surface. The adult has a dark gray body with a black wing. Adults drift on surface until their wings are dry, then fly off the water quickly. Females dive underwater to oviposit on structure, so fish a diving soft-hackle spinner. After ovipositing, they resurface and drift spent. This can be imitated with a soft-hackle egg-laying caddis fished first dead drift, then pulled underwater and fished on a swing, or dead drift as the ascending egg-laying female.

A member of the longhorn sedge family, the antennae on these caddis are over twice their body length. They have frequent hatches, especially on trout rivers in upstate New York, where they are found flying over slow-water stretches. Since they hatch at midday with a high sun, trout on some rivers won't surface-feed on them. Later in the day toward the evening, trout will begin to take notice and rise to them.

## PUPA

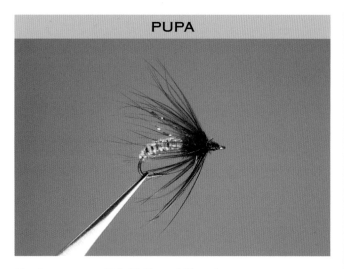

| Hook: | #18-20 Curved Nymph |
|---|---|
| Thread: | Black |
| Abdomen: | Green Flashabou ribbed over black thread |
| Thorax: | Brown rabbit and brown Ice Dubbing Mix |
| Winglets: | Copper Krystal Flash |
| Hackle: | Black hen cape |

## EMERGER PUPA

| Hook: | #10-18 Tiemco 200R |
|---|---|
| Thread: | Black 8/0 UNI-Thread |
| Abdomen: | Green ostrich herl |
| Thorax: | Black ostrich herl |
| Wing: | Gray partridge marked with Prismacolor Goldenrod |
| Hackle: | Partridge aftershaft wound |

## Green Sedge (*Rhyacophila*)

### East to West, hatches May through August (#14-16)

These are free-living larvae with a bright green body and a tan head. Large and free, these caddis larvae are an important source of food for trout. The larvae rappel between rocks with a brown silk line they produce. They are found in riffle water year round.

Pupae have a bright green abdomen and tan thorax. They are fast swimmers that emerge on the surface. Imitate them with an active soft-hackle pupa, fished with imparted action of

strips and lifts, drops and lifts, or rod-tip twitches. Adult males have a bright green abdomen and tan thorax, females are tan, and wings are brown. They emerge in the late afternoon, and mating flights occur at the same time. Females dive or crawl underwater to oviposit. Afterward, they dead drift back up toward the surface, where they drift spent. Heavy mating flights are obvious and create a good chance for fishing a Diving Egg-Laying Soft-Hackle. You don't need to imitate the egg sack on females, which is internal.

## TRANSITIONING ROCKWORM

| Hook: | #14-16 Eagle Claw L055 |
|---|---|
| Thread: | Olive 8/0 Orvis |
| Shuck: | Olive Z-Lon |
| Abdomen: | UTC Medium vinyl rib over thread |
| Thorax: | Hareline peacock Ice Dub |
| Hackle: | Olive grizzly marabou |

## PUPA

| Hook: | #14-16 Eagle Claw L063 (hand-bent) |
|---|---|
| Thread: | Camel 8/0 UNI-Thread |
| Abdomen: | Chartreuse Sparkle Braid |
| Rib: | Black Hareline Rabbit Dubbin |
| Thorax: | Brownish-tan ostrich herl |
| Hackle and Antennae: | Ginger India hen back |
| Eyes: | Chameleon .010 Maxima |

**Note:** Rib dubbing is on a section of marked black thread. Eyes are burnt with a lighter.

## PUPA/DIVING EGG-LAYER

| | |
|---|---|
| **Hook:** | #14-16 Eagle Claw L055 |
| **Thread:** | Camel 8/0 UNI-Thread |
| **Abdomen:** | Olive UTC Medium vinyl rib |
| **Thorax:** | Natural Hareline Rabbit Dubbin and olive Hareline Ice Dub |
| **Wing:** | Tan Brahma hen saddle fibers |
| **Hackle:** | Light brown grizzly marabou |

**Note:** Abdomen vinyl rib is over tying thread. Natural dubbing mixed with a small amount of olive.

## Autumn Sedge (*Neophylax oligius*)
### Northeast and Midwest, hatches September through October (#14-18)

Larvae have a light tan body and are tube case makers. Pupae have a light tan abdomen and a tan thorax. They emerge in the surface film; match with a tan soft-hackle pupa fished under and in the surface with a smooth swing, rod-tip twitches, short one-to-two-inch strips, or dead drifted. Adults have a light olive abdomen, tan thorax, and mottled light brown wing. Hatches occur midmorning to afternoon, and adults drift and fly off the water quickly, though trout do feed on the adults on the surface. Egg layers dive or skitter along the surface laying eggs in the evening. Watch the water surface for the natural's behavior. The mating flights and egg laying offer heavy feeding opportunities for the trout.

## PUPA

| | |
|---|---|
| **Hook:** | #14-18 Tiemco 2487 |
| **Thread:** | Black 8/0 UNI-Thread |
| **Abdomen:** | Yellow Holographic Tinsel under UTC vinyl rib (medium) |
| **Rib:** | Natural Hareline Rabbit Dubbin |
| **Rear Thorax:** | Natural Hareline Rabbit Dubbin |
| **Hackle:** | Brown partridge |
| **Front Thorax:** | Black Hends #45 Spectra Dubbing |
| **Head:** | Gold bead (#14 $^{3}/_{32}$", #16-18 $^{5}/_{64}$") |

**Note:** For rib, dubbing is lightly dubbed on thread and wound between the vinyl rib.

## EMERGER

| | |
|---|---|
| **Hook:** | #14-18 WR-396 (hand-bent) |
| **Thread:** | Olive 6/0 Danville Flymaster |
| **Shuck:** | Brown Z-Lon |
| **Abdomen:** | Rusty brown Ultra Wire (small) |
| **Rib:** | Small brown wire |
| **Thorax:** | Natural Hareline Rabbit Dubbin |
| **Wing:** | Two strands Pearl Krystal Flash |
| **Hackle:** | Hen pheasant |
| **Head:** | Tan ostrich herl or white ostrich herl marked with Prismacolor Goldenrod |

## Little Western Weedy Water Sedge (*Amiocentrus aspilus*)

**West, hatches occur in late July through early August in Yellowstone, while other regions often see a hatch in May and another in September. (#16-22)**

Small in size, yet they can hatch in large numbers. Sometimes this is a hidden hatch, as fish are rising, taking pupae or adults that at first aren't apparent. Larvae have a cream body and tan head. This casemaker is found in slow current, often attached to aquatic plants. Pupae have a bright green abdomen and tan thorax. Fish the pupa from streamed all the way up to the surface with a swing or animation. Adults are green with mottled dark brown wings. They drift on the surface to dry their wings, and then fly off the water. Egg layers dive underwater to lay eggs.

PUPA

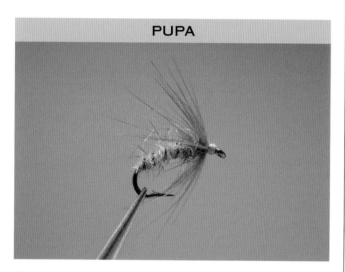

| | |
|---|---|
| **Hook:** | #16-22 Eagle Claw L063 Hand-bent |
| **Thread:** | Tan 8/0 Orvis |
| **Abdomen:** | Caddis green Hare's Ear Plus Dubbing |
| **Rib:** | Black Ultra Wire (small) |
| **Thorax:** | Rusty brown Hare's Ear Plus Dubbing |
| **Hackle:** | Light brown India hen cape |

## McKenzie Caddis (*Arctopsyche*)

**West, hatches in May (#8-10)**

This is an important hatch on some western rivers. Their large size will bring trout to the surface to feed. The free-living larvae found in riffles are green with a brown head. Pupae are also green. They emerge near the surface at midday. Fish a pupa from streamed all the way up to the surface dead drift with animation. Adults, also green with a light brown wing, drift on the surface drying their wings. After ovipositing, egg layers drift spent on the surface.

PUPA

| | |
|---|---|
| **Hook:** | #8-10 WR-396 Hand-bent |
| **Thread:** | Black 6/0 Danville Flymaster |
| **Shuck:** | Olive Z-Lon |
| **Abdomen:** | Olive Hareline Rabbit Dubbin, olive Antron Dubbing |
| **Ribbing:** | Black 6/0 Danville Flymaster |
| **Winglets:** | Two furnace hen cape tips |
| **Hackle:** | Brown partridge |

**Note:** Hen cape tips are shaped with a wing burner, olive dubbing for abdomen should be mixed with a small amount of brown olive Hareline Rabbit Dubbin mixture.

PUPA

| | |
|---|---|
| **Hook:** | #8-10 Tiemco 200R |
| **Thread:** | Camel 8/0 UNI-Thread |
| **Abdomen:** | Caddis green Hareline Rabbit Dubbin over rust brown UTC Wire (small) |
| **Thorax:** | Seal brown Hareline Rabbit Dubbin |
| **Winglets:** | Two furnace hen cape feather tips |
| **Hackle:** | Brown partridge |

## PUPA

| | |
|---|---|
| **Hook:** | #8-10 Tiemco 2457 |
| **Thread:** | Dark brown 8/0 UNI-Thread |
| **Abdomen:** | Caddis green Hareline Rabbit Dubbin |
| **Rib:** | Dark brown 8/0 UNI-Thread |
| **Wing:** | Two copper Krystal Flash strands |
| **Thorax:** | Brown Hareline Rabbit Dubbin |
| **Hackle:** | Brown partridge |

**Note:** Rib brown dubbing dubbed lightly with natural Hareline Rabbit Dubbin mixture.

## PUPA

| | |
|---|---|
| **Hook:** | #10 Tiemco 2487 |
| **Thread:** | Black 8/0 UNI-Thread |
| **Abdomen:** | Natural rubberband |
| **Thorax:** | Black Hareline Rabbit Dubbin and light gray Antron Mixture |
| **Hackle:** | Brown partridge behind dun hen cape |

**Note:** For abdomen, color with Prismacolor Avocado, then overlap wrapped.

## PUPA

| | |
|---|---|
| **Hook:** | #10 Mustad C49S |
| **Thread:** | Tobacco brown 6/0 Danville Flymaster |
| **Abdomen:** | Green Hareline Rabbit Dubbin |
| **Rib:** | Ostrich herl marked with Prismacolor Black |
| **Antennae:** | Two Mallard dyed wood duckfibers |
| **Hackle:** | Tan Whiting Brahma hen saddle |
| **Head:** | Rusty Hareline Rabbit Dubbin |

## PUPA

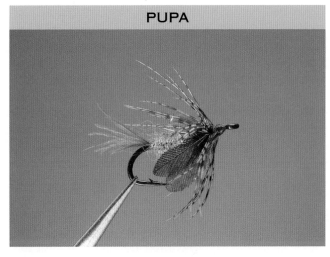

| | |
|---|---|
| **Hook:** | #8-10 Mustad S82 (hand-bent) |
| **Thread:** | Camel 8/0 UNI-Thread |
| **Tail:** | Ginger Woolly Bugger marabou |
| **Abdomen:** | Caddis green Hareline Rabbit Dubbin and Brassie UTC Copper Wire |
| **Winglets:** | Two dark dun hen saddle feather tips |
| **Thorax:** | Seal brown Hareline Rabbit Dubbin and golden brown Hareline Ice Dub mixture |
| **Hackle:** | Brown partridge |

**Note:** For abdomen, dubbing loosely dubbed over wire. Winglet feather tips should be wing-burner-shaped.

### ADULT

| | |
|---|---|
| **Hook:** | #8-10 Daiichi 1190 |
| **Thread:** | Olive 6/0 Danville Flymaster |
| **Body:** | Green and olive Superfine Dubbing mixture |
| **Rib:** | Black 6/0 Danville Flymaster |
| **Wing:** | Coastal deer |
| **Hackle:** | Light brown India hen cape |

### PUPA/DIVING EGG LAYER

| | |
|---|---|
| **Hook:** | #8 Eagle Claw L063 |
| **Thread:** | Tobacco brown 6/0 Danville Flymaster |
| **Abdomen:** | Amber Hareline Rabbit Dubbin |
| **Rib:** | Gold Ultra Wire (small) |
| **Thorax:** | Hen pheasant aftershaft feather |
| **Hackle:** | Hen pheasant |
| **Head:** | Reddish brown Hare's Ear Plus |

## October Caddis (*Dicosmoecus*)
### West, hatches September through mid-October (#6-8)

Cream-body larvae with burnt-orange head are case-builder species found in moderate-to-fast water. As they grow, they must leave the case and often are exposed and available to trout if they are dislodged into the drift, or when they are moving during behavioral drift. These behavioral drifts occur in June and July, in late afternoon. In August they hunker down and await pupation in September or October. Pupae have a creamy orange body and black head. They either crawl out of the water to emerge, or do so in shallow water. This makes the pupa less important than the adult stage. Adults are light tannish orange with a dark dun wing. They drift on the surface drying their wings, and fly off the water. Egg laying occurs from late afternoon to after sunset. After the mating flight, the adults fall on the water. The females skitter or drift on the surface laying eggs, before drifting spent. Fish soft-hackle egg-laying caddis patterns dead drift, skittered and sunken both dead drift and with a line strip or two, to activate the soft-hackle. Even though a sunken egg layer is spent, it still moves as its body parts undulate in the current.

### ADULT

| | |
|---|---|
| **Hook:** | #6-8 Tiemco 200R |
| **Thread:** | Orange 6/0 Danville Flymaster |
| **Body:** | Light hare's mask |
| **Wing:** | Natural dun CDC |
| **Hackle:** | Whiting Greenwell hen cape |

**Note:** Body dubbing dubbed loosely and fluffy on the thread.

## White Miller (*Nectopsyche albida*)

**East to West, hatches May through June and again from mid-August through November (#14)**

Larvae have a cream body with a yellow head. This is a tube casemaker found in slower, warmer water with aquatic vegetation, a source of food in their larval stage. Pupae are also cream in color. They emerge on the surface in the morning and late afternoon, in weedy, slower-moving waters, allowing trout to somewhat leisurely sip and rise to the naturals as they are breaking out of their pupal shuck, suspended in the surface film. Often this appears as a head-and-tail rise from the trout. In this case, use a floating emerger like a soft-hackle dry with a trailing shuck. Presenting a slowly swung soft-hackle caddis pupa just under the surface works as well, especially if the water has some current or is slightly broken. Adults are white with a pale yellow head and white wing. They drift on the surface drying their wings, and then fly off the water. Mating flights and egg laying occur in the evening, with the females skittering and skating on top of the water, creating a noticeable disturbance of which trout take advantage.

These caddis are especially important in the waters of the Yellowstone area. On some waters, they now outnumber *Hydropsyche* due to the geological hot springs becoming even more pronounced and warming these streams.

### SHUCK EMERGER

| | |
|---|---|
| **Hook:** | #14 Mustad R50 |
| **Thread:** | Olive 12/0 Benecchi |
| **Shuck:** | White Z-Lon |
| **Body:** | White Superfine dry-fly dubbing |
| **Wing:** | Natural mallard flank under white CDC |
| **Hackle:** | Grizzly hen cape |

### PUPA/DIVING EGG LAYER

| | |
|---|---|
| **Hook:** | #14 Tiemco 3761 |
| **Thread:** | Olive 12/0 Benecchi |
| **Body:** | Cream Hareline Rabbit Dubbin |
| **Hackle:** | Partridge side breast feather |

### ADULT/SKITTERING AND SPENT EGG LAYER

| | |
|---|---|
| **Hook:** | #14 Mustad R50 |
| **Thread:** | Olive 12/0 Benecchi |
| **Body:** | White Superfine dry-fly dubbing |
| **Wing:** | White CDC |
| **Hackle:** | Grizzly hen cape |

## Universal Caddisflies

Because you can never have enough, use these patterns for general searching, or to match species with a common appearance.

### KELLS CADDIS

| Hook: | #14-16 Eagle Claw L055 |
|---|---|
| Thread: | Camel 8/0 UNI-Thread |
| Abdomen: | Fluorescent green Wapsi Antron Yarn |
| Wing: | Copper Krystal Flash |
| Thorax: | Seal Brown Hareline Rabbit Dubbin |
| Hackle: | Brown partridge |

### SWIMMING CADDIS

| Hook: | #12-16 Tiemco 206BL |
|---|---|
| Thread: | Coffee 6/0 Danville Flymaster |
| Shuck: | Ginger Z-Lon |
| Rib: | Copper Ultra Wire (small) |
| Abdomen: | Coffee 6/0 Danville Flymaster, |
| Back: | Two peacock herls |
| Wing: | Two strands Pearl Krystal Flash |
| Thorax: | Natural Hareline Rabbit Dubbin |
| Hackle: | March Brown Whiting Brahma hen saddle |
| Head: | Tan ostrich herl or white ostrich herl marked Prismacolor Goldenrod |

**Note:** Alternatives for abdomen are Summer Brown Coats and Clark #8360 thread, or DMC 25 #869 embroidery floss.

### GENERAL PUPA

| Hook: | #10-16 Tiemco 2487 |
|---|---|
| Thread: | Camel 8/0 UNI-Thread |
| Shuck: | Brown Z-Lon |
| Abdomen: | Brown Flashabou under UTC Medium (#10-12) or Midge (#14-16) vinyl rib |
| Thorax: | Golden brown Hareline Ice Dub |
| Hackle: | Brown or Prismacolor Goldenrod Partridge |
| Head: | Copper bead (³⁄₃₂" #10-12 or ⁵⁄₆₄" #14-16) |

### CRACKLE PUPA

| Hook: | #12-16 Tiemco 206BL |
|---|---|
| Thread: | Tan 8/0 Orvis |
| Tail and Body: | Ginger blood marabou fibers |
| Rib: | Rust Ultra Wire (small) |
| Back: | Two peacock herls dyed bright green |
| Wing: | Pearl Krystal Flash |
| Rear Thorax: | Ginger blood marabou fibers |
| Hackle: | Whiting tan Brahma hen saddle |
| Head: | Dyed bright green peacock herl |

## ALL-CADDIS PUPA (GREEN)

| | |
|---|---|
| **Hook:** | #10-18 Eagle Claw L055 |
| **Thread:** | Cream 6/0 Danville Flymaster |
| **Shuck:** | Cream 6/0 Danville Flymaster |
| **Abdomen:** | Fluorescent green Wapsi Antron Yarn |
| **Rib:** | Black Ultra Wire (small) |
| **Thorax:** | Rusty brown Hareline Rabbit Dubbin |
| **Antenna:** | Wood duck mallard flank |
| **Hackle:** | Gray partridge |

**Note:** Thread should be colored with reddish-brown marker. Variations for the abdomen: orange, tan, cream.

## SPLITBACK PUPA

| | |
|---|---|
| **Hook:** | #12-16 Eagle Claw L055 |
| **Thread:** | Tobacco brown 6/0 Danville Flymaster |
| **Abdomen:** | Fluorescent green Wapsi Antron Yarn |
| **Back:** | Black Krystal Flash |
| **Rib:** | Silver Ultra Wire (small) |
| **Antennae:** | Two Mallard dyed wood duckfibers |
| **Thorax:** | Rusty Hareline Rabbit behind black dubbing |
| **Hackle:** | Brown partridge |

**Note:** Rib wire should be marked in sections with a black marker before being wound.

## EMERGING SEDGE

| | |
|---|---|
| **Hook:** | #12-18 Tiemco 2487 |
| **Thread:** | Camel 8/0 UNI-Thread |
| **Shuck:** | Amber rabbit dubbing |
| **Abdomen:** | Fluorescent chartreuse Wapsi Sparkle Braid |
| **Thorax:** | Light olive Hends #6 Spectra Dubbing, Black Hareline Rabbit Dubbin |
| **Hackle:** | Brown partridge |

**Note:** Abdomen variations include bronze, copper, fluorescent orange, fluorescent blue, black, fluorescent pink.

A classic spring creek may just be the culmination of what fly fishing stands for. The rarest of all trout waters, it offers the greatest challenges for the angler and the most ideal habitat for fish and fly, not to mention the intricate, lush beauty and technical personality. Due to the consistent water temperatures, midge patterns can and should be fished year round on these waters, as they are one of the most commonly available food sources for trout.

# STONEFLIES (PLECOPTERA)

On many western rivers like the Firehole River canyon section, the Box Canyon of the Henry's Fork, the Big Hole River, the Yellowstone River, the Gallatin River canyon, the Madison River, the Colorado River, and the Deschutes River, stonefly nymphs are a year round food source and a large part of a trout's diet. Stoneflies range in size from the half-inch Snowfly to the two-inch *Pteronarcys californica* or Salmonfly. Stoneflies are pollution intolerant and an indicator of water quality. They are generally less populous in the East and Midwest, but fishing stonefly nymphs as prospecting flies often works well, especially in the fast-riffle water where they live. In the West, stoneflies make up much of the biomass in many rivers. They are not good swimmers and their large size makes an easy, hearty meal, fattening up fish fast. Winter brings hatches of the little dark stoneflies. As the year progresses into spring, the large *Perlodidae* offer some of the first good dry-fly fishing. Springtime brings the large *Pteronarcys californica*, followed by the Golden Stoneflies; summer, the Little Yellow Stoneflies (*Perlodidae*) and the green *Chloroperlidae* hatch.

Stonefly nymphs migrate to the shore or in-stream structure like boulders to hatch out of the water. As they migrate, trout will hold near the banks of the stream or structure to intercept the nymphs. Although the adults hatch out of the water, many flying adults are blown back into the river by strong wind, so trout commonly see Salmonflies drifting on the surface. But more important are the egg layers and spent egg layers drifting on the surface. After they hatch, stonefly adults can eat and drink, allowing them to live longer outside of the water, like caddis and midge, but unlike the mayfly. They can live up to a month before returning to the river to mate, lay eggs, and

die. Don't forget about fishing a soft-hackle dry underwater to imitate spent, sunken egg layers.

I especially like to prospect nymph with stonefly nymphs in the winter, when the water is cold and fish are lethargic, as this fly will reach the depths at which the fish hold, and is a big enough meal that it will entice them to strike if it's placed right in front of their noses. Two all-season fast-water prospecting rigs that I like are a heavy #8 Brown Stonefly Nymph point fly and a #16 Hare's Ear Soft-Hackle, either at the tippet blood knot or trailed off the hook bend; and a #8 Orange Dry Stone with a 12-inch monofilament hook bend dropper and a #16 Pheasant Tail Soft-Hackle.

Shucks on rocks can indicate that trout are looking for and feeding on the nymphs. Tie on a soft-hackle stonefly nymph and fish it near protruding structure and the banks.

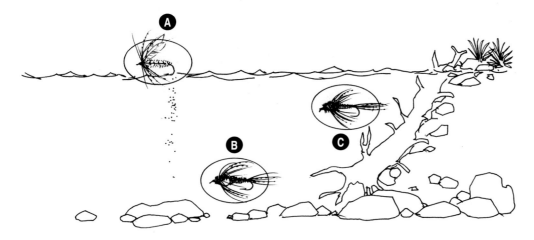

**Stonefly Lifecycle**
The stonefly lifecycle is matched with the adult and nymph as the emergence takes place out of the water on structure. Stonefly Lifecycle Patterns include Soft-Hackle Stonefly Nymph, Soft-Hackle Stonefly Dry, and Sunken Egg Layer.
**A.** Soft-Hackle Dry/Wet Adult
**B.** Bead Thorax Heavy Nymph
**C.** Light Nymph

## Black Stone (*Taeniopteryx nivalis*)
**East and Midwest, hatches late February through April (#14-18)**

These stoneflies are more pollution-tolerant than the rest of the stoneflies. They can be found in a wide variety of warmer and colder waters. Nymph bodies are dark brown or black. They migrate to structure or shore, and crawl out of the water to emerge in the warmest part of a sunny day. Drift the nymph near the bottom at the tailouts of pools and runs, or at the head of the next pool downstream, as the mature nymphs often get swept into the current from their migration route. Egg-layer bodies are dark gray or black with dark dun wings. Egg layers drift and drop eggs in the current, then drift spent.

## Little Brown Stone (*Strophopteryx fasciata*)
**East and Midwest, hatches late February through April (#16-18)**

The dark brown nymphs migrate to structure or shore, and crawl out of the water to emerge in the warmest part of sunny days. Drift the nymph downstream, as the mature nymphs often get swept into the current from their migration route. Egg layers have brown bodies with medium tannish dun wings. They drift and drop eggs in the current, then drift spent.

These stoneflies can cause surface feeding on warm, early-spring days. Fish near the banks or structure protruding from the water, with a soft-hackle stone nymph, especially if you see signs of empty stonefly cases near structure like rocks or timber above the water.

**NYMPH**

**NYMPH**

| Hook: | #14-18 WR-396 |
|---|---|
| Thread: | Rusty brown 70-denier Ultra Thread |
| Tail and Abdomen: | Ginger blood marabou |
| Rib: | Copper Ultra Wire (small) |
| Hackles, Rear Abdomen: | Ginger blood marabou from abdomen, two rusty-brown Woolly Bugger marabou fibers, brown starling |

**Note:** For hackles, fibers are tied in by tips and wound.

| Hook: | #16 WR-396 (hand-bent) |
|---|---|
| Thread: | Camel 8/0 UNI-Thread |
| Tail: | Prismacolor Goldenrod Partridge |
| Abdomen: | Brown Superfine dry-fly dubbing mixture |
| Rib: | Gold UNI Micro-Tinsel |
| Thorax: | Ginger Nature's Spirit hare's mask dubbing |
| Antennae: | Mallard flank wood duck |
| Hackle: | Brown starling |

## Giant Black Stone (*Pteronarcys dorsata*)
### East and Midwest, hatches April through June (#2-4)

Black nymphs migrate, crawling out of the water to hatch at night. Found in riffle water, nymph fishing should be done there as well. The nymph takes three years to mature, all the time available as trout food. Drift the nymph near the bottom downstream, as the mature nymphs often get swept into the current from their migration route. Egg layers are dark brown with dun wings. Surface feeding can occur when the females lay eggs on the surface at night. These are the largest stonefly found in the East.

Little Yellow Stonefly adult. JON RAPP

### ARTICUNYMPH

| | |
|---|---|
| **Hook:** | #12 Eagle Claw L063 |
| **Thread:** | Camel 8/0 UNI-Thread |
| **Tail:** | Rusty brown turkey biots |
| **Abdomen:** | Seal brown Hareline Rabbit Dubbin |
| **Rib and Abdomen** | |
| **Thread:** | Tobacco brown 6/0 Danville Flymaster |
| **Rear Hackle:** | Brown partridge or rusty brown hen cape |
| **Thorax:** | Seal brown Hareline Rabbit Dubbin and ⅛" copper bead |
| **Hackle:** | Brown partridge |

## Little Yellow Stonefly (*Isoperla*)
### East to West, hatches March through May (#10-16)

Nymphs are tannish yellow and brown, and live in rocky-bottomed riffle water with faster currents. The nymph crawls to shore or structure to hatch out of the water, usually in the evening. It migrates to shore or structure in shallow water, to hatch out of the water at dawn and dusk. Fishing a soft-hackle stonefly nymph dead drift or on a slow swing near shore is effective. Also, drift the nymph near the bottom at the tail-outs of pools and runs, or at the head of the next pool downstream, as the mature nymphs often get swept into the current from their migration route. Egg-layer bodies are yellow with a translucent light yellow wing. Mating flights with floating egg layers occur in the afternoon and evening. Fish a soft-hackle dry stonefly with dead drifts, or small amounts of skittering to animate the fly.

Nymphs are similar in appearance to Golden Stoneflies, but *Isoperla* have longer tails and antennae, and lack thoracic gills underneath their body.

### NYMPH

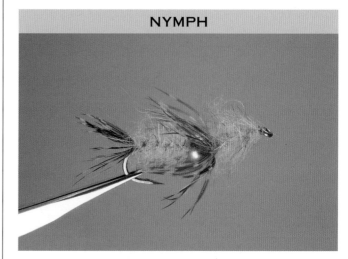

| | |
|---|---|
| **Hook:** | #10-16 Mustad R73 (hand-bent) |
| **Thread:** | Tobacco brown 6/0 Danville Flymaster |
| **Tail:** | English grouse split into two sections |
| **Body:** | Natural Hareline rabbit on a dubbing loop |
| **Rib:** | Copper Ultra Wire (small) |
| **Thorax:** | ⁵⁄₃₂" (#10), ⅛" (#12-16) gold bead |
| **Hackle:** | English grouse |

## ADULT

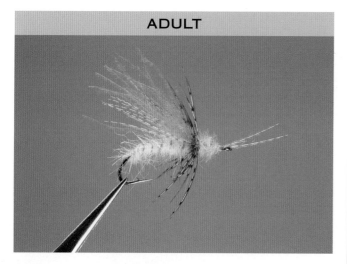

| Hook: | #10-16 200R |
|---|---|
| Thread: | Orange 6/0 Danville Flymaster |
| Abdomen: | Pale yellow Hareline Rabbit Dubbin |
| Rib: | Orange 6/0 Danville Flymaster |
| Wing: | Mallard dyed wood duck under tan CDC |
| Hackle: | Brown partridge marked with Prismacolor Sunburst Yellow |
| Head: | Amber Hareline Rabbit Dubbin |
| Antennae: | Mallard flank wood duck |

## NYMPH

| Hook: | #4-8 Mustad R74 (hand-bent) |
|---|---|
| Thread: | Tobacco brown 6/0 Danville Flymaster |
| Tail: | English grouse split into two sections |
| Body: | Medium hare's mask in a dubbing loop |
| Rib: | Gold Ultra Wire (medium) |
| Thorax: | $5/32$" gold bead |
| Hackle: | English grouse |

## Golden Stone (*Acroneuria lycorias*)
### East and Midwest, hatches early June through mid-July (#4-8)

Nymphs are tannish yellow and migrate from fast riffles to slower water, and structure or the bank. Fish a nymph near these features, as trout will follow the migration of the bugs, holding close to the bank. Also, drift the nymph near the bottom of the next pool downstream, as the mature nymphs often get swept into the current from their migration route. The belly of the nymphs is much lighter than the back. Also, when they molt, they are a creamy color before darkening again. A lighter shade nymph to imitate this makes a great prospect-nymphing pattern, as it's highly visible to trout. Egg layers are also tannish yellow, with medium dun wings. After hatching and mating at night, females swarm, flying over the river the next afternoon, laying eggs, and falling on the surface. Dead drift or skittered soft-hackle stoneflies are effective either above the water or underwater as a sunken-stonefly imitation. Good fishing with adult stoneflies can extend into the evening and after dark.

## ADULT

| Hook: | #6-8 Mustad R43 |
|---|---|
| Thread: | Orange 6/0 Danville Flymaster |
| Abdomen: | Amber and antique gold Hareline Rabbit Dubbin mixture |
| Palmered Hackle: | Bleached grizzly hen cape |
| Wing: | Natural dun CDC |
| Hackle: | Light brown partridge |
| Head: | Orange Hareline Rabbit Dubbin |

**Note:** Hen cape is palmered from hook bend to thorax. The head is ribbed with Hareline Hare's Ear Rabbit Dubbin.

## Appalachian Springfly (*Isogenoides hansoni*)
### East, hatches April through July (#12-16)

Nymph body is yellow with brown mottled sections. Nymphs crawl to shore or structure to hatch out of the water. Fish the next pool downstream from emergence, as the mature nymphs often get swept into the current from their migration route. Egg layers have a brown abdomen, yellow thorax, and mottled medium dun wings. Mating flights occur with floating egg layers.

Though this Eastern stonefly is not found in abundance, *Isogenoides hansoni* nymphs can be fished throughout the year in riffles where they are found. An egg-laying event in the riffles may be encountered as well, with a few spinners landing on the water.

### ARTICUNYMPH

| | |
|---|---|
| **Hook:** | #16-18 Tiemco 3761 |
| **Thread:** | Tobacco brown 6/0 Danville Flymaster |
| **Tail:** | Rusty brown Woolly Bugger marabou |
| **Abdomen:** | Natural Hareline Rabbit Dubbin |
| **Thorax:** | Rusty brown Hareline Rabbit Dubbin |
| **Hackle:** | Mottled gray Whiting Brahma hen saddle |
| **Head:** | ⁵⁄₆₄" gold bead |

**Note:** Hackle feather is in back of a rusty brown Woolly Bugger marabou wound around the hook shank.

## Sallyflies: Yellow Sally/Green Sally (*Chloroperlidae*)
### East, Midwest, West, hatches May through August (#12)

The nymph's body is yellow and brown or green and brown. Drift the nymph near the bottom at the tailouts of pools and runs, or at the head of the next pool downstream, as the mature nymphs often get swept into the current from their migration route. Egg layers are yellow or light green with light dun wings. Fish a floating soft-hackle dry fly, a sunken soft-hackle stone, or a traditional soft-hackle, like a Partridge and Yellow, in the surface and just under the surface, to imitate the egg-laying females, both floating and sunken.

This family includes the Yellow Sallies and Green Sallies. You often find them in the summer, hatching on small mountain streams on the East Coast. My recommendation is to be prepared to imitate the nymphs, both deep and shallow, and a floating soft-hackle egg layer. Then watch for rising trout and notice their surface-feeding behavior. If you see adults on the water or air, fish a floating fly or wet fly to imitate egg layers. You can fish the nymphs anytime, especially from April through August during the migration to hatch.

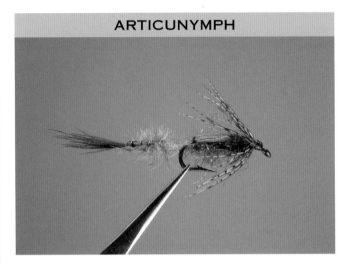

### ARTICUNYMPH

| | |
|---|---|
| **Hook:** | #16 Eagle Claw L063 |
| **Thread:** | Tobacco brown 6/0 Danville Flymaster |
| **Tail:** | Brown blood marabou |
| **Abdomen:** | Tan ostrich herl |
| **Rib:** | Copper Ultra Wire (extra small) |
| **Abdomen Back and Wing Case:** | Brown Swiss Straw |
| **Thorax:** | Seal brown Hareline Rabbit Dubbin and Hareline rusty brown Ice Dub mixture |
| **Hackle:** | Brown partridge |

### ARTICUNYMPH

| | |
|---|---|
| **Hook:** | #16 Eagle Claw L063 |
| **Thread:** | Coffee 6/0 Danville Flymaster |
| **Tail:** | Brown ostrich herl |
| **Abdomen:** | Golden tan and golden stone Wapsi Antron dubbing mixture |
| **Rib and Wing Case:** | Brown ostrich herl |
| **Thorax:** | Amber Hareline Rabbit Dubbin |
| **Hackle:** | Tan Whiting Brahma hen saddle |

## Winter Stonefly (*Capniidae*)
### West, hatches January through April (#12-16)

Light brown nymphs are the first of the western stoneflies to hatch. They crawl to shore or structure to hatch out of the water. Fish next pool downstream of emergence, as the mature nymphs often get swept into the current from their migration route. Egg layers are black or dark brown with mottled brown wings. Females drop eggs while floating on top of the water.

**NYMPH**

| | |
|---|---|
| **Hook:** | #12-16 WR-396 eye straigthened |
| **Thread:** | Rusty brown 70-denier Ultra Thread |
| **Tail and Abdomen:** | Peach blood marabou |
| **Rib:** | Copper Ultra Wire (small) |
| **Hackle:** | Peach blood marabou from abdomen, two wound rusty brown Woolly Bugger marabou fibers, brown starling |
| **Head:** | $\frac{3}{32}$" (#12-14), $\frac{5}{64}$" (#16) copper bead |

## Skwala Stonefly (*Skwala americana*) (#6-10)
### West, hatches in February through April

The yellowish olive and brown nymphs are found in bouldered riffle water. The nymph crawls to shore or structure to hatch out of the water. Mature nymphs often get swept into the current from their migration route. Egg layers, with their brown-olive bodies and brown wings, prefer calm days with sunshine to lay eggs. Mating flights occur with floating egg layers. The females drift on the current laying eggs. They don't make much commotion, unlike some of the other stonefly species when ovipositing.

This early season stonefly doesn't hatch in great numbers, but what does hatch gets eaten by eager trout. The Yakima River and the Bitterroot River have good hatches of this stonefly.

**ARTICUNYMPH**

| | |
|---|---|
| **Hook:** | #12-14 Tiemco 3761 |
| **Thread:** | Tobacco brown 6/0 Danville Flymaster |
| **Tail:** | Rusty brown Woolly Bugger marabou |
| **Abdomen:** | March Brown Hareline Rabbit Dubbin |
| **Rib:** | Brown ostrich herl |
| **Thorax:** | Rusty brown Hareline Rabbit Dubbin |
| **Hackle:** | Mottled Gray Whiting Brahma hen saddle |
| **Head:** | Ostrich herl marked with Prismacolor Goldenrod |

**ADULT**

| | |
|---|---|
| **Hook:** | #6-10 Tiemco 200R |
| **Thread:** | Burnt orange 70-denier Ultra Thread |
| **Abdomen:** | Amber and orange Hareline Rabbit Dubbin blend |
| **Rib:** | Coffee 6/0 Danville Flymaster |
| **Wing:** | Natural mallard flank under natural dun CDC |
| **Hackle:** | Brown partridge behind grizzly hen cape marked Prismacolor Mineral Orange |
| **Head:** | Rust orange Hareline Rabbit Dubbin ribbed with Hareline brown Rabbit Dubbin |
| **Antennae:** | Two natural mallard flank fibers |

Salmonfly adult. MONTANA RIVERBOATS

## Salmonfly (*Pteronarcys californica*)
### West, hatches April through July (#4-8)

Light reddish to dark brown nymphs live in bouldered riffle-water sections. They migrate to shore or structure, to hatch out of the water at dawn and dusk. Fishing a soft-hackle stonefly nymph dead drift, or on a slow swing near shore, is effective. Nymphs often get swept downstream into the current from their migration route. Egg layers have yellowish orange abdomens and orange heads, with dark brown wings. Imitate this life stage with floating dry flies. After the mating flights, the ovipositing females fly low over the water and drop their egg sacks. Sometimes the wind blows them onto the water, and otherwise they will lay eggs while drifting on the surface. Either way, they make a commotion when they are on the water, and trout rise to feed. After they are spent, they will either drift a little longer with wings splayed out on the water, or sink. Fishing a soft-hackle spinner dead drift and then sunken is effective.

This hatch works its way upriver, because it starts in the warmer water downstream, then moves upstream as the water warms. Nymphs are particularly effective before, during, and after the hatch season, as trout become conditioned to this large protein source. The nymphs live three years in the river before they mature enough to hatch. This whole time they are growing, making it natural to fish smaller, then larger nymphs. As the hatch moves upriver, lasting only a few days in each location, one can stay ahead of the adults, targeting the aggressive fish feeding on the nymph. Fish upriver from the adults and fish Salmonfly nymphs, as the trout are actively feeding on the migrating nymphs below the surface. There are fewer anglers here as well.

### NYMPH

| | |
|---|---|
| **Hook:** | #4-8 Mustad R74 (hand-bent) |
| **Thread:** | Tobacco brown 6/0 Danville Flymaster |
| **Body:** | Seal brown Hareline Rabbit in a dubbing loop |
| **Rib:** | Copper Ultra Wire (medium) |
| **Tail:** | English grouse split into two sections |
| **Thorax:** | 5/32" Copper bead |
| **Hackle:** | English grouse |

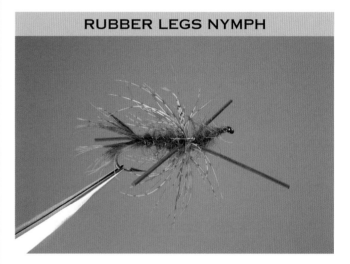

### RUBBER LEGS NYMPH

| | |
|---|---|
| **Hook:** | #4-8 Mustad R74 Hand bent Nymph |
| **Thread:** | Coffee 6/0 Danville Flymaster |
| **Body:** | Seal brown Hareline Rabbit in a dubbing loop |
| **Tail:** | Marginal covert partridge fibers split into two sections |
| **Rib:** | Amber Ultra Wire (medium) |
| **Thorax:** | Brown rubber legs |
| **Hackle:** | Brown partridge |

## ADULT

**Hook:** #4-8 Tiemco 200R
**Thread:** Burnt orange 70-denier Ultra Thread
**Body:** Rust orange Hareline Rabbit Dubbin
**Rib:** Black Coats and Clark #0002 thread
**Wing:** Mallard dyed wood duck under natural dun CDC
**Hackle:** Grizzly hen cape feather, half feathers marked Prismacolor Mineral Orange
**Head Rib:** Natural Hareline Rabbit Dubbinon burnt orange thread
**Antennae:** Mallard flank wood duck

**Note:** The thread in the rib is lightly dubbed with Natural Hareline Rabbit Dubbin.

## ADULT

**Hook:** #4-8 Tiemco 200R
**Thread:** Orange 6/0 Danville Flymaster
**Abdomen:** Cinnamon Superfine Caddis dry-fly dubbing
**Wing:** Coastal deer
**Hackle:** Brown India hen back
**Head:** Amber Superfine dry-fly dubbing

**Note:** For the abdomen, the dubbing should be ribbed with Hareline Hare's Ear Rabbit Touch Dubbing on black 8/0 UNI-Thread; and the dubbing for the head ribbed with light hare's mask dubbing on orange thread.

## ADULT

**Hook:** #4-8 Tiemco 200R
**Thread:** Orange 6/0 Danville Flymaster
**Abdomen:** Orange Nature's Spirit Fine Natural Dubbing
**Rib:** Black 8/0 UNI-Thread
**Thorax:** Sulphur orange Nature's Spirit Fine Natural Dubbing
**Wing:** Coastal deer
**Hackle:** Palmered brown partridge

Golden stonefly. MONTANA RIVERBOATS

## Golden Stonefly (*Calineuria californica, Hesperoperla pacifica*)
### West, hatches May through June (#6-8)

Both of these stonefly nymph species are yellow and brown. Hatches occur primarily on freestone streams. Golden Stoneflies grow for three years in rocky-bottomed riffle water with faster currents. They migrate to shore or structure in shallow water to hatch out of the water at dawn and dusk. Fishing a soft-hackle stonefly nymph dead drift or on a slow swing near shore is effective. Also, drift the nymph near the bottom of the next pool downstream, as the mature nymphs often get swept into the current from their migration route. Egg layer bodies are brownish yellow with an orange head and translucent mottled brown wings. Mating flights with floating egg layers occur in afternoon and evening. Fish a soft-hackle dry stonefly with dead drifts and skittering to animate the fly and imitate the clumsy behavior of the naturals.

In the West, two species are known as Golden Stoneflies: *Calineuria californica* (larger of these two by about a hook size, prominent in the West Coast states) and *Hesperoperla pacifica* (prominent in the Rocky Mountain states). Both of these large stoneflies share many of the same traits and behaviors as the even larger Salmonfly (*Pteronarcys californica*). The Salmonfly and Golden Stone patterns are interchangeable in fly design, the former reddish orange, and the latter a golden-yellow body color.

## NYMPH

| Hook: | #6-8 Mustad R73 |
|---|---|
| Thread: | Camel 8/0 UNI-Thread |
| Tail: | Bleached partridge split into two sections |
| Abdomen: | March Brown Hareline and pale yellow Rabbit Dubbin mixture |
| Rib: | Brown Ultra Wire (medium) |
| Thorax: | Brown rubber legs |
| Hackle: | Bleached partridge |
| Head: | Hareline Hare's Ear Rabbit Dubbin |

Note: Bleached partridge for hackle should include some fluffy base fibers.

## ADULT

| Hook: | #6-8 Tiemco 200R |
|---|---|
| Thread: | Orange 6/0 Danville Flymaster |
| Body and Head: | Amber Hareline Rabbit Dubbin |
| Rib: | Bronze UNI Micro-Tinsel |
| Wing: | Dun CDC feather |
| Hackle: | Gray partridge marked with Prismacolor Goldenrod |
| Antennae: | Two wood duck mallard flank fibers |

Note: For body and head, amber dubbing is lightly dubbed over thread to allow thread to show through, then dubbed over again lightly with Hareline Hare's Ear Touch Dubbing. Wing feather is tied flat on top of the hook with the stem intact.

The Big Hole River is one of the world's best stonefly habitats. Hatches include the Skwala in April, Salmonflies in June, Golden Stoneflies in June and July, the overlooked Nocturnal Stonefly in July, and Little Yellow Sallies in late June through July.

## CHIRONOMIDS: MIDGES

Though small in size, midges can be the largest biomass of insects in many streams, and in concentrated populations trout can grow large feeding on them as a primary food source. They hatch every month of the year, and trout can feed on them year round. Some midges are so small fly patterns can't effectively imitate them, but most are #14-28. There are so many species of chironomids that identifying and using their Latin names would require microscopic inspection of the species. Instead, as their behaviors are the same, matching life stage size, color, and behavior is all that is required, and effective enough.

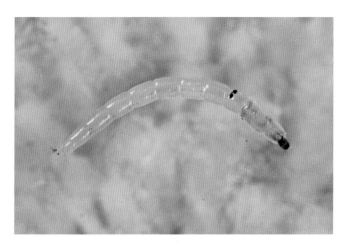

Midge larvae are found in a variety of colors, depending on the alkalinity and substrate in which they burrow or the vegetation that sustains them. JON RAPP

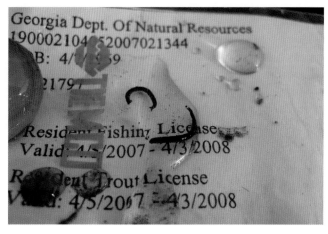

The red bloodworms live in silt and can thrive in low-oxygen environments, due to the hemoglobin they carry that holds oxygen.

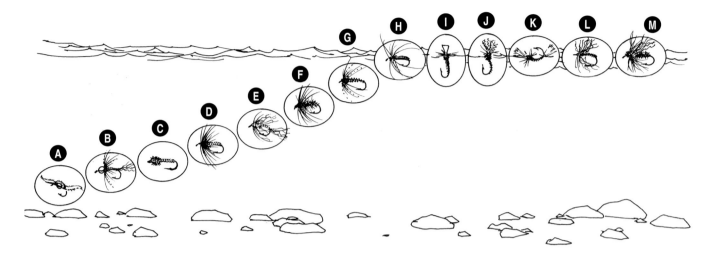

**Midge Life Cycle**
The midge life cycle imitated with soft-hackle fly patterns. When fishing the subsurface pupa, it's often helpful to use a dry/dropper rigging with a midge soft-hackle dry and a pupa dropper for visible traceability, dead drift ability, strike detection, and depth-level suspension. Midge life cycle patterns include Soft-Hackle Larva, Soft-Hackle Pupa, Floating Pupa, Soft-Hackle Dry Fly, and Soft-Hackle Dry Fly with Egg Sack.

**A.** Larva Bloodworm; **B.** Deep Larvae; **C.** Brassie Flymph (Nymph Hook); **D.** Brassie Flymph (Dry Fly Hook); **E.** Z-Lon Shuck Pupa; **F.** Fuzzy Pupa; **G.** Soft-Hackle Pupa; **H.** Light Pupa; **I.** Foam Post Midge Pupa; **J.** CDC Post Midge Pupa; **K.** Suspended V-Pupa; **L.** Soft-Hackle Dry Fly and Egg Layer (Thread Body); **M.** Soft-Hackle Dry Fly and Egg Layer (Dubbed Body).

Midge larvae live in silt, on aquatic plants, or in silk tubes they construct in burrows in the substrate. They feed on algae, detritus, and even wood. They are often bright red, cream, or gray. Midge pupae are the most important stage to match. The movement of the emerging midge pupae is similar to that of a mayfly. They swim to the surface with abdominal kicks that are fast and noticeable, and lifting and swimming a midge pupa with short strips or tugs of line is effective.

A #18 Midge V-Pupa hook bent in vise. White Antron yarn on the front and bend imitates gills and helps visibility to some degree. Use floatant on the Antron yarn to imitate a suspended emerging midge.

When midges reach the surface, some can break through the surface water tension by themselves and crawl out of their shuck. More commonly, though, the midge anchors both head and posterior under the surface film, and uses the anchoring to give the fly leverage to crawl out head first through the surface film. The midge at this anchoring stage is U-shaped, magnified by a mirror image on the underside of the water surface. This shape is distinct, and trout will key in on the appearance and the drag-free drift. Trout target the vulnerable pupae, as most adults can escape off the water quickly.

After emergence, adults fly off the water to streambank vegetation. After mating, they return to the water where the ovipositing females can bring trout to the surface. This life stage may be mistaken for a hatch. In this situation, a dead-drifted soft-hackle dry fly to rising trout produces results. After the dry fly has drifted past the fish or begins to drag, you can pull it under and fish it as a sunken egg layer, or pull it under upstream of the fish so that it's sunken when it reaches the riser.

## Midges
### East to West, hatches year-round (#14-28)

Larvae are colored cream and red. They mature on the streambed where they pupate. Pupa bodies occur in black, gray, red, green, chartreuse, cream, and brown. They can hatch at any time of day, and are particularly abundant on stillwaters and slow, flat sections of rivers and streams. They ascend to the surface by swimming, during which they are susceptible to trout. Even though small, they make a lot of commotion, easily catching the interest of trout on their way from the streambed to the surface. Pupae attach themselves underneath the water surface, where they are trapped and trout can feed at will. Adult bodies appear in black, gray, red, green, chartreuse, cream, brown. They drift on top of the water for a short distance until their wings dry, and then quickly fly off. Egg layer bodies are black, gray, red, green, chartreuse, cream, and brown. Sometimes mating couples or groups of mating midges may fall onto the surface of the water in clusters of two or more. This is attractive to trout who get more food per mouthful. Sometimes, the midges mate away from the water, and the females return and lay eggs by drifting on the surface and dropping the eggs. A colorful orange egg sack is present on these females. After ovipositing, they drift spent, eventually sinking.

Midge pupae are often the invisible "hatches" when trout are rising in flat water and you don't see any bugs on the surface, just delicate sipping rises. Trout can often be ultraselective about naturals. Matching the size of the natural midge is the first step. The difference between a #24 and a #22 hook may seem small to the angler, but to the trout it is a large difference and perceptible, especially when there are many naturals on the water. After determining the appropriate hook size to match the body, then life stage, color, and shape need to be matched, and finally appropriately presented in front of trout. Naturally we aim to match the other midges in both movement and behavior, namely, a moving bug or a statically dead-drifted bug moving at the same speed and direction of the current.

Sometimes, if a trout rejects the dead-drift presentation, I will present the fly again with a more active presentation and get an induced take from the trout. My standard rig is a 12-to-14-foot monofilament hand-tied dry-fly leader with a 30-inch 7X fluorocarbon tippet. If fish are approaching and rejecting a fly at the last second, it could mean either the fly is correct in other respects but is a size too large, or the fish detects drag. Use a smaller pattern and a better drift. I fish midge pupae by using either a small fly, like a McGee SCS or a Wire Flymph, and fishing a dead-drift nymphing presentation. I let the fly dead drift just under the surface to a rising trout, then make a slow swing with a few short line strips or tugs to animate the fly as it is swinging down and below me, to imitate the pupa swimming up to the surface. I also fish floating pupae with a standard dry-fly presentation to visibly surface-feeding fish. Another way is to drop a soft-hackle midge pupa a few inches off a midge soft-hackle dry fly, or even an ant, to allow the dry fly to suspend the pupa under the surface.

## BLOODWORM LARVA

| | |
|---|---|
| **Hook:** | #18-20 Tiemco 200R |
| **Thread:** | Red 12/0 Benecchi |
| **Body:** | UTC Midge vinyl rib over thread |
| **Thorax:** | Red Hareline Rabbit Dubbin |
| **Hackle:** | Red hen cape |

## MIDGE SPARKLE WORM

| | |
|---|---|
| **Hook:** | #18-20 Tiemco 2487 |
| **Thread:** | Red 12/0 Benecchi |
| **Body:** | Red UTC Midge Sparkle Braid |
| **Thorax:** | ⅝" copper bead |
| **Hackle:** | Bobwhite quail neck feather |

## REFLEX PUPA

**Hook:** #16-22 Dai-Riki #060
**Body:** Black 12/0 Benecchi
**Rib:** Silver Ultra Wire (extra small)
**Thorax:** Caddis green Hareline Ice Dub
**Hackle:** Starling

**Note:** Thread color can be changed to match natural.

## VEILED MIDGE

**Hook:** #14-22 Tiemco 100
**Thread:** Black 12/0 Benecchi
**Body:** Black Hareline Rabbit Touch Dubbing over red Ultra Wire
**Hackle:** Starling

**Note:** For body, dubbing can be applied over small (#14-16) or extra small (18-22) wire. Body variations can be black, gray, yellow, green, chartreuse, white, rusty brown, gold or copper wire body.

## TW PUPA (CHARTREUSE)

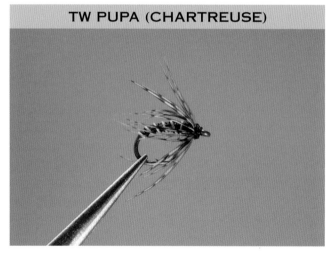

**Hook:** #18-24 Tiemco 2488
**Body:** Black 12/0 Benecchi thread
**Rib:** Fluorescent chartreuse Ultra Wire (extra small)
**Hackle:** Brown partridge

## TW PUPA

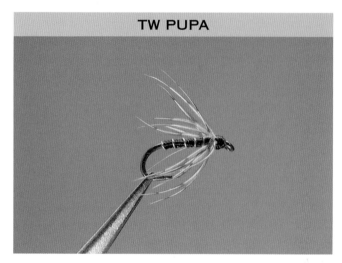

**Hook:** #18-26 Tiemco 100
**Body:** Black 12/0 Benecchi thread
**Rib:** Silver or other color variations Ultra Wire (extra fine)
**Hackle:** Gray partridge

## CONTRAST BRASSIE

**Hook:** #14-18 Mustad S82
**Thread:** Camel 8/0 UNI-Thread
**Abdomen:** Copper and Green Metallic Ultra Wire (small)
**Thorax:** Peacock herl
**Hackle:** Bobwhite quail

## TW PUPA (SILVER)

**Hook:** #18-26 Tiemco 2488
**Body:** Black 12/0 Benecchi thread
**Rib:** Silver or other color variations Ultra Wire (extra small)
**Hackle:** Silver Whiting Badger Hen Cape

## SHUCKED PUPA

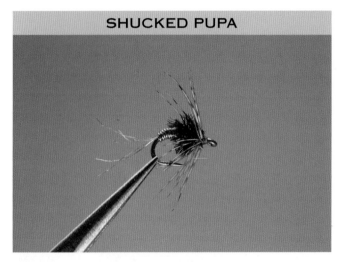

**Hook:** #16-24 Tiemco 2488
**Thread:** Brown 8/0 UNI-Thread
**Shuck:** Amber Z-Lon
**Abdomen:** Copper wire (extra small)
**Thorax:** Peacock
**Hackle:** Brown partridge

## ENGINE MIDGE

**Hook:** #18-22 Dai-Riki #060
**Body:** Camel 8/0 UNI-Thread
**Tail:** Ginger India hen neck
**Abdomen:** Camel 8/0 UNI-Thread
**Thorax:** Chartreuse Hends Body Quill
**Hackle:** Starling
**Head:** Copper bead (#18 ⁵⁄₆₄", #20-22 ¹⁄₁₆")

## BRASSIE SOFT-HACKLE

| | |
|---|---|
| **Hook:** | #14-20 Tiemco 200R |
| **Thread:** | Camel 8/0 UNI-Thread |
| **Abdomen:** | Hot orange Ultra Wire (small) |
| **Thorax:** | Peacock herl |
| **Hackle:** | Brown partridge |

**Note:** Abdomen wire color variations include red metallic, golden olive, amber, fluorescent pink.

## BRASSIE SOFT-HACKLE

| | |
|---|---|
| **Hook:** | #14-22 WR-396 Wet |
| **Thread:** | Tobacco brown 6/0 Danville Flymaster |
| **Abdomen:** | Copper Ultra Wire (small) |
| **Thorax:** | Peacock herl |
| **Hackle:** | Bobwhite quail |

**Note:** Hook can be Mustad R50 Dry, depending on the desired weight.

## THREAD PUPA

| | |
|---|---|
| **Hook:** | #18-26 Tiemco 100 |
| **Body:** | Black 12/0 Benecchi thread |
| **Hackle:** | Starling |

## SUSPENDER MIDGE (SILVER)

| | |
|---|---|
| **Hook:** | #14-24 Tiemco 100 |
| **Body:** | Black 12/0 Benecchi thread |
| **Rib:** | Silver Ultra Wire (extra small) |
| **Thorax:** | Peacock herl |
| **Wing Case and Gills:** | Light dun CDC |
| **Hackle:** | Starling |

## SUSPENDER MIDGE (RED)

| | |
|---|---|
| **Hook:** | #14-24 Tiemco 2488 |
| **Body:** | Black 12/0 Benecchi thread |
| **Rib:** | Red Metallic Ultra Wire (small, #14-16; extra small, #18-24) |
| **Thorax:** | Peacock herl |
| **Wing Case and Gills:** | Light dun CDC |
| **Hackle:** | Starling |

## U-MIDGE

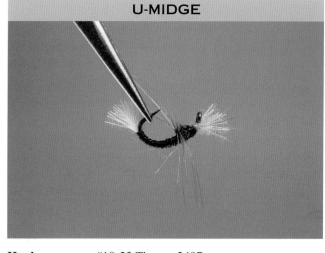

| | |
|---|---|
| **Hook:** | #18-22 Tiemco 2487 |
| **Body:** | Black 8/0 UNI-Thread |
| **Hackle:** | Dun hen cape |
| **Gills:** | White Antron Yarn |

## HI-VIZ PUPA

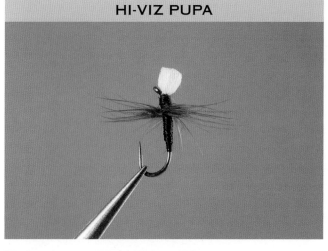

| | |
|---|---|
| **Hook:** | #18-24 Tiemco 100 |
| **Body:** | Black 12/0 Benecchi thread |
| **Hackle:** | Dun hen cape |
| **Post:** | White Foam |

## SURFACE MIDGE

| | |
|---|---|
| **Hook:** | #14-26 Tiemco 100 |
| **Thread:** | Black 12/0 Benecchi |
| **Body:** | Tying thread |
| **Wing:** | Dun CDC |
| **Hackle:** | Dun hen cape |

**Note:** For #14-20 use black Superfine dubbing for the body.

| **SURFACE MIDGE** | **MIDGE SOFT-HACKLE DRY** |
| --- | --- |

| | |
| --- | --- |
| **Hook:** | #18-26 Tiemco 101 |
| **Body:** | Olive 12/0 Benecchi thread |
| **Wing:** | Natural dun CDC puff |
| **Hackle:** | Olive hen cape |

**Note:** Body thread variations include black, cream, gray.

| | |
| --- | --- |
| **Hook:** | #18-26 Tiemco 2488 |
| **Body:** | Black 12/0 Benecchi thread |
| **Wing:** | Dun CDC puff |
| **Hackle:** | Grizzly hen cape |

**Note:** Variations include bodies tied with black, gray, red, green, chartreuse, cream, and brown thread.

A 20-inch Beaverhead River brown trout caught on a #18 Beaverhead Midge. The amazing midge flats right below the Clark Canyon dam can offer terrific sight fishing to large trout rising for egg laying and emerging midges.

# Match-the-Hatch Soft-Hackles: Other Insects and Baitfish

## Dragonfly (Odonata-Aeshnidae)
### East to West, hatches peak mid-July (#4-8)

Nymphs are brownish olive, and associated patterns are the Articulated Soft-Hackle Nymph and Steven Bird's Dragonfly Nymph. These climber-type predatory nymphs live in stillwaters and slow sections of streams and rivers, and are available year round. They mature for three years before becoming adults. Nymphs use water for jet-like propulsion. They are best imitated near the streambed with drifts and foot-long line strips or Figure-8 retrieves with pauses, to imitate the spurts of movement the natural makes.

Wading deep below the Ashton dam on the Henry's Fork of the Snake River.

Dragonfly nymph. MONTANA RIVERBOATS

### BIRD'S DRAGONFLY NYMPH

| | |
|---|---|
| **Hook:** | #4-8 Tiemco 200R |
| **Thread:** | Olive 6/0 Danville |
| **Tail:** | Four strands olive Flashabou, olive mallard flank and yellow-olive grizzly marabou |
| **Rib:** | Chartreuse Metallic Brassie Ultra Wire |
| **Body:** | Peacock herl |
| **Hackle:** | Welsummer Hen palmered midhook shank forward |
| **Front Hackle:** | Olive Whiting Brahma hen saddle |
| **Head:** | Caddis green Superfine with a small amount of pale morning dun dry-fly dubbing |

## Damselfly (Odanata-Zygoptera)
### East to West, hatches peak in July (#8-12)

The nymph has a brown, green, or yellow-green body with three tails. Associated patterns include Soft-Hackle Nymph and Articulated Soft-Hackle Nymph. Predatory nymphs that are available year round, they live in weedy sections of still-waters and slow sections of streams and rivers. The nymphs can swim slowly. They are best imitated near vegetation with dead drifts or slow Figure-8 retrieves with pauses, to imitate the movement the natural makes. Nymphs migrate to shore or structure to emerge as adults out of the water. This migration can cause trout to hold inches under the water, near banks or structure in slow-water habitats, to intercept the migrating nymphs. The adult's body is blue or green with black markings along the abdomen, with three tails. Its associated pattern is the Soft-Hackle Damselfly. Hatches occur on stillwaters and slow-moving sections of streams and rivers. After emergence

on land, the adults live for a few weeks, feeding on mosquitoes and small flies like midges. During this time, they may accidently become trapped on the surface of the water, or be blown in by wind. Trout will rise and feed on them, but this is sporadic. The adults return a few weeks later to lay eggs on the vegetation in which the nymphs live. The egg layers crawl underwater where trout may occasionally intercept them.

A close relative of the dragonfly, damselflies are even more common. While trout occasionally eat the adults, the nymphs are by far the most important life stage for trout food.

### NYMPH

| | |
|---|---|
| **Hook:** | #14-16 Eagle Claw L063 |
| **Thread:** | Tobacco brown 6/0 Danville Flymaster |
| **Tail:** | Brown grizzly marabou |
| **Abdomen:** | Seal brown Hareline Rabbit Dubbin and golden brown Hareline Ice Dub mixture |
| **Thorax:** | Natural Hareline Rabbit Dubbin and golden brown Hareline Ice Dub mixture |
| **Hackle:** | Brown partridge |

### EGG LAYING ADULT

| | |
|---|---|
| **Hook:** | #14-16 Eagle Claw L063 |
| **Thread:** | Black 8/0 UNI-Thread |
| **Abdomen:** | Damsel blue Superfine dry-fly dubbing |
| **Thorax:** | Damsel blue Superfine dry-fly dubbing |
| **Wing:** | Dun Swiss Straw |
| **Hackle:** | Grizzly hen cape marked with BIC Misty Blue |
| **Eye:** | BIC Black Marker |

Cressbug. MONTANA RIVERBOATS

## Cress Bug/Sowbug (Isopoda)
### East to West, year round (#8-18)

Body is light translucent gray with light brown shading. Associated patterns are Soft-Hackle Sow Bug, Soft-Hackle. They live their entire life underwater and are ever present for trout, which often will turn head-down and rout them out of the streambed vegetation where they cling, feed, and grow. They produce multiple broods per year, one every two months, making for a significant population and protein base where they are found.

Sow bugs live mainly on aquatic vegetation like water milfoil and watercress, which supplement their diet as they eat many kinds of organic matter. They are not good swimmers and only become available to trout if dislodged from their habitat, or if trout rout them out from the vegetation. They tend to inhabit high-pH limestone and spring creeks. If you know a particular section or river has them in the vegetation, fishing the run just downstream from the population is often highly effective. Trout will hold in this water, intercepting nymphs and the sow bugs that inevitably get washed into the drift. Though they don't swim and a natural dead-drift presentation is most natural, it's effective every now and then to animate a soft-hackle sow bug when fishing them. First, dead drift the presentation over the vegetation habitat or through the run; then, as the line tightens, give the fly a small rod-tip lift and drop it like a jig—this is the dangle. As the fly begins to swing, let it. Then make a line strip or two at the end of the swing or through the swing. Don't pick up the fly too early; let it hang downstream in the current for a few seconds. Trout often hit a hanging fly. I most commonly fish a #14 or a #16.

### SOFT SOW

| | |
|---|---|
| **Hook:** | #8-18 Mustad S82 |
| **Thread:** | Light Dun 12/0 Benecchi |
| **Tail, Head, Hackle:** | Whiting Grizzly hen saddle |
| **Body:** | Gray Hareline Rabbit Dubbin |
| **Back:** | Sparkle Organza |

**Note:** One side of the feather should be stripped. For body dubbing, add a small amount of gray Hareline UV Ice Dub Mix.

Scud. MONTANA RIVERBOATS

## Scud (Amphipoda)
### East to West, year round (#8-24)

Scuds have different colored bodies, with olive, tan, and gray the most common. They may have translucent shades of green, pink, and blue as they grow after a new molt of their exoskeletons. They may acquire an orange shade, caused by parasites or from built-up fat reserves, and particularly when carrying an orange egg sack. Associated patterns include the Soft-Hackle Scud. Scuds are born from eggs, grow, mate, lay eggs, and die. They live their entire life underwater and are ever present for trout. As they do with sowbugs, trout often will turn head-down and rout them out of the streambed vegetation. They need stable water temperatures and levels, and high pH, as the alkalinity promotes the aquatic vegetation and the crustacean's shell growth. Alkaline spring creeks, limestone streams, and fertile tailwaters tend to be their most common habitats.

Where scuds exist, it is usually in such numbers that they make up the largest macroinvertebrate populations in the trout stream. In turn, they provide trout with a nearly endless food source, available year round. Being freshwater crustaceans (i.e., shrimp), they can fatten trout to sizes of which anglers dream. There are two main species that are important. *Hyalella* (3 to 5 mm) is the less common, and *Gammarus* (10 to 25 mm), the more common and the larger of the two.

Scuds tend to curl up, though not completely, and when they swim, they straighten out the body, so a standard straight-shank nymph hook is also a natural shape. Some may initially think that wrapping a soft-hackle around the hook and tying the fly in the round might not create a natural look, but scuds swim right side up, on their side, and even flipped over, meaning that trout see them from all angles.

Using nymphing tactics, I fish soft-hackle scuds and sowbugs within their habitat of aquatic vegetation and streambed rocks. It's also effective to fish these patterns just below the habitat in the faster chutes and riffles, as the dislodged crustaceans will be swept and directed into these areas. Fish hold in these locations of faster water below slower water, waiting for food to be swept toward them. Sampling the aquatic vegetation in certain stream sections gives the population density, general size, and color to use. Fish them up to 12 inches off the streambed or over the top of aquatic vegetation. Imitate the movement of a dislodged or swimming scud with a dead drift, or swim it with short line strips of 6 to 12 inches. Pause for a couple of seconds between each strip to allow the fly to sink, and then strip, causing the fly to rise and then shoot forward, just like the swimming naturals. Or use a Figure-8 line retrieve. At the end of the drift, let them hang for a second downstream before picking up the line. When scuds are pregnant, the egg sack is held in a pouch on the underside of their thorax. Since their exoskeleton shell is semitranslucent, the bright-orange egg sack is highly visible from the outside. It can be effective to imitate this with an orange hot spot on the thorax. Scuds are also sometimes orange when they develop a parasite that causes the color and results in erratic behavior that puts them into the drift. Still another reason is that they build up fat reserves that cause an orange shade. Also, when scuds die, they often turn an orange color. Sometimes this happens when water levels have dropped, and the scuds get stranded out of the water and die. A good time to fish an orange scud is when the water level rises back up after a good rain, washing scud downstream and back into the flow.

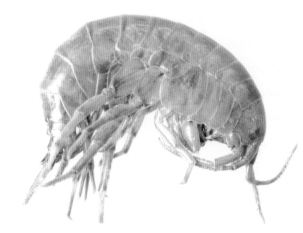

When scuds die, they turn orange due to the high amount of beta-carotene in their body. When alive, the scud matches the habitat in which it's found, as the living color is a masking pigment to protect them from being too visible to predators. Tying scuds with the living color and a hot spot of orange or pink lets the angler match living, pregnant with egg sack, and dying scuds all at the same time. The eye-catching contrast of color is also a feeding trigger for trout.
MONTANA RIVERBOATS

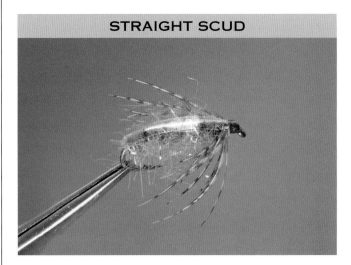

## STRAIGHT SCUD

| | |
|---|---|
| **Hook:** | #14-16 Tiemco 3761 |
| **Thread:** | Iron gray 8/0 UNI-Thread |
| **Body:** | Light gray Hareline Rabbit Dubbin and gray Hareline UV Ice Dub |
| **Thorax:** | Shrimp pink Hareline UV Ice Dub |
| **Rib:** | Black 6/0 Danville Flymaster |
| **Hackle:** | Gray partridge |
| **Back:** | Ziploc Bag Strip |

**Note:** Straight-shank hooks imitate the longer outstretched body when scuds swim. Scuds curl up when resting, but are often straight and extended when in the drift.

## PREGNANT SCUD

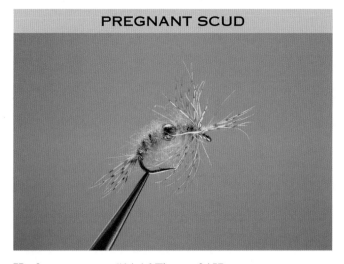

| | |
|---|---|
| **Hook:** | #14-16 Tiemco 2457 |
| **Thread:** | Black 12/0 Benecchi |
| **Tail, Antennae,** | |
| **Hackle:** | Gray partridge |
| **Rib:** | Black Ultra Wire (small) |
| **Body:** | Light gray Hareline Rabbit Dubbin and a small amount of gray Orvis Hare' E Ice Dub mixture |
| **Thorax:** | Sulphur orange Nature's Spirit Hare's Mask Dubbing with an Orange bead, ³⁄₃₂" (#14) or ⁵⁄₆₄" (#16) in the middle |

## HENRY'S FORK SCUD

| | |
|---|---|
| **Hook:** | #14-16 Tiemco 2487 |
| **Thread:** | Black 12/0 Benecchi |
| **Tail and Antennae:** | Grizzly hen cape |
| **Body:** | Gray Hareline Rabbit Dubbin mixed with gray Orvis Hare' E Ice Dub |
| **Thorax:** | Silver bead, ³⁄₃₂" (#14), ⁵⁄₆₄" (#16) |
| **Hackle:** | Gray partridge |

## RED BALLER SCUD

| | |
|---|---|
| **Hook:** | #14-16 Tiemco 2487 |
| **Thread:** | Light dun 12/0 Benecchi |
| **Tail and Antennae:** | Grizzly hen cape |
| **Abdomen:** | Hareline Gray Rabbit Dubbin |
| **Rib:** | Black Coats and Clark #0002 thread |
| **Thorax:** | Red bead, ³⁄₃₂" (#14), ⁵⁄₆₄" (#16) |
| **Hackle:** | Gray partridge |

**Note:** For abdomen, add chopped up Orvis Hare' E Ice Dub Hare's Ear mixture.

## HOT SPOT SCUD

| | |
|---|---|
| **Hook:** | #14 Tiemco 2487 |
| **Thread:** | Light Dun 12/0 Benecchi |
| **Abdomen:** | Orvis Hare' E Ice Dub Hare's Ear |
| **Rib:** | Black 6/0 Danville Flymaster |
| **Thorax:** | Orange bead, ³⁄₃₂" |
| **Hackle:** | Gray partridge |

## DEAD SCUD

**Hook:**             #14 Tiemco 2487
**Thread:**        Orange 6/0 Danville Flymaster
**Body:**           Amber Hareline Rabbit Dubbin and yellow
                            Wapsi Antron dubbing mixture
**Rib:**               Coffee 6/0 Danville Flymaster
**Hackle:**        Bleached partridge

**Note:** For body dubbing, pick out with bodkin after ribbing.

## KILPATRICK SCUD

**Hook:**                     #14 Tiemco 2487
**Thread:**               Light dun 12/0 Benecchi
**Tail and Antennae:**   Grizzly hen cape
**Body:**                  Hareline Gray Rabbit Dubbin and
                            blue #11 Spectra Dubbing mixture
**Rib:**                       Black 6/0 Danville Flymaster
**Hackle:**                Gray partridge

# SOFT-HACKLE TERRESTRIALS

Trout relish terrestrials, but maximum success requires fishing them correctly at the right time and place. These insects usually find themselves on the water by accident, having fallen in off the bank. Fishing wet terrestrials is an underfished method. Ants, flying ants, grasshoppers, crickets, beetles—any insect that gets blown into the stream or lands there will float for a while, but eventually they sink. Trout feed on sunken terrestrials as voraciously as they do on the surface bugs; I dare say more. Also fish them during hatches; sometimes they are one way to make your fly stand out, increasing the odds of a fish eating your artificial when there are a lot of naturals on the water.

## Ant (Formicidae)
### East to West, spring through fall (#10-16)

The ant's body is black, black and red, orange, or rusty brown. Associated patterns are the Soft-Hackle Dry and the Wet Ant. The flying ant, with black body and amber wings, has its own dedicated patterns, the Soft-Hackle Flying Ant and Wet Flying Ant. Individual ants either fall into or are blown onto the water near banks. Flying ants can cover the water anywhere, bank to bank. There are two types of flying ants: alates, which are reproductive male ants, and queen ants. When new queens are born in a colony, they leave in a migration flight to establish new colonies. The mating swarms of many species often take place over water, as they are attracted to light sources, in this case the light reflected off the water. After mating, males frequently fall onto the water in large quantities. Effective presentations include Surface or Subsurface Dead Drift.

    Ants are the most numerous of all insects, and trout relish them. Perhaps it's for their taste, but if trout see an ant land, the trout will likely eat it sooner rather than later. I have witnessed some of the best surface fishing in the summer when a population of flying ants ends up on the water. The floating ants create what amounts to a hatch, and trout rise to them with intent. It's one of those onstream experiences that imprint themselves on your mind and stick with you throughout your angling lifetime. A "hatch" of flying ants is that important, and you will always be waiting and ready for the next time it happens.

At first it can be difficult to understand to what the trout are rising. If you look closely at the water surface, you can notice the flying ants drifting here and there. If you see winged ants on the surface, tie on an imitation and start presenting it with wet/dry-fly tactics. Chances are that fish will eat the fly. Many people think of fishing ants only on the surface, but ants will sink eventually if not eaten by trout. I have found a Wet Ant to be one of the most effective subsurface flies. I use it as a prospecting pattern, and fish it through likely holding lies, dead drift like a nymph or wet fly. These work especially well on smaller meadow streams that have a lot of ants falling in from the streambank grasses. On windy streams, it may be more effective to concentrate on the banks on the side from which the wind is blowing, as streamside insects will get blown into the water here. Trout will lie in wait for these terrestrials, both those floating on the surface and those that have sunk. Many years ago, I wrote a letter with a self-addressed stamped envelope enclosed to George Harvey. One of the questions I asked him was what fly he had caught the most fish on in his life. When I received my letter back, his answer, written under my question read "a black ant!" Enough said.

A soft-hackle flying ant pattern can imitate both male flying ants (seen here) and parasitic wasps when they are found drifting on the water surface, as well as when they eventually sink. Sparkle Organza is a great imitation of the clear, yet highly visible and reflective wing.

### FLYING ANT

| | |
|---|---|
| **Hook:** | #16-18 Tiemco 100 |
| **Thread:** | Black 8/0 UNI-Thread |
| **Body:** | Black Superfine dry dubbing |
| **Wing:** | Sparkle Organza |
| **Hackle:** | Black hen cape |

### DRY/WET ANT

| | |
|---|---|
| **Hook:** | #12-18 Eagle Claw L059 |
| **Post:** | White Antron Yarn |
| **Abdomen Thread:** | Black 8/0 UNI-Thread |
| **Thorax Thread:** | Tan 8/0 Orvis |
| **Abdomen:** | Black Superfine dry dubbing, black foam back |
| **Hackle:** | Rusty brown India hen neck |
| **Thorax:** | Cinnamon Superfine Caddis dry-fly dubbing |

**Note:** For thorax, orange foam should be tied in, then cut and split, pulled around the post, and tied down in front of the post.

## DRY/WET ANT

**Hook:** #12-18 Tiemco 100
**Thread:** Rusty brown 70-denier Ultra Thread
**Abdomen**
**and Thorax:** Rusty brown Superfine dry-fly dubbing
**Hackle:** Welsummer hen saddle

## WET FLYING ANT

**Hook:** #14-18 Eagle Claw L063
**Thread:** Black 8/0 UNI-Thread
**Abdomen**
**and Thorax:** Tying thread built up, then black
Loon Hard Head
**Wing:** Sparkle Organza
**Hackle:** Black hen cape

**Note:** First build body, let dry, then tie in wing and hackle. For abdomen and thorax, alternative colors are red, orange, or combinations of these.

## WET ANT

**Hook:** #14-18 Eagle Claw L063
**Thread:** Red 12/0 Benecchi
**Abdomen**
**and Thorax:** Tying thread built up, then red Holographic
Tinsel
**Hackle:** Rusty brown India hen neck

**Note:** Tinsel is wrapped over thread, then a few coats of clear loon hard head are built up over abdomen and thorax. Rotate in the vise to create an even distribution of the epoxy. Color variations are black, orange, black/orange, black/red.

Even in the chilly early season, trout still will eat ants, in this case, a hard-body sunken wet ant fished upstream.

MY IMAGES-MICHA/SHUTTERSTOCK.COM

## Beetle (Coleoptera)
### East to West, spring through fall (#12-18)

The terrestrial beetle has long been known as an important summer source of trout food. On forested and meadow streams, trout relish these insects, and the floating dry beetle can be used as a searching pattern, and even during a hatch. Trout will frequently take a properly presented beetle. If a fish does not take the beetle on the surface, it will eventually sink. Fishing a sunken beetle is often overlooked, but can be rewarding. Try using beetles during the midday lull when nothing is rising on spring creeks, drifted over or deeply through the undercut banks of the deeper S-curves of a stream, and along its banks. They also can work to select trout during a hatch. Also, try a beetle/soft-hackle dropper searching combo in meadow streams along the bank.

### SUNKEN BEETLE

| | |
|---|---|
| **Hook:** | #12-18 Mustad S82 |
| **Thread:** | Black 8/0 UNI-Thread |
| **Body:** | Fluorescent chartreuse Ultra Wire |
| **Hackle:** | Black Woolly Bugger marabou |

**Note:** The Ultra Wire should be under a lightly dubbed black Hareline Rabbit Dubbin and caddis green Hareline Ice Dub mixture.

### DRY/WET BEETLE

| | |
|---|---|
| **Hook:** | #12-18 Mustad R50 |
| **Thread:** | Black 8/0 UNI-Thread |
| **Body:** | Black Hareline Rabbit Dubbin |
| **Rib:** | Black ostrich herl |
| **Legs:** | Black ostrich herl |
| **Hackle:** | Black hen cape |
| **Antennae:** | Fibers from hackle collar |

**Note:** Apply floatant to hackle and legs for a surface presentation. Antennae fibers should be pulled forward and whip finished under the head.

## Grasshopper (Orthoptera)
### East to West, July through early October (#8-12)

These are often blown or fall into the stream from bankside vegetation, or fly over the water. Grasshoppers are a favorite food source for trout, and an exciting way for fishermen to fish in late summer on meadow-stream stretches with tall grasses lining the banks. The insects may be blown by the wind or accidently jump into the water. As with other terrestrials, fishing the banks nearest the direction of the wind will often result in the most fish, as this is where terrestrial insects find themselves blown into the stream. If there is a good population, trout will hold on this bank in anticipation. When the insects do find their way into the water, they "plop," usually near the bank and loud enough that trout hear them, like the dinner bell. When you fish hoppers, it's important for them to hit the water hard enough to make the noise. Also, the natural doesn't stop moving once it lands on the water. It will struggle and move clumsily about on the surface. Often, I'll be on the lookout when I'm walking to the river through meadows to fish. If I see a hopper or two on the tall grass, I know what to prospect with. Also, don't forget about the hopper/dropper. Tie a 12- to 24-inch section of 5X off the hook bend of the point hopper, and attach a soft-hackle nymph, ant, or even a wet hopper. In addition to a single fly, a deadly combo is a #12 Soft-Hackle Dry Hopper, with a fly like a #16 bead thorax Pheasant Tail Soft-Hackle Nymph dropped off the hook bend. It covers both terrestrials and nymphs, two enticing insects, in a single presentation.

The "hopper banks" are the grassy banks on open-meadow streams that will have the wind blowing from behind them onto the stream. On particular rivers, this will be blowing hoppers onto the water, and you want to imitate the "splat" they make. You will be casting into the bank, and thus into the wind. If there is a strong wind, shorten the leader down to about 8 feet and use a 4X tippet. Make a sidearm cast low over the water to find the lowest wind resistance, and check the rod by stopping it abruptly at the end of the forward cast, even giving it a little pull back to shock the leader and cause the hopper to drop with a thud onto the water surface.

There's a special hopper technique that is used on the Henry's Fork. It's called "Walking the Dog." It's a way to get a long drift of the hopper down the streambank. First, make the shock cast into the bank from mid-river with a dry-fly reach cast, pulling back when the line straightens, to drop the fly onto the water. Then, walk downstream parallel to the fly, at the same speed as the current. This works on shallow rivers with a flat bottom and no obstacles. You can get long drifts this way, and cover a lot of water without drag.

Grasshoppers that aren't eaten by fish when they are floating will soon sink. They are then available as subsurface food, and while these feedings may go unnoticed by anglers, they don't by trout! The Soft-Hackle Grasshopper is a dry/wet fly. It can be fished exclusively dry on the surface, wet subsurface, or both.

Try fishing the Soft-Hackle Grasshopper as a dry, then as a sunken hopper near the bank. Slowly swing it away from the bank into the middle of the stream, in front of any trout holding near the banks, or center-middle channel. A grasshopper right in front of the fish under the surface will tempt it into striking. It's simply irresistible.

To further enhance the grasshopper, make short skitters by twitching the rod tip or small line strips throughout the presentation; but first try it dead drift/dead swing. Try to think like the bug and send the urgency it feels to your fly. Trout love a helpless insect, and a big one is even better. Finally, sometimes the best hopper success comes by using a smaller fly. My favorite hopper is a size 12.

## SOFT-HACKLE GRASSHOPPER

| | |
|---|---|
| **Hook:** | #8-12 Mustad R50 |
| **Thread:** | Light olive 6/0 Danville Flymaster |
| **Body:** | Insect green Hareline Rabbit Dubbin |
| **Rib:** | Spice Coats and Clark #8150 Thread |
| **Wing:** | Coastal deer |
| **Legs:** | Four pheasant tail fibers |
| **Hackle:** | Olive partridge |
| **Head:** | Two tan ostrich herls |

**Note:** Pheasant tail fibers should be jointed with an overhand knot on each side of the hook.

## BAITFISH

Baitfish.

### Baitfish
#### East to West, year round (#2-14)

All trout species can potentially be cannibalistic, either out of hunger or territorialism. Winter and early spring, or in the weeks before spawning, are especially good times to fish streamers, because fish will strike out of sheer territoriality. An effective trick in fishing them is to make the trout think the fly is an injured fish trying to escape. An injured minnow would not try to swim upstream against the current to escape a trout. It would likely take the path of least resistance and try to swim with the current. So, instead of casting across and downstream, and stripping the fly back upstream, use a strip-and-mend presentation. This injured behavior can also be imitated with lifting and dropping of the fly, or drifting across and downstream or with a soft-hackle jig presentation. Try to give the streamer a broadside presentation to the trout. You can present the streamer broadside by mending the line as the streamer drifts downstream. I like to cast upstream of the target and make a mend to let the fly sink. After the fly drifts across stream from me and starts to drift below me, I start a series of mends and strips to keep the fly drifting broadside as long as possible. Whether deep or shallow, streamers need to be right in front of the fish. Trout hold facing into the current, even if it's reverse current. An example is in an eddy, where it looks like the fish are facing downstream, but are actually facing into the water flow from their perspective. Trout like to attack smaller fish by going for the head.

Baitfish can be imitated with streamers anytime of the year. Some periods are better than others, such as early spring for prespawning rainbows and cutthroats, and fall for pre-spawning brook and brown trout, when these fish more aggressively defend their territory, and their hormone levels are raised. Also, streamers are good in the winter when trout are lethargic from a low metabolism and not actively feeding, yet still territorial enough to strike. Other good conditions are during higher water after a rain in freestone streams, at night when larger brown trout feed, or when large trout are spotted holding deep in prime lies.

The fact is that streamers are anytime-anywhere flies that can work to trigger fish to strike. Soft-hackle streamers are the best, because they have constant movement like a fish. When fishing streamers to imitate baitfish, the most important consideration is first to get your fly in front of the trout, at whatever depth they are holding. Sometimes that means on the streambed, and this takes either mends or weight, but a combination of both is best. Trout look for an easy meal, and while baitfish are a large source of protein, they can be difficult to catch. For this reason, trout will often ambush them or lie in wait until the baitfish swims too close. Brown trout over 14 inches rely on other trout and baitfish for their protein requirements. As they get even larger, they turn their attention more and more to a fish-based diet. Other trout species don't have such cannibalistic tendencies, but all trout species will eat baitfish and, in turn, streamers if presented where they are holding, at the right time and in the right way. Choosing the size streamer and color means either picking one that imitates a natural fish found in the stream, or basing the choice on general attractor characteristics like color and flash. Another consideration is water turbidity that affects the ability of trout to see prey. A dark-colored fly will not be as visible as one with flash materials or brighter colors, especially white.

Another way to make the baitfish streamer more appealing and visible is to incorporate an acoustic element in the design and character of the fly. Trout use not only their eyes to find food sources, but also their sense of sound. By using their inner ears and lateral lines, they can both hear as we do, and feel the vibration in their body as sound waves travel through the water and vibrate against their lateral line. They use their lateral line not only to sense the sound, but also to locate the direction, and thus the source. The Acoustic Streamer is one such fly. It uses two large beads that can freely slide across the length of the hook shank, with stops on each end. When the beads slide into each other or the lead wire ends, they make a tapping noise. As the fly drifts or is stripped, the combinations of the currents and the retrieve causes the beads to slide and produce the noise. It's another tool in the arsenal of the tier and the angler, to help get the attention of the fish to our fly, and entice them to strike.

In some streams, sculpins can be an important food source for trout. They are found living between rocks on the streambed. These fish are fast and have a darting movement. A proper presentation would be strip, pause, strip near the streambed, over rocks, and in the tailouts of pools. After making your cast, stack mending or hump mending will allow the fly to sink to depth, before either dead drifting the fly or imparting a strip-and-pause retrieve, a jig. To imitate sculpins, fish olive and brown Chickabou Wolf streamers. Always keep some contact with the fly, as trout will hit these hard, as they have to do when chasing the speedy naturals.

**BLOODY SHINER**

| | |
|---|---|
| **Hook:** | #8-14 Tiemco 5262 (eye straightened) |
| **Thread:** | Black 6/0 Danville Flymaster |
| **Tail:** | March Brown Whiting Brahma Hen chickabou |
| **Body:** | Caddis green Hareline Ice Dub |
| **Rib:** | White ostrich herl |
| **Lateral Lines:** | Red Krystal Flash |
| **Hackle:** | Red hen cape behind March Brown Whiting Brahma hen saddle |

**Note:** Mark the ostrich herl with Prismacolor Goldenrod, then the middle stem with black.

## CHICKABOU COYOTE

| | |
|---|---|
| **Hook:** | #10 Eagle Claw L055 |
| **Thread:** | Light olive 8/0 UNI-Thread |
| **Body:** | Olive Hareline grizzly marabou |
| **Head:** | Gold bead, 1/8" |

## CHICKABOU WOLF

| | |
|---|---|
| **Hook:** | #10 Tiemco 2457 |
| **Thread:** | Wood duck 70-denier Ultra Thread |
| **Body:** | Brown Hareline grizzly marabou |
| **Eyes:** | Gold Fly Eyes, 1/8" |

## BIG SKY PERCH

| | |
|---|---|
| **Hook:** | #10 Tiemco 5262 |
| **Thread:** | Camel 8/0 UNI-Thread |
| ***Rear Hook:*** | |
| **Tail:** | Brown Woolly Bugger marabou |
| **Lateral Line:** | Copper Holographic Tinsel |
| **Body:** | Rusty Hareline Rabbit and golden brown Ice Dub mixture |
| **Hackle:** | Olive Woolly Bugger marabou |
| ***Front Hook:*** | |
| **Connection:** | .010 Monofilament Loop |
| **Body:** | Rusty Hareline Rabbit and golden brown Ice Dub mixture |
| **Lateral Line:** | Copper Holographic Tinsel |
| **Hackle:** | Brown Woolly Bugger marabou |
| **Eyes:** | 7/32" Gold Fly Eyes with dubbing wrapped between |
| **Head Hackle:** | Brown partridge |

**Note:** Rear Hook Hackle should have marabou wrapped, then a lateral line of copper Holographic Tinsel, and then at the front brown Woolly Bugger marabou.

## SILVER FOX

| | |
|---|---|
| **Hook:** | #10 Tiemco 5262 |
| **Thread:** | Tobacco brown 6/0 Danville Flymaster |
| **Body and** | |
| **Lateral Line:** | Red Holographic Tinsel |
| **Rib:** | Silver Ultra Wire (small) |
| **Hackle:** | White Woolly Bugger marabou |
| **Front Hackle:** | Gray partridge |
| **Head:** | Silver bead, ⅛" |

**Note:** Marabou is wound around hook shank.

## ACOUSTIC STREAMER

| | |
|---|---|
| **Hook:** | #8-12 Mustad R73 |
| **Thread:** | Coffee 6/0 Danville Flymaster |
| **Beads:** | Two ⁵⁄₃₂" gold beads |
| **Bead Stops:** | .015 lead-free wire |
| **Lateral Lines:** | Copper Holographic Tinsel |
| **Hackle:** | Two golden brown grizzly marabou feathers |
| **Head:** | Golden brown grizzly marabou aftershaft feather wound as a collar |

**Note:** Gold beads face inward toward each other. For bead stops, wire is attached with thread, one at the bend and one at the thorax. One strand of tinsel goes on each side of the hook. Hackle feather stem tips are cut out and tied in and spun around the hook facing toward the bend. Then use one of the aftershaft feathers to wind a hackle collar head. The two beads will knock against each other and the bead stops, creating acoustical vibration in the water.

The King's River flows through the Wicklow Mountains of Ireland. The trout here are not selective, but they are ultraspooky. I like to fish here with an upstream presentation, using a soft-hackle dry and an 8-inch wet-fly dropper off the dry. Soft-hackle dry flies make excellent indicator flies as well as depth suspenders for a wet fly dropper.

# *Modern Prospecting Soft-Hackle Flies*

When I tie and pick soft-hackle flies to fish, I think of each pattern as either a prospecting, generic yet buggy looking fly or a match-the-hatch pattern designed to imitate a specific trout-food species and life stage. This book divides the flies into these two general categories for the sake of organization and approach to imitating, tying, presenting, and organizing patterns in your fly box. I separate the design into these groups to allow me to instantly recognize and choose flies as necessary onstream. The flies in this chapter are prospecting nymphs, flymphs, wet flies and dry/wet flies that are fished with nymphing techniques, wet-fly techniques, or dry-fly presentations, depending on

the category. I use these patterns when trout are not rising or keying in on an obvious insect.

When I'm nymphing in water and fish are not rising, I choose flies that will allow me to search the water efficiently and thoroughly with prospect nymphing. First, I take into consideration where I think trout may be holding, and at what depth. Along with the speed of water and its turbidity, all of these considerations go into choosing one, two, or three flies to fish on a leader. I usually begin with a point fly that is weighted enough to reach the streambed. This may be augmented with split shot on the tippet, about 4 to 18 inches up from the point fly, depending on how low to the streambed I

Hooked up on the Big Wood River, Ketchum, Idaho. The Ernest Hemingway house is on the hill.

When prospect nymphing during a nonhatch situation, I often use two or three flies to show fish different options, and also fish in different water-column depths.

want the fly to ride. My dropper flies would then usually become progressively lighter up the leader. This is a multilevel fly rig. If the fish are holding near the surface, visibly rising, or in low water, I will fish one or more unweighted flies. Also, getting strikes only on the top dropper indicates trout feeding just under the surface.

Prospect nymphing really is covering the likely trout lies thoroughly in the most efficient manner. If you are catching all the fish at a certain depth, whether deep or shallow, you could remove the other weighted flies and target that depth alone for as long as you keep catching. If the water is turbid and stained, I try to fish more visible flies like white, chartreuse, or light gray colors. Bead thorax and bead-head flies also are good in stained and turbid water. I often use bead flies for point flies in deep water, as they will sink deep and reflect flash better in low-light environments on the bottom of the stream. If the water is clear or shallow, I like to use more naturally colored nymphs like brown or olive, perhaps with a hot spot on one fly. This gives fish a choice, and while they might not strike the bright fly, it gets their attention and they hit one more muted. Some of the intense colors of the naturals may surprise you, such as orange mayfly nymphs (PMDs) or bright green caddis larvae.

# BEAD HEAD NYMPHS

## REDNECK SWINDLER

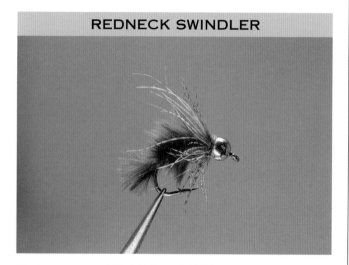

| Hook: | #10-16 Mustad C49S |
|---|---|
| Thread: | Tobacco brown 6/0 Danville Flymaster |
| Brown: | Brown marabou |
| Hackle: | Gray partridge |
| Head: | Gold bead |

**Note:** Follow these bead size rules for other bead-head flies: ⅛" (#10), ³⁄₃₂" (#12-14), ⁵⁄₆₄" (#16).

## RUBY NYMPH

| Hook: | #10-16 Mustad S82 |
|---|---|
| Thread: | Tobacco brown 6/0 Danville Flymaster |
| Tail: | March Brown Whiting Brahma base fibers |
| Abdomen: | Rusty Hareline Rabbit Dubbin |
| Rib and Thorax: | Peacock herl |
| Hackle: | March Brown Whiting Brahma hen saddle |
| Head: | Copper bead |

## FANTAIL NYMPH

| Hook: | #10-14 Mustad S82 (shown) or |
|---|---|
| Thread: | Tobacco brown 6/0 Danville Flymaster |
| Tail: | Brown Whiting Brahma hen chickabou aftershaft feather |
| Abdomen: | Copper Ultra Wire (small) |
| Thorax: | Olive grizzly hen cape |
| Hackle: | Brown Brahma Hen chickabou |
| Head: | Copper bead |

**Note:** Alternative hook is Tiemco 5262 for a longer appearance.

## INSPIRATION NYMPH

| | |
|---|---|
| **Hook:** | #12-16 Mustad S82 |
| **Thread:** | Olive 8/0 UNI-Thread |
| **Tail:** | Bleached partridge |
| **Abdomen:** | Yellow Danville rayon floss |
| **Rib:** | Copper Micro Tinsel |
| **Thorax:** | Caddis green Hareline Ice Dub |
| **Hackle:** | Bleached partridge in back of olive hen cape |
| **Head:** | Gold bead |

## LIBERTY NYMPH

| | |
|---|---|
| **Hook:** | #12-16 Eagle Claw L063S (straighten eye) |
| **Thread:** | Fluorescent blue 6/0 Danville Flymaster |
| **Tail:** | Sparkle Organza |
| **Tag:** | Red Holographic Tinsel |
| **Abdomen:** | Blue Holographic Tinsel |
| **Rib:** | Silver Ultra Wire (small) |
| **Thorax:** | Bluish-gray Hends #11 Spectra Dubbing |
| **Hackle:** | Gray partridge behind red hen cape or red ostrich herl |
| **Head:** | Glass bead 3.2 mm (#12), 2.4 mm (#14), 2.0 mm (#16) |

## NEW WESTERN NYMPH

| | |
|---|---|
| **Hook:** | #12-16 Tiemco 5262 |
| **Thread:** | Tobacco brown 6/0 Danvill Flymaster |
| **Tail:** | Bleached partridge feather base fibers |
| **Abdomen:** | Tan Orvis Spectrablend Nymph |
| **Rib:** | Fluorescent orange Ultra Wire (small) |
| **Thorax:** | Reddish brown Hare's Ear Plus |
| **Hackle:** | Bleached partridge |
| **Head:** | Copper bead (optional) |

**Note:** Bead size corresponding to hook size: ⅛" (#12), ³⁄₃₂" (#14), ⁵⁄₆₄" (#16).

## GOLD PROSPECTOR

| | |
|---|---|
| **Hook:** | #12-16 Tiemco 3761 |
| **Thread:** | Light olive 8/0 UNI-Thread |
| **Tail:** | Yellow grizzly marabou |
| **Abdomen:** | Hot yellow Ultra Wire (small) |
| **Thorax:** | Brown grizzly hen cape |
| **Hackle:** | Yellow grizzly marabou |
| **Head:** | Gold bead |

## PANTHER PUPA

| | |
|---|---|
| **Hook:** | #10-16 Mustad C49S |
| **Thread:** | Black 8/0 UNI-Thread |
| **Abdomen:** | Green Holographic Tinsel and chartreuse wire |
| **Thorax:** | Black Hareline Rabbit Dubbin and Wapsi black UV Ice Dub Mix |
| **Antennae:** | Olive mallard flank |
| **Hackle:** | Green Woolly Bugger marabou |
| **Thorax:** | Olive and black ostrich herl |
| **Head:** | Black bead |

**Note:** Abdomen tinsel and wire should be under black marker edged Scud Back. Ostrich herl should have one side marked black, the other olive.

## CASTLE NYMPH

| | |
|---|---|
| **Hook:** | #12-16 Eagle Claw L063S |
| **Thread:** | Tobacco brown 6/0 Danville Flymaster |
| **Tail:** | Sand Wapsi blood marabou |
| **Abdomen:** | Copper Ultra Wire (small) |
| **Thorax:** | Brown Hareline Rabbit Dubbin and rusty brown Ice Dub mix |
| **Hackle:** | Ginger hen saddle behind tan CDC |
| **Head:** | Gold bead |

## BARKER'S *BAETIS*

| | |
|---|---|
| **Hook:** | #18 Tiemco 3761 |
| **Thread:** | Black 12/0 Benecchi |
| **Tail:** | Coq De Leon |
| **Abdomen:** | Black thread |
| **Rib:** | Chartreuse Hends Body Quill over chartreuse Ultra Wire (extra small) |
| **Hackle:** | Purple starling |
| **Head:** | Silver tungsten or regular bead, depending on the desired sink rate |

## GNEISS CREEK NYMPH

| | |
|---|---|
| **Hook:** | #12-16 Tiemco 3761 |
| **Thread:** | Black 12/0 Benecchi |
| **Tail:** | Black blood marabou |
| **Abdomen:** | Green Hareline Ice Dub |
| **Thorax:** | Peacock Hareline Ice Dub |
| **Hackle:** | Gray partridge |
| **Head:** | Copper bead |

# BEAD THORAX NYMPHS

## CODY PEAK NYMPH

| | |
|---|---|
| **Hook:** | #12-16 Tiemco 5262 |
| **Thread:** | Tobacco brown 6/0 Danville Flymaster |
| **Tail and Abdomen:** | Bleached pheasant tail (shown) or bleached peacock herl |
| **Rib:** | Copper Ultra Wire (small) |
| **Thorax:** | Light olive Hends #89 Spectra Dubbing and copper bead |
| **Hackle:** | Light brown partridge |

**Note:** Use these bead sizes for the corresponding fly sizes: ⅛" (#12), ³⁄₃₂" (#14), ⁵⁄₆₄" (#16-20).

## GRIZZLY NYMPH

| | |
|---|---|
| **Hook:** | #12-14 Tiemco 5262 |
| **Thread:** | Tobacco brown 6/0 Danville Flymaster |
| **Tail:** | Brahma aftershaft wound hackle collar |
| **Abdomen:** | March Brown Hareline Rabbit Dubbin |
| **Rib:** | Brown ostrich |
| **Thorax:** | Copper glass bead |
| **Hackle:** | March Brown Whiting Brahma hen saddle |
| **Head:** | Brown ostrich |

**Note:** For thorax, use following bead sizes with corresponding hook size: 3.2 mm (#12), 2.4 mm (#14), 2.0 mm (#16).

## CASHEL NYMPH

| | |
|---|---|
| **Hook:** | #12-16 Mustad S82 |
| **Thread:** | Tobacco brown 6/0 Danville Flymaster |
| **Shuck:** | Golden brown Hareline Ice Dub |
| **Abdomen:** | Midge vinyl rib over green Flashabou |
| **Thorax:** | Brown ostrich and gold bead |
| **Hackle** | Gray partridge |

## THE CHIEFTAIN

| | |
|---|---|
| **Hook:** | #12-16 Mustad S82 |
| **Thread:** | Orange 6/0 Danville Flymaster |
| **Abdomen and Tail:** | Ginger Woolly Bugger marabou |
| **Thorax:** | Nickel bead |
| **Hackle:** | Brown partridge |

**Note:** For hackle, lower back is tied with compensation method.

## FUZZY HORNED NYMPH

**Hook:** #12-18 Eagle Claw L063S
**Thread:** Tobacco brown 6/0 Danville Flymaster
**Tail, Hackle**
**and Antennae:** Light brown partridge
**Abdomen:** Light orange rabbit and Hends #98 Orange Spectra dubbing mixture
**Thorax:** Copper bead

## GENERAL NYMPH

**Hook:** #10-20 Tiemco 200R
**Thread:** Tobacco brown 6/0 Danville Flymaster
**Tail:** Brown partridge
**Abdomen:** Copper Wire (small)
**Thorax:** Light olive Hareline UV Ice Dub behind a copper bead
**Hackle:** Brownish gray partridge hackle

**Note:** For thorax, use bead sizes corresponding to hook sizes: 1/8" (#10-12), 3/32" (#14), 5/64" (#16-20).

## DEEP GREEN HOLOGRAPHIC NYMPH

**Hook:** #12-18 Eagle Claw L063S
**Thread:** Olive 12/0 Benecchi
**Tail and Hackle:** Light brown partridge
**Abdomen:** Olive Hareline Rabbit Touch Dubbing and green Holographic Tinsel
**Thorax:** Copper bead

**Note:** Abdomen touch dubbing over tinsel.

## FOUNTAIN NYMPH

**Hook:** #12-16 Mustad S82
**Thread:** Tobacco brown 6/0 Danville Flymaster
**Abdomen:** Hareline Light Hare's Ear Plus
**Thorax:** Orange Orvis Hare' E Ice Dub and gold bead
**Hackle:** Gray partridge
**Head:** White ostrich

## COMPLEX SPIDER

| | |
|---|---|
| **Hook:** | #12-16 Tiemco 3761 |
| **Thread:** | Tobacco brown 6/0 Danville Flymaster |
| **Tag:** | Copper Holographic Tinsel |
| **Abdomen:** | Light hare's mask dubbing |
| **Rib:** | Copper Ultra Wire (small) |
| **Thorax:** | Orange Orvis Hare' E Ice Dub and gold bead |
| **Hackle:** | Brown partridge |

## SUNFLAIR NYMPH

| | |
|---|---|
| **Hook:** | #12-16 Mustad S82 |
| **Thread:** | Orange 6/0 Danville Flymaster |
| **Tag:** | Sulphur Orange Nature's Spirit Hare's Mask Dubbing |
| **Body:** | Nature's Spirit Hare's Mask Dubbing |
| **Thorax:** | Gold bead |
| **Hackle:** | Natural Brahma Hen Cape colored with Prismacolor Sunburst Yellow. |

## GREAT HORNED NYMPH

| | |
|---|---|
| **Hook:** | #12-15 WR-396 |
| **Thread:** | Tobacco brown 6/0 Danville Flymaster |
| **Shuck:** | Ginger Wapsi Antron Dubbing |
| **Abdomen:** | Pheasant tail |
| **Rib:** | Copper Ultra Wire (small) |
| **Thorax:** | Copper bead |
| **Hackle and Antennae:** | Gray partridge |

**Note:** Partridge feather should include soft base fibers. Pull two fibers forward for antennae.

## CONTINENTAL NYMPH

| | |
|---|---|
| **Hook:** | #10-18 Eagle Claw L063S |
| **Thread:** | Tobacco brown 6/0 Danville Flymaster |
| **Abdomen:** | Bleached peacock herl |
| **Rib:** | Copper Ultra Wire (small) |
| **Thorax:** | Gold bead |
| **Hackle:** | Gray partridge |

## RED ROCK NYMPH

| | |
|---|---|
| **Hook:** | #10-18 Mustad S82 |
| **Thread:** | Tobacco brown 6/0 Danville Flymaster |
| **Abdomen:** | Pale yellow DMC 25 #745 embroidery floss |
| **Rib:** | Brown ostrich |
| **Thorax:** | Brown Hareline Rabbit and golden brown Hareline Ice Dub mix |
| **Wing Case:** | Olive Flashabou |
| **Tail and Hackle:** | Partridge body side feather hackle to hook point. |

## OVERWEIGHT SPIDER

| | |
|---|---|
| **Hook:** | #12-18 Tiemco 2487 |
| **Thread:** | Black 12/0 Benecchi |
| **Tail:** | Brown partridge |
| **Abdomen:** | Brown Hends Body Quill |
| **Thorax:** | Copper bead |
| **Hackle:** | Brown partridge |
| **Head:** | Black Hends Spectra Dub |

## PHEASANT TAIL SOFT-HACKLE (VARIANT)

| | |
|---|---|
| **Hook:** | #12-18 Mustad S82 |
| **Thread:** | Tobacco brown 6/0 Danville |
| **Tail and Abdomen:** | Bleached pheasant tail |
| **Rib:** | Copper Wire (small) |
| **Thorax:** | Gold bead |
| **Hackle:** | Speckled brown India hen back |

**Note:** Use bead size for corresponding hook size: ⅛" (#12), ³⁄₃₂" (#14), ⁵⁄₆₄" (#16, #18).

## PEARL DIVER

| | |
|---|---|
| **Hook:** | #10-16 WR-396 |
| **Thread:** | Black 6/0 Danville Flymaster |
| **Tail:** | White Woolly Bugger marabou |
| **Abdomen:** | Pearl Ice Dub |
| **Thorax:** | Gray partridge and copper bead |

## FIREHOLE DRIFTER

| | |
|---|---|
| **Hook:** | #12-16 Eagle Claw L063S |
| **Thread:** | Tobacco brown 6/0 Danville Flymaster |
| **Tail:** | Rusty brown blood marabou |
| **Abdomen:** | Natural Rabbit Dubbin and golden brown Ice Dub mixture |
| **Thorax:** | Copper bead |
| **Hackle:** | Brown partridge |

**Note:** For abdomen, use the tag ends of the tail to make a hackle collar.

## HEAVY METAL NYMPH

| | |
|---|---|
| **Hook:** | #12-18 Eagle Claw L063S |
| **Thread:** | Tobacco brown 6/0 Danville Flymaster |
| **Tail:** | Rusty brown blood marabou |
| **Abdomen:** | Amber Ultra Wire (small ) |
| **Thorax:** | Gray partridge |

**Note:** Solid color variations: yellow, orange, red, blue, purple, black, silver, gray, white, chartreuse, green. Contrast color variations using two wire colors wrapped side by side: yellow/red, orange/green, red/black, blue/white, purple/silver, black/yellow, gray/olive, white/black, chartreuse/amber, green/gold.

# WIRE-BODY NYMPHS

## BUFFALO NYMPH

| | |
|---|---|
| **Hook:** | #12-16 Eagle Claw L063S (eye straightened) |
| **Thread:** | Tobacco brown 6/0 Danville Flymaster |
| **Abdomen:** | Copper Ultra Wire (small) |
| **Thorax Hackle:** | Hen aftershaft feather |
| **Thorax:** | Rusty Hareline Rabbit Dubbin |
| **Front Hackle:** | Speckled hen saddle |

## HEAVY METAL NYMPH (RED)

| | |
|---|---|
| **Hook:** | #12-18 Eagle Claw L063S |
| **Thread:** | Red 12/0 Benecchi |
| **Tail:** | Rusty brown blood marabou |
| **Abdomen:** | Orange UTC Ultra Wire |
| **Thorax:** | Peacock herl |
| **Hackle:** | Light brown partridge |

## MOSSY CREEK NYMPH

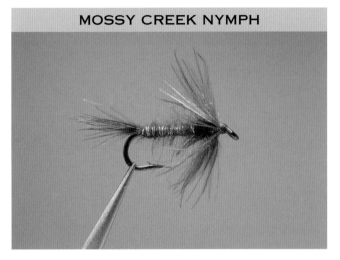

| | |
|---|---|
| **Hook:** | #12-16 Eagle Claw L063S |
| **Thread:** | Camel 8/0 UNI-Thread |
| **Tail:** | Mixture of olive and brown chickabou |
| **Abdomen:** | Chartreuse Ultra Wire (small) under rusty brown Hareline Rabbit Touch Dubbing |
| **Thorax:** | Black Hareline Rabbit Dubbin |
| **Hackle:** | Olive and brown chickabou tied in together |

## KETCHUM CADDIS

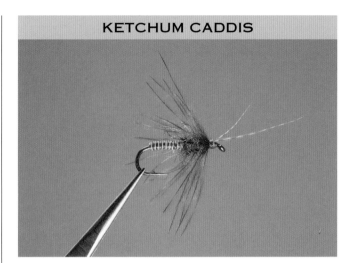

| | |
|---|---|
| **Hook:** | #12-18 Tiemco 5262 |
| **Thread:** | Camel 8/0 UNI-Thread |
| **Abdomen:** | Copper UTC Ultra Wire (small) and chartreuse UTC Ultra Wire (small) |
| **Thorax:** | Peacock Orvis Spectrablend Nymph |
| **Hackle:** | Tan Hareline grizzly marabou |
| **Antennae:** | Mallard flank dyed wood duck |

## TIPPERARY SEDGE

| | |
|---|---|
| **Hook:** | #12-18 Tiemco 5262 |
| **Thread:** | Olive 8/0 UNI-Thread |
| **Abdomen:** | Chartreuse UTC Ultra Wire (small) |
| **Thorax:** | Brown Woolly Bugger marabou |
| **Wing:** | Two mallard flank dyed wood duck fibers |
| **Hackle and** | |
| **Antennae:** | Speckled gray Wapsi hen saddle patch |

## THE KIMBERLEY

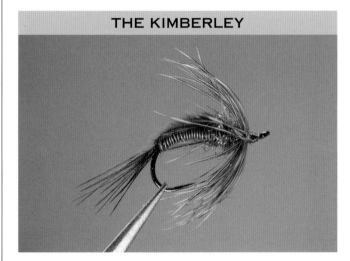

| | |
|---|---|
| **Hook:** | #12-16 Tiemco 206BL |
| **Thread:** | Tobacco brown 6/0 Danville Flymaster |
| **Tail:** | Reddish brown blood marabou |
| **Abdomen:** | Rust Ultra Wire (small) |
| **Thorax:** | Golden brown Hareline Ice Dub |
| **Hackle:** | Hen pheasant |

**Note:** For abdomen, pull tail marabou over the back.

## HI-VIS CONTRAST NYMPH

| | |
|---|---|
| **Hook:** | #12-16 WR-396 |
| **Thread:** | Tobacco brown 6/0 Danville Flymaster |
| **Abdomen:** | Copper Ultra Wire (small) |
| **Thorax:** | Sulphur Orange Nature's Spirit Hare's Mask Dubbing |
| **Tail and Hackle:** | Brown partridge |

## NYMPHS

## PHEASANT TAIL FLYMPH

| | |
|---|---|
| **Hook:** | #12-20 Eagle Claw L063 |
| **Thread:** | Tobacco brown 6/0 Danville Flymaster |
| **Shuck:** | Brown Z-Lon |
| **Abdomen:** | Pheasant tail |
| **Rib:** | Copper Ultra Wire (small) |
| **Thorax:** | Peacock herl |
| **Hackle:** | Brown partridge |

## LAVA CREEK NYMPH

| | |
|---|---|
| **Hook:** | #10-16 Mustad S82 |
| **Thread:** | Tobacco brown 6/0 Danville Flymaster |
| **Tail:** | Brown partridge |
| **Abdomen:** | Copper Flashabou |
| **Wing:** | Two amber turkey biots |
| **Thorax:** | Natural and sulphur orange Nature's Spirit Hare's Mask Dub |
| **Hackle:** | Brown partridge |

**Note:** Flashabou should be under black edge marked tan Scud Back.

## IRON SPRING NYMPH

| | |
|---|---|
| **Hook:** | #12-16 Mustad S82 |
| **Thread:** | Black 12/0 Benecchi |
| **Tail:** | Gray Whiting Brahma chickabou |
| **Abdomen:** | Gray Hareline Rabbit |
| **Rib and Thorax:** | Peacock herl |
| **Hackle:** | Gray Whiting Brahma hen saddle |

## PEACOCK DOUBLE WING

| | |
|---|---|
| **Hook:** | #10-18 Eagle Claw L063S |
| **Thread:** | Black 12/0 Benecchi |
| **Tail:** | Gray partridge |
| **Body:** | Peacock herl |
| **Hackle:** | Tan CDC behind gray partridge |

## KATHY'S FURY

| | |
|---|---|
| **Hook:** | #12-14 Mustad S82 |
| **Thread:** | Olive 12/0 Benecchi |
| **Tail:** | Olive Brahma Hen chickabou |
| **Body:** | Olive Brahma Hen aftershaft |
| **Hackle:** | Olive Brahma hen saddle |
| **Head:** | Black ostrich |

## CARRIGATHA NYMPH

| | |
|---|---|
| **Hook:** | #10-16 WR-396 |
| **Thread:** | Tobacco brown 6/0 Danville Flymaster |
| **Shuck:** | Brown Z-Lon |
| **Abdomen:** | Brown Z-Lon under medium vinyl rib |
| **Thorax:** | Peacock herl |
| **Hackle:** | Whiting Brahma hen saddle |

## WEST FORK NYMPH

| | |
|---|---|
| **Hook:** | #12-16 Eagle Claw L063S |
| **Thread:** | Camel 8/0 UNI-Thread |
| **Abdomen:** | Orange Danville rayon floss |
| **Rib:** | Copper Ultra Wire (small) |
| **Thorax:** | Brown Hareline Hare's Ear Plus |
| **Wing case:** | Gold Flashabou |
| **Tail and Hackle:** | Partridge body side feather |

## MONEY SEDGE

**Hook:** Tiemco 2487 #12-16
**Thread:** Camel 8/0 UNI-Thread
**Tail:** Olive turkey biots
**Abdomen:** Clear Scud Back over olive Flashabou
**Thorax:** Rusty brown Hareline Rabbit Dubbin
**Hackle:** Brown partridge

**Note:** For abdomen, leave with gaps for thread to show.

## ADAPTOR CADDIS

**Hook:** #10-16 Tiemco 2487
**Thread:** Tobacco 12/0 Benecchi
**Shuck:** Yellow Z-Lon
**Abdomen:** Vinyl rib over yellow Z-Lon
**Thorax:** Medium Hare's Mask Dubbing
**Hackle:** Brown partridge

**Note:** Variations are yellow, green, and brown.

## CONTRAST NYMPH

**Hook:** #10-18 Tiemco 3761
**Thread:** Light dun 12/0 Benecchi
**Tail:** Gray partridge
**Abdomen:** Light gray Hareline Rabbit Dubbin
**Rib:** Gold UTC Ultra Wire (small)
**Thorax:** Dark dun Hareline Rabbit Dubbin
**Hackle:** Brown partridge

## TWO FORK NYMPH

**Hook:** #12-16 Mustad S82
**Thread:** Tobacco brown 6/0 Danville Flymaster
**Tail:** Brown turkey biots
**Abdomen:** Cream Hareline Rabbit Dubbin
**Rib:** Green Ultra Wire (small)
**Thorax:** Peacock herl
**Hackle:** Brown partridge

## MP ARTICUNYMPH (#1)

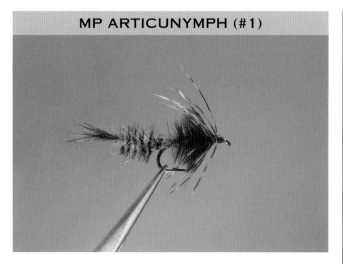

| | |
|---|---|
| **Hook:** | #14-16 WR-396 |
| **Thread:** | Tobacco brown 6/0 Danville |
| **Tail:** | Rusty brown Woolly Bugger marabou |
| **Abdomen:** | Natural Hareline Rabbit Dubbin |
| **Rib:** | Brown ostrich |
| **Thorax:** | Rusty brown Woolly Bugger marabou |
| **Hackle:** | Gray Whiting Brahma hen saddle |

**Note:** MP stands for multi-purpose. Strip one side of the hackle feather.

## BRASS LAWBREAKER

| | |
|---|---|
| **Hook:** | #10-16 Tiemco 2487 |
| **Thread:** | Camel 8/0 UNI-Thread |
| **Tail:** | Golden brown grizzly marabou |
| **Abdomen:** | Amber UTC Brassie Ultra Wire |
| **Thorax:** | Rusty brown Hareline Rabbit Wing: Amber Z-Lon |
| **Hackle:** | Bobwhite quail |

**Note:** For abdomen, pull chickabou from the tail ends over the back. For thorax, add a touch of rusty brown Hends #19 Spectra Dubbing Blend.

## SALMONFLY ARTICUNYMPH

| | |
|---|---|
| **Hook:** | #14-16 Eagle Claw L063S |
| **Thread:** | Camel 8/0 UNI-Thread |
| **Tail:** | Brown turkey biots |
| **Abdomen:** | Hareline Hare's Ear Rabbit Dubbin |
| **Thorax:** | Brown Hareline Rabbit |
| **Wing case:** | Pheasant tail fibers |
| **Hackle:** | Brown partridge |

## NEW PALE WATERY DUN

| | |
|---|---|
| **Hook:** | #14 Eagle Claw L059S |
| **Thread:** | Primrose Pearsalls's Silk |
| **Body:** | Natural Hareline Rabbit Touch Dubbing |
| **Hackle:** | Mallard duck marginal covert feather |

## SPECKLED QUILL

**Hook:** Mustad S82 (bent eye)
**Thread:** Claret Pearsall's Silk Thread
**Tail and Hackle:** Mallard flank dyed wood duck
**Body:** Hare's mask

## AUTUMN SEDGE

**Hook:** #12-16 Eagle Claw L063S (hand bent)
**Thread:** Iron gray 8/0 UNI-Thread
**Abdomen:** Hareline Hare's Ear Rabbit Dubbin
**Rear Thorax**
**Hackle:** Whiting Tan Brahma Enveloping Hackle
**Thorax:** Hareline Hare's Ear Rabbit Dubbin and Hareline Gray UV Ice Dub mixture
**Hackle:** Whiting Tan Brahma hen saddle

## PHEASANT TAIL SOFT-HACKLE

**Hook:** #12-18 Eagle Claw L063S
**Thread:** Cream marked purple 6/0 Danville Flymaster
**Tail and Abdomen:** Pheasant tail dyed purple
**Rib:** Blue Metallic Ultra Wire
**Thorax:** Peacock herl
**Hackle:** Gray partridge

**Note:** Variations include purple, red, green, yellow, and brown.

## COPPER HOLOGRAPHIC OSTRICH

**Hook:** #12-18 Eagle Claw L063S
**Thread:** Cream 6/0 Danville Flymaster
**Tail and Hackle:** Brown partridge
**Abdomen:** Copper Holographic Tinsel
**Rib:** Copper Ultra Wire (small)
**Thorax:** White ostrich herl marked green

**Note:** Thread marked with a green marker to match thorax.

## SUNRISE HOLOGRAPHIC OSTRICH

| | |
|---|---|
| **Hook:** | #12-18 Eagle Claw L063S |
| **Thread:** | Cream 6/0 Danville Thread |
| **Tail and Hackle:** | Partridge body side feather |
| **Abdomen:** | Yellow Holographic Tinsel |
| **Rib:** | Copper Ultra Wire (small) |
| **Thorax:** | White ostrich herl marked orange |

**Note:** Thread marked orange to match thorax.

## COPPER RABBIT

| | |
|---|---|
| **Hook:** | #12-18 Eagle Claw L063S |
| **Thread:** | Tobacco brown 6/0 Danville Flymaster |
| **Tail and Hackle:** | Brown partridge |
| **Abdomen:** | Copper Holographic Tinsel |
| **Thorax:** | Rusty Hareline Rabbit Dubbin and Hends #2 Rusty Spectra Dubbing mixture |

## VIOLET HOLOGRAPHIC OSTRICH

| | |
|---|---|
| **Hook:** | #12-18 Eagle Claw L063S |
| **Thread:** | Cream 6/0 Danville |
| **Tail and Hackle:** | Gray partridge |
| **Abdomen:** | Purple Holographic Tinsel |
| **Rib:** | Silver Ultra Wire (small) |
| **Thorax:** | White ostrich herl marked purple |

**Note:** Thread marked light purple to match thorax.

## SILVER HOLOGRAPHIC OSTRICH

| | |
|---|---|
| **Hook:** | #12-18 Eagle Claw L063S |
| **Thread:** | Rusty dun 8/0 UNI-Thread |
| **Tail:** | Gray partridge |
| **Abdomen:** | Silver Holographic Tinsel |
| **Rib:** | Silver Ultra Wire (small) |
| **Thorax:** | Dark gray ostrich herl |
| **Hackle:** | Gray partridge |

**Note:** Half of partridge stem fibers should be marked with a light brown marker.

## CHARTREUSE HOLOGRAPHIC OSTRICH

| Hook: | #12-18 Eagle Claw L063S |
|---|---|
| Thread: | Cream 6/0 Danville |
| Tail and Hackle: | Gray partridge |
| Abdomen: | Chartreuse Holographic Tinsel |
| Rib: | Chartreuse Ultra Wire (small) |
| Thorax: | White ostrich herl marked green |

**Note:** Thread marked green to match thorax.

## TANNED-GREEN HOLOGRAPHIC OSTRICH

| Hook: | #12-18 Eagle Claw L063S |
|---|---|
| Thread: | Cream 6/0 Danville Flymaster |
| Tail, Hackle, and Antennae: | Light brown partridge |
| Abdomen: | Green Holographic Tinsel |
| Rib: | Green Ultra Wire (small) |
| Thorax: | White ostrich marked tan |

**Note:** Thread marked tan to match thorax.

# WET FLIES

## CLEARWATER SOFT-WING

| Hook: | #12-16 Mustad S82 |
|---|---|
| Thread: | Camel 8/0 UNI-Thread |
| Shuck: | Reddish brown Hare's Ear Plus |
| Abdomen: | Golden brown Orvis Hare' E Ice Dub |
| Thorax: | Rusty brown Orvis Ice Dub |
| Hackle: | Gray partridge |

## BRAIDED FLYCATCHER

| Hook: | #10-16 Tiemco 2487 |
|---|---|
| Thread: | Black 12/0 Benecchi |
| Abdomen: | Red and black Midge Sparkle Braid |
| Thorax: | Black Hareline Rabbit and peacock Hareline Ice Dub mix |
| Wing: | Orange mallard flank |
| Hackle: | Black hen cape behind red hen cape one size smaller |

## ORANGE MARAUDER

**Hook:** #10-16 Mustad 2487
**Thread:** Orange 6/0 Danville Flymaster
**Abdomen:** Orange Danville rayon floss
**Rib:** Silver Ultra Wire (small)
**Thorax:** Amber Hareline Rabbit Dubbin and golden brown Ice Dub mix
**Tail and Hackle:** Bleached partridge

**Note:** Variations include orange, green, and purple.

## PICABO MAYFLY

**Hook:** #12-18 Eagle Claw L063S
**Thread:** Tobacco brown 6/0 Danville Flymaster
**Tail and Body:** Rusty brown blood marabou
**Wing and Hackle:** Rusty orange starling

**Note:** Variations include orange, yellow, olive, and brown.

## WESTERN LADY

**Hook:** #12-16 Eagle Claw L063S
**Thread:** Camel 8/0 UNI-Thread
**Abdomen:** DMC E130 embroidery floss
**Thorax:** Rusty Hareline Rabbit Dubbin
**Tail and Hackle:** Brown partridge

## FUZZY CATERPILLAR

**Hook:** #12-16 Eagle Claw L063S (bent and curved)
**Thread:** Black 6/0 Danville Flymaster
**Abdomen:** Olive ostrich
**Rib:** Copper Holographic Tinsel
**Thorax:** Caddis green Hareline Ice Dub
**Hackle:** Olive marabou
**Head:** White ostrich

## BROWN TWO-STAGE FLYMPH

| | |
|---|---|
| **Hook:** | #12-16 Eagle Claw L063S |
| **Thread:** | Tobacco brown 6/0 Danville Flymaster |
| **Abdomen:** | Tobacco brown 6/0 Danville Flymaster |
| **Rib:** | Copper Ultra Wire (small) |
| **Thorax Hackle:** | March Brown Whiting Brahma hen saddle |
| **Thorax:** | Golden brown Hareline Ice Dub |
| **Hackle:** | March Brown Whiting Brahma hen saddle |

**Note:** For thorax hackle, base feather fibers should be stripped off the stem and tied in using an enveloping compensation method.

## ORANGE TWO-STAGE FLYMPH

| | |
|---|---|
| **Hook:** | #12-16 Eagle Claw L063S |
| **Thread:** | Orange 6/0 Danville Flymaster |
| **Abdomen:** | Orange 6/0 Danville Flymaster |
| **Rib:** | Gold Ultra Wire (small) |
| **Thorax Hackle:** | Hen aftershaft |
| **Thorax:** | Orange UV Lightning Dubbing |
| **Hackle:** | Ginger India hen saddle |

**Note:** For thorax hackle, tie in using an enveloping compensation method.

## TRANSITION CADDIS

| | |
|---|---|
| **Hook:** | #16 WR-396 |
| **Thread:** | Tobacco Brown 6/0 Danville Flymaster |
| **Abdomen:** | Ginger Hareline Rabbit Dubbin |
| **Thorax:** | Chartreuse Hends #89 Spectra Dubbing |
| **Hackle and** | |
| **Antennae:** | Brown partridge |

**Note:** Thorax dubbing should be cut into a finer mixture and dubbed.

## TRANSITION CADDIS

| | |
|---|---|
| **Hook:** | #12-18 WR-396 |
| **Thread:** | Tobacco brown 6/0 Danville Flymaster |
| **Abdomen:** | Rusty brown Hareline Rabbit Dubbin and Ice Dub mixture |
| **Thorax:** | Caddis green Hareline Rabbit Dubbin and Ice Dub mixture |
| **Tail and Hackle:** | Brown partridge |

## OUTLAW SOFT-WING

| | |
|---|---|
| **Hook:** | #12-14 WR-396 |
| **Thread:** | Tobacco brown 6/0 Danville Flymaster |
| **Tab:** | Orange Holographic Tinsel |
| **Abdomen:** | Black Hareline Rabbit Dubbin |
| **Rib:** | Copper Ultra Wire (small) |
| **Thorax:** | Light orange Hends #98 Spectra Dubbing behind Yellow ostrich herl |
| **Hackle:** | Gray Whiting Brahma hen saddle |

## EAGLE CREEK NYMPH

| | |
|---|---|
| **Hook:** | #12-16 Mustad S82 |
| **Thread:** | Tobacco brown 6/0 Danville Flymaster |
| **Shuck:** | Yellow Hareline Rabbit Dubbin |
| **Abdomen:** | Natural Hareline Rabbit Dubbin and tan Antron mix |
| **Rib:** | Copper Ultra Wire (small) |
| **Thorax:** | Yellow Hends #6 Spectra Dubbing and yellow ostrich |
| **Hackle:** | Partridge side body feather |

**Note:** Variations are yellow, red, green, brown.

## FLOWERING PUPA

| | |
|---|---|
| **Hook:** | #10-16 Tiemco 2487 |
| **Thread:** | Camel UNI-Thread |
| **Tail:** | Olive turkey biots |
| **Abdomen:** | Scud Back over green Flashabou |
| **Thorax:** | Reddish brown Hareline Hare's Ear Plus |
| **Hackle:** | Brown partridge |

**Note:** Rib abdomen with black thread.

## HALO PHEASANT

| | |
|---|---|
| **Hook:** | #12-16 Eagle Claw L063S |
| **Thread:** | Tobacco brown Danville Flymaster 6/0 |
| **Abdomen:** | Hen pheasant palmered aftershaft |
| **Thorax:** | Reddish-purple Hends #7 Spectra Dubbing |
| **Hackle:** | Hen pheasant |

## WHITE CLOUD

**Hook:** #12-16 Tiemco 200R
**Thread:** Light olive 8/0 Orvis
**Body:** Caddis green Hareline Rabbit Dubbin and caddis green Hareline Ice Dub mixture
**Tail and Hackle:** Natural Whiting Brahma hen cape

## FLUORESCENT SPIDER

**Hook:** #12-18 WR-396
**Thread:** Orange 6/0 Danville Flymaster
**Body:** Orange Holographic Tinsel under orange UV Lightning Touch Dubbing
**Hackle:** Bobwhite quail

## FLUORESCENT SPIDER

**Hook:** #12-18 WR-396
**Thread:** Red 6/0 Danville Flymaster
**Body:** Red Holographic Tinsel under red UV Lightning Touch Dubbing
**Hackle:** Bobwhite quail

## FLUORESCENT SPIDER

**Hook:** #12-18 WR-396
**Thread:** Light olive 6/0 Danville Flymaster
**Body:** Green Holographic Tinsel under chartreuse UV Lightning Touch Dubbing
**Hackle:** Bobwhite quail

## REFLECTION NYMPH

| | |
|---|---|
| **Hook:** | #12-16 Tiemco 5262 |
| **Thread:** | Tobacco brown 6/0 Danville Flymaster |
| **Body:** | Natural Hareline Rabbit, middle golden brown Hareline Ice Dub |
| **Hackles:** | Gray partridge |

## WHITE SULPHUR SOFT-WING

| | |
|---|---|
| **Hook:** | #12-16 WR-396 |
| **Thread:** | Coffee 6/0 Danville Flymaster |
| **Tail and Abdomen:** | Ginger marabou |
| **Thorax:** | Brown Woolly Bugger marabou |
| **Rib:** | Copper Ultra Wire (small) or Micro Tinsel |
| **Hackle:** | White or light dun hen cape |

## MAHOGANY CREEK DUN

| | |
|---|---|
| **Hook:** | #14-16 WR-396 (shown) or Mustad R50 |
| **Thread:** | Tobacco brown 6/0 Danville Flymaster |
| **Abdomen and Thorax:** | Mahogany Superfine dry-fly dubbing |
| **Rib:** | Summer brown Coats and Clark #8360 thread |
| **Tail and Hackle:** | Light brown India hen back |

## SULPHUR FLASH

| | |
|---|---|
| **Hook:** | #14-18 Dai-Riki #070 |
| **Thread:** | Light Cahill 8/0 UNI-Thread |
| **Underbody:** | Yellow Flashabou |
| **Overbody:** | Sparse yellow Spirit River Far and Fine Dry-Fly Dubbing |
| **Hackle:** | Light dun hen cape |

**Note:** Underbody Flashabou ribbed over thread.

## VENUS MAYFLY

| | |
|---|---|
| **Hook:** | #12-16 Mustad S82 |
| **Thread:** | Orange 6/0 Danville Flymaster |
| **Abdomen:** | Orange DMC 25 floss or tying thread |
| **Rib:** | Fluorescent orange Ultra Wire |
| **Wing:** | Gray Hareline UV Ice Dub |
| **Thorax:** | Orange Hends #98 Spectra Dubbing |
| **Tail and Hackle:** | Orange partridge or gray partridge |

**Note:** Partridge marked with Prismacolor Mineral Orange.

## EAST FORK SPIDER

| | |
|---|---|
| **Hook:** | #12-18 Mustad S82 |
| **Thread:** | Orange 6/0 Danville Flymaster |
| **Body:** | Light hare's mask (touch dub) and orange Danville rayon floss |
| **Hackle:** | Hen pheasant |

## VENUS MAYFLY

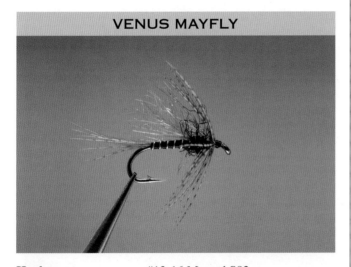

| | |
|---|---|
| **Hook:** | #12-16 Mustad S82 |
| **Thread:** | Black 6/0 Danville Flymaster |
| **Abdomen:** | Black DMC 25 floss or tying thread |
| **Wing:** | Gray UV Ice Dub |
| **Thorax:** | Black Hends #45 Spectra Dubbing |
| **Tail and Hackle:** | Brown partridge |

## NORTH FORK SPIDER

| | |
|---|---|
| **Hook:** | #12-20 Eagle Claw |
| **Thread:** | Black 6/0 Danville Flymaster |
| **Body:** | Black Hareline Rabbit and green Antron Dubbing mix, copper Holographic Tinsel |
| **Hackle:** | English grouse |

**Note:** Body dubbing lightly applied with gaps over tinsel.

## GERMAN BROWN SPIDER

| | |
|---|---|
| **Hook:** | #12-18 Mustad S82 |
| **Thread:** | Tobacco brown 6/0 Danville Flymaster |
| **Body:** | Gold and red medium Holographic Tinsel |
| **Rib:** | Black Ultra Wire (small) |
| **Thorax:** | Black Hareline Rabbit Dubbin |
| **Hackle:** | Bobwhite quail |

## NEW PINK LADY

| | |
|---|---|
| **Hook:** | #10-18 Tiemco 200R |
| **Thread:** | Black 6/0 Danville Flymaster |
| **Body:** | Pink Wapsi Antron Dubbing |
| **Rib:** | Gold tinsel |
| **Tail and Hackle:** | Brown partridge |

## HORNED SOFT-WING SEDGE

| | |
|---|---|
| **Hook:** | #12-16 Eagle Claw |
| **Thread:** | Tobacco brown 6/0 Danville Flymaster |
| **Body:** | Orvis Hare' E Ice Dub Hare's Ear |
| **Hackle and** | |
| **Antennae:** | Golden brown Whiting Brahma hen |

## CALDERA SPIDER

| | |
|---|---|
| **Hook:** | #12-16 Mustad S82 |
| **Thread:** | Orange 6/0 Danville Flymaster |
| **Shuck:** | Light Hare's Ear Plus |
| **Abdomen:** | Orange 6/0 Danville Flymaster |
| **Rib:** | Gold Micro Tinsel |
| **Thorax:** | Light brown ostrich |
| **Hackle:** | Brown partridge |

## GREEN FLICKER

| | |
|---|---|
| **Hook:** | #12-16 Eagle Claw |
| **Thread:** | Camel 8/0 UNI-Thread |
| **Rib:** | Gold Ultra Wire (small) |
| **Abdomen:** | Olive ¹⁄₆₄" small Holographic Tinsel |
| **Thorax:** | Black Hends #45 Spectra Dubbing |
| **Hackle and Tail:** | Bleached grizzly hen cape |

**Note:** Tinsel variations include orange, copper, blue, purple, silver, chartreuse, gold, red black, and green Holographic Tinsel.

## ELEGANT LADY

| | |
|---|---|
| **Hook:** | #14-18 Tiemco 200R |
| **Thread:** | Fluorescent blue 6/0 Danville Flymaster |
| **Body:** | Blue Danville rayon floss |
| **Palmering:** | Yellow ostrich herl |
| **Wing:** | Hareline Clear Wing |
| **Head:** | Amber and pale yellow Hareline Rabbit Dubbin mixture |
| **Hackle and Tail:** | Gray Whiting Brahma hen saddle |

## FUZZY HORNED NYMPH

| | |
|---|---|
| **Hook:** | #12-18 Eagle Claw |
| **Thread:** | Tobacco brown 6/0 Danville Flymaster |
| **Tail, Hackle and Antennae:** | Light brown partridge |
| **Abdomen:** | Amber Hareline Rabbit and golden brown Hareline Ice Dub mixture |
| **Thorax:** | Olive Hareline Rabbit and caddis green Hareline Ice Dub mixture |

## WOLF SPIDER

| | |
|---|---|
| **Hook:** | #12-18 WR-396 |
| **Thread:** | Tobacco brown 6/0 Danville Flymaster |
| **Abdomen:** | Rusty brown Hareline Rabbit Dubbin |
| **Thorax:** | Amber Hareline Rabbit Dubbin |
| **Hackle and Tail:** | Brown grizzly marabou |

## ACTION FLYMPH

**Hook:** #14-16 Daiichi 1530
**Thread:** Olive 8/0 UNI-Thread Light
**Body:** Light olive Nature's Spirit Hare's Mask Dubbing
**Hackle:** Gray partridge

## PMD LETHAL WEAPON

**Hook:** #14-18 Mustad S82
**Thread:** Light olive 8/0 UNI-Thread
**Shuck:** Golden Tan Wapsi and Hare's Ear Antron Mixture
**Body:** Pale yellow 727 and tan 437 DMC 25 embroidery floss
**Thorax:** Pale yellow and yellow-olive Hareline Rabbit Dubbin mixture
**Wing:** Medium Dun hen cape feather tip
**Hackle:** Light tannish-dun hen cape

## SILKY EMERGER

**Hook:** #14-18 Eagle Claw Nymph
**Thread:** Orange 6/0 Danville Flymaster
**Shuck:** White Z-Lon
**Body:** .010 clear monofilament over thread
**Thorax:** Mixture of amber, pale, yellow Hareline Rabbit and orange Hends Spectra Dubbing
**Hackle:** Medium blue dun hen cape

**Note:** Body thread variations include green, yellow, purple, black, gray, red, and blue.

## SPECKLED CADDIS

**Hook:** #10-18 Dai-Riki #075
**Thread:** Tobacco brown 6/0 Danville Flymaster
**Egg Sack:** Chartreuse 6/0 Danville Flymaster
**Body:** Light hare's mask
**Wing:** Tan mallard flank
**Hackle:** Bleached starling

## ORANGE LANTERN

| | |
|---|---|
| **Hook:** | #12-18 Eagle Claw L063S |
| **Thread:** | Rusty dun 8/0 UNI-Thread |
| **Abdomen:** | Bright orange .010 monofilament |
| **Thorax:** | Peacock Hareline Ice Dub |
| **Hackle and Antennae:** | Gray partridge |

## SLEDGEHAMMER SEDGE

| | |
|---|---|
| **Hook:** | #12-16 Mustad C49S |
| **Thread and Rib:** | Tobacco brown 6/0 Danville |
| **Abdomen:** | March Brown Hareline Rabbit Dubbin |
| **Rib:** | Rusty brown turkey feather fiber |
| **Thorax:** | Brown Hareline Rabbit Dubbin |
| **Winglets:** | Brown turkey biots |
| **Hackle and Antennae:** | Brown India hen back |

**Note:** One side of hen back fibers should be stripped.

## HOTWIRE NYMPH (OLIVE)

| | |
|---|---|
| **Hook:** | #12-18 WR-396 |
| **Thread:** | Light olive 8/0 Orvis |
| **Body:** | Green Danville rayon floss |
| **Rib:** | Rust Ultra Wire (small) |
| **Thorax:** | Rusty brown Hareline Rabbit Dubbin |
| **Tail and Hackle:** | Gray partridge |

## HOTWIRE NYMPH (RUSTY BROWN)

| | |
|---|---|
| **Hook:** | #12-18 WR-396 |
| **Thread:** | Tobacco brown 6/0 Danville Flymaster |
| **Body:** | Rusty brown Danville rayon floss |
| **Rib:** | Green Ultra Wire (small) |
| **Thorax:** | Caddis green Hareline Rabbit Dubbin |
| **Tail and Hackle:** | Gray partridge |

# ONE-FEATHERS AND STREAMERS

## VAGABOND SEDGE

| | |
|---|---|
| **Hook:** | #10-14 Tiemco 2487 |
| **Thread:** | Black 6/0 Danville Flymaster |
| **Tail, Body, and Hackle:** | Gray Brahma saddle |
| **Rib:** | Hot yellow Ultra Wire (small) |

## OLIVE ONE-FEATHER MAYFLY

| | |
|---|---|
| **Hook:** | #14-16 Eagle Claw L063S |
| **Thread:** | Olive 8/0 Orvis |
| **Tail, Body, and Hackle:** | Golden olive Brahma hen saddle |

## GOLDEN ONE-FEATHER MAYFLY

| | |
|---|---|
| **Hook:** | #14-16 Mustad S82 |
| **Thread:** | Tobacco brown 6/0 Danville Flymaster |
| **Tail, Body, and Hackle:** | March Brown Brahma saddle |

## RUSTY ONE-FEATHER MAYFLY

| | |
|---|---|
| **Hook:** | #14-16 Eagle Claw L063S |
| **Thread:** | Tobacco brown 6/0 Danville Flymaster |
| **Tail, Body, and Hackle:** | Brown hen cape |
| **Rib:** | Hot Yellow Ultra Wire (small) |

## TAN ONE-FEATHER MAYFLY

| | |
|---|---|
| **Hook:** | #14-16 Eagle Claw L063S |
| **Thread:** | Tobacco brown 6/0 Danville Flymaster |
| **Tail, Body, and Hackle:** | Tan Whiting Brahma hen saddle |

## GRAY ONE-FEATHER MAYFLY

| | |
|---|---|
| **Hook:** | #14-16 Eagle Claw L063S |
| **Thread:** | Tobacco brown 6/0 Danville Flymaster |
| **Tail, Body, and Hackle:** | Gray Whiting Brahma Saddle |

## SPECKLED ONE-FEATHER MAYFLY

| | |
|---|---|
| **Hook:** | #14-16 Eagle Claw L063S |
| **Thread:** | Tobacco brown 6/0 Danville Flymaster |
| **Tail, Body, and Hackle:** | India hen saddle |
| **Rib:** | Gold Ultra Wire (small) |

## SILKY WATER SEDGE

| | |
|---|---|
| **Hook:** | #12-14 WR-396 |
| **Thread:** | Tan 8/0 Orvis |
| **Tail, Body, and Hackle:** | Ginger hen saddle |

**Note:** Body should be clipped and palmered.

## CLOUD STREAMER

| | |
|---|---|
| **Hook:** | #12 Tiemco 3761 |
| **Thread:** | Black 6/0 Danville Flymaster |
| **Tail, Body, and Hackle:** | Gray partridge feather |

## GRAY BAITFISH

| | |
|---|---|
| **Hook:** | #12 Mustad S82 |
| **Thread:** | Tobacco brown 6/0 Danville Flymaster |
| **Tail, Body, and Hackle:** | Gray partridge feather |
| **Head:** | Gray partridge aftershaft feather |

## SODA BUTTE STREAMER

| | |
|---|---|
| **Hook:** | #12 Mustad S82 |
| **Thread:** | Black 6/0 Danville Flymaster |
| **Tail, Body, and Hackle:** | Pale yellow Whiting Brahma hen saddle |
| **Rib:** | Hot yellow Ultra Wire (small) |
| **Head:** | Pale yellow Whiting Brahma hen saddle aftershaft feather |

## FOX CREEK MINNOW

| | |
|---|---|
| **Hook:** | #12 Mustad S82 |
| **Thread:** | Tobacco brown 6/0 Danville Flymaster |
| **Body and Hackle:** | Bleached partridge |
| **Head:** | Aftershaft feather from hackle feather |

## CHICKABOU WOLF

| | |
|---|---|
| **Hook:** | #10 Tiemco 2457 |
| **Thread:** | Wood duck 70-denier Ultra Thread |
| **Body:** | Golden brown Hareline grizzly marabou |
| **Eyes:** | 7/32" Gold Fly Eyes |

## DALMATIAN STREAMER

| | |
|---|---|
| **Hook:** | #12 Tiemco 3761 |
| **Thread:** | Black 6/0 Danville Flymaster |
| **Tail:** | Feather base fibers |
| **Body and Hackle:** | Gray partridge |

# SOFT-HACKLE DRY FLIES

## ORANGE MORNING GLORY

| | |
|---|---|
| **Hook:** | #12-14 Mustad R50 |
| **Thread:** | Camel 8/0 UNI-Thread |
| **Tag and Rib:** | Gold tinsel |
| **Abdomen:** | Orange Hareline Rabbit Dubbin |
| **Hackle:** | Brown Woolly Bugger marabou |
| **Thorax:** | Superfine PMD Dry Fly Dubbing |
| **Wing:** | Coastal deer |
| **Legs:** | Wood duck mallard flank |

## SUNBURN CADDIS

| | |
|---|---|
| **Hook:** | #12-16 Mustad R50 |
| **Thread:** | Orange 6/0 Danville Flymaster |
| **Body:** | Reddish brown Hare's Ear Plus |
| **Rib (Optional):** | Silver Ultra Wire (fine) |
| **Wing:** | Tan CDC |
| **Hackle:** | Bleached grizzly hen cape |

## LAMAR DRIFTER

**Hook:** #12-16 Tiemco 200R
**Thread:** Tan 8/0 Orvis
**Shuck:** Brown Z-Lon
**Abdomen:** Natural Hareline Rabbit Dubbin
**Wing:** Amber Poly yarn
**Hackle:** Ruffed grouse
**Head:** Rusty Hareline Rabbit Dubbin

## LONGHORN TAN SEDGE

**Hook:** #12-16 Eagle Claw L059
**Thread:** Coffee 6/0 Danville Flymaster
**Shuck:** Golden tan Wapsi and Wapsi Hare's Ear Antron dubbing mixture
**Underbody:** Coffee 6/0 Danville Flymaster
**Rib:** Coffee 6/0 Danville Flymaster
**Body:** Natural Hareline Rabbit Dubbin
**Wing:** Natural dun CDC
**Hackle:** Brown Variant India hen neck
**Antennae:** Two fibers from hackle collar

**Note:** Underbody thread is colored with Harvest Orange BIC Mark It. Rib thread is colored with Woodsy Brown BIC Mark It.

## SURFACE RUNNER

**Hook:** #12-14 Mustad R50
**Thread:** Camel 8/0 UNI-Thread
**Tag and Rib:** Copper Holographic Tinsel
**Body:** Ginger Nature's Spirit Hare's Mask Dubbing
**Thorax:** Sulphur orange Nature's Spirit Hare's Mask Dubbing
**Hackle:** Brown starling or rusty brown marabou (shown)
**Wing:** Coastal deer
**Legs:** Wood duck mallard flank

## FLITTING SEDGE

**Hook:** #12-14 WR-396 (heavier, shown)
**Thread:** Tobacco brown 6/0 Danville Flymaster
**Tail:** Hen pheasant
**Body:** Gold rabbit fur
**Rib:** Amber ostrich herl
**Wing:** White Antron Yarn
**Hackle:** Tan CDC
**Head:** Black Hend #45 Spectra Dubbing lightly applied on thread. Dub with gaps to allow the thread to show through. Hook choice is Mustad R50 (lighter), depending on flotation needs.

## EMULATOR

| | |
|---|---|
| **Hook:** | #10-16 Tiemco 200R |
| **Thread:** | Tobacco brown 6/0 Danville Flymaster |
| **Tail:** | Light dun CDC |
| **Abdomen:** | Amber Hareline Rabbit Dubbin |
| **Abdomen Hackle:** | Ginger hen cape palmered |
| **Wing:** | Light dun CDC |
| **Head:** | Orange Hareline Rabbit Dubbin |
| **Thorax Hackle:** | Palmered grizzly hen cape |

## JONES SEARCHER

| | |
|---|---|
| **Hook:** | #12-18 Eagle Claw L059 |
| **Thread:** | Orange 6/0 Danville Flymaster |
| **Body:** | Natural Hareline Rabbit Touch Dubbing |
| **Wing:** | Coastal deer |
| **Hackle:** | Gray partridge |
| **Head:** | Orange Hareline Rabbit Dubbin |

## IRISH HUMMINGBIRD

| | |
|---|---|
| **Hook:** | #12-14 Mustad R50 |
| **Thread:** | Tobacco brown 6/0 Danville Flymaster |
| **Tail:** | Tan CDC |
| **Butt:** | Caddis green Hareline Ice Dub |
| **Abdomen:** | Cream Superfine Dry Dubbing |
| **Wing:** | Deer |
| **Hackle:** | Gray partridge |
| **Thorax:** | Rust orange Hareline Rabbit Dubbin |

## YELLOW AND GRAY HIGH RIDER

| | |
|---|---|
| **Hook:** | #12-16 Eagle Claw L059 |
| **Thread:** | Camel 8/0 UNI-Thread |
| **Body:** | Yellow and natural spun deer |
| **Hackle:** | Brown partridge |

## CREAM HIGH RIDER

**Hook:** #12-16 Eagle Claw L059
**Thread:** Camel 8/0 UNI-Thread
**Body:** Spun bleached deer
**Hackle:** Brown partridge

## SPECTRUM HIGH RIDER

**Hook:** #12-16 Eagle Claw L059
**Thread:** Wine 6/0 Danville Flymaster
**Body:** Mixed bleached, yellow, orange, and red spun deer
**Hackle:** Brown partridge

## HALF AND HALF HIGH RIDER

**Hook:** #12-16 Eagle Claw L059
**Thread:** Light Cahill 8/0 UNI-Thread
**Body:** Natural and yellow spun deer
**Hackle:** Bleached partridge

## YELLOW AND ORANGE HIGH RIDER

**Hook:** #12-16 Eagle Claw L059
**Thread:** Orange Hareline Flymaster
**Body:** Yellow and orange spun deer
**Hackle:** Yellow partridge or gray partridge

**Note:** Partridge should be marked with Prismacolor Sunburst.

The Upper Green River near Pinedale, Wyoming, offers miles of fantastic freestone-fly water. The river flows out of the Green River lakes, there's camping, and the fishing is great just below them. Don't forget about the river below Highway 191. Spring creeks flow in there and keep the water cold and fertile.

For a good hook set it's important to set the hook in different ways (slip strike, rod tip lift, line hand set, or just letting the fly smoothly set itself on the swing such as during a one-handed presentation) depending on the angle one is relative to the fish. When playing fish, I often use side pressure for more leverage, and on large, strong fish I place my line hand on the blank to shorten the fulcrum point and guide the fish with the rod tip either high or combined with side pressure for the greatest leverage possible.

# Presentation Tactics

As the sun fell behind the mountains of the Cherokee National Forest, it silhouetted them against the rich blue dusk. The stars began to appear as numerous as the trout breaking the water surface and rising in all directions, in a frenzy for the protein that had suddenly appeared in front of them, as if on cue (and maybe it was). Sunset had triggered the Sulphur spinnerfall on the fertile upper South Holston River tailwater, and although the Sulphurs had been hatching for hours, it grew more intense with the overlapping spinner activity. The fish began feeding even more heavily due to the reassuring safety they felt from the darkening sky. Even the big ones started to feed on the surface. I tied on a sparser fly, a #16 dry fly hook with a pale yellow thread body, a rabbit thorax, and a yellowish-green hen soft-hackle collar. I was fishing it to rising fish that I couldn't always see, but which I could hear in the fading light. I didn't need to see the soft-hackle, as I had feel from the semitight line drifts and swings, and the strikes were vicious. High-sticking across and downstream, and then dropping the rod tip, the fly would sink a few inches below the surface and allow me to raise the fly with an emerger lift. I was able to make the Sulphur wet fly appear as a newly emerged adult at the surface, or as a sunken spinner. This was good in light of the overlapping emergence accompanying the spinnerfall. I was able to match the location of the naturals where the trout were feeding, in and just under the surface. The fly would set itself in the mouth of the trout if I maintained tension on the leader. I caught some nice fish that evening.

This wasn't the first time that soft-hackles had been successful for me in a low-light situation. On many streams, egg laying and emergences of caddis and mayflies happen at dusk and later. This is probably a defense mechanism of the aquatic insects, as they are harder to see. But it also benefits the trout, as they are also harder for their predators, herons and osprey, to see. The combination of food and safety prompts their feeding behavior.

Dusk, the last 45 minutes of visible light, on the South Holston River in summer, is Sulphur-spinner time. The fisherman doesn't need to be able to see wet flies, because the trout can, and strikes will be felt and hooks set.

The South Holston Sulphur hatch and spinnerfall are among the longest lasting (from mid-April through early November) and most intense, in terms of numbers of bugs, that I've ever experienced. While the daytime Sulphur hatches are great, I've found that the largest fish, such as this brown trout, feed during the spinnerfall, in the fading light over the rock shelves that create riffle-water seams.

### SOUTH HOLSTON SULPHUR (EPHEMERELLA INVARIA)

| | |
|---|---|
| **Hook:** | #16 Tiemco 101 |
| **Body:** | Saffron Coats and Clark #7560 thread |
| **Tail:** | Mallard flank wood duck |
| **Thorax:** | Pale yellow Hareline Rabbit Dubbin |
| **Hackle:** | Light dun Whiting American hen cape |

**Note:** Use a Velcro strip to pull out and sweep back the thorax dubbing over the abdomen. The South Holston Sulphur (SHS ) can be fished wet to imitate subsurface emergers and sunken spinners, or in the film to imitate floating duns and spinners. For extra flotation, lightly treat the hen-cape hackle with floatant.

The fishing method that you choose depends on the depth at which your targets are holding or feeding; then the insect species and life cycle you will imitate; then how deep you will fish this pattern and what behavior you want the fish to see the fly exhibit. This combination of factors will dictate your presentation strategy. For instance, if no fish are visibly rising, but you see caddis emerging, it would be logical to fish a caddis pupa imitation, because the fish are holding just under the surface, taking pupae. In this situation, a lightly weighted soft-hackle caddis pupa in the appropriate size and color could be fished with a reach mend, with the line aerialized; or a hump mend just upon entry into the water, to let the fly sink a few inches, then swung or stripped through a likely feeding lane.

Throughout the day, adjustments to leader and fly are always possible. If one method is working, stick with it; if not, change not only the fly life stage or species, but perhaps also the leader length, fly depth, and presentation, including angle of approach to the fish. Often, fishermen don't fish deep enough. They drift their flies right over the heads of the fish. If the fish don't have a reason to be near the surface looking for food, such as during strong hatch times or terrestrial activity on the water, they like to hold near the bottom for safety and energy savings (hydraulic friction of the streambed creates a slower current). Interesting these fish requires using weighted flies or a leader to reach them. This is why I consider the whole water column when designing flies. The presentation methods will complement the fly design and allow the fly to behave like a natural. Soft-hackles work well not just because of movement, but also because of the natural behavior they exhibit.

Why do both natural and unnatural presentations catch fish? The short answer is that trout are both selective and opportunistic, from moment to moment and from fish to fish. When fishing wet flies at the end of a swing or drift, I will often hold the fly downstream in the current before making another presentation. This is really not natural, as no insect except perhaps a silk rappelling caddis larva can hover in the current near the surface. But trout often strike even after the fly has been held there for many seconds. At the end of the cast, I sometimes will strip a small wet fly back upstream toward me, just under the surface; again, not a realistic presentation. Small aquatic insects aren't strong enough to swing against most stream currents, but as the fly travels back upstream and passes by, trout often strike. This is why when I'm fishing, I mix up my presentations between natural dead drifts or slow ascending swings of the fly, and more active retrieves like line strips, rod-tip shakes, or faster-than-current retrieves. The combination of presentations allows me to target any and all trout, and give them different looks at appealing versions of the same fly. It's neither only the fly nor only the presentation, but a combination of both that makes various behavior characteristics and life-stage imitation successful.

Many times, I like to make the first drift of a wet fly through a run a high-stick dead drift presentation with no added animation. If no fish strike, on the second presentation I will fish a wet-fly swing that has more animation. The third presentation usually combines dead drift, swing and rise, and some activation of the fly such as short strips of line or twitching the rod tip. The presentations get more animated as I prospect through the run. Some fish are spooky enough to be put off by an overly animated fly, and want a slowly inactive fly. On the other hand, animated flies excite some fish, and they get caught only with line manipulation to activate the fly. This is why I progress from low-activation to high-activation presentations.

A large part of fly fishing is about confidence. Call it intuition or experience, it comes through time spent on the water, and never leaves you. It builds skills on which you can draw wherever you go and wherever you fish. Confidence is the untold and unteachable secret of the best anglers. It only comes through the experiences of trial, error, and ultimately the consistency of proven methods of the catch. Believe in yourself and your flies from the beginning; then comes lots of time on the water and field-testing your beliefs. When you have fine-tuned them to satisfy the fish consistently, you have arrived. Then it's just a matter of fishing as many different locations and conditions as possible. It all adds up to experience, and ultimately confidence in your angling skills. This is what the 10 percent who catch 90 percent of the fish know and possess.

## CURRENT AND DRAG

Mayfly nymphs cannot swim upstream in water any faster than just under a half mile per hour. On many waters, this slow speed only occurs where frictional drag near the bottom of the stream occurs. The type of streambed also affects the speed of the current. For example, at a depth of up to about half an inch above the bottom, sand bottoms slow the current down to speeds at which nymphs can move upstream. Gravel the size of a small pea to a marble will slow the bottom current up to about two inches above the streambed. Large gravel of golf-ball size and larger will slow the current to allow upstream movement to about four inches above the streambed. These factors are important in determining how deep a nymph needs to be fished during nonhatch time periods. Thus, as adrift nymphs go downstream, they remigrate upstream in the boundary layer of slower water on or near the bottom of the streambed. All of this highlights the active lifestyle of the nymph, and shows that a natural presentation need not be strictly dead-drift if you fish the fly deep enough near the streambed.

In moving water, the changing speeds of the currents will move a natural fly in and out of current lanes, changing its drifting speed accordingly. Anglers can achieve drag-free drifts by using mending, and holding line off the surface of the water. Short drag-free drifts are often better and just as effective if made just upstream and in front of the targeted fish location. In slower-water situations, naturals often emerge at angles across the stream, as they can swim or drift sideways. This means that some drag on a fly, and even line strips and swings, can still look natural and match the angles of emergence.

Current influences the behavior of the nymphs and determines how anglers should fish their artificials. For instance, in waters like the Madison River, the large *Pteronarcys*

*californica* stonefly nymphs are ultraimportant to trout diets. They generally live in highly oxygenated, fast, rocky water over 30 inches deep, and with boulders more than a foot in diameter. These are prime feeding lies for large trout. Above the streambed in fast-water currents, no trout-stream aquatic insect, even the large stonefly nymphs, can swim against the currents, so a dead-drift is a natural way to fish them. This is not to say the nymphs will drift without movement, because as they are swept off the rocks they will twist, undulate, and contort, trying to regain footing and the safe shelter of another rock. For anglers, this means a dead-drift nymph presentation with line control to detect strikes, and a fly that has movement from the fur body and soft-hackle collar, even an articulated abdomen, will correctly combine fly design, stream-current influence, and natural behavior. The nymphs migrate to shore on the streambed slow-water layer, and emerge on land. Fish the streambanks with nymphs leading up to and during the hatch.

Hydraulic stream dynamics are important to the angler because they determine the effect the currents will have on flies. Understanding hydraulic current properties helps you know how much weight you need in the flies or on the leader, as well as the mends to use. Recognizing that every stream is different, yet the physics are still relatively the same from stream to stream, here's an example.

Let's say that in this stream the depth is 5 feet and the current is 1 foot per second at the surface. Two to three feet deeper, the current is slightly more than 1 foot per second. This is the fastest current; trout don't hold in the middle stream column depth because food moves too fast for them to easily capture it. They would expend more calories capturing food than they would gain from ingesting it. At the streambed, the current is one-third the speed of the surface current, due to hydraulic friction. Streambanks have similar effects on the current. Five feet from the bank, the current speed is about one and a half feet per second. At the bank, the current speed is about a quarter foot per second. In some faster-current rivers where the midchannel speed is fast, the bank is even more important for food concentration, as insects will be found concentrated in eddies and back currents. With the dynamics of the stream current in mind, we can generally say that fishing in the middle of the stream, where water is often deeper, requires more weight to keep the fly on the streambed and slow the drift down, as the floating fly line will drag the fly at the speed of the surface current. Also, fishing near the bank will require a slower drift, as these currents are slower. A fly line floating across midstream currents will drag a fly fished near the bank faster than it should be drifting, requiring mending or moving closer and holding line off the water to slow the drift down.

Study the waterway before fishing. Look at the prime lie locations and current seams, and watch for rising fish. The water level, water temperature, water clarity and depth, insect activity, and whether or not you see risers will all dictate fly selection, rigging technique, fishing depth, casting choice, and presentation tactics.

Trout will concentrate in seams and riffle water leading into flat water, as the riffle water is home to many invertebrates that are often washed into the current downstream, where hungry trout await their arrival. Fishing wet flies in these seams is ideal, as seen here on the River Liffey.

## Angles

In wet-fly fishing, presentation angles are critical. You can set up the fly for a drift in front of a fish with both casting and mending. The fly arrives in front of the fish rising or descending, depending on the life cycle of the species you want to imitate. It's important to understand how the flies will behave with mends on upstream, across-stream, and downstream presentations. Once you learn this, you will know how to approach small streams and large streams differently, and be in position for the right angle to get the best drift of the fly and achieve the behavior and movement you want to imitate.

It is more difficult to reposition yourself on small streams without spooking trout. On bigger waters, negotiating into a better position above or across from the trout can be easier, as long as wading into that position is possible. Before casting, think of how you want the fly to appear to the trout, and at what angle; i.e., what location best allows that presentation. As we are imitating behavior, the setup to get that fly to behave naturally is essential for the appearance of the fly to the fish,

and requires consideration of physical location, approach, and execution of the cast. With experience, this knowledge will become second nature and spontaneous.

Fishing where others don't fish, and in unique ways, shows fish new flies and methods. Approaching the river from angles at which others don't fish shows flies moving differently than other anglers' flies. For example, if it seems like everyone fishes a certain riffle or run section of the river from one side, try crossing over to the other side and fishing it from a different angle. I believe, for instance, that a wet fly rising to the surface at a different angle than other people's looks unique and interesting to trout that see a lot of flies.

When striking fish on a downstream presentation, the hook can pull out of a fish's mouth, due to the physics of the current flow and the weight of the fish putting strain on the leader and the hook point. The catenary curve is a rod angle established by holding the rod tip high during the swing, creating a curve in the line belly from rod tip to the line entering the water. This way, the line has more slack or "give" upon

Holding line off the water at the proper angle through the drift allows the line to create the Catenary Curve and is the secret to both allowing wet flies and nymphs to sink deeper, if designed to, as well as being able to make soft-strikes that cushion the hook set instead of pulling the fly out of the fish's mouth.

hooking a trout. Once the fish strikes, the belly absorbs the tension and will start to straighten, but the hook will penetrate deeper without pulling tight on the leader until the hook has set; i.e., it's a shock absorber. It's also a drift-lane preserver, as it allows the rod to be lowered through across-stream drift, which keeps the fly in the current lane longer before it swings across the stream.

## LINE GATHERING AND LINE MANAGEMENT

The line hand manages line to keep line/leader control when it's floating back toward the angler from an upstream presentation; feeds out line on a down-and-across presentation; or gathers line during a shorter cast or another presentation to animate and swim a wet fly. Finally, line gathering helps keep the line from tangling when it's off the reel during float tubing or fishing from the bank in tall meadow grasses, and still lets the angler feed out line as necessary. Feeding out the

line keeps the fly in a drift lane and at the same speed as the current, to prevent the fly from dragging and swinging across currents. There are two primary methods of line gathering: the bunch and gather and the Figure-8 method.

The bunch and gather method has a major advantage when you hook a fish. You can release the line from the line hand quickly by just opening the hand so the line drops out. However, you must trap the line running through the guides against the rod handle with the rod hand, while the line is gathered quickly onto the reel, then played off the reel alone.

The Figure-8 method is good for gathering line, but even better for manipulating the fly. You can gather the line fast or slow, and the fly can move through the water imitating a swimming motion. When a fish is hooked, the fingers must release the line all at once so the fly reel can pick it up on. The Figure-8 is also good for a controlled release of line to keep speed with the current, since the amount released is easy to feed out by pointing your fingers forward and letting it release. If a fish is not too big, it can be played by hand, by gathering line with either of these methods, and not even using the reel.

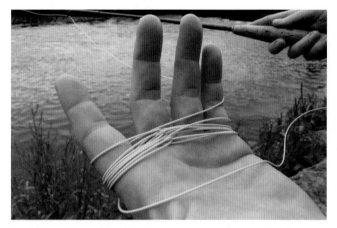

The Figure-8 line method is often used as a retrieve, but it's also very useful as a line management strategy. Whether high-stick nymphing or wet-fly fishing across- and downstream, it can be used to manage the drift and then release line into the current by pointing your fingers out toward the stripping guide and allowing the current to pull the line off at a natural rate. The Figure-8 method is also useful for downstream sweeping methods to let the current drift the fly into holding and feeding lies and then retrieving the flies back upstream through precise drift lane locations.

The Figure-8 line retrieve is important in line management. As a line retrieve method, it can activate the fly, especially in slower currents. As a line release method, it allows the fly to drift longer in a current lane before dragging across current, and keeps line/leader control out at the point fly to detect even subtle strikes. This works best in medium and faster currents, as they will pull the line out from your fingers if you keep an open hand and fingers pointed out toward the rod tip.

The Figure-8 retrieve is also effective for crawling nymphs on the bottom of the stream, using a weighted nymph and split shot. The speed of the hand-twist retrieve should relate to the natural species being imitated. Usually this is a slow retrieve, not only to appear natural, but also to keep the nymph from lifting too far off the streambed. The innovative nymph fisherman, Charles Brooks, quantified the movement into hand-twist-retrieve speeds. The same logic applies to line-stripping speed. Mayflies and cased caddis should have slow hand-twist retrieves.

*Ephemera* are some of the slower swimming mayflies. They move at about ten hand twists per minute, followed by *Ephemerella, Potomanthus,* and *Siphlonurus,* which move at about twenty hand twists per minute. Next are *Baetis,* at about thirty hand twists per minute. *Isonychia,* one of the fastest of the mayfly swimming species, move at about thirty hand retrieves per minute. Stoneflies dead drift when dislodged, but can scurry along the streambed. To imitate this, consider a deep hand-twist retrieve over streambed rocks. Stoneflies should be fished in faster water, their preferred habitat due to the water oxygen content they require. Large stonefly nymphs are underutilized, and in fast, deep water they should be on leader, along with a caddis larvae or mayfly nymph. Scuds can be fast swimmers and a move-pause-move pulsating swimming action hand-twist retrieve, with frequent stops and starts, imitates this behavior.

Down-and-across is an effective way to fish a nymph, both drag-free and with line manipulation. By raising and lowering the rod tip, a nymph can be lifted off the streambed, or lowered back down to keep the fly drifting at a proper level. You can either pull line off the reel or feed line off the line hand from a Figure-Eight retrieve, keeping enough slack in the line to make the line feed out, and extend the drift without dragging and swinging across-stream until you want it to swing.

## PRESENTATIONS

When fishing soft-hackles, we want to imitate two main appearances, depending on the water conditions. First is a fly of general attraction. This doesn't necessarily imitate a specific food source, but rather one that may pass for multiple species, such as caddis, mayfly, stonefly, or midge; or it may just look so good and have movement in general that fish can't resist it. The second appearance is species-specific: matching a specific insect species and its behavior, often during a hatch. The fly choice, rigging method, and presentation should match one of the two intended appearance scenarios.

Slack-tight is a state in which the angler fully controls the line out to the leader, tippet, and fly, but fly and line also drift in a somewhat drag-free state. This fine line between "slack" and "tight" is achieved by mending, high sticking, and dropping the rod tip as the fly drifts up, across, and down, and across-stream, so that the rod receives and telegraphs any fish strikes to the angler, who can then quickly set the hook. Slack-tight allows the fly to drift naturally, yet in the angler's full control. It allows for a degree of dead-drift nymphing, sinking the fly, and swinging the fly, all in the same cast and presentation. It may also require feeding line quickly off the reel with the line hand, or free-line nymphing, to keep pace with the water current and allow the fly to drift downstream in a current lane without swinging across-stream.

When the cast is made, the angler employs aerial reach mends, hump mends, stack mends, or a combination of these to achieve initial total dead drift. Then, as the slack in the fly line is tightened, the slack-tight zone is achieved. This can be targeted to a specific portion of water where the likeliest prime lie exists. In this moment, the fly is both drifting naturally, established by mending, yet controllably for manipulation if the angler desires, with rod-tip twitches, small line tugs, or strips; or lifting the fly to simulate an emerging life stage.

Dry-fly fishing uses mending to slow down the drift and avoid drag. Similarly, wet-fly fishing can use mends not only to slow down the drift of the fly or flies, but also to keep the fly drifting in a current zone, and to sink the fly to various depths according to which mend and how many the angler makes, when they are made, and how big they are.

Two very important casts for introducing slack in your line, along with the basic reach cast, are the slack line cast and the parachute cast. The parachute cast and slack-line cast have the similarity of presenting a dead-drift fly, but are the reverse motion of each other. The parachute cast lowers the rod tip to present the fly, while the slack-line cast raises the rod tip through the presentation.

On small streams like the Kells Blackwater in Ireland, I can get a wet-fly swing from bank to bank by roll casting to the opposite bank and letting the fly swing across-stream. The downstream presentation of the wet fly will put the fly in front of the fish before anything else, keeping you camouflaged if you stay low.

To make a slack line cast, make a regular forward cast upstream of and over the target, so the fly will drift into the fish's window, stopping the rod at two o'clock. Use a 12-foot-plus leader and long tippet, so that the fly line is not visible. When the line has nearly extended out on the forward cast, drop your elbow straight down to bring the line down to a lower plane. Keep the rod at two o'clock. This will introduce slack to the tippet. Lower the rod tip down to the water. As the fly drifts back downstream toward you, lift the rod tip to lift the line off the water and keep the line from dragging the fly.

During heavy hatches and on flat-water streams, fishing flies on a downstream presentation is a better method, as you can't line the fish, and drag is largely counteracted. You can be accurate with the location of the fly, putting it right in front of the trout without any drag, by lowering the rod tip at the same speed as the current. And since you are casting and presenting the fly in one current lane, there is less possibility of conflicting currents causing microdrag on the fly. It is the preferred method on the most technical waters, like the Henry's Fork, Silver Creek, and (for me) the South Holston River.

To make a downstream parachute cast, position yourself about 20 to 25 feet directly upstream of the targeted trout. Make a standard forward cast, and when the line is almost fully extended, pull back with the rod tip, to bring the fly down on the water well upstream of the fish's window. Lower the rod tip to keep pace with the current, and drift the fly at the same rate. The fly will drift right into where the trout is rising.

One of the most important pieces of advice I can offer is not to false-cast too much, if at all. Shoot line if you need to, and let the presentations play out; don't pick the fly up too soon, as strikes often occur when the fly is hanging in the current. I see a lot of fishermen make way too many false casts. Over the course of a fishing day, this adds up to less time that the fly was in the water. If your line and fly are in the water more often than not, you'll catch more trout. When surface dry-fly fishing, let the cast drift and play out before picking it up to recast, so as not to disturb the water in the trout's field of vision and alert them to an angler.

## Water Hump Mend

This mending technique is important for sinking flies and slowing drift. It can be done in the air on the forward cast before the line lands, or on the water after the fly has landed, to help it sink. When performed on the water right after the line lands, the fly has begun sinking and this mend gives it a little twitch of animation that sometimes triggers a trout to strike right away, only seconds after the fly enters the water.

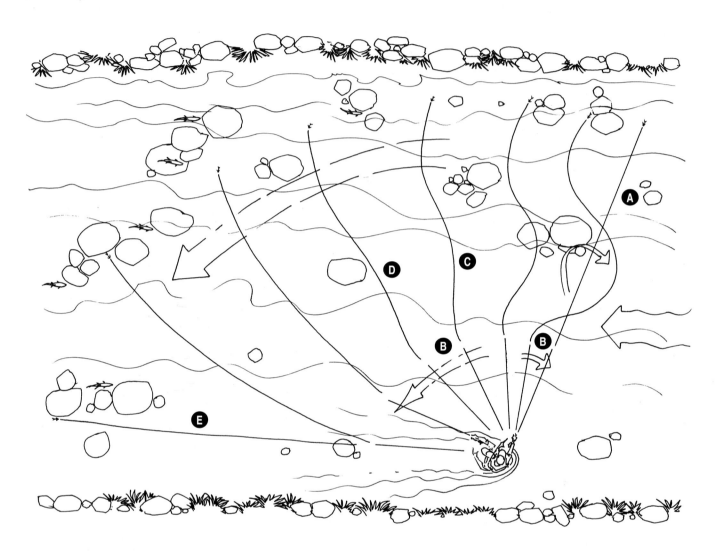

### Water Hump Mend

**A.** Make a straight-line cast from two to ten feet above and upstream of targeted trout. The faster the water, the farther the fly needs to land upstream from the holding position of the trout that is across, or down and across-stream.

**B.** As the line lands on the water, immediately make an upstream or downstream mend by lifting the closest line up and off the water, and flipping it in the direction that will slow the point fly at the end of the leader. A current seam creating two different current speeds between you and the fly will determine which direction you make the mend. Mend upstream for a faster current closest to you; for a slower current, mend downstream. If the current is the same, mend upstream. You can make one or two mends immediately, and more if desired, as the fly drifts through the whole presentation. The idea is to slow the leader-rig flies and let them sink or just drift at the current speed they are in, without crosscurrent dragging them too fast or across-stream prematurely.

**C.** After mending, the presentation starts. Often the strike comes right after the mend, as the fly is sinking right under the surface. Be ready for that one, it's a guaranteed smile and one of the best surprise quick strikes you'll get! It's important to visualize the point fly, and focus on its depth and drift in your mind's eye.

**D.** Once the fly has sunk to the streambed or desired depth, fish it across-stream, down and across, and downstream.

**E.** Don't forget to let the fly hang for a few seconds in the current below you. Then you can strip the fly back upstream, or Figure-8 retrieve before re-presenting.

## Aerial Hump and Reach Mend

A reach cast combined with a hump mend is a good way to not line a fish from across-stream, as well as to get a drag-free drift of nymph or dry fly.

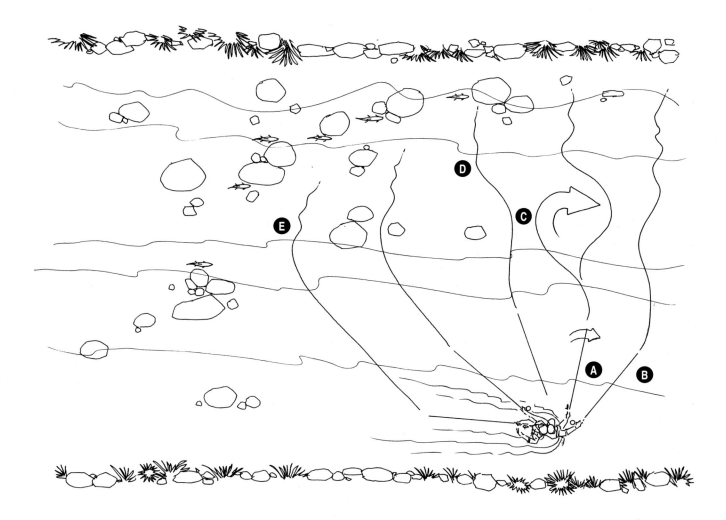

**Aerial Hump and Reach Mend**

**A.** Cast slightly farther up and across-stream than the targeted across and down and across-stream fish lies.

**B.** Make a straight-line cast and, as the line is unfurling and before it lands, throw a hump mend to either the left or right side, or a reach mend to either your left or right. You can also combine them, with a reach mend first, and then a hump mend at the last second before the line lands. Both mends combat current drag by introducing extra line above or below the fly to give it an extended drift, either on the surface or as a sinking aid.

**C.** Hold the rod out to the side of the mend. The fly will sink or drift without drag in the surface, depending on the type of fly. The direction of the mend depends on the currents between you and the fly. Reach to your right (upstream) if the water is faster closer to you, and slower in the current lane you want to fish; or reach left (downstream) if the water is slower closer to you, and faster in the current lane you want to fish. This compensates for the differing speeds and keeps the fly from dragging across-stream.

**D.** The fly is across-stream and drifting without drag. As the fly drifts down and across-stream, follow the fly with the rod tip, and lower it smoothly and at the pace of the stream current, to allow for a smooth swing and reduce drag. Concentrate on the fly's drift and watch the line, leader, and the water itself for any sign of the strike. Then set the hook with a slip strike or a slight lift of the rod tip.

**E.** Fish out the presentation with a swing, swing and dangle, or other line-action manipulations.

## Stack and Slack

The stack and slack presentation is a way to get a fly deep, then be able to swing the fly to the surface with or without any weight. The stack mending at the beginning of the presentation is key. The first half of the presentation is used to achieve depth, not for actually catching fish. It's with the second half of the presentation, after the fly has sunk and the line and leader begin to straighten, that the fishing begins. This means that to fish a targeted location, the cast needs to be made well upstream of the intended target. The fly can be swung to the surface with the current raising it up, or lifted with the rod tip, which accelerates the rise but allows more control. After the rise of the fly, you can do the dangle by lowering and raising the rod tip slightly when the fly is swinging or hanging downstream.

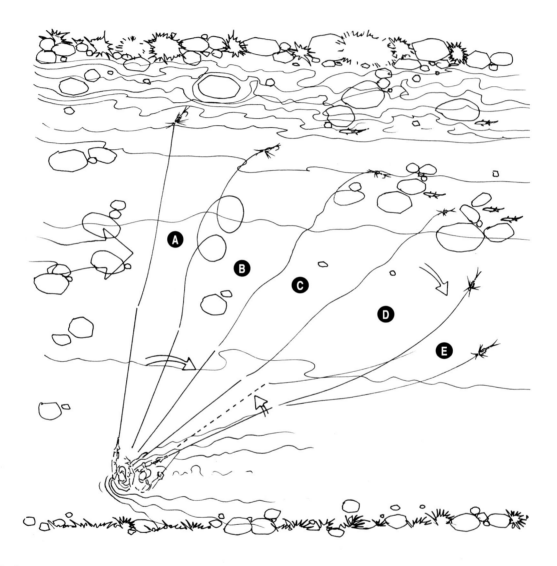

### Stack and Slack

**A.** Make a straight-line cast across-stream and farther than needed, for the current lanes you want to fish down and across-stream.

**B.** Immediately after the fly enters the water, make two stack mends by lifting the rod tip, thus pulling back on the line, and then throwing two short roll-cast motions to introduce two stack mends, and also drop the rod tip down to the water by dropping your elbow and making a plane-level change, the same as when making the slack-line cast. This allows maximum slack and lets the fly sink without any tension, setting up the rising swing and letting you get down to the streambed quickly.

**C.** The fly or flies will be deep as the current begins to straighten out the line. This is when the opportunity to catch trout really begins. Follow the fly with your rod tip as it begins to swing.

**D.** The swing will be slow, and the fly will lift from the streambed up to the surface as all the slack line begins to straighten. You can strip short sections (2 to 5 inches) of line, make line tugs without shortening the line, or simply raise the rod tip at different speeds to increase the rise rate. This is when most strikes occur.

**E.** Follow the fly through the swing until it's downstream of you. Don't lift it out of the water too quickly, as strikes can happen as it's hanging.

## Strip and Mend

Stripping the flymph in short 3- to 6-inch strips as it swings down and across-current can elicit violent strikes. But this also shortens the drift, as it pulls the fly both across-current and back toward the angler. Using a series of downstream hump mends, then strips or tugs, prolongs the fly's downstream drift, and also looks more natural to the fish. A small invertebrate doesn't swim against the current near the surface, but during emergence will drift and swim upward at the same time.

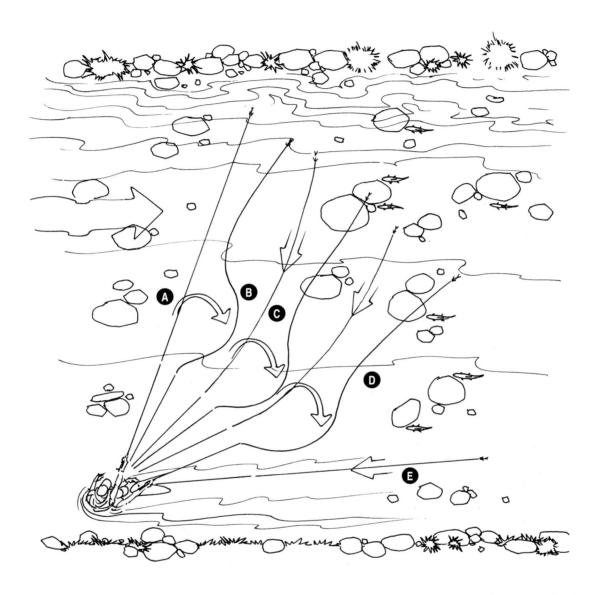

### Strip and Mend

**A.** Make a straight-line cast across-stream and farther than the targeted current lanes down and across-stream.

**B.** After the fly enters the water, make a downstream hump mend to allow the fly to sink.

**C.** Strip the fly (2 to 5 inches of line) or just tug on the fly line once. This animates the fly by giving it a sudden burst of movement, as though it had just propelled itself through the water with its legs or abdomen. This excites trout.

**D.** Keep making a series of hump mends followed by strips or tugs throughout the down-and-across swing, until the fly is straight downstream.

**E.** Don't pick it up too quickly; let it hang. You can also strip it back upstream or use a Figure-8 retrieve to bring it back upstream before casting again.

## The Soft-Hackle Swing and Dangle

If there were only one presentation that I could use for fishing soft-hackles, the soft-hackle swing and dangle would be it. This wet-fly swing variation makes the fly hitch and jump a little at the end of the swing, then rise and appear as a swimming nymph that is making practice runs or otherwise trying to swim to the surface to emerge. The soft-hackle swing and dangle can be used for fishing wet flies or streamers equally effectively.

**1** Make a quarter cast across and upstream from the intended target fish holding down and across-stream. If the water is fast or has multiple current seams, or if you want a deep sinking of the fly, make two hump mends right after the line lands on the water. Keep contact by following the fly with the rod tip as it's sinking and drifting.

**2** Hold the rod tip high enough for a catenary curve to form out to the fly. Let the fly drift across-stream and down and across, without affecting the drift, but still keeping line/leader control with a slack-tight drift. Now is the time to manually release line off the reel if you want to extend the drift, or don't and instead allow the fly to start to swing and rise across the current lanes and toward the surface.

**3** As the fly nears the end of the swing, it should be right in front of a targeted trout or lie. As this happens, release a little bit of line by letting the line slip between your line-hand fingers, and then stop it with your fingertips. Right then, lift the rod tip a little, and immediately drop it. The fly will jump up toward the surface and then quickly drop down again. This is called the dangle. After the fly has swung, lift the rod tip to raise the fly, then drop the rod tip down. Continue this three or four times in a slow, steady manner. Work your way around the stream, setting yourself in positions to achieve the correct setup for making this presentation to targeted fish or likely-looking holding water.

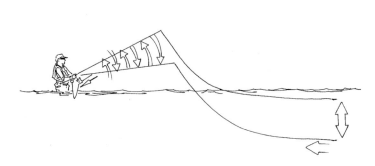

### Practice Run Method

The practice-run method aka soft-hackle jig is a presentation method that imparts level changes and action to the fly through a series of rod-tip lifts and drops, made either across-stream during a drift, or back upstream toward the angler when the fly is downstream. In between each drop, a little bit of line is pulled (stripped) with the line hand, until the line has been fully retrieved. The method is good for fishing to mayflies like *Siphlonorus* and *Leptophlebia* nymphs, as these make a number of surface practice runs to emerge, until they finally break the water surface. Each surface-rise attempt is a chance for a trout to eat the mayfly, and this method mimics that behavior well. This presentation can be use for midge pupae, mayfly nymphs and caddis pupae attempting to rise to the surface to emerge, and the repeated efforts that it takes some of them to do so. Use different lift and drop speeds for different effects.

## Greased-Line Technique

This method uses upstream and downstream hump mends to keep the fly drifting longer in a single current lane, before the cross-current swing begins. It is useful for bank fishing, where the fish are holding in the shallow water and the angler drifts the fly along the bank, then swings away from the bank out into the midstream current. This presentation is especially good for matching stonefly nymphs, caddis pupae, or mayfly nymphs that migrate the shore to hatch out of the water, as it allows you to cover the bank current lane for some distance.

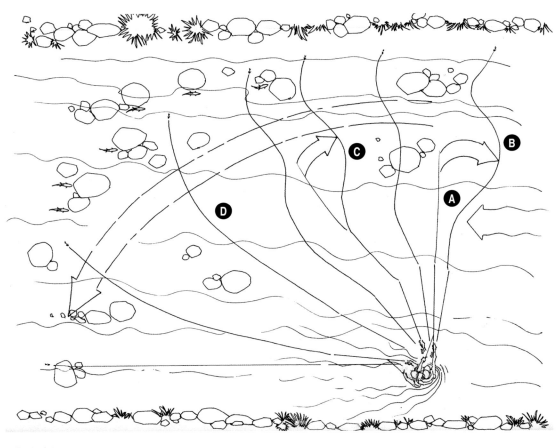

**Greased-Line Technique**

**A.** Either make a tuck cast or a straight up-and-across-stream cast.

**B.** After the line lands, make an upstream or downstream hump mend, depending on the crosscurrents between you and the fly (see water hump mend for more information), to allow the fly to sink to depth. This sets up the presentation, and sometimes this little bit of animation from the mend triggers the instinctive response from a trout to strike a fleeing food source.

**C.** The fly is sinking and directly across-stream. Hold the rod at about two o'clock. This creates the catenary curve. Farther upstream or downstream, make hump mends if needed to slow the fly or allow it to drop and rise.

**D.** Follow the fly with the rod tip through the swing downstream, lowering the rod tip as the fly swings, to allow for less drag and a smoother swing.

## Downstream Walk

The downstream walk method allows a fly that has drifted through an across-stream presentation to get to very deep and target fish in tailouts of pools. It works well in the winter when water temperatures are very cold and fish are holding on the bottom and require the fly to placed, sometimes held in front of them for them to strike.

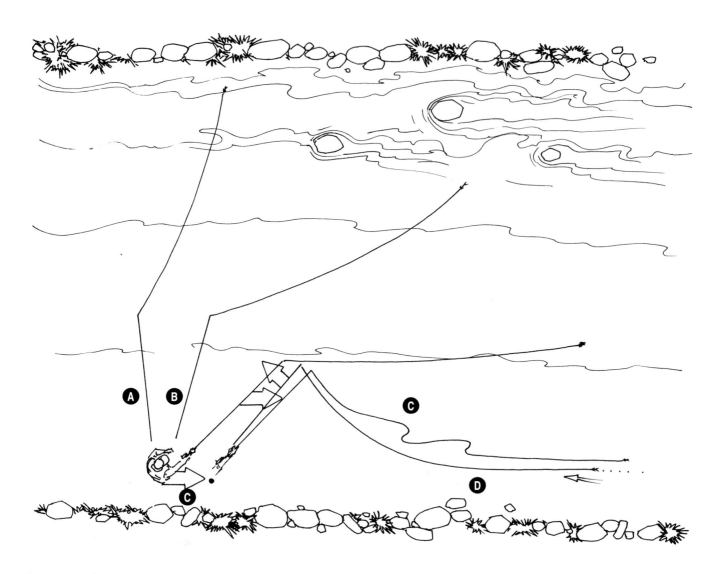

**Downstream Walk**

**A.** Cast across-stream with enough line to reach any target current lanes either across-stream, down and across or downstream.

**B.** Fish the nymphs with a high stick nymphing presentating. Then let them swing down and across-stream.

**C.** When the fly or flies begin to swing across-stream, reach with the rod hand to steer them into the middle channel while also taking a step or two downstream. Drop the rod tip down to the water surface all at the same time. This will introduce slack into the fly line and let the fly drop to the streambed.

**D.** The fly will hang deeply in front of fish that are holding deep for a second. Then slowly lift the rod tip as the line tightens in the current, raising the fly in front of the fish. Strikes will be vicious when they happen, so be ready, and when it happens don't pull the fly out of the fish's mouth; just raise the rod tip slightly to set the hook.

## High-Stick Nymphing

Use this presentation to keep soft-hackle nymphs drifting deeply, with control to steer them through current lanes, and to defeat drag and keep them drifting at the same rate or slower than the surface current. This is important because the deeper currents are slower, as the drift of naturals will be the deeper you go. High-stick nymphing also allows for great line/leader control and transmits the strike of the fish excellently, both of which also allow for a quick hookset.

When I'm high-stick nymphing a fast chute of water, I'll often manage the line with a Figure-8 in my line hand. I can feed line into the current at the same rate as the current, to keep my fly drifting downstream farther in a current lane without swinging across-stream too soon. It's important to hold the rod tip horizontal and high, to keep as much line as possible off the water when the line is feeding out from the Figure-8, so that the current pulls the line at the correct speed.

High-stick nymphing is good in fast pocketwater where you want to target trout around boulders or riffle-water structures. This method is also one of the best ways to steer flies through channels such as in vegetated spring creeks. It's not just for deep nymphs; it also works well for lightweight nymphs and surface or near-surface soft-hackle drifts.

High-stickin' in South Korea. Holding the line over current seams lets the fly drift longer through one current lane, potentially staying deeper and not swinging across-stream as fast.

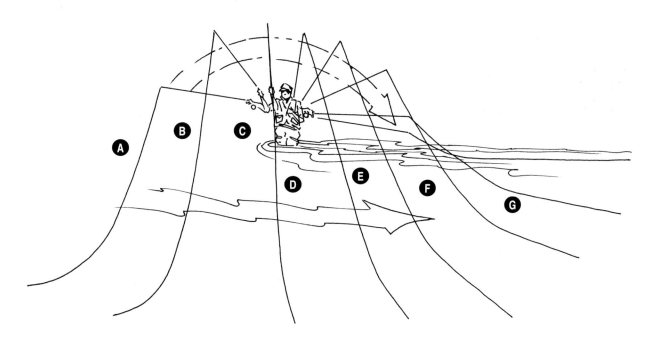

**High-Stick Nymphing**

**A.** Cast up and across-stream with either a straight-line cast or a tuck cast.

**B.** Hold the rod tip high to keep as much line off the water as possible.

**C.** You can make a hump mend if you want to momentarily let the fly sink, as if it were untethered. Lift the rod tip throughout the drift here.

**D.** The fly drifts across stream. You will feel the strike if you have good control all the way out to the point fly. You can even change hands with the fly rod here for more downstream reach and a prolonged drift, or just keep the rod in the rod hand.

**E.** As the fly passes across from you, begin to lower the rod tip to keep it from swinging, and in the current lane.

**F.** The fly is now on the far down-and-across-stream point of the drift. This is when the most violent strikes occur. Fish hit the fly hard here, because they see a meal that is rising to the surface and trying to escape, and they jump on it.

**G.** The rod tip has been completely lowered to compensate for the position. The fly will swing across-stream here. You can slow down the swing with a mend, swung at the same speed as the current, by following it with the rod tip; or speed up by stripping line, or twitching the rod tip up and down or left and right. The presentation is not over. Allow the fly to fully swing until it is directly downstream. Hold it there for about five seconds, since strikes often occur at this point. Then, either strip the fly upstream back toward you, or pick it up immediately and make another presentation.

The high-stick swing combines elements of high-stick nymphing and the classic wet-fly swing.

1.  Cast across or slightly up and across-stream, holding the fly rod nearly parallel to the water surface to keep as much line off the water as possible.

    Follow the fly through the drift, slowly lowering the rod tip as the fly drifts across and downstream.

    Keep lowering the rod tip. The fly will swing until it's directly downstream from you. As the fly is swinging, you may lift the rod tip to raise the fly more quickly. You can also wait until the fly is downstream, then lift the rod tip and the fly; or you can raise, drop, and raise the fly throughout the drift and/or swing, simulating the practice runs some mayflies make to emerge.

2.  Hold the fly in the current below you a few seconds. Strikes often happen here as the fly hangs in the current. If desired, you can strip the fly back upstream as little or much as you want, which covers more water and exposes the fly to more fish.

## Modified Leisenring Lift

The highly effective Leisenring Lift fits medium-depth and speed stream conditions and their fish holding locations. This method casts the fly across-stream, then drifts as the current is swinging. Raising the fly, the angler lifts the rod tip to raise the fly slightly faster in front of fish. I use a variation of this, called the Modified Leisenring Lift, to sink the fly a little deeper before it rises. To perform this presentation, simply make an across-stream cast and mend before the line straightens, allowing the fly a fast sink to depth and then to be set up for either a natural rising swing, quick lift, or deep dead drift before lift (as the angler sees fit).

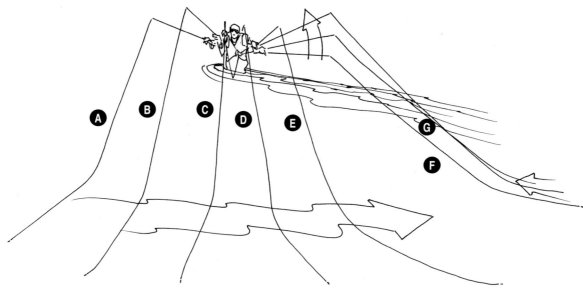

**Leisenring Lift**

**A.** Make an up-and-across-stream cast farther than the targeted current lanes across and down and across-stream.

**B.** Hump mend once or twice to sink the fly to depth.

**C.** Lift the rod tip and follow the fly across-stream.

**D.** Keep following the fly with the rod tip, raising the rod tip to the highest point when the fly is directly across-stream. The fly is at the deepest point.

**E.** The fly passes down and across-stream.

**F.** As the fly drifts down and across-stream, lower the rod tip. When the rod tip is at the lowest point, smoothly begin lifting the rod tip either slowly or fast, depending on current speed, species-imitation intended, fly weight, or fly animation you intend.

**G.** The fly lifts to surface and enticingly imitates an emerging insect species.

## Feeding Line

To keep a fly drifting in a current lane for a long distance downstream, it's necessary to feed line so the line doesn't drag and pull the fly across the current. Mending can achieve this for a short distance, but a long distance requires a constant amount of line feeding out of the rod-tip top guide, to keep the fly drifting without dragging.

Feeding line downstream into hard-to-reach lies, particularly in small streams, lets you target fish that lie in difficult places like undercut banks, or under half-sunken logs or overhanging tree branches. The angler feeds out line while standing upstream from the target lie, until the fly reaches the fish, then lets the fly hang in the current there right in front of the trout. If the fly is at the right depth, the fish will usually strike.

One method of feeding line is to do it manually. During a drift, use the line hand to strip line from the reel, to let the fly drift at the same speed as the current for a drag-free drift. It should be controlled, and you should only pull off enough at a time to accomplish the goal. Feed line, prestripped off the reel before the presentation, into the drift of the fly, to sink it deeper or extend the drift in a current lane before drag and swing occur. After you cast, and as the fly just starts to pass alongside and across-stream, begin to feed line off the reel and into the drift by pulling it off the reel and feeding it into the down-and-across drift of the fly, to keep it from dragging and swinging across-stream. Use a combination of the line hand releasing the line and the current speed pulling the line out through the rod guides to keep pace with the current. The speed of the feed depends on the speed of the current. After you have fished through the drift, eventually allow the fly to swing, and fish out the presentation. After the presentation is over, gather the line in loose coils to retrieve for another presentation.

## Free-Line Nymphing

Free-Line Nymphing is a technique I developed fishing the lower tall-grass meadows of LeTort Spring Run, which has what I consider the spookiest trout I've ever encountered. Merely approaching the water while standing is enough to scatter the fish, even from a distance of 100 feet. You have to stay low when fishing from the banks, especially if you are fishing downstream as they are facing toward you.

Free-Line Nymphing on the River Suir in Ireland. Notice that the line hand isn't holding the line, and it can freely spool off the reel at the same rate as the current if the pawls are disengaged.

I discovered that by bending the pawl spring to allow the pawl to completely disengage from the gear when the drag is all the way off, the spool turned freely, allowing the line to feed off the reel at the same rate as the current. The line must be carefully managed when fishing to avoid line overrun. This method reduces cross-stream drag and is great for the lightest of tippets on the biggest of trout.

Cast across-stream and make one or two hump mends up-stream. With the drag off, the current will pull the line off the reel as the fly drifts down and across-stream. The fly won't swing across-stream until you stop the spool by grabbing the line coming off it. This presentation only uses the rod hand to hold the rod, and the line hand waits for the time to stop the line. The line can then be reeled back onto the reel, to make another presentation.

The advantage of this is that the fly can cover a lot of water downstream while the angler stays far upstream from fish, remaining invisible to them. Trout will set themselves upon striking the fly because the line is under some tension, yet drifting naturally. You don't even have to be able to watch the end of the line, as strikes can be felt in the rod hand. Use this presentation on all types of water. In faster currents, apply some light drag by palming the spool, so the line doesn't travel off the spool too quickly. This presentation requires enough current speed to pull line off the spool. If a large fish strikes and you need drag, reach over your rod hand, and turn it on with your line hand after you set the hook.

I fish with the freespool and drag completely off on my reels most of the time. This low resistance of the spool also benefits manually feeding line out and allows me to fish regularly with line in the line hand or to Free-Line nymph from cast to cast. The freespool also has a mental aspect to it in that it helps me keep the idea of a unencumbered system in mind all the way out the fly that let's me feel freer and fish more loosely. This helps the fly look more natural and alive.

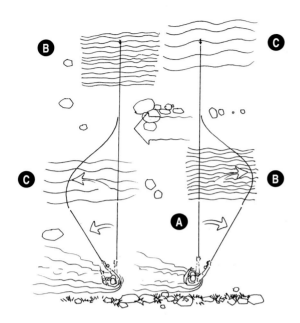

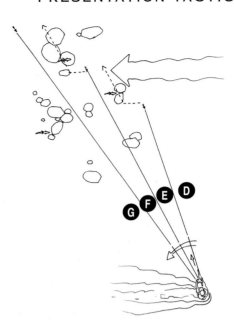

**Free-Line Nymphing**
**A.** Cast across-stream. Make two surface hump mends upstream or downstream, depending on the crosscurrents between you and the fly. **B.** Fast current. **C.** Slow Current.

**D.** Follow the fly with the rod tip as it drifts across and downstream. If the reel is adjusted properly, the line will pull off the reel at the same rate as the current. **E.** The line will continue to be pulled off the reel. Eventually the fly will swing across-stream, but at a slower rate, as the line is still traveling off the reel. **F.** Lift the rod tip slightly to set the hook when you feel a strike. **G.** Tighten up the drag on reel if you need to, or palm-drag the reel spool edge to slow down the fish.

## High-Line Nymphing

This presentation lets the fly achieve a long drift through a single current lane before dragging, by keeping a lot of line off the water and drifting at the same speed as the current. This method lets the fly sink as far and as fast as the fly's weight and design allow.

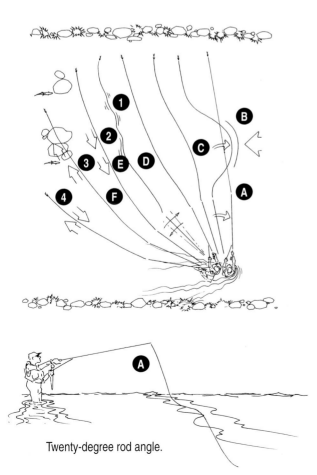

Twenty-degree rod angle.

**For Adding Extra Action to the Presentation:**
Animation of wet flies is important at times to add extra enticement to the appearance of the fly. Here are some rod-and-line manipulations that can be added to activate the fly more. Many, if not all, of these presentation strategies work best with the across-, downstream, and sweeping presentations. I use both active and nonactive presentations, depending on the mood of the fish, the water type, and the insect species I'm trying to imitate. In fact, highly active species such as caddisflies demand this to look natural. Here are some fly animations to imitate nymphs, emergers, and diving egg layers: (1) horizontal rod shakes parallel to the water surface, (2) stripping in line at varying retrieve rates, (3) feeding/releasing line from the reel into the drift, or (4) stripping in some line followed by releasing out some line or line tugs/releases without making the line distance overall effectively shorter at the end of the presentation. **A.** Make a cast across-stream holding the rod high, nearly level with the top of the stream surface. Let go of the line with the line hand. **B.** Keeping the rod tip high, completely let go of the line from the rod hand momentarily and make two upstream hump mends, pulling line off the water and through the guides of the rod until it's tight to the reel. This allows slack and sinking of the fly to achieve depth. The rest of the presentation is made with only the rod hand on a lifted plane, at about a 20-degree angle to the water. **C.** This becomes a one-handed presentation. Keep holding the rod high and parallel to the stream surface. **D.** Begin dropping the rod in a vertical plane, but keeping the angle nearly parallel to the stream surface. Drop the rod-hand elbow straight down, but don't change the angle of the rod. **E.** Lower the rod tip and track the fly as the drift continues. The line is straight and down and across-stream. Strikes commonly happen; always prepare for them. **F.** Fish the fly across the stream with a swing and rise.

## Sweeping Methods

Sweeping methods can be used on any-size moving water, but they are often the only way to present dries, wets, and nymphs in small streams that aren't wide enough for across-stream presentations yet still be able to activate the soft-hackle collars on the flies. If the stream is too narrow to effectively cast across-stream and mend to get the fly to sink before rising, then a shorter, sharper downstream angle presentation and swing is called for. This is accomplished by casting downstream with a reach mend that throws slack into the line, then allowing the fly to sink and swinging from the middle of the stream toward the bank, from the bank to the middle, or from bank to bank, depending on where you first land the fly.

A down-and-across-stream cast can be made on any size stream. On smaller streams, the flies can be fished from bank to bank. I call this the Sweeping Method. Make a reach mend cast, or a hump mend, before swinging the fly across the entire stream from bank to bank. The downstream presentation allows you to stay far enough upstream to avoid detection before moving downstream for the next presentation. The presentation can be a simple swing, strips, mends and drift, or a combination of all these, to discover what the trout find most interesting under particle conditions. The upstream hump mend sets up the presentation, as it keeps the fly drifting naturally, sinking for the swinging rise, and allows for line manipulations throughout the entire drift.

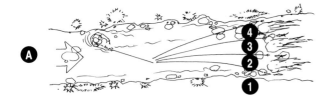

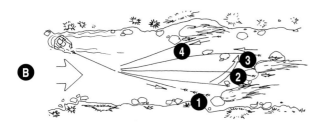

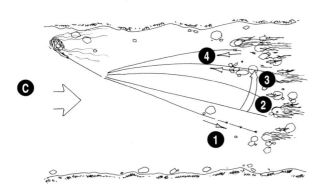

### Sweeping Methods

**A.** The basic sweeping method is a downstream presentation, in this case covering the small stream midstream to bank, bank to midstream, or bank to bank, and then moving downstream and presenting again. This method covers the water thoroughly and targets nearly every fish available in the stream. The diagram shows landing the fly on the far bank (1) and sweeping it across-stream (2, 3, 4). The fly could alternatively be landed in any of numbered locations and swept across to any other numbered location (i.e., 4-1, 3-4, 4-3, 1-2, or 2-1).

**B.** A Figure-8 sweep in a small stream. Working a small stream bank to bank with Figure-8 line management allows for the release of line into the current, while remaining able to make line strips for distance coverage and fly enhancement. (1) Cast the fly down and across to the far bank, then (2) release line from the line hand by allowing the current to pull it off the hand. The fly will swing across to midstream while (3) still allowing the line to pull off the line hand if desired or otherwise held on to and not released. (4) When the fly swings downstream, begin to retrieve line back upstream using the Figure-8 retrieve while directing the fly over to the near-side bank with the rod tip to cover an arc from bank to bank.

**C.** A Figure-8 sweep in a large stream. On fast, large-volume waters like the Madison and the Yellowstone, and even on technical spring creeks, I often use a downstream presentation only and target fish with distance, then sweep, then distance again for a more accurate drift and pinpoint presentation to holding water. This allows me to guide the flies where I want them, and at what depth, and determine how long the stay in the feeding lanes. When I'm fishing the sweeping method downstream, I look for feeding fish or likely holding lies and target them with a narrower presentation width than when I fish across-stream, working section by section. (1) Cast down and across-stream and allow a Figure-8 line release current to feed the line out. (2) Swing below and across-stream. (3) Cover the water back upstream with a Figure-8 retrieve. (4) Direct the rod tip to the near side of the angler as much as desired to cover a narrow or wider arc of drift with the fly. In larger water, move across-stream and repeat the presentation to cover another section.

A hefty native Yellowstone River Cutthroat caught on the surface in shallow water along the bank, with a #16 Gray Soft-Hackle Dry Caddis. Catching some of the larger fish in this river requires being there right around opening day as they migrate upstream to Yellowstone Lake.

## Upstream Presentations

Trout-feeding behavior (whether or not there is a hatch), water temperature, and water levels are important in determining the level of fly presentation called for in the water-column. Consistently successful surface wet-fly fishing requires water or air temperature warm enough for stream and terrestrial invertebrates to be active enough for trout to look to the surface for food. If trout are feeding either selectively or opportunistically on the surface, then a low-floating soft-hackle that rides in the film like a helpless emerger or adult, with the hackle collar

movement showing signs of life, generally will excite these fish into striking. Upstream soft-hackles are also a great way to work up a small stream. They allow you to approach the fish from their blindspot and show them only the fly. Fishing upstream requires more timing of rod and line handling and more focus than any other angle of wet-fly fishing. The rod, line, and leader are drifting back toward the angler, and slacking up if not managed well. This will cause strikes to be missed, unless the angler lifts the rod tip and gathers line with the line hand, to manage a direct connection out to the fly.

A wet fly fished on the surface sits low in the film. You have to watch how the fly line is drifting back to know where the fly is, and raise the rod at the same rate to keep line/leader control. The deeper the upstream fly is fished, the more challenging the line/leader control is to maintain. The rod lift must be both smooth and paced to the water speed through which the subsurface fly is traveling, even though the surface current is often drifting the floating fly line faster than the deeper currents. This requires practice and focus. A 9- or 10-foot fly rod helps minimize the amount of fly line on the water; helps control and feel for what the fly is actually doing; and, most importantly, makes it do what it should be doing: drifting deep back downstream at the same speed as the current level where it's located.

Fishing up and across in Millionaire's Pool on Henry's Fork of the Snake River. A wide variety of soft-hackle designs work well here and show flies and presentations to these rainbow trout that they may never have seen before.

# *Favorite Rigs*

The number of flies I fish, as well as how I rig them, depends on many factors, but especially the water conditions. If I'm nymphing, most of the time I fish two flies. If the water is cold, fast, or deep, I'll often tie on another dropper and fish three flies. Now, if the water is clear, shallow or slow-moving, and the fish are spooky, or if there is a visible hatch and I can sight-fish to a specific fish, I'll fish one fly and target the fish. In all of these scenarios, I will change flies not only to offer a different size or insect type, but also to change the depth or relationship of depth between the flies.

Single Wet Fly Benefits:
* Simpler for presentation with less bulk on the leader
* Easy to cast
* Good for targeting rising fish, as you can focus on the fly and fish
* Less commotion that risks spooking selective trout

Tandem or Multifly Dropper Leader Benefits:
* Covers different stream levels
* Able to present different sizes and colors for prospect nymphing, or life stages for hatches
* Flies balance each other and stay sunk
* Able to cover more water and, in turn, more fish during a presentation

Notice how the Duncan Loop Dropper slid up from the blood knot after the fish took the fly, but this is actually a good thing as it allows some give in the tension of the fly under pressure instead of pulling out of the fish's mouth.

The ultimate goals of both fly design and appearance in the water are bugginess, movement, and matching natural behavior. To achieve these goals, an angler must account for stream depth and current speed; the color, size, and shape of the fly; the speed of the rise and drift; and all the elements of fly design such as body construction and hackle-collar choice. In addition, the leader, the cast, perhaps a mend and the drift combine to make the fly appear to a targeted or suspected lie of a fish as a naturally acting insect, full of life . When combined properly, the fly will often elicit a strike from a trout, either as a feeding response or an induced take (i.e., when the fish strikes not out of aggressive hunger, but with an instinctive response to prey that's easy to catch). The placement and weight of droppers on the leader will determine the drift depth of the whole rig, and each fly's relationship to the others. A weighted fly as a point fly will help keep the leader tight all the way out to the point fly. A weighted fly on the dropper(s) and lighter point fly will allow the point to ride higher than the droppers off the leader, similar to using a split shot placed farther up the tippet. When fishing two or three flies, choose different sizes, shapes, colors, or weights. By offering different flies and weights, you will find the most effective flies and cover different water depths to search for where the fish are holding. If you find you are taking trout at a specific depth on one fly over and over, you may want to change the rest of the flies to that pattern and fish them all at the most productive depth. Fishing two or three flies of a single productive pattern on a leader can reap huge rewards. Rigging goes hand in hand with presentation.

1. Consider the species of insect you want to imitate and the life stage; these determine depth and location in the river. Decide if you will match any natural fly hatch conditions with droppers and fly choice, or if you will prospect with nymphs or dries with droppers, and then make the fly choices.
2. Decide on leader length and tippet length to get the best presentation on the water you are fishing.
3. Decide on dropper methods: how many flies, weight of each, and location on leader.

The best benefit of fishing two flies, or more, at once is the chance of catching two or more trout on a single cast.

4. Decide if extra weight on the tippet with split shot will be necessary or not, and how this will affect the drift and depth of the point fly and any droppers.
5. Decide on fly-attachment method, depending on fly size, fish size, and stream velocity.

## DROPPER RIGS

### Hook Eye Dropper
This method lets you insert a dropper in-line on the leader or at the end of the tippet attaching a dropper off the hook eye of the point fly. In-line droppers tangle less but have less free movement. It leaves the point fly hook point un-obstructed to trout so as to not alert them to the monofilament and rejecting the fly, like sometimes hook bend droppers can when trout feel the monofilament as they come in to strike the point fly. This is also a good dropper rigging for fishing two dry flies.

### Blood Knot Dropper
In this method, the dropper comes off the leader at a right angle and if kept to 2"–4" in length will not tangle. The Blood Knot Dropper is created by leaving a tag end of one of the two monofilament sections when you build a leader. The heavier of the two monofilaments would usually be the tag end for the dropper fly as it's stiffer and will hold the dropper at a 90 degree angle to the leader and minimizes tangles, but due to mono sizes it's really only appropriate for the tippet blood knot.

### Hook Bend Dropper
If you want a quick way to attach a dropper to the point fly or want to let the dropper float differently than it would with a tippet knot dropper (longer and more freely), or you want to rig a wet fly off a dry point fly (i.e., a dry/wet fly dropper), the hook bend dropper off the point fly is the method you want to choose. This rigging method will accentuate the movement of the dropper and also let you reach farther out, as it effectively lengthens your leader. It's best to keep the trailer dropper 4"–24" from the point fly to reduce tangles. Using a Duncan Loop around the point fly hook bend allows it to be removed or reattached by opening up the loop or drawing it tight. This method is good for two wet flies or two dry flies. Use either 4X, 5X, or 6X fluorocarbon for its stiffness and sinking properties depending on the size of the dropper.

### Dry/Dropper
This method is good for suspending a nymph or pupa under a soft-hackle dry or terrestrial. The dry acts as a depth suspender for life stage imitation. It's a great method for fishing egg-laying caddis as you can imitate both the surface adult (skittered or drifted) and a diving egg-layer at the same time. You can also fish a mayfly or caddis hatch matching both the surface adult and emerger at the same time. It's also the best system for upstream presentations in pocket water small mountain streams.

### Free Sliding Dropper
Thread a fly onto a leader section when building the leader between two blood knots. The fly will be able to slide along the leader, and it won't get tangled. Use either a straight eye hook or up-turned eye hook to keep the hook point exposed.

## Duncan Loop Dropper

I use the Duncan Loop both for attaching flies to the tippet and attaching dropper to the leader. When used to attach the fly to the tippet, the loop allows the fly to move freely giving the fly more life in the water. This versatile loop can be adjusted easily and even pulled tight, making it a quick way to attach, remove, and reattach a hook bend dropper without cutting the knot.

One technique that works well, especially for midges, is to fish a midge, caddis, or mayfly soft-hackle dry on the point, with Duncan Loop dropper on the tippet to suspend a midge pupa two inches or less under the surface. Not only does this gives the trout two choices of life stage to eat and provide a built in strike indicator, but the pupa will stay drifting at a set level and not sink too far.

After the first half of a dry-fly presentation, you can also pull the soft-hackle dry under and fish out on the swing, imitating a sunken egg-laying midge. This system can also apply to other insect species for the same purposes. To fish this system, use a soft-hackle dry fly or floating soft-hackle point fly and a Duncan Loop dropper attached between the tippet blood knot and along the 30-inch tippet section, not above the tippet blood knot. This allows you to slide the dropper along the tippet section and position it where it can be most effective. I often slide the dropper only 6 to 8 inches above the point fly, placing the two flies in essentially the same place and allowing me to fish to targeted rising trout,. The fish see both flies together and choose their preference of subsurface fly or dry fly. This method works better than a hook-bend dropper to avoid alerting a fish closing in on the dry fly to the presence of the monofilament dropper.

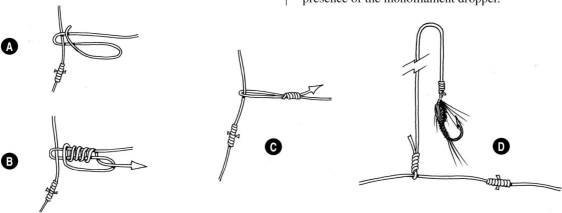

## Tying the Duncan Loop Dropper

**A.** Wrap an 8- to 10-inch section of 4X mono around the leader above the blood knot on your leader where you want the dropper. The blood knots on each end of the section act as stops. Make a small loop.

**B.** Pass the tag end around the standing line and through the loop five times. Hold the Duncan Loop and tighten, pulling on the tag end and loop.

**C.** Trim the tag end. Tighten up the loop against the leader.

**D.** Slide the dropper to reposition it. If you want to move it onto another monofilament section loosen up the loop and slide it over a blood knot then retighten it. You can open the loop up and remove the dropper from the leader completely by sliding it over the point fly.

## Dropper Position on the Leader

There are different reasons to put the heaviest fly as either the point fly or as an upper dropper, and they are determined mainly by water depth and the behavior you want from the flies. For deciding on where the heaviest fly should go on the leader, the thinking and practice go like this. When High-Stick nymphing in deep water (2' and deeper), I usually put the heavier fly on the point. This allows me to have a tight line all the way out to the point fly as it helps keep the line tight. The dropper flies higher up the leader are higher up in the water allowing me to fish more vertical depths of water. If you put the heavier fly as the dropper, it's an anchor for the flies out to the tippet. This is similar to using split shot.

When fishing shallow water (2' or less), I don't high stick. I fish a more horizontal leader drift because I need the flies to be drifting in a more similar horizontal plane. In this case I put the heaviest fly at the topmost dropper on the leader. Then I am able to achieve a better drift with all the flies at the same

level but covering different lanes of the river. The dropper fly needs to be separated enough from the point fly so that it can lift off the bottom. Usually this distance is 15 to 30 inches. This shows the fish two life stages, a streamed nymph, and a rising transitional emerger.

Another difference between the riggings is the way the point fly will behave. A light point fly will dance in the current more and be more active; the fly will shake side to side and rise and fall off the streambed as well. But, strike detection can suffer slightly if you don't maintain line/leader control, just as using split shot as the heavy dropper will not transmit strike detection as well from the light point fly. Vice versa, a heavy point fly will not be as animated, but the strike detection from flies along the entire leader will be more sensitive; this is because there is no deadening from a mid-point weight on the leader. There are uses for both methods of riggings depending on the water depth and whether you want more horizontal or more vertical coverage.

**Fly Depth**

**A.** Fast Water: Multiple Split Shot 2"–6" Up From the Point Fly. This is the type of weight rigging you use in the fastest, deepest water situations to get the fly deep. It will pin the fly to the streambed if you use proper line management holding as much line off the water as possible and mending when needed. If you want even more weight use a weighted fly and slow down your casting. **B.** Medium Fast Water: Split Shot 10"–20" Up From the Fly. The further the split shot is up from the fly the higher off the streambed the fly has the ability to lift. Fly

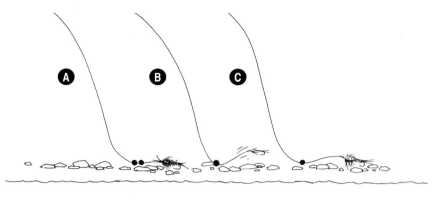

weight also affects this ability to lift. The most movement effect by the current lifting the fly off the streambed and letting it dance can be achieved with a lightweight fly and one or more size #1 split shot that hold the weight lower than the fly depth. **C.** Single Split Shot 10"–15" Up From Heavy Point Fly. This setup allows for less split shot weight to hold the fly deep as the nymph is heavy enough to drop. The disadvantage can be less action of the fly and its ability to "dance."

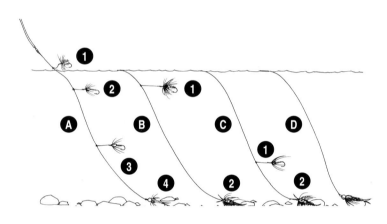

**Rigs for Different Depths**

**A.** This setup shows how you can cover top to bottom with multiple flies. Usually I only use the sub-surface lower three flies when nymphing, but you can leave off the second dropper and still have a very manageable leader rig. The keys to fishing multiple flies like this are proper rigging, fly weight selection and placement, proper casting form and line management during the drift. **1.** Surface Soft-Hackle Dry or Surface Wet Fly, **2.** Unweighted Soft-Hackle, **3.** Medium Weight Soft-Hackle Nymph, **4.** Point Fly Heavy Weighted Brass or Tungsten Bead. **B.** You can fish deep and just under the surface using a two-fly rig like this. These two zones are where fish hold most of the time and are where you can usually catch them. **1.** Fur Dubbing Flymph,

**2.** Stonefly Soft-Hackle Nymph. **C.** In very fast water, high water, or in the winter when the water is colder, fish often hold on the streambed. This rig puts two flies deep in front of trout. **1.** Soft-Hackle Dropper, **2.** Stonefly Soft-Hackle Nymph. **D.** This single fly nymphing setup gets the fly deep by using a heavy enough point fly, a 9' or 10' long fly rod to the line off the water as much as possible, a long 12' or longer leader depending on the water depth and where fish are holding, a long 30"–50" 6X fluorocarbon tippet that sinks fast as it cuts through the water, and a High Stick Nymphing presentation that holds line off the water to avoid drag pulling the fly off the bottom. Further depth is achieved with mends like hump mends and stack mends. All of this can often be achieved without any weight on the leader. When prospect nymphing in the fastest water, try using a tungsten bead head soft-hackle nymph like the Orange Hare Thorax Nymph.

**A.** Micro Split Shot. This setup uses only one small #6 or #8 size split shot to hold the fly a few inches underwater—sometimes necessary when the flies are very light or for fishing faster water to keep them from planing up to the surface. **B.** Dry/Nymph Dropper. This tandem fly surface rig allows you to fish a surface fly and sub-surface wet fly at the same time. The combination of flies is up to you and the fishing conditions. For example, during

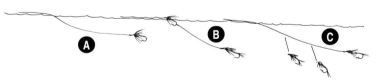

conditions when trout are visibly rising, and you want to fish with an adult pattern and emerger or floating nymph. Another situation is when you are prospect fishing upstream in a small stream or pocket water where you want to be able to detect drift easily and where opportunistic trout strike quickly yet carefully. Some fish in pocket water will take a surface fly while others prefer to feed on subsurface fare. This rig allows you to target both. Don't just use the Hook Bend Dropper rigging method; try the point fly Hook Eye Dropper as well. Soft-Hackle Dry Fly or Greased Spider (top fly), Lightweight Flymph or Nymph (bottom fly). **C.** Shallow Drift Wet Fly. This rigging uses either 1, 2, or 3 light wet flies or nymphs to fish only inches under the water surface. Using Duncan Loops, you can put on or remove the #1 and #2 droppers by opening up the loop and sliding the rig off the end of the leader with fly still attached to it. Keep it in your vest, and you can add it again to the leader whenever you want by sliding the open loop back over the point fly, up the leader to a position you want and gently tightening it against the leader. Remember to use 4X for the droppers and keep them about 4" or less for best performance. From top to bottom: Optional dropper #2, optional dropper #1, and unweighted flymph or nymph.

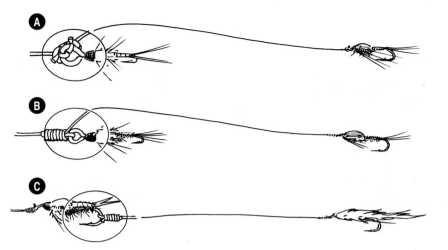

**Connections**
**A.** Hook Eye Dropper connected with Davy Knots.
**B.** Point fly tied with an extra long tag and then droppers attached.
**C.** Hook Bend Dropper tied off a wet or dry fly.

**Fly Attachments**
**A.** Davy Knot. The smallest bulk knot for fly attachment. Great for midges and uses less material than most knots. I use this knot the most except when fishing in streams with consistently large trout as it isn't the strongest knot.
**B.** Clinch Knot. A stronger knot but uses more material. Good, but not the strongest. On smaller diameter mono it must be lubricated with water before being drawn closed to avoid friction kinking of the tippet material.
**C.** Improved Clinch Knot. For the biggest fish in the strongest currents. This knot doesn't fail. It uses the most material and must be lubricated with water before tightening. A must on Madison River and Yellowstone due to the size and strength of the fish and the fast water.

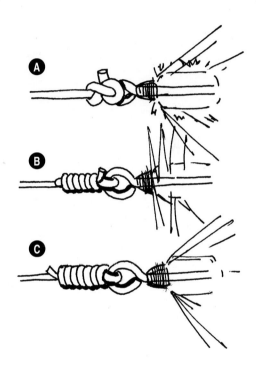

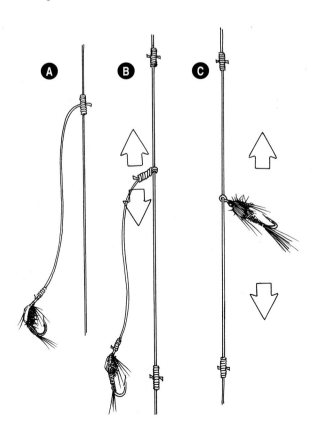

**Dropper Options**
**A.** Blood Knot tag dropper.
**B.** Duncan Loop Dropper. The blood knots act as stops.
**C.** Free Sliding Dropper. The blood knots act as stops.

# COVERAGE AREA FOR WET-FLY RIGS

Controlled mends let fly(s) sink yet still able to detect strikes on the semi-slackless leader because of good line/leader control.

These arcs represent one, two, and three flies on a standard dropper leader, and the importance of not only the stream-depth levels at which the flies drift, but also the distance between them. Knowing where the subsurface flies will drift tells you where you need to make your casts. I cast and target trout positions with the point fly or a dropper, depending on the fly and its likelihood to take a fish. The other flies cover where they cover, and often it's places you didn't expect a fish to be. Controlled mends let the flies sink, drift, and then rise through the swing, yet still enable you to detect strikes on the drift of the semislack leader through line/leader control.

## Stacking Dropper Flies

We can use flies of very different sizes and weights not only for matching insect species, but also to get the correct drift-depth and speed. Triple stacking means using a large, medium, and small fly on a leader rig. The large, heavy dropper is the top fly, used to weigh down the whole set of flies. The best way to rig these is with Hook Eye Dropper connections that keep the heavier flies from tangling. The smallest fly is the point fly, and it will ride higher than the droppers. This is a good prospecting nymph rig for fast, medium, or deep-riffle water.

A more balanced method of dropper fly size choice is to use three consecutive fly sizes for rigging multiple flies. This I call the concept of 12/14/16. On big rivers, the point is usually a heavy #12, the Blood Knot Dropper a medium weight #14, and up two blood knots from that a light weight #16. With this graduated system, there is no slack point or hinge in the setup and it is easier to detect strikes. The flies will ride at three different drift levels in the water column, with the point fly being the deepest and the top dropper nearest the surface.

If I fish two flies, then many combinations come into play, but it's usually a #12 point, #14 tippet dropper or a #14 point, #16 tippet dropper. Sometimes I'll have more drastic size differences, like a #12 point, #16 dropper. This 12/14/16 is a middle-ground system. If you are fishing a stream with primarily smaller species, try a 14/16/18 setup or even 16/18/20. Substitute larger or smaller flies, depending on the water conditions and active insects. It's a good place to start for prospect nymphing. In choosing the flies, a stonefly point fly, mayfly nymph tippet dropper, and caddis pupa top dropper make size, weight, and life cycle sense for determining what trout prefer.

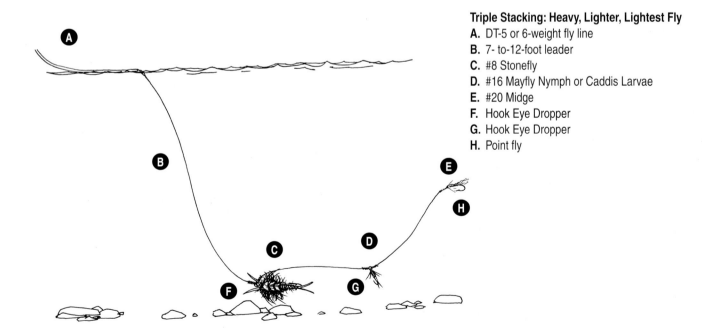

**Triple Stacking: Heavy, Lighter, Lightest Fly**
A. DT-5 or 6-weight fly line
B. 7- to-12-foot leader
C. #8 Stonefly
D. #16 Mayfly Nymph or Caddis Larvae
E. #20 Midge
F. Hook Eye Dropper
G. Hook Eye Dropper
H. Point fly

## Dredge Rig

In the winter when water temperatures drop, trout will hold on the streambed in the deeper pools and tailouts of runs. To reach these fish you have to get the flies deep, on the bottom and in front of these trout. This is not graceful fly fishing but rather short high-sticking and a deep drift. Fish the fly low and slow as a trout's metabolism slows down and they eat less and move less to eat the food. Using a long leader and tippet will help in getting this depth drift. This rigging works throughout the year on deep holding trout. For the deepest presentation try this with the downstream walk.

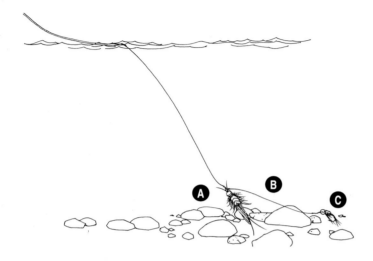

**Dredge Rig**
**A.** #8 Soft-Hackle Stonefly Nymph
**B.** 12" Hook Eye Dropper
**C.** #14 or #16 brass or tungsten bead head nymph

Silver Creek requires the right fly, at the right time, in the right way, and correct tackle and leader design help complete the transaction. Always have a well thought out and careful approach before you even begin fishing to trout in environs like this.

## Two Dry Flies

In a complex hatch where multiple species of mayflies or caddis are hatching at the same time, fishing two dry flies at the same time can help identify the species to which a trout is rising. Also, on turbulent small streams with fast chutes or pocket water, the two flies help float each other and aid visibility for tracking each other's drift. Fishing two dry flies is easy to rig. I like to use a longer-than-normal tippet, about 45 inches. Thread the first dry fly onto the tippet and use a Davy Knot to tie the fly on, leaving 12 to 20 inches of tag, and then tying the second dry fly onto the tag. This keeps the two flies separated by the distance of the tag. You can even attach a short subsurface nymph dropper off the hook bend of either dry fly. Two attractor dry flies are deadly on small streams, with an upstream presentation for opportunistic trout.

A two-fly match-the-hatch approach applies to matching life stages as well, i.e., rising emerger, floating emerger, floating spinner not traditional by any means but so deadly and that matters more to me. Which fly do you use to target a specific fish with? The answer is the one you feel will be more effective. Whether it's the dropper or the point fly. This is the one you focus on when fishing to riser with two dry flies. You fish that fly as if it's by itself and the other fly is along for the ride and yet not too far away that it can't also catch the targeted fish's eye or the eye of another fish near your target. If the fish doesn't take the first fly whether point or dropper then I cast again making the other fly the primary one. In another match-the-hatch scenario where I'm using two wet flies, I use the same principle. I focus on whichever fly I feel is most appropriate and will be most effective in catching a rising trout. Any dropper would be used as the primary fly only after I tried the first choice. The casting would be tailored to presentation either point fly or dropper in the most accurate and effective manner to both target the fish and imitate the behavior of the naturals. Finally, when the fish aren't rising and I'm prospect nymphing with a wet fly leader and a point fly and droppers tied off the leader, I focus on and use the point fly as if it's by itself making sure it rides at the right depth and speed. The droppers are along for the ride, but I'm focused on that point fly when casting and drifting the rig through the presentation.

## Two-Level Flies: Ovipositing Caddis or Mayfly Spinners

Two flies are a great way to fish a spinnerfall of mayflies or an ovipositing caddis event. These riggings enable you to fish both a floating soft-hackle fly and a subsurface egg-laying caddis or sunken spinner, covering two water levels and offering the fish more choice.

Tip: Cast far enough above the feeding trout to present the subsurface dropper to the rising fish first, and then let the point fly drift over the fish. Reverse if fishing downstream.

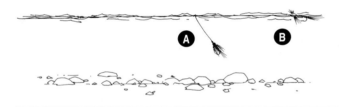

**Two-Fly Match-the-Hatch Spinner or Egg-Laying Caddis Rig**
**A.** Diving Caddis or Soft-Hackle Sunken Mayfly Spinner
**B.** Soft-Hackle Dry Fly, either Egg-Laying Caddis or Mayfly Spinner

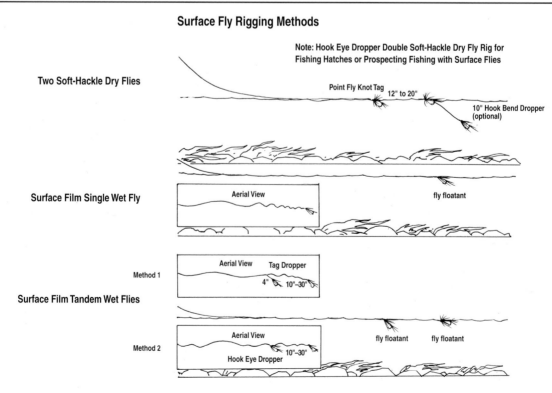

**Surface Fly Rigging Methods**

Two Soft-Hackle Dry Flies

Note: Hook Eye Dropper Double Soft-Hackle Dry Fly Rig for Fishing Hatches or Prospecting Fishing with Surface Flies

Point Fly Knot Tag   12" to 20"

10" Hook Bend Dropper (optional)

Surface Film Single Wet Fly

Aerial View

fly floatant

Method 1

Aerial View   Tag Dropper

4"   10"–30"

Surface Film Tandem Wet Flies

Aerial View

10"–30"

fly floatant   fly floatant

Method 2

Aerial View

10"–30"

Hook Eye Dropper

Soft-hackle dry flies are good for surface fishing in fast water, as they are capable of floating high, and also are visible. They are used to match the hatch, as searching patterns or as depth suspenders.

Target the fish with either fly first. For example, when fishing upstream or downstream, I am far enough upstream of a trout so that all flies will float over the target, exposing it to the flies and giving it choice by exciting it into a frenzied strike at appetizing food items. Across-stream doesn't allow this, but you can present one fly at a time by putting each fly in front of the fish on successive casts. Start with the one you feel most confident in first.

## Double Dry-Fly Rig

There are a couple of scenarios in which I like to fish two dry flies at the same time. First is when I'm fishing a small, fast mountain stream, and drifts are short through a small pocket of holding water. Two surface flies give the trout more chance of seeing, moving, and then striking one of the flies. It's also easier to see the flies and track their drift in fast water. The second is in a multiple-species hatch, where trout are selectively feeding on one species, but you can't tell what they are taking. By offering them two different surface flies, you can help narrow that list down to the right species, size, or life stage (emerger, dun, or spinner).

A good way to rig two surface flies is with a Duncan Loop dropper off the hook bend of the point fly. This is easy to cast and quick to rig, and the dropper can be taken on and off quickly. You can also attach the second fly to a long-connection knot tag of the point fly. Some examples of two-fly species combination rigs are mayfly and mayfly, caddis and caddis, caddis and mayfly, terrestrial and caddis, and mayfly and terrestrial. These combinations can be replicated with two different sizes or two different life stages of the same species, to uncover the selectivity of the feed. Some trout will only take a fly that is one size smaller than what's hatching, so fishing the correct size and one smaller is sometimes the key. Size is king in this regard, whether small or large, and it's of utmost importance to find the right one and fish it correctly. I find trout usually key in on size initially if they are feeding on a particular species of bug, and only then will they consider the other traits.

## Weighted Flies and Split Shot Selection and Placement

I use split shot not only for depth but also to slow the drift speed down, whether in deep or shallow water. I only go to heavy split shot if the tuck cast, mending and fly weight are not enough to either sink the fly or keep it drifting deep if the fish are holding there. This doesn't always mean fishing on the streambed, but rather from just under the surface down to the streambed. To accomplish this weight I use two primary split shot sizes and add them together to get the right weight on the tippet. For fishing deep I use one to three size 1 shot to get the fly deep. For shallower water and just to sink the flies under the surface, I like the #6 size as it's small enough to be easy to cast.

## Micro Split Shot

Small or unweighted fur bodied flies often need a micro split shot on the leader about 10 inches up from the point because they tend to want to float or buoy and plane on the surface. I use micro split shot on the leader just enough to pull the fly underwater and keep it submerged. Not so much for a deep drift but for a complete drift underwater a few inches down to a foot underwater. I often fish a single fly with this system. The small #6 split shot weighs 0.1 grams. It's practically unnoticeable when casting but will sink a team or single fly underwater and keep them from buoying up to the surface. Sometimes I add two of these split shot 10 inches up from the point fly and about an inch apart, but usually one does the job. The micro split shot are particularly effective when fishing midge larva and pupa on small #20 or smaller hooks that you want to drift a few inches or so under the surface.

A channel of the River Suir near Golden, Ireland. This excellent stretch of water while not wide is 3-5 feet deep and holds a fine stock of native brown trout. Don't miss out on the Suir's excellent tributaries like the River Multeen, Aherlow, Tar, Nire, and especially the Anner.

## Hook Bend Dropper Two-Life-Stage Rig

A Hook Bend Dry/Dropper works well during hatches or prospecting. For example, a two-life-stage caddis rig uses a soft-hackle dry to imitate surface adults or egg layers; and a 6- to 12-inch Hook Bend Dropper attached to a wet fly to imitate caddis pupae, diving egg layers, or sunken egg layers, depending on the patterns used and naturals on the water. One fly often gets the attention of the fish, but then they strike the other fly, finding it more attractive—an induced take of sorts.

One trout-stimulating dry-fly presentation is to sparingly apply some fly floatant to the soft-hackle dry caddis wing, hold the rod with the tip pointed upward after making the cast, and use quick, short rod-tip twitches to skate the fly over the surface, imitating the skittering movement of the egg-laying caddis. This is effective on windy days when the wind will belly the line off the water, helping to give the fly lift and skitter it. This rigging and method can also apply to other species of mayfly, caddis, and midge, with appropriate flies and behaviors.

## FAVORITE FLY RIGS

**Prospect Nymphing: #16 Contrast Nymph (Tippet Knot Dropper) #14 Beaverhead Nymph**

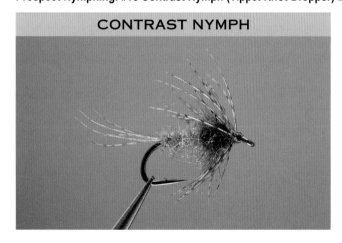

CONTRAST NYMPH

BEAVERHEAD NYMPH

**Nymphing in Deep Water: #8 Steven Bird's Depthcharge Nymph (Hook Bend, 20" 5X Fluorocarbon) #16 Heavy Metal Nymph**

## DEPTHCHARGE NYMPH

## HEAVY METAL NYMPH

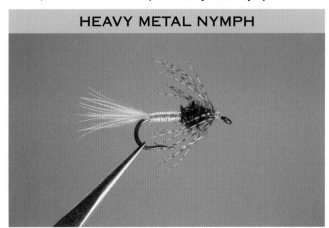

**Prospect Nymphing, Downstream Walk: #16 Teton Sunset (Tippet Knot Dropper) #12 Marabou Egg (Point Fly)**

## TETON SUNSET

## MARABOU EGG

**Prospect Nymphing, Medium Depth and Speed Current: #14 Geyser Pupa (Tippet Blood Knot Dropper) #14 Appalachian Springfly ArticuNymph**

## GEYSER PUPA

## APPALACHIAN SPRINGFLY

**Prospect Nymphing Shallow, Clear Water: #16 Holo Spider (Tippet Knot Dropper) #14 Clinger Nymph**

| HOLO SPIDER | CLINGER NYMPH |
|:-----------:|:-------------:|
|  |  |

**PMD or Sulphur Mayfly Hatch: #16-18 PMD Soft-Hackle Dry (Hook Bend Dropper, 4" to 12") #16-18 Pale Morning Sulphur Wet Fly**

| PMD SOFT-HACKLE DRY | PALE MORNING SULPHUR |
|:-------------------:|:--------------------:|
|  | 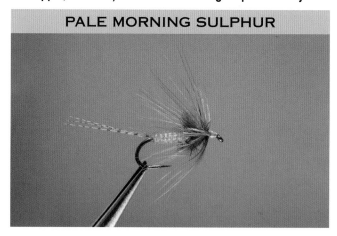 |

**Caddis Hatch (Double Pupa): Cahir Caddis (Tippet Knot Dropper) Evergreen Pupa**

| CAHIR CADDIS | EVERGREEN PUPA |
|:------------:|:--------------:|
|  |  |

*Hydropsyche* Caddis Hatch and Egg Laying Overlapping: Skittering Egg-Laying Soft-Hackle Dry (Hook Bend Dropper) Egg-Laying Diving Caddis or Pupa

**SKITTERING EGG-LAYING SOFT-HACKLE DRY**

**EGG-LAYING DIVING CADDIS OR PUPA**

Midge Hatch: Soft-Hackle Dry Midge (Hook Bend Dropper) Midge Pupa Soft-Hackle

**SOFT-HACKLE DRY MIDGE**

**MIDGE PUPA SOFT-HACKLE**

Terrestrial Fishing: #12 Soft-Hackle Dry/Wet Grasshopper (Hook Bend Dropper, 6" to 18" of Tippet) #16 Wet Ant

**SOFT-HACKLE DRY/WET GRASSHOPPER**

**WET ANT**

**Three-Depth Rig: #18 Fluorescent Spider (Duncan Loop Dropper) #16 Ice Pheasant (Tippet Knot Dropper) #14 Heavy Metal Nymph**

FLUORESCENT SPIDER

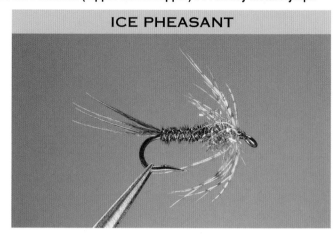

ICE PHEASANT

HEAVY METAL NYMPH

**Action Rig: #16 Hare's Ear Soft-Hackle (Tippet Knot Dropper) #16 Pheasant Tail Soft-Hackle**

HARE'S EAR SOFT-HACKLE

PHEASANT TAIL SOFT-HACKLE

## Small-Stream Soft-Hackle Rigs and Methods

Living near the Blue Ridge and Great Smoky Mountains, I've spent many days fishing the small creeks that run down through those mountain ridges and gorges. The native brook trout are only found in the uppermost headwaters nowadays. Fishing for them is as much physical as it is mental, due to the tight quarters that one must negotiate to catch them. Many of the bigger creeks have boulders and waterfalls of various sizes that you have to crawl over and hike around to keep traveling and fishing upstream. Often the only casts made are roll casts or bow-and-arrow casts, due to the streambank vegetation, overhanging rhododendron, mountain laurel, and the narrow width. These creeks don't require long casts or long leaders. They require stealth, concentration, patience, and fitness. There are two ways to fish them: fishing upstream, casting to pockets and pools, then moving upstream; or fishing downstream. Since casting is often tight, fishing downstream can be easier, as you can use the drift to carry the fly to the target. When I fish upstream, I usually use a high-floating surface soft-hackle dry fly, often with a wet fly or soft-hackle nymph as a hook-bend dropper, or one or two soft-hackles fished in the surface film. The upstream soft-hackle on small water can be deadly, and fish will rise and strike aggressively. The drifts are often short due to the fast, shallow pocket water. Fish will either strike or they won't. I don't waste too much time on each small hole; if strikes happen, they usually happen on the first, second, or sometimes third cast. Then I move up to the next holding lie. You can make the downstream approach with the same rigging, or remove the dry fly in favor of only a wet fly, flymph, or soft-hackle nymph. Many times, the best downstream fly selection is a #12 soft-hackle streamer, with or without a smaller #14-18 wet fly attached to the streamer on a 12- to 16-inch Hook Eye Dropper. I sometimes go with a short 6-foot fly rod, but usually fish a 7-foot, 6-inch 4-weight, as it's short enough for some of the tight overhanging vegetation,

yet long enough to hold some line off the water to reduce drag. Leaders are usually only 5 to 7 feet long. Since you are not fishing across the current, but rather upstream and downstream with smaller angles, having droppers off the point fly will expose the fish to both flies.

Here are some of the main factors that I consider when I fish small mountain creeks.

1. In tightly covered small streams, the 6-foot-6-inch mountain leader is long enough, and will allow some fly line to load the rod enough to make short and precise casts or roll casts.
2. Present upstream with a dry/dropper setup like a Soft-Hackle Stimulator or Soft-Hackle Dry Caddis, and a #16 soft-hackle dropper off the hook bend.
3. Try fishing upstream with one or two soft-hackle dry flies.
4. If fishing downstream, stay far enough upstream and away from the water you are fishing, to not spook the fish. Feed line down into the pool with a streamer, streamer/soft-hackle dropper, or double soft-hackle nymph.
5. Fish a skated soft-hackle dry fly downstream, with or without a soft-hackle nymph as a Hook Bend Dropper.
6. Triple stack rigging to give trout a wide range of nymph choices.
7. In higher water, try a white streamer along the streambed.
8. Move slowly, kneel down to cast, stay low, and wear camouflage, if for no other reason than to remind you to be stealthy and avoid detection.
9. If the stream is tight or there is a lot of overhanging vegetation, use the Downstream Line-Feed Method to put the fly in front of the trout. This keeps the angler hidden and doesn't even require casting.
10. Try a one-handed presentation for better concentration on a drag-free drift.

Staying low and invisible to trout can be critical in spring creeks, where trout have low-depth holding water and a highly reflective window to the world above. When these conditions are present, trout can often see you better than you can see them. These situations in particular call for roll casts and long leaders, in additon to clothing, flies, and presentations that are not alarming. Put together, these factors fool trout all day. Remember, approach and positioning will ultimately affect your fly presentation choices. Study the stream and fish, and become the heron. Then begin fishing.

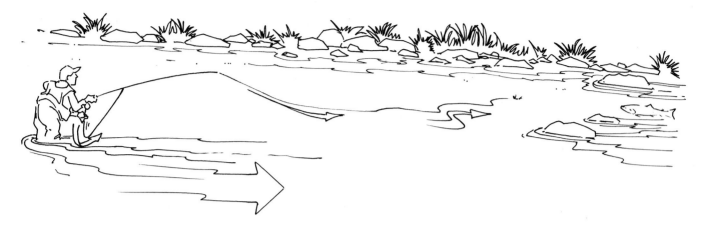

A downstream manual line feed into a prime lie gets a fly into an undercut bank or other prime lies for trout, where you want the fly to entice a fish by appearing right in front of him. Feed line off the reel, or turn off the drag and let the reel free spool the fly into the feeding lie.

## *Examples of Mountain Stream Prospecting Rigs*

Caddis Dry Fly/Mayfly Nymph Dropper: #16 Tan and Orange Soft-Hackle Dry Caddis (*12" 6X Hook Bend Dropper*) #16 Pheasant Tail Soft-Hackle

Yellow Sally Stonefly Dry/Prospecting Nymph Dropper: #14 Yellow and Orange Soft-Hackle Stimulator (*12" 6X Hook Bend Dropper*) #16 Green and Copper Wire Flymph

Double Surface Film Spiders: #14 Bukcheon Spider (*12" 6X Hook Eye Dropper*) #16 Bukcheon Spider both greased to float the flies in the surface film

Mayfly Dry Fly/Sunken Terrestrial: #16 Gray Soft-Hackle Dry Mayfly (*12" 6X Hook Bend Dropper*) #16 Soft-Hackle Wet Ant Hook Bend Dropper

Surface Terrestrial/Mayfly Nymph: #14 Orange Soft-Hackle Ant (*12" 6X Hook Bend Dropper*) #16 Gold Beadhead Soft-Hackle Pheasant Tail Nymph

Double Caddis Dry Fly: #16 Tan and Orange Soft-Hackle Dry Caddis point fly (*14" Davy Knot tag end*) #16 Tan and Orange Soft-Hackle Dry Caddis

## *Streamer/Nymph Dropper Rig: #12 Weighted Soft-Hackle Streamer (18" 5X) #16 Bead Head Orange Hare Thorax Nymph*

The streamer/dropper rig is great for fishing the undercut banks of small meadow streams. Streamers imitate baitfish venturing under the bank looking for a home, and resident trout often eat them. Fish the streamer tight to the bank, then swing it into the middle of the stream, as if the small bait-fish were trying to escape from the area. The small trailer fly will go along for the ride and be active in the current. Fish often will strike the larger fly, but if not, it gets their attention and sometimes makes the smaller, less obtrusive fly more attractive.

A wet ant is a great meadow-stream fly that also works well just about everywhere. I fish them in orange, cinnamon, black, and (my favorite) the black/red ant, in soft-hackle dubbed or epoxy-wet versions.

## *Dry/Dropper Rigs*

On narrow waterways with heavy bank foliage, where you have to wade in the water to fish and move upstream, I often fish with a dry/dropper rig. The dry fly serves as a strike in-dicator, allowing for drag-free drift of the trailing dropper; offers another fly for the fish to strike; and allows for an un-detected approach from behind trout's blindspot. There is also the benefit of line/leader control and a direct connection out to the nymph dropper. The leader can't belly underwater causing loss of connection out to the point fly and missed trout strikes.

Furthermore, you can fish two levels at the same time, giving the trout their choice. The dropper connects to the hook bend of the dry fly with a length of an 8- to 18-inch section of 5X mono or fluoro. The water depth and, in the case of a hatch, the depth at which the fish seem to be feeding determine the length. I like to keep the length of dropper as short as will work, so that I can cast the rig easily, avoid tangles, and see a strike on the dropper transmitted quickly to the dry fly so I can set the hook immediately. On small, fast waters with opportunistic trout, target casts to holding lies. Be ready for quick strikes that can happen fast.

Dry/droppers aren't just relegated to small streams or upstream presentations. On big waters like the middle Henry's Fork of the Snake, they can be a great searching rig. For instance, in May the river can be high due to the runoff of tributaries like the Warm River and Robinson Creek. But the fishing can still be good if you target the banks where the fish hold in the higher water. Using an unweighted #8 PT Stone Nymph dropped 12 inches off a #6 Soft-Hackle Stone dry fly can be effective for searching, and realistic as well. This is the time period leading up to the Salmonfly hatch, and fish will be looking for these nymphs migrating and along the banks before the hatch begins. When you fish a dry/dropper instead of just the dead drift another method is to skitter the dry fly across the surface back toward you with rod tip twitches combined with the streamflow. This gives the impression of an egg-laying caddis and the soft-hackle dropper appears as a swimming, darting nymph.

When fishing dry and droppers, especially on small streams, I sometimes use only my rod hand to make casts and presentations, with the line trapped under my finger on the rod handle. This technique offers several advantages. First, it allows for maximum reaching out and over currents, which lets the fly drift longer with less drag possibilities. There is a more direct feel out to point fly, making drift control and strike detection more precise. It feels right for upstream dry-fly presentations on small streams. Hook sets are quicker—merely lifting the rod tip—than they are using the line hand to pull the line, which helps in fast water. The one-handed presentation method is also good for high-stick nymphing and lifting the line over multiple currents, when fishing in all directions: upstream, up and across, across and down and across. It can even benefit the classic wet-fly swing, as you can't accidentally pull on the line, making the swing smoother. Finally, it's also good for high-stick nymphing with a fixed length of line. However, I wouldn't use a one-handed presentation when I need to be able to gather line to manage line/leader control, such as when I'm fishing a deep nymph upstream; or when I may want to impart line strips or tugs, or manage line with a Figure-Eight retrieve; or when I may want to feed out line to extend the drift, either from line prestripped off the reel or by stripping it off the reel as the flies are drifting.

## HI-VIS CADDIS

| | |
|---|---|
| **Hook:** | #12-#16 Mustad R50 |
| **Thread:** | 6/0 Danville Flymaster Yellow |
| **Shuck:** | Hend's #94 Golden Yellow Spectra Dubbing |
| **Abdomen:** | Yellow Ostrich Herl |
| **Wing:** | Bleached Deer Hair |
| **Hackle:** | Bleached Partridge |
| **Head:** | Orange Ostrich Herl |

**Note:** A Hi-Vis Caddis is used for strike detection but more importantly to suspend the wet fly 4 to 18 inches under water.

On small streams, I often fish with an upstream dry-fly one-handed presentation. There's no chance for even the slightest pullback on the line, resulting in a better drag-free drift. If I want to lengthen the cast, I let go of the line held against the grip while making false casts, and the line is pulled off the reel if the drag is light. When false casting reaches the length of line I want out, I trap it against the grip again and lay the line down on the presentation to the fish. After the strike, I play the trout on the reel with my line hand.

## Leader Designs

These are my basic leader designs. I use these interchangeably for nymphing, wet fly and dry fly fishing based on the stream size, depth and fish location. I carry all of them in my vest and change them out connecting them with loop to loop connection to a 1-inch section of .017 Maxima Chameleon superglued into the ends of my fly lines. Fluorocarbon has less reflectivity; it's great for wet flies as it will stay underwater better while monofilament doesn't necessarily float but it does tend to buoy up more toward the surface. Monofilament also is often better for the slack line dry fly presentation as it's limper and allows the tippet to pile up and create S-curves to decrease drag.

First is the standard 3-fly leader rig for nymphing. Depending on the stream and fishing conditions sometimes only one or two flies are fished. Second, on small streams and when I fish a shorter leader the droppers and point fly can be closer together. A sighter leader offers the benefits of the hi-vis mono sections that can help you detect strikes and drift speed. Hold as much line off the water as you can to allow the flies to sink out the point in a direct connection.

When nymphing, a thinner diameter tippet is going to cut through the water column and sink faster than a heavier material. Also, fluorocarbon material sinks faster; therefore using a thin 6X diameter and a long tippet 5' or more, along with weighted soft-hackle nymphs and keeping as much line off the water by using a long fly rod, will sink those fly(s), and they will stay down in the strike zone faster and longer. These are the keys to catching trout holding at depth and are mandatory to learn and use.

**Standard Nymphing Leader Formulas**

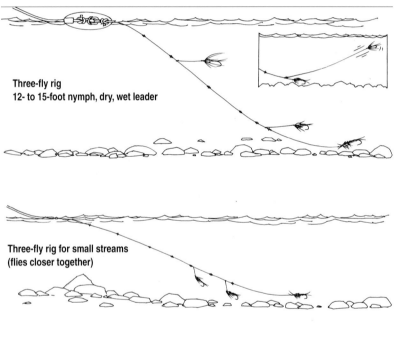

**Three-fly rig**
**12- to 15-foot nymph, dry, wet leader**

**Three-fly rig for small streams**
**(flies closer together)**

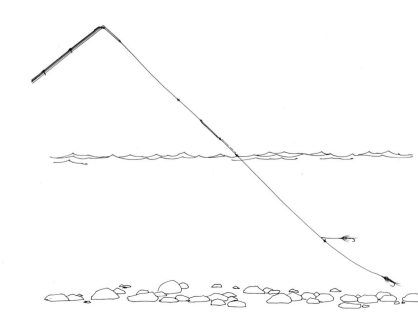

**Sighter Leader**

## *Other Effective Leader Designs*

mch = maxima chameleon; p = rio powerflex; f = fluorocarbon; ra = red amnesia

Small Eastern Mountain Streams 6' 6"

| 10" .017mch | 10" .015mch | 10" .013mch | 10" .011mch | 6" .010p | 6" .008p | 8" .006p | 18" .005p or f | 6X |
|---|---|---|---|---|---|---|---|---|

| 6" .008p | 8" .007p | 18" .006p or f | 5X |
|---|---|---|---|

| 14" .008p | 18" .007p or f | 4X |
|---|---|---|

6-foot, 6-inch leader for small Eastern mountain streams.

8'–10' Standard Multi-Purpose Nymph and Dry Fly Leader

| 15" .017mch or ra | 15" .015mch | 15" .013mch | 12" .010p | 12" .009p | 12" .008p | 26"–40" depending on depth .005p or f | 6X |
|---|---|---|---|---|---|---|---|

| 26"–40" .006 p or f | 5X |
|---|---|

| 26"–40" .007 p or f | 4X |
|---|---|

| 26"–40" .008 p or f | 3X |
|---|---|

8- to 10-foot standard multi-purpose nymph and dry fly.

12–15 Spring Creek or Deep Water Nymph and Dry Fly Leader

| 10" .017mch or ra | 20" .015mch | 20" .013mch | 20" .011mch | 20" .010p | 12" .008p | 12" .006p | 30–60" .004p or f depending on water depth for nymphing or fish spookiness | 7X |
|---|---|---|---|---|---|---|---|---|

| 12" .008p | 12" .006p | 30–60" .005p or f | 6X |
|---|---|---|---|

| 12" .008p | 12" .007p | 30–60" .006p or f | 5X |
|---|---|---|---|

| 12" .009p | 12" .008p | 30–60" .007p or f | 4X |
|---|---|---|---|

| 12" .009p | 30–60" .008p or f | 3X |
|---|---|---|

12- to 15-foot spring creek.

15' Spring Creek or Deep Water Nymph and Dry Fly Leader

| 60" .017mch | 60" .013p | 12" .010p | 36" .007p | 12" .004p or f | 7X |
|---|---|---|---|---|---|

| 36" .007p | 12" .005p or f | 6X |
|---|---|---|

| 36" .008p | 12" .006p or f | 5X |
|---|---|---|

| 36" .008p | 12" .007p or f | 4X |
|---|---|---|

15-foot spring creek.

Eastern mountain rivers like the Raven's Fork near Cherokee, North Carolina, often require roll casting into a wet-fly presentation. I'm casting so that my wet flies will drift along current seams, as well as through depth changes, to where trout hold, awaiting food.

## RECIPES

### CONTRAST NYMPH

| | |
|---|---|
| **Hook:** | #12-18 Mustad S82 |
| **Thread:** | Tobacco brown 6/0 Danville Flymaster |
| **Abdomen:** | Antique gold Hareline Rabbit Dubbin mixed with yellow and pink Wapsi Antron Dubbing |
| **Thorax:** | Seal brown Hareline Rabbit Dubbin mixed with yellow and pink Wapsi Antron Dubbing |
| **Tail and Hackle:** | Brown partridge |

### BEAVERHEAD NYMPH

| | |
|---|---|
| **Hook:** | #10-16 Tiemco 200R |
| **Thread:** | Tan 8/0 Orvis |
| **Tail:** | Rusty brown blood marabou |
| **Body:** | Orvis Hare' E Ice Dub Hare's Ear |
| **Rib:** | Fine gold tinsel |
| **Hackle:** | Partridge marginal covert and Brown India hen neck |
| **Head:** | Copper bead |

**Note:** Bead sizes corresponding to hook size: $\frac{1}{8}$" (#10), $\frac{3}{32}$" (#12-14), $\frac{5}{64}$" (#16). Hackle feathers wrapped together.

## DEPTHCHARGE NYMPH

| | |
|---|---|
| **Hook:** | #6-10 Tiemco 200R |
| **Thread:** | Black 6/0 Danville Flymaster |
| **Tag:** | Flourescent blue 6/0 Danville Flymaster |
| **Underbody:** | .015 lead-free wire |
| **Body:** | Peacock herl |
| **Rib:** | Gold Ultra Wire (medium) |
| **Wing:** | Four strands of Pearl Krystal Flash |
| **Hackle:** | Brown partridge |

## HEAVY METAL NYMPH

| | |
|---|---|
| **Hook:** | #12-18 Eagle Claw L063 |
| **Thread:** | Yellow 6/0 Danville Flymaster |
| **Tail:** | Ginger blood marabou |
| **Abdomen:** | Hot yellow metallic Ultra Wire (small) |
| **Thorax:** | Peacock |
| **Hackle:** | Brown partridge |

## TETON SUNSET

| | |
|---|---|
| **Hook:** | #12-16 Eagle Claw L063 |
| **Thread:** | Tobacco brown 6/0 Danville Flymaster |
| **Abdomen:** | Amber Hareline Rabbit Dubbin |
| **Thorax:** | Amber Hareline Rabbit Dubbin mixed with golden brown Ice Dub |
| **Hackle:** | Golden brown Hareline grizzly marabou behind Whiting Furnace hen cape |

**Note:** Abdomen light dubbed to allow the underbody to show a little.

## MARABOU EGG

| | |
|---|---|
| **Hook:** | #10-18 Tiemco 2457 |
| **Thread:** | Light Cahill 8/0 UNI-Thread |
| **Body:** | Yellow and orange Woolly Bugger marabou fibers |
| **Head:** | Gold bead |

**Note:** Body fibers tied in at the hook bend with the tips facing back, then wound forward together and the tail clipped. Bead sizes and corresponding hook size: ⅛" (#10), 3/32" (#12-14), 5/64" (#16-18).

## GEYSER PUPA

| | |
|---|---|
| **Hook:** | #12-16 Eagle Claw L055 |
| **Thread:** | Rusty brown 70-denier Ultra Thread |
| **Tail:** | Golden brown grizzly chickabou |
| **Abdomen:** | Amber Ultra Wire (small) |
| **Wing:** | Golden brown grizzly marabou |
| **Thorax:** | Orvis Hare' E Ice Dub Hare's Ear |
| **Hackle:** | Tan Whiting Brahma hen saddle |

## APPALACHIAN SPRINGFLY

| | |
|---|---|
| **Hook:** | #14 Tiemco WR-396 |
| **Thread:** | Tobacco brown 6/0 Danville Flymaster |
| **Tail:** | Rusty brown Woolly Bugger marabou |
| **Abdomen:** | Natural Hareline Rabbit Dubbin |
| **Thorax:** | Rusty Hareline Rabbit Dubbin |
| **Hackle:** | Gray Whiting Brahma hen saddle |

## HOLO SPIDER

| | |
|---|---|
| **Hook:** | #12-20 Mustad R50 (light) |
| **Thread:** | Black 12/0 Benecchi |
| **Body:** | Red Holographic Tinsel, medium hare's mask touch dubbing |
| **Hackle:** | English grouse |

**Note:** Body tinsel ribbed over black thread, then touch dubbing on thread tag wrapped sparsely (ribbed) over tinsel. Alternative hook is Mustad S82 depending on sink rate.

## CLINGER NYMPH

| | |
|---|---|
| **Hook:** | #12-16 Mustad S82 |
| **Thread:** | Tobacco Brown 70-denier Ultra Thread |
| **Tail:** | White partridge body side feather fibers |
| **Abdomen:** | Brown DMC 25 #435 embroidery floss |
| **Gills:** | DMC 25 #746 embroidery floss |
| **Thorax:** | Seal brown Hareline Rabbit Dubbin and golden brown Hareline Ice Dub mixture |
| **Hackle:** | Partridge side body feather |

## PMD SOFT-HACKLE DRY

| | |
|---|---|
| **Hook:** | #16-#18 Tiemco 100 |
| **Thread:** | Light Cahill 8/0 UNI-Thread |
| **Tail:** | Wood duck |
| **Body:** | Pale Morning Dun Superfine dry-fly dubbing |
| **Rib:** | Yellow 6/0 Danville Flymaster |
| **Wing:** | Medium dun CDC |
| **Hackle:** | Metz dun hen cape |

## PALE MORNING SULPHUR

| | |
|---|---|
| **Hook:** | #16-#18 Tiemco 100 (light) |
| **Thread:** | Light Cahill 8/0 UNI-Thread |
| **Tail:** | Wood duck |
| **Abdomen:** | Sulphur orange turkey quill |
| **Thorax:** | Brown ostrich herl |
| **Hackle:** | Medium dun hen cape |

**Note:** Alternative hook is Tiemco 3761 depending on sink rate.

## CAHIR CADDIS

**Hook:** #12-#16 L055
**Thread:** Black 8/0 UNI-Thread
**Abdomen:** UTC Medium vinyl rib over chartreuse Antron Yarn
**Thorax:** Rusty brown Hareline Ice Dub
**Hackle:** March Brown Whiting Brahma hen saddle

**Note:** Abdomen—vinyl rib over yarn with gaps, to let thread show through and create more contrast.

## EVERGREEN PUPA

**Hook:** #12-18 Tiemco 2487
**Thread:** Black 12/0 Benecchi
**Abdomen:** Green Hareline Rabbit Dubbin
**Rib:** Black Ultra Wire (small)
**Thorax:** Golden brown Hareline Ice Dub
**Hackle:** Tan CDC wound

## SKITTERING EGG-LAYING SOFT-HACKLE DRY

**Hook:** #10-20 Tiemco 100
**Thread:** Camel 8/0 UNI-Thread
**Egg Sack:** Caddis green Superfine dry-fly dubbing
**Body:** Tan Superfine dry-fly dubbing
**Wing:** Coastal deer
**Hackle and Antennae:** Light brown partridge

## EGG-LAYING DIVING CADDIS OR PUPA

**Hook:** #10-18 Eagle Claw L063
**Thread:** Light dun 12/0 Benecchi
**Abdomen:** Olive 12/0 Benecchi thread
**Rib:** Silver Ultra Wire (small)
**Rear Hackle:** Partridge base fibers
**Thorax:** Rusty brown Hareline Rabbit Dubbin
**Hackle:** Brown partridge

**Note:** Rear hackle, use enveloping hackle method.

## SOFT-HACKLE DRY MIDGE

**Hook:** #18-24 Tiemco 100
**Body:** Black 12/0 Benecchi thread
**Rib:** Silver Ultra Wire (extra small)
**Thorax:** Olive Hends #6 Spectra Dubbing
**Wing:** Dun CDC
**Hackle:** Starling

## MIDGE PUPA SOFT-HACKLE

**Hook:** #16-22 Tiemco 2488
**Body:** Black 12/0 Benecchi thread
**Rib:** Silver Ultra Wire (extra small)
**Hackle:** Starling

## SOFT-HACKLE DRY/WET GRASSHOPPER

**Hook:** #8-12 Mustad R50
**Thread:** Light Olive 6/0 Danville Flymaster
**Body:** Insect green Hareline Rabbit Dubbin
**Rib:** Spice Coats and Clark #8150 thread
**Wing:** Coastal deer
**Legs:** Four Pheasant tail fibers
**Hackle:** Olive partridge
**Head:** Two tan ostrich herls

**Note:** Leg fibers jointed with an overhand knot on each side of the hook.

## WET ANT

**Hook:** #12-18 Eagle Claw L063
**Thread:** Black 8/0 UNI-Thread
**Body:** Tying thread and black Loon Hard Head
**Hackle:** Black hen cape

**Note:** Build up abdomen and thorax with tying thread, then coat with black Loon Hard Head; let dry and then hackle.

## FLUORESCENT SPIDER

**Hook:** #14-20 WR-296
**Thread:** Light olive 8/0 UNI-Thread
**Body:** Pale yellow diced UV Lightning Touch Dubbing over thread
**Hackle:** Bobwhite quail

## ICE PHEASANT

**Hook:** #12-18 Eagle Claw L063
**Thread:** Tobacco brown 6/0 Danville Flymaster
**Tail and Abdomen:** Pheasant tail
**Rib:** Copper Ultra Wire (small)
**Thorax:** Caddis green Hareline Ice Dub
**Hackle:** Gray partridge

## HEAVY METAL NYMPH

**Hook:** #10-16 Eagle Claw L063
**Thread:** Brown 12/0 Benecchi
**Tail:** March Brown Whiting Brahma hen chickabou or saddle fibers
**Abdomen:** Copper UTC Ultra Wire, Brassie (#10-12) or small (#14-16)
**Thorax:** Brown Hareline Rabbit Dubbin and golden brown Hareline Ice Dub mixture
**Hackle:** March Brown Whiting Brahma hen saddle
**Head:** Copper bead (optional)

**Note:** Variations: olive, chartreuse, yellow, purple, gray, black, silver, orange, blue, white. Bead sizes and corresponding hook size: ⅛" (#10), ³⁄₃₂" (#12-14), ⁵⁄₆₄" (#16).

## HARE'S EAR SOFT-HACKLE

**Hook:** #10-18 Mustad S82
**Thread:** Tobacco brown 6/0 Danville Flymaster
**Body:** Light hare's mask dubbing or Light Hare's Ear Plus Dubbing
**Rib:** Copper Ultra Wire (small)
**Thorax:** Gold bead
**Hackle:** Brown partridge

**Note:** Bead sizes and corresponding hook size: ⅛" (#10), ³⁄₃₂" (#12-14), ⁵⁄₆₄" (#16-18).

## PHEASANT TAIL SOFT-HACKLE

**Hook:** #10-20 Eagle Claw L063
**Thread:** Tobacco brown 6/0 Danville Flymaster
**Body:** Pheasant tail
**Rib:** Copper Ultra Wire
**Thorax:** Gold bead
**Hackle:** Partridge side body feather

**Note:** Bead sizes and corresponding hook size: ⅛" (#10), ³⁄₃₂" (#12-14), ⁵⁄₆₄" (#16-20). Use small size wire for #10-16 and extra small for #18-20.

A #24 SCS took this 20-inch brown in near darkness, too dark to possibly see a dry fly, and everybody else had left the water. Because insects and trout, particularly browns, are active in lower light, it's often my favorite time to be fishing soft-hackles.

Target trout in the seams between slack water and fast water chutes. Getting closer to trout in pocket water lets you fish a shorter line, giving you a direct feel out the fly to detect quick strikes in the fast water and less line to drag, allowing for a slower drift, keeping the fly in front of the fish longer, and giving them more opportunity to strike.

# Soft-Hackles on the Water

**10**

You can spend a lot of time tying flies and studying rigging and techniques at home but on-stream is where the practical knowledge is applied and lessons are really learned and imprinted for future use. In addition to on the water practice, try to fish as many different waters as you can. In my opinion, the more experience you have fishing all different types of trout streams the more confidence and skills you have to draw on when you go to new waters to fish. You can draw on past experience from a similar waterway and conditions and apply that to the water you are on. I live in the southeastern United States and fish the tailwaters and mountain streams of North Georgia, North Carolina, and Tennessee year round, but I also fish the spring creeks, rivers, and tailwaters of Pennsylvania, New York, Missouri, Iowa, Minnesota, Wisconsin, South Dakota, Idaho, Wyoming, or Montana every year. On each trip I fish familiar waters, but I also am constantly trying to find off-the-beaten-track secret waters and locations to further expand the testing and development of my flies and methods.

On-stream experience and fishing many different waters is going to help you learn what works. Then your knowledge can be applied to customizing the equipment, the actions of rods you prefer, leader preferences, fly weight preferences, fishing methods, and reading water skills to compile a style of fishing that is your own. When you develop this, you will gain confidence in your fish catching ability and in turn you will be a more consistent angler in terms of catching fish. You will be able to take this confidence and style to trout streams anywhere in the world and be able to fish them successfully by using your style to tune your skills to each waterway you encounter on a day by day and season by season basis. This process of style development is an ongoing one throughout your fishing life and one that is based on continual open-minded learning about trout and insect behavior, on-stream practice, and application of the learned observation and knowledge to fly tying and tackle considerations anywhere and everywhere you fish. The correct choices will equal success catching trout on all streams, especially challenging streams, and thus will convey confidence—and that is the true secret and most valuable character trait of a successful angler.

I always consider my motto to be, "The right fly, at the right time, in the right place, in the right way." Try keeping this in mind, and I hope it will help you as you consider what, when, where, and how to fish. Now let's go out on on the water and have a look at some diverse trout habitats and approaches to fishing them with soft-hackles.

An art marker colored the burnt mono eyes on the Looker Pupa, a *Hydropsyche* caddis imitation. The monofilament and marker combination creates a nice glowing translucence.

253

## Davidson River, May

Tackle: 8-foot, 6-inch 4-weight; 4-weight DT line; 12-foot, 36-inch 7X fluorocarbon tippet; #22 McGee's SCS.
Presentation: Up and across-stream cast, mend, drift across, and then down and across with an occasional subtle strip.

The Davidson River gets a charge of fertility from the hatchery effluent. This creates an insect-rich environment and a massive chironomid population that grows large trout.

The Spring Creek Special (SCS) is impressionistic, yet imitates the small midge of the Davidson River well. It darkens when it gets wet.

The Davidson is a unique fishery. Like many other Blue Ridge Mountain freestone streams, it starts with brook trout in the headwaters, and then mostly smaller rainbows in the upper river. As it flows through the Pisgah Forest and the NC State Fish Hatchery property, it picks up effluent and nutrients from the hatchery outflow pipes. This raises the pH and fosters insect life. The half-mile section is home to some of the largest fish in the Southeast, and they are tough to catch, let alone land. Approaching them is easy. They are used to anglers and will just swim a few feet away if one gets too close. They gorge on black, gray, and cream midges, the basis of their diet, all year round. Many of these fish are over 20 inches, and some approach double digits in weight. You need to be able to fish both floating midge pupae and subsurface midge larvae to catch fish here. #22-#24 Copper Brassie Soft-Hackles and Peacock and Partridge Soft-Hackles fished just under the surface dead drifted or with short slow strips are great midge pupa imitations. Some Cahills and Drakes appear in May, but mostly it's the midges that catch the most trout. Small soft-hackle midges are deadly if you can fish them slow and get good drifts to the fish.

## Gangwon-do, South Korea, June

Tackle: 8-foot, 6-inch 4-weight; 4-weight DT line; 12-foot, 5X leader; Bukcheon Spider.
Presentation: Upstream surface wet fly.

A healthy resident of South Korea's Gangwon-do Province. The Korean cherry trout, *Oncorhynchus masou*, is a close relative of the rainbow trout, *Oncorhynchus mykiss*.

A #16 Bukcheon Spider has two hackle collars, CDC and a gray partridge. The CDC collar allows better surface floatability, while still sitting low in the film and providing movement similar to a live insect's legs kicking. The partridge collar provides contrast and a segmented leg and wing appearance.

After traveling halfway around the world and driving four hours from Seoul, I'm eager to fish. I don my waders and string my rod, and wade slowly into the cold, swift waters of Buk-cheon. The longer I fish, and the more *sancheoneo* I catch, the more familiar the setting becomes. The fish, the water, and the mountains all provide the same peace and contentment I seek wherever I fish. The sounds of flowing water and a trout stripping line from my Orvis CFO are universal. The same good flies and stealthy casts that bring success in the mountain trout streams of America's Southeast bring success in the mountain trout streams of Korea, and the fly fishermen here all lead familiar lives. Finally, here in Korea as at home, I let go of all conscious thought and blend into my surroundings, relaxed, in the zone, fishing well. Eventually, releasing another fine cherry trout, I began to sense what Korean Buddhists call *Inyeon*, the belief that everything is ultimately connected and all is one.

The northeastern corner of South Korea is a mountainous area known as Gangwon-do. In the mountains and valleys of this province, there are many trout streams that hold native cherry trout and *lenok*. Streams such as Buk-Cheon, Kiwha-Cheon, Naerhin-Cheon, and many others remind me of the streams I fish back in the Blue Ridge Mountains of Georgia and North Carolina. "Cheon" means stream. These waterways range in size from small mountain headwaters to large valley-wide rivers. In Korean, the native cherry trout are called

"sancheoneo": San (mountain), Cheon (stream), O (fish, or mountain trout). They are close relatives to rainbow trout; no surprise as rainbows are native to eastern Russia and Alaska, where there once existed a land bridge. Perhaps that is where the ancient relative once connected to the Korean Peninsula in some way or another. Cherry trout are anadromous on coastal streams, but in the mountains there are resident populations. They are also found in Japan. They are interesting in that they retain their parr marks throughout their entire lifespan. They are a hard-fighting fish whose strength can often belie their size.

Fishing upstream, staying low, moving slow, and fishing the tail, middle, and head of pools are the best methods of approach. These streams have a lot of pocket water and pool chutes.that feed the pools where most of the fish hold, awaiting food. There aren't many hatch events; rather, the fish are opportunistic feeders. Over the seasons, these freestone rivers have dramatic shifts in water level. Midsummer is monsoon season, and the best times to fish are spring and fall. Fly fishermen in Korea are a small but devoted and friendly group. You will often have rivers totally to yourself, even on weekends. You don't even need a fishing license. I developed the Bukcheon Spider here. It's effective on all these rivers, and has accounted for many trout and some *lenok* as well. If you ever find yourself in Seoul, South Korea, stop into one of the city's fly shops, get some directions, and then catch a ride across the peninsula, about a four-hour drive.

## Mossy Creek, June

Tackle: 8-foot, 6-inch 4-weight; 4-weight DT line; 14-foot 6X leader; #12 Golden Softie Bugger.
Presentations: Up and across high stick, across high stick and down, and across subsurface swing.

Virginia's Mossy Creek is one of the southern-most classic spring creeks in the eastern United States. It offers an entrenched stream channel that is often deeper than it is wide, providing a food-rich environment for trout and a challenge for the angler.

**Right:** A Golden Softie Bugger imitating a brown trout fingerling often proves a wise choice of point fly here, where fish don't have to feed much on the surface. As brown trout grow, their diet moves to piscatorial interests, and if they reach about 14 inches, the fingerling is one of their primary food sources.

This stream is one of the southernmost spring creeks on the East Coast. It's a lovely meadow spring creek that holds some large brown trout. It's challenging fishing, and these fish are difficult to approach without spooking them. It also requires a special permit that is free, but has to be acquired from the Virginia Department of Game and Inland Fisheries, along with a Virginia fishing license. The stream has a heavy biomass of caddis, Sulphurs, BWOs, and Tricos. Being a meadow stream, it also has terrestrials in the summer. But, in my opinion, the largest fish are caught using scuds, nymphs, or (even better) soft-hackle streamers. Remember, large brown trout are cannibalistic for a large percentage of their diet. I like to fish a #12 Golden Softie Bugger to imitate brown trout parr. Add one or two small split shot on the tippet and target the drop-off points and deeper holes. If you ever fish Mossy, please be nice to this stream; it's special.

## Willowemoc Creek, June

Tackle: 8-foot, 6-inch 4-weight; 4-weight DT line; 12-foot leader with 30 inches of 6X monofilament; #16 Winged Wet Sulphur, #18 Winged Wet Sulphur

Presentation: Mended classic wet-fly swing with dangle.

Willowemoc Creek below Livingston Manor holds a good population of 10-to-15-inch brown trout, thanks in part to good habitat and a no-kill section. The many deep runs and long flats beg to be fished with a cast of flies. You can feel the history of this river when you fish there in the birthplace of American fly-fishing.

This brown trout took a Sulphur wet fly fished in the middle of the day in June, when there were no rises. Trout will often aggressively eat wet flies during nonhatch periods, making them patterns that can be fished at any time.

The last week of May into June is known as "bug week" on the trout streams of the Catskills in New York. This is due to the multiple species that can be encountered, such as Blue-Winged Olives, Slate Drakes, Green Drakes, Golden Drakes, March Browns, Light Cahills, Spotted Sedges, Little Sister Sedges, Dark Blue Sedges, Short-Horned Sedges, *Hydropsyche*, Green Sedges, Chironomids, and Sulphurs, species that all overlap. I was fishing the water behind the Catskill Fly Fishing Museum, and as evening approached, trout began to rise. The flat-water sections below the riffles looked like good Sulphur water, so I tied on two Sulphur winged wet flies, a #16 on the point and a #18 on the tippet knot dropper. The combination intended to match both the larger *Ephemerella invaria* and the smaller *Ephemerella dorothea dorothea*, both

of which hatch at that time of year. Although there were some sporadic rises, I was prospecting with these flies using a high-stick wet-fly drift and a classic wet-fly swing, with a dangle at the end of the drift. Many nice browns were brought to hand with this method.

On this trip, I was attending the first International Brotherhood of the Flymph conclave at the museum. A great time was had by all, and it's now an annual event. The Willowemoc and Beaverkill are bug factories, where some of the first fly fishing in America took place. Fishing these waters is a special experience. For sheer insect numbers, the nearby East and West Branches of the Delaware River offer some of the most challenging match-the-hatch fishing in the East and the country.

## Madison River, July

Tackle: 9-foot 5-weight; 5-weight DT line; 12-foot 6-inch leader with 30 inches of 5X fluorocarbon tippet; #12 Tungsten Bead Orange Hare Thorax Nymph, #16 Diving Caddis, #16 Caddis Pupa.

Presentations: Deep nymph across stream, mend, slow deep drift and swing, dead drift nymph and swing with line strips, sweeping methods

The Madison River just below Hebgen Lake. This short section is fishable even during runoff, as it stays clear, but will be high in the early season.

**Left:** Tan Horned Sedge. The body is cinnamon caddis Hareline Rabbit Dubbin and the hackle and antennae are speckled brown Wapsi soft-hackle hen saddle patch.

The runoff had lasted well into late July that year, and the Madison River was chocolate milk below Cabin Creek. But as we were driving from West to Ennis, we found a section of high, fast, and clear water right below the outflow of Hegben Lake. We pulled the car to the side of the road, and I fished from the bank, as the velocity of the water was fast. I weighted the leader with two split shot and had two #12 Tungsten Bead Orange Hare Thorax nymphs, one a point fly, and one a tippet knot dropper. This was a heavy rig, but it got the flies to the bottom where the fish were sheltering in this high, fast riffle water. As the flies began to swing into a deeper riffle channel, I felt the line stop. The fly had set itself on the swing. I lifted the rod tip a little and immediately knew it was a good fish. The large fish was below me, and the fast water was stressing the tippet and knot. I couldn't follow the fish downstream to get a better position below it, because of riprap, bushes, and another angler below me. I had to use side pressure and choke up on the rod to gain leverage.

I slowly was able to reel a little line in at a time, all the while hoping the improved clinch knot would hold. I got the fish up, but I didn't have a net with me and worried it would break off as I tried to land it. I noticed the angler below me had a net, and got an idea. My wife was with me on this trip, and I asked her to please go and ask him if I could borrow his net. While I held the fish in current, she brought the net, and I was able to net the fish and land a nice 22-inch brown trout. I thanked the other angler and talked with him for a few minutes before we got back in the car and left. About a quarter mile below this, Cabin Creek entered and the rest of the Madison was brown water from snowmelt runoff. This was a true case of the right fly at the right time, in the right place, and in the right way, with a little help from a borrowed net.

The Madison River, especially in midsummer, is special. Brooks described it as the "world's longest riffle" and the "world's largest chalkstream," due to its high alkalinity from the calcium bicarbonate present in the rocky streambed. It has tremendous diversity of hatches, and caddisflies abound in the summer months. This water is perfect for them, and thus for soft-hackle imitations. The quantity of caddis hatching and egg laying, along with the large rainbow and brown trout and fast water, combine to produce hard-fighting and aggressive fish, and intense, even chaotic, fishing. The open sky and bright moon allow fishing well past ten o'clock at night without any additional light. The *Hydropsyche* hatches can be large, and start about seven or eight o'clock at night. There's no need to wade into the middle of the river, as the fish are mostly along the banks or not too far out. Look for any boulders, timber, or structure, and the current seams to find the prime lies through which you can fish flies. That evening, I rigged a Diving Caddis on the point fly and a Soft-Hackle Caddis Pupa tippet knot dropper. This let me match both egg-laying and emerging adults. Fishing from the bank out into the river, and then swinging the fly down and across back toward the bank, produced many fish. Getting the strike isn't always the hardest part. I had to follow many of these large fish a ways down along the bank in the darkness, before they were ready to be landed.

The Old Kirby Ranch (look for the trellis bridge) is an access point on the Madison that has some intense July-evening caddis egg-laying events. The fish get aggressive in the lower light, and fishing is best from eight o'clock until after dark. I was fishing the river earlier that evening, using a fly I now call the Miracle Caddis. It simulates the #18 *Hydropsyche* diving egg layers. I fished this as a point fly and a #16 Green Lantern pupa imitation as a dropper at the tippet blood knot. The best presentation for fishing caddis on the fast water is using a down-and-across presentation, and managing it with a Figure-8 line retrieve that lets you both feed out line as the current pulls it out of your fingers, and swim the flies on the swing. As the fly was below me, I began to retrieve it back upstream, and hooked what felt like a good fish. Little did I know that it would end up being the most stressful battle with a trout that I'd ever had.

The fish dropped to the streambed, but soon jumped, and I could see it was a fat, strong rainbow. The Madison's powerful currents hold some of the strongest fish I've ever caught, and this trout began running downstream. I had to follow, and at the same time work it over to the slower water of the bank. This fish had other ideas, and kept taking out line. I was able to work the fish back upstream and just hold him there for a couple of minutes, trying to tire him out. He fled again, and then I watched as a rather large tree branch floated right over my leader and got tangled in it. I had the weight of the trout and the tree branch, as well as the fast current, pulling on the line and stressing the leader. Somehow, after a minute or so, the tree branch worked loose and I was able to battle the trout again. Then, as I followed the fish downstream, the line encountered a subsurface boulder and the current pressed the line against it. I worried that this would be the end of the fight. Amazingly, after a bit I was somehow able to work and lift the line over the boulder. and again the fish was out in the current.

This Madison River brown trout was caught in the middle of a deeper run on a #12 bead head Orange Hare Thorax Nymph. The current and depth made me play him from the bank; I even had to horse him back upstream on a 5X tippet.

I decided this was enough; it had been nearly 20 minutes. I used side pressure and choked up on the rod blank to work the fish to the bank. I reached down and lifted the worn out trout out of the river, quickly took a picture, and let the trout return to its world. I've caught bigger fish and more selective fish, but this fish and the resulting battle were the most intense so far.

When caddis are visible on the water, Madison River browns and rainbows won't necessarily be rising. Instead they will most often hold just under the surface in the seams created by boulders in the river eating the diving caddis or emerging pupa. This is when I use the Figure-Eight Sweep Method almost straight downstream to feeding lies, fishing sub-surface soft-hackles.

## Silver Creek, June

Tackle: 9-foot 5-weight; 5-weight DT line; 14-foot leader with 6X-7X fluorocarbon tippet; marabou nymph and flymph during hatch, soft-hackle spinner during the spinnerfall.
Presentations: High-stick swing, high-line nymphing during hatch, slack-line dry-fly cast during spinner egg laying.

Awaiting the Brown Drake spinnerfall at Silver Creek East. This creek off North Picabo Road has a heavy population of these mayflies, due to the combination of fine gravel and silty streambed.

Chickabou Soft-Hackle Nymph (Light Brown) has a rib of tan ostrich herl and golden brown grizzly marabou tail and hackle.

The Brown Drake Marabou Nymph has some of the most active materials of any soft-hackle nymph. This mimics the naturals' strong swimming ability when they actively swim to the surface to hatch near dusk. Nymphs often work better than dry flies, due to their quick-emergence behavior. Target rising fish during the hatch with an actively fished rising nymph right in front of them.

The spinners allow for easier targeting by trout, as the dun takes off quickly. The spinners can even bring some of the largest browns to the surface to feed, which usually don't.

In June, anglers on Silver Creek near Picabo await the Brown Drake hatch and spinnerfall with baited breath and readied fly rods. The large #10 Drake nymphs emerge from their silty dens and begin their emergence into adults from late afternoon into evening. Some fish are caught then, with emergers and nymphs. The main event starts near dusk, when the adults return in large swarms of mating spinners over the water. As the spinners fall, the trout feed heavily until the activity tapers off after dark. Don't leave, though; often you will see a caddis hatch and egg-laying event after the spinnerfall, which you can fish with soft-hackles even if you can't see your fly on the water. The Brown Drake hatch only occurs on the middle and lower slow, silty sections of the creek.

Mayflies or caddis often hatch on the creek in huge numbers and overlapping hatches. The fish get into selective feeding modes, and even rhythmic feeding. This makes fishing Silver Creek special, difficult, yet rewarding, more than anywhere else I've ever fished.

I've found a method that works to match many of the smaller fly hatches, whether they are midge, caddis, or mayfly. I use a 12-to-14-foot leader with a long 30-inch 6X or 7X fluorocarbon, and a #18 Pheasant Tail Flymph fished down and across to rising fish. The flymph uses a partridge marginal covert for the hackle collar because of the unique mottling of this feather. I usually fish this fly unweighted on either a fine-wire dry-fly hook or a 2X heavy nymph hook, depending on how heavy and fat I want the flymph. First I cast the fly above

the fish, and make a mend or two to let it sink. Then I swing it in front of the fish, and sometimes use a rod-tip twitch or short strips to animate the fly and activate the hackle collar even more. At other times, I may use a Free-Line Nymphing presentation to reach out to fish and prevent drag. The flymph works fished upstream, across-stream, down and across, or downstream, stripped back upstream. I also tie and fish it with a bead thorax for a quicker-descending fly, or for better lift and drop during a Practice-Run Method presentation.

Silver Creek is home to brown and rainbow trout. The Brown Drakes appear on the creek downstream below the Highway 20 bridge. On streams that have large Brown Drake populations, fishing soft-hackle Drake nymphs can catch fish year round.

## Middle Fork Provo River, July

Tackle: 9-foot 5-weight; 5-weight DT line; 12-foot 6X leader and 30 inches of fluorocarbon tippet; #16 Green Antron Caddis Pupa and #16 PMD Soft-Hackle tippet blood knot dropper or a three-fly rig consisting of a #14 Green Caddis Pupa point fly, #16 PMD Thread Soft-Hackle tippet knot dropper, #16 Pheasant Tail Soft-Hackle Sparkle Flymph above .010 blood knot.
Presentation: High-Stick Dead-Drift Nymphing with Swinging Rise.

Fishing with a high-stick presentation and a wet fly upstream on the Provo River. Make this cast like you would for High-Stick Nymphing. Don't drop the rod tip down to the water to set the line down; instead, keep the rod high on the forward cast and let the leader achieve the distance on the water. Using a 9- or 10-foot fly rod and a 12-foot leader allows me to fish 30 feet in front of me with only minimal line on the water, for line/leader control and reduced dragging of the fly.

The Middle Fork of the Provo River in Park City, Utah, is a beautiful section of water that is full of strong and wise brown trout, and smaller populations of cutthroats and rainbows. The river has about 3,500 fish per mile, and though these fish are rather challenging, a good wet-fly fisherman will have fun here. The river flows out of Jordanell Reservoir and offers about 12 miles of public access. The nice thing about this river is that this is a walk-and-wade fishery with ample opportunities to find solitude if you are willing to hike away from the main access points. There can be some good caddis hatches throughout the day in the summer, and fishing caddis pupa to rising fish can be rewarding. Be ready for a fight with these fish; once hooked, they know their habitat well and seem to be able to dive into structure immediately and break off tippets. Don't leave too early, as the late evening sees good caddis hatches and egg laying, with the fish feeding more heavily and rising more than they do in the middle of the day. I'm impressed by the strength of these fish. They find soft-hackle patterns attractive, and they let you know it when they strike.

The Looker Pupa matches the summer evening *Hydropsyche* pupa on the Middle Provo, where the fish aggressively rise to the overlapping emergence and egg-laying. You can imitate both by fishing a soft-hackle caddis pupa dropper and a diving caddis egg-layer point fly to match both life cycles.

## Ireland, July

Tackle: 8-foot, 6-inch 4-weight; 4-weight DT line; 12- to 14-foot leader and 6X and 7X fluorocarbon tippet; 14-18 Kells Caddis, Suir Caddis, Hare's Ear Soft-Hackle Bead Thorax, Pheasant Tail Soft-Hackle Bead Thorax, Copper and Orange Wire Flymph, Yellow Stonefly Soft-Hackle Dry Fly, Soft-Hacked Dry Midge, Tan Soft-Hackle Dry Caddis Deer-Hair Wing, Gray Mayfly Soft-Hackle Dry Fly.

Presentations: High-Stick Nymphing, High-Line Nymphing, Classic Wet-Fly Swing, Flymph Mending Swing, Upstream Wet Fly, Dry/Dropper.

The River Suir, with Athassel Abbey in the background, is a fertile limestone spring creek with heavy hatches of mayflies, and especially evening sedge. In midsummer, the evening sedge hatch raises nearly every trout in the river. It is a long river with many different looks. Most of all, it's a great fishery, with memories that will last a lifetime for those fishermen who have the opportunity to experience a day or more on the river.

**Right:** The Kells Caddis imitates many common caddis species that share a green abdomen and brown thorax. The chartreuse Antron yarn and copper Krystal Flash make this fly vibrant, while the movement of the partridge hackle imitates the rowing motion of the legs of the pupa as it swims toward the surface. Imitate this behavior for the full effect with strips and intermittent horizontal rod-tip shakes.

I visited Ireland in July 2014, for a two-week trip around the country to sample the trout fishing, experience the culture of my Irish roots, and see how Guinness direct from the brewery a few blocks away tasted at the Brazen Head, the oldest pub in Ireland, established in 1198. If you're ever in Dublin, I also recommend Kehoe's and Bowe's pubs for great pints of Guinness. In mid-summer, the best fishing is in the early morning, and again at dusk and after dark. Being so far north of the equator, sunset is around nine thirty, and the fishing gets better and better as the light fades. Sedges begin to hatch around nine o'clock, and by ten thirty on calm, warmer evenings, they are heavy. A river seemingly devoid of fish in the afternoon comes alive with rising brown trout as the light fades and caddis emerge. Rivers like the Kells Blackwater, the upper Suir around Holycross and Cahir and its tributaries, and the Liffey are some of the best bets at dusk in the summer. The River Suir has been ranked as one of the best trout streams in Europe, and when I fished it I found it lived up to its reputation. While spring sees day-long fishing opportunities, in July and August you can sightsee in the day, eat dinner, and casually get ready for the evening rise. Just be prepared to fish late. The caddis hatch from about nine to eleven o'clock. Then there is about a two-hour break and another hatch begins, with another two hours of night fishing.

During the evening sedge hatches, I fished a #16 chartreuse and brown soft-hackle caddis pupa that I now call the Kells Caddis, on a dropper with a #16 bead thorax Hare's Ear Soft-Hackle on the point. Sometimes, I added a second dropper like a Suir Caddis, and fished three flies. As the light was low, you could see and hear rising fish, but tracking a floating dry was difficult. At night, a wet-fly rig was not only easier to fish, but more effective as well, as I was imitating ascending pupae. I fished up and across stream, mending to let the fly sink to depth, and then fished out the presentation down and across, sometimes with a slow swing and other times imparting short line strips or tugs to the line, to activate the hackle and give the impression of the pupa swimming to the surface with propulsion from its legs. Strikes were easy to detect, even in the dark, and all it took was slight lift of the rod tip to set the hook.

If you visit Ireland for trout fishing, the town of Cahir makes a great home base, and I can recommend the Tinsley House Bed and Breakfast. The owners know the local fisheries well, particularly the Suir, and they make a great breakfast. Try the Lazy Bean Café for lunch, and then head downstream a couple of miles to the Suir at Ballybrado, to the "Trout Stream" for afternoon nymphing, and then caddis into the evening. Location doesn't get much better than this, and perhaps it's why the Swiss Cottage was built here for a hunting-and-fishing retreat on the banks of the River Suir.

The King's River flows through the Wicklow Mountains of southeastern Ireland. This is a spate river that has a tannin color to the water, like a cup of tea. I found the brown trout here to be spooky, and any lining or visibility of the angler sent them scurrying for cover. I used an upstream dry-fly approach with a #16 Gray Soft-Hackle Dry Mayfly and a #16 Copper and Orange Wire Flymph tied with a bobwhite quail hackle on an 8-inch 6X fluorocarbon hook bend dropper. Most productive was targeting pocket-water holding lies around boulders and eddies, fishing slowly and methodically from bank to bank. The upstream dry/dropper technique is the best for small streams you must fish with a subsurface wet fly, with trout that are easily spooked.

In Ireland, native brown trout are the most widely distributed freshwater fish. In this fertile limestone tributary stream of Lough Corrib, this trout was visibly rising to mayflies, but a weighted Hare's Ear Bead Thorax Soft-Hackle moved him to strike just under the surface—another reminder that trout often feed subsurface, even during hatches.

# Index